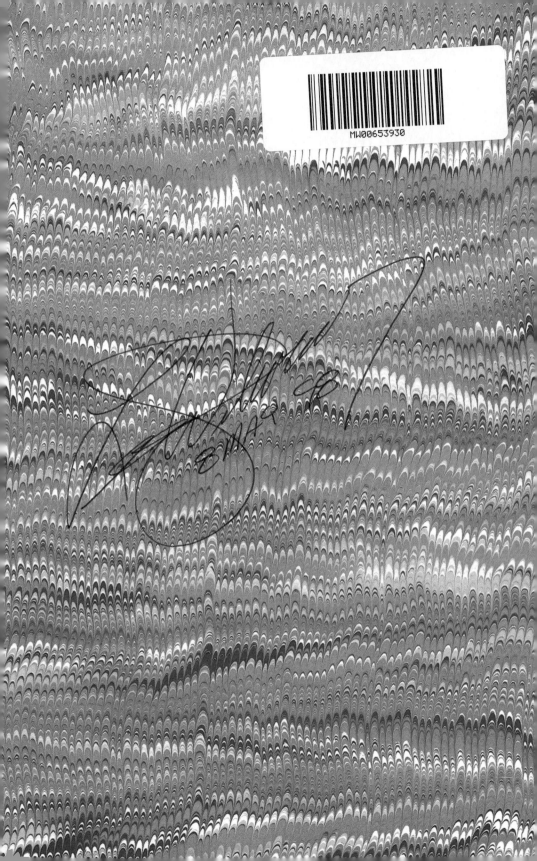

Engineering the Victory
The Battle
of the Bulge

Engineering the Victory
The Battle
of the Bulge
A History

Col. David Pergrin

Schiffer Military/Aviation History
Atglen, PA

DEDICATED TO:

THOSE UNSUNG HEROES—THE COMBAT ENGINEERS
THE GEORGES AND EDOUARD DE HARRENNE FAMILIES-
MY VERY DEAR BELGIAN FRIENDS AND THE PEOPLE OF THE ARDENNES.
TO THE AMERICAN SOLDIERS WHO DIED THERE

Book Design by Ian Robertson.

Copyright © 1996 by Col. David Pergrin.
Library of Congress Catalog Number: 96-68183

Printed in the United States of America.
ISBN: 0-7643-0163-2

We are interested in hearing from authors with book ideas on related topics.

Published by Schiffer Publishing Ltd.
77 Lower Valley Road
Atglen, PA 19310
Phone: (610) 593-1777
FAX: (610) 593-2002
Please write for a free catalog.
This book may be purchased from the publisher.
Please include $2.95 postage.
Try your bookstore first.

Table of Contents

FOREWORD

The Battle of the Bulge, in December 1944, was Hitler and the Wehrmacht's last great battle of World War II in the West. After losing the war for the beaches and hedgerows of Normandy, and barely escaping with huge losses from the Falaise pocket, the German Army fell back to just West of the Rhine and the German border. Hitler and his Generals planned a massive counter stroke and marshaled the forces to make it work. Striking in surprise on December 16, 1944 in the weakly defended Ardennes, German thrusts moved quickly to put Allied forces on the defensive. The Battle of the Bulge was that ensuing great battle.

Much has been written of that great battle: stories of Clarke at St. Vith; McAulliffe and the 101st Airborne at Bastogne; Patton turning his rapidly advancing Third Army 90 degrees to move 120 miles to the north; Abrams, in the first tank leading his 37th Tank Battalion into the lines at Bastogne to break the siege; and the "damned engineers" earning that accolade from SS Colonel Peiper, blowing bridges to stop the advance of his SS Panzer Grenadier column.

In this book Colonel David Pergrin reaches out for the other stories of that battle. Assisted by the Army Engineer Association, he has gathered numerous battlefield stories, anecdotes, and experiences told by those who were there and who lived them. With his own battlefield experience providing an understanding of people in war, he has crafted an interesting book that tells those stories of engineers in battle.

Many of the participants in that great battle have never been recognized for their exploits. The stories Dave Pergrin has collected in this book bring attention to engineer soldiers in combat and construction units who fought and died with their comrades of infantry, tankers, artillery, and the others – units that have not before been accorded their due. Weaving these stories and vignettes together into the framework of the overall battle, this book honors the many engineer soldiers, their companies and battalions, that contributed greatly to the allied defeat of the Germans.

This is not just a story of strategy, or the story of Generals, but the story of combat and construction engineers, trained to build and destroy and also to fight. They carried the day just as their Sapper ancestors carried the day at Yorktown, Fredericksburg, Petersburg, and at the Marne.

Richard S. Kem
Major General (USA Ret)
Honorary Colonel of the Engineer Regiment

PREFACE

The Congress of the United States, May 28, 1945. Congressman Hinshaw was recognized by the Speaker for 20 minutes.

Mr. Hinshaw: Mr. Speaker, I rise to call to the attention of the Congress and the American people a few facts on a subject that is about to be neglected. This subject is the largely unrecognized but indispensable role which has been acted out, and will be acted out by engineer troops in making the victory over Italy and Germany—also a victory over Japan.

What I have in mind is that members of Congress as representatives of the American people should make known to the War Department the American people's wish to honor the Engineer soldiers who have helped to put the Army into Africa, Sicily, and into Italy, into and across France, across the Rhine, and now further into the far East—both with additional pay and with some special

insignia. I think that two special cloth shoulder patches would be the answer. One an expert Engineer emblem—to be worn only by those Engineer soldiers who under such tests of proficiency in their assigned mission of their unit as the War Department will prescribe have proved themselves to be outstandingly proficient as military engineers.

The Congressman went on to cite three Engineers who had received Congressional Medals of Honor. The Corps of Engineers is the oldest professional service of the United States. June 16th of this year will be the one-hundred-seventieth anniversary of the appointment of the first Chief Engineer of General George

Washington's Continental Command. The Corps of Engineers has been in continuous existence since March 16, 1802, when it was constituted as the military academy of West Point, charged with the mission of infusing science into the army. Although the Academy passed to the army as a whole in 1866, it still reserves to its highest ranking cadets the choice of accepting commissions in the Corps of Engineers. The Academy's present efficiency owes much to the high standards set for it by the Corps during its first 60 years.

Now there are 700,000 of these Army Engineers, a group larger than any branch of the service except infantry and the Air Corps. It is an Engineer's war (very mobile). In the next three months alone, the Pacific theater could use every engineer soldier now in Europe— and more. For the engineers the big job—and really big job—is just getting started.

The American people may think the Normandy landings were easy. American Engineers know that those landings went in over the blasted bodies of Engineers who went in first and cleared paths through the German obstacles and mines. To date the survivors of no less than seven engineer battalions have been awarded "Battle Honors" citations for what they did on the beaches of Normandy.

Each Member of Congress is now receiving from the War Department a little booklet entitled "Engineering the Victory", which tells part of the story of the Corps of Engineers in the European Theater. The booklet was given to each engineer soldier in Europe to help him know what other Engineer Soldiers working for other engineer commands were doing in carrying out the overall mission: construction and destruction to facilitate the movement of our own troops and to impede the movement of the enemy.

The Chief of Engineers, Lt. General Eugene Reybold, summed it up this way when he noted that what the Engineers were doing today is a pretty accurate index of what the army intends to do tomorrow. The other part of the story is that when the engineers are committed to action as infantry, it means that the tactical commander is having to commit his last combat-trained reserves, his irreplaceable engineer specialists, to action. And he doesn't want the enemy to know it.

ENGINEERS IN COMBAT

The Congressman went on to explain to the Congress the actions of the Engineer units in construction as well as the engineers in combat in other areas such as the Pacific, Italy, Sicily and North Africa. Now he becomes specific about the following campaign:

ENGINEERS IN THE BATTLE OF THE BULGE

On the night of December 17th, east of Bastogne, the 158th Engineer Combat Battalion was ordered to hold its ground in the face of the German thrust. It held. Two days later the 101st Airborne Division moved in to receive credit for the defense of Bastogne. When Patton's Army broke through to reestablish contact with the 101st, the first men to rise out of the snowy foxholes to greet their buddies were Engineers.

Mr. Hinshaw continued: I want to read the unit citation for battle when the 30th Infantry Division relieved the 291st Engineer Combat Battalion. Major General Leland Hobbs, the division commander, wrote that the Engineers had 'strengthened their position both locally and in depth every day during their occupancy.' It was the day after Christmas when the 291st was relieved of its combat assignment to the 30th Division. In February the unit was building bridges across the Roer River at the Huertgen Forest. Between March 8th and 10th, the 291st Engineer Combat Battalion helped complete the first pontoon bridge the Allies threw across the Rhine.

It took them only two days to build the bridge, despite severe German artillery fire that was zeroed in on the pontoon bridge as well as the Ludendorff bridge which we captured nearby. Artillery smashed into their pontoons, their trucks and their men. They lost more men building that Pontoon bridge under German attack than were lost when the Ludendorff bridge collapsed.

THE LUDENDORFF BRIDGE, REMAGEN

You remember the Ludendorff bridge at Remagen. That is the bridge on which the Germans fumbled the ball. It was the Engineers that grabbed the fumble to give us first down and goal to go on the other side of the Rhine. Still looking out for the Army, a second lieutenant of engineers, John Mitchell, led the men who clipped the wires on the demolitions which had not yet exploded. What Lt. Mitchell did that afternoon was the talk of the whole expeditionary force that night. He had a commanding general, William Hoge, the combat commander of the 9th Armored Division who had captured the bridge. Within 36 hours Hoge had rushed enough men, tanks, and guns across the damaged but still-standing bridge to hold a bridgehead on the other bank. Any German plans for defending the Rhine River collapsed right there.

Eventually the bridge went down, but it went down fighting, carrying down with it some fighting Engineers still battling to repair the accumulated damage piled up by the registered German shells scoring one hit after another.

The Congressman went on to extol the Combat Engineers; however, the grand effort to award some badge to the valiant Engineers who have led the Armor and Infantry in the attack in the Korean, the Vietnam, and the Gulf Wars has never come about. The writings in this book will tell the long overdue story of the courageous and dedicated Engineers in the "Battle of the Bulge," so the reader may learn about some long unsung heroes since Washington's time that have made our country safe and secure in the largest battle in American history.

I want to read you the unit citation for battle honors awarded in the name of the President to Company "C" of the 55th Armored Engineer Battalion and Company "C" of the 9th Armored Engineer Battalion. The engineer companies who among others (the 35th and 158th) held Bastogne. Here are the words of the citations: "These units distinguished themselves in combat against powerful and aggressive enemy Nazis forces composed of no less than eight enemy German Divisions during the period from December 18th to 24, 1944. By extra heroism and gallantry in defense of the key communications center of Bastogne, Belgium. Essential to a large scale exploitation of his breakthrough into Belgium and Northern Luxembourg, the enemy attempted to seize Bastogne by attacking constantly and savagely with the best of his armor and infantry. Without the benefit of prepared defenses, facing almost overwhelming odds, and with limited and fast dwindling supplies, these units maintained a high combat morale and an impenetrable defense against extremely heavy bombing, intense artillery fire, and constant attacks from armor and infantry on all sides of their cut-off and encircled position. This master and determined defense denies the enemy even momentary success in an operation for which he paid dearly, in men, material, and eventually morale. The outstanding courage, resourcefulness, and undaunted determination of this gallant force are in keeping with the highest treatment of the service."

ACKNOWLEDGMENTS

Stephen M. Ruseicki, Major in the U.S. Infantry, Assistant Professor at West Point Military Academy. Major Rusiecki did a fine, thorough job, and his own writing experience about the Battle of the Bulge added much integrity to his edit.

Randy and Patricia Brown for their patient assistance in editing, spell checking, and placing the final manuscript on computer discs prior to submission to the publisher. They also were assisted by Janeen Weinstock, Meg and Bill Bohn, Bernadette Marriott, and David E. Pergrin Jr.

Major Adam Chubinski for providing excellent historical photographs of the actions of the Battle of the Bulge.

Serge Fontaine, Belgian historian, for his excellent material on the actions of the 1st SS in the Stavelot-Trois Ponts area.

Charles A. Hammer, Writings on the history of the 285 Field Artillery Observation Battalion.

Colonel Frank Rhea, for his untiring effort to bring the 291st history up to date and to Raymond Nice for his assistance.

General Arthur Williams and his Corps of Engineers history staff under the leadership of Dr. Paul Walker.

Colonel Mike Morgan for assistance through the AEA publication in acquiring the histories and personal experiences of the men and engineer units that were engaged in the Battle of the Bulge.

Rick Ferris and Captain Charles Mitchell for their material about the 526th Armored Infantry.

Sergeant Mort Tuftadol for the first hand information on the 99th Norwegian Battalion.

Corporal Fran Currey, Medal of Honor winner, first hand information about the battles at Malmedy and Thiramont.

General James Gavin, 82nd Airborne Division after action reports.

General Bruce Clarke, personal accounts of the actions of the 7th Armored Division.

Henry and Janice Giles, the collection of facts from the men of the 291st.

Francois des Harrenne, collection of facts concerning the movement of Kampfgruppe Peiper.

Stan Wojtusik, National Commander of the Veterans of the Battle of the Bulge, history of the 106th Infantry Division.

George Linthicum, the actions of the 26th Infantry Division.

Peter Munger, story of his first combat action in the Battle of the Bulge as an infantryman with the 30th Division.

Unit Histories from National Archives.

Major General William Carter, First Army Engineer, personal papers.

Brigadier General H. Wallis Anderson, personal papers covering three wars.

Sergeant Calvin Chapman, 291st Battalion's photographer, for all the action pictures used in the manuscript.

Earl Hart, member of V.B.O.B., for WWII photographs.

Sergeant Joe Geary for writings of the actions of his unit in the Battle of the Bulge.

To the members of the Veterans of the Battle of the Bulge and particularly Bill Greenville for supporting the effort to tell this story.

INTRODUCTION

The story of the Corps of Engineers was given to each engineer soldier near the close of Hitler's war in Europe. The booklet was entitled "Engineering The Victory". On the first page was a picture of the Bailey bridge, which is considered one of the outstanding erector sets that won the war in the huge chunk of land that Hitler attempted to overrun and rule.

The second page shows a picture of Major General Cecil B. Moore, Chief Engineer of the Corps of Engineers. General Moore's comments are most apropos for the American soldier and the times: "This booklet records briefly the achievements of the Engineer soldiers in the European Theater of Operations. It cannot tell the complete story—a story of magnificent accomplishment and heroism among individuals and units of the Corps of Engineers in every element in our Army. If it were possible to fittingly dedicate this book, I should like it to be to all who serve—at home or abroad—as an example of what citizens of the American Democracy can and have done to defeat a determined enemy whose aggressions threatened its very existence. Every Engineer soldier can take pride in the work he has done to help write this brilliant record. I hope sincerely that we may all rededicate ourselves to the task of speeding victory over the Nazi enemy so that we can again turn our engineering talents to the works of peace."

General Moore, through many pages with pictures and wording, extols the courageous efforts of the engineer men and units. Due to the fact that the "Battle of the Bulge" and the Remagen bridgehead were the highlights to victory in the European war, the Chief Engineer's comments on these two major events are hereby expressed:

"In December 1944, when the German's counter-thrust hit Luxembourg and Belgium, engineers in the threatened areas set up barrier zones of minefields, road blocks, and demolitions, then picked up weapons to help defend them. Typical of their activities during this period was the performance of the 159th Engineer Combat Battalion. In the path of a vicious Nazi thrust, they waited until they could see the whites of the enemy's eyes. Then opening fire, they stopped the Germans in their tracks, literally dropping them in the same formation in which they had attacked, a "V", but not for German victory. As rampaging Panzers met successive barriers they were slowed, stopped, and finally turned from a triumphant moment to a costly debacle. Engineers batted von Runstedt groggy; should some apologist write the story of the battle of the bulge, he can blame the Wehrmacht's failure on the U.S. Army Engineers."

East of Bastogne, the 158th Engineer Combat Battalion dug-in on the night of December 17th. As the German juggernaut came crashing forward, it met the attack head-on and for two days, by skillful shifting of forces, hurled back every enemy attack, thereby allowing the 101st Airborne to move in for its famous defensive stand.

Typical of the 158th's heroes was Private Bernard Michin, from Providence R.I. From his foxhole, Michin saw an enemy tank advance cautiously through the night and with-held his bazooka fire until the tank was only ten yards away. Realizing the blasts might wipe him out along with the target, he let go, completely destroying the tank and crew.

Blinded and burned by the explosion, Michin crawled back to the covered position of his shallow foxhole, now raked by enemy fire. Infiltrating Germans were now machine gunning his fellow engineers. Still blinded, he located the machine gun by sound and, as the Citation awarding him the Distinguished Service Cross reads, With complete disregard for his own safety he hurled a hand grenade which silenced the gun and killed the entire crew.

Throughout the First Army area, as General Hodges' men fought to stave off the massive German blow, Engineers dropped shovels and grabbed rifles. With the enemy only a few miles east of Malmedy, the 291st Engineer Combat Battalion, together with a few infantrymen, dug-in to defend the vital road center.

They constructed and manned road blocks, evacuated civilians and the wounded, and held out against savage enemy attacks from December 17th until the 26th. Battered by its own and enemy artillery and aerial bombardment, the 291st slugged it out 24 hours of the day. Fighting as infantry, battling fires and digging for wounded was a sideline.

Simultaneously, elements of the battalion set up road blocks south of Stavelot and Trois Ponts where the destruction of the lead vehicle in a German armored column southeast of Werbomont marked the halt of the German prong in this direction.

When Engineers at Malmedy were finally relieved by the 30th Infantry Division, Major General Leland Hobbs, Commanding General, wrote a letter of commendation which won a Presidential Citation for the 291st. General Hobbs wrote, 'Not only did the Engineers hold out against continuous enemy assault, but they strengthened their position locally and in depth every day during their occupancy.'

This was not the only Engineer unit to be cited during the desperate action. The 51st Engineer Combat Battalion, ordered to prevent the Germans from crossing the Ambleve and Salm Rivers, held Trois Ponts against artillery supported enemy attacks for three days until the 82nd Airborne Division arrived.

At Hotton, the 51st held the bridge against overwhelming German odds, using every available weapon to fight Nazis armor to a standstill. One private manned a 37mm while his Commanding Officer passed the ammunition. In the face of such resistance, Germans moved away before it became necessary to blow the bridge.

All up and down became the same. The 36th Engineers, who had fought their way across Africa, Sicily, Italy and southern France, had taken their toll of the enemy at Anzio. Along the bloody banks of the Volturno, they celebrated New Years day, 1945, by taking up guns again to relieve an infantry regiment.

Earlier as the 7th Army pushed north, two typical G.I.s, Sgt. Charles M. Schwartz, of Philadelphia, PA, and Sgt. Charles B. Dombroskie, of Verbank, NY, completely confused an enemy company. When assigned to scout strong points behind enemy lines, they accomplished their mission by night. By day they harassed Nazis with hand grenades thrown from various positions reached by running at top speed. The enemy feared a counterattack, assuming the engineers to be a large force.

PROLOGUE

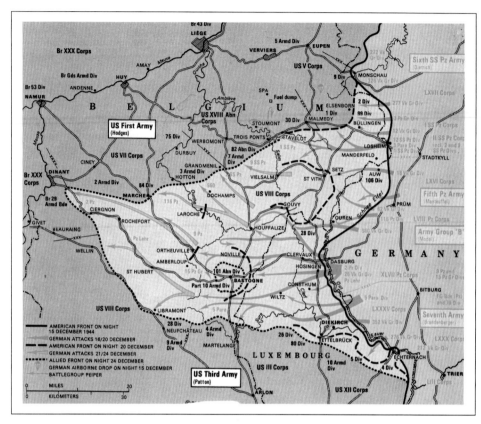

The 291st Engineer Combat Battalion now experienced being up near the infantry and armor of General Courtney Hodges' First Army in the drive across France and into Belgium. It was September 28th, 1944 and we had just completed a timber trestle bridge that could carry tanks up to 70 tons. The bridge, built by Captain James Gamble's "A" Company and Captain Larry Moyer's "C" Company, was located in Luxembourg at the village of Ettlebruck.

This bridge was a short distance from Germany and its vaunted Siegfried line. Just a few days prior, the rapidly retreating Nazi and Volkestorm divisions had fallen back into their homeland, demolishing bridges as they went.

At this time the 291st had built 23 timber trestle bridges, 34 Bailey bridges, and cleared over 5000 mines. There had been numerous prisoners of war captured. We had seen bombed-out German Infantry and armored columns, and dead people by the thousands on the beaches, farms, and in the villages. We had witnessed the saturation Bombing at St.Lo prior to the breakout. We had seen the assault crossing of the Vire River near St. Lo. by the 30th Divi-

American assault troops, along with equipment from landing craft, wade ashore on Omaha Beach in northern France June 7, 1944.

American assault troops land on the northern coast of France at Omaha Beach.

sion. And in the Mortain, France area we bore witness to the results of the 7-time counter-attack of the 30th Division by two Nazi Panzer Divisions.

In fact, at Mortain village, our A Company deactivated unexploded bombs with Sgt. Dolcha performing the hazardous mission. Having come from the beaches of Normandy in four months and seen and participated in many combat engineer missions, we were now a hardened and experienced group of Americans at war.

Conducting assault crossings of rivers, opening up bombed-out road nets, and building a by-pass under fire were only a few of the things we did to aid the infantry and the armor.

Now we were building bridges close up to the pillboxes and dragons-teeth of the Siegfried line in the front of First Army from Monschau to Echternach. Little did we know that just before Christmas, Hitler would unleash the largest counter-attack of WWII in this very area.

We would witness as we spread our forces throughout the Ardennes, the crushing defeat of three of our infantry divisions in the Huertgen forest: the 9th, the 4th, and the 28th. We would see four of our divisions form along the line from Echternach to Monschau: the 99th, the 106th, the 28th and the 4th. We often wondered why this line was so thinly spread with infantry over 88 miles. Some of us wondered why the high brass didn't attack into Germany in this lightly held area.

Sgt. Frank Dalcha with Company "A" clearing mines at Normandy Beach.

American Air knocks out a German tank at St. Jean de Daye.

One of the points of interest is that in the Ardennes area many other Engineer units were completing missions just like the 291st. Thus when one says the Ardennes area was lightly held, it would be wrong, for with over 21 Engineer Combat Battalions on hand it represented more than one full division with combat engineer weapons and tools.

During the course of the years following my retirement, I have enjoyed returning to Europe and meeting with the people in the Ardennes and in Remagen, Germany, where the 291st built the longest tactical bridge across the Rhine under withering fire. During these years I met many civilian and military personnel whose lives had become involved in WWII at these locations. Fifteen years ago I was most fortunate to meet with Major General Mike Reynolds, the British commander of the NATO ACE Mobile Force Land.

Since meeting Mike in the environment where the "Battle of The Bulge" occurred, we have both studied the battle of the Ardennes in great depth. Now in 1997 we are publishing the interesting results of our efforts. Mike in an effort to add to his well-written "The Pied Peiper". And my attempt to add the full story of the combat engineers to my previously published writings, "First Across The Rhine" and "Damned Engineers".

General Mike Reynolds' book entitled "The Devil's Adjutant" is the full story of Colonel Jochen Peiper, the commander of the 1st SS Panzer Division's leading Combat Group in the counter offensive of Adolf Hitler in the battle of the Ardennes.

1

Hitler's Secret War Plan

Adolf Hitler suffered greatly following the attempt by his generals to assassinate him in July 1944. After his escape, this incident caused him to turn the war in Germany around in his favor. He spent many hours in closely guarded quarters, with maps and charts of the conditions on the Eastern and Western fronts. Finally, in late summer he had formulated his final counter-offensive against the Allies.

The map of his detailed planning showed the 6th Panzer Army of General Sepp Dietrich spearheading the main thrust of the attack with two army corps: the 1st and 2nd SS Panzers. The mission of this formidable "Battle Group" was to break through the Loshiem gap at the Belgium border, capture the bridges over the Meuse River south of Liege, Belgium in 48 hours, and then drive on to the port of Antwerp.

The 5th Panzer Army, made up of the 58th and the 47th Panzer Corps, was to crash through the Siegfried line into Belgium, cross the Oure River, capture the bridges over the Meuse River near Namur, Belgium and then cover the left flank of the 6th Panzer Army. Hitler's favorite General was Sepp Dietrich, and he was chosen over General Hasso von Manteuffel to lead the assault. Manteuffel was to command the 5th Panzer Army.

The Army was made up of mostly infantry divisions that, along with the 67th Corps, would act as defensive blocking forces on the northern and southern shoulders of the drive.

Despite the fact that Hitler's own Generals at the top level attempted to assassinate "The Fuhrer" in July of 1944, he still had the will and the backing to mount this amazing counter thrust. And it was through the same terrain that had been used so successfully in 1940 and on two other occasions when the Germans attempted to expand a smaller state into a larger, more economically sound country with land bordering the seas.

Hitler planned to cut off the British Army from the main supply base, Antwerp, and force them into another, Dunkirk, and out of the European Continent. He believed that with Britain out of the war, American resolve would weaken. He could then concentrate his forces in the east against Russia to produce a stalemate out of which would come a negotiated peace.

The code name for the counteroffensive was "Wacht am Rhein" and the overall commander would be seventy-year-old Field Marshall Gerd von Runstedt. The Executive officer was Field Marshall Model. Hitler anticipated that as the British and Canadian Armies

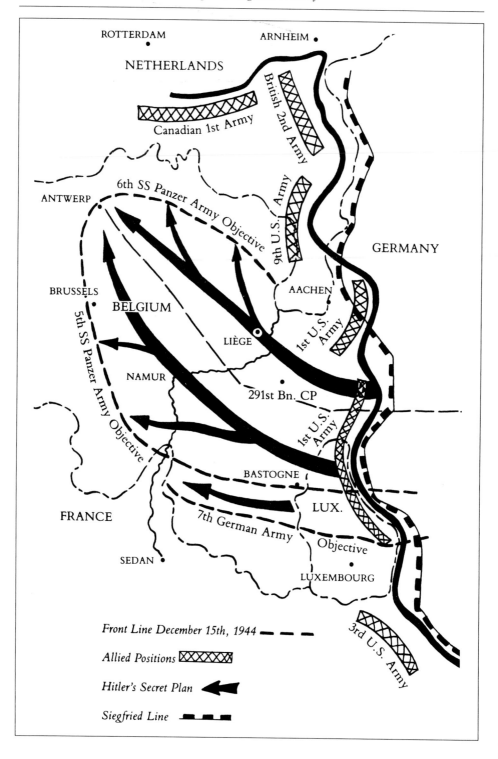

ROTTERDAM   ARNHEIM

NETHERLANDS

Canadian 1st Army

British 2nd Army

6th SS Panzer Army Objective

ANTWERP

9th U.S. Army

GERMANY

BRUSSELS

BELGIUM

AACHEN

5th SS Panzer Army Objective

LIÈGE

1st U.S. Army

NAMUR

291st Bn. CP

1st U.S. Army

BASTOGNE

FRANCE

LUX.

7th German Army   Objective

SEDAN

LUXEMBOURG

3rd U.S. Army

Front Line December 15th, 1944 — — —

Allied Positions ⊠⊠⊠⊠

Hitler's Secret Plan ⬅

Siegfried Line ▬ ▬ ▬

swung to meet the Sixth Panzer Army as it crossed the Meuse River on D plus 2, the 15th Panzer Army would attack them in the north, when the British had exposed their left flank.

For this total offensive, seven Panzer and thirteen infantry divisions were made available with an additional eight divisions and two brigades in reserve. To concentrate undetected, a force of 200,000 men, and 1,400 tanks and self-propelled assault guns, called for superb organization and rigid security arrangements. Hundreds of trains reached the concentration area west of the Rhine from all over the Reich. It is a measure of German success that the Allied Intelligence staffs completely failed to warn their Commanders of the forthcoming offensive.

The Sixth Panzer Army was the strongest of the three Armies. Dietrich's attack plan required the 67th Corps to establish a shoulder northwest of Monshau. The main thrust would come from the 1st SS Panzer Corps. After three infantry divisions had broken through the American defenses, he planned to unleash the 12th SS Panzer Division "Hitler Jugend" and the 1st SS Panzer Division "Leibstandarte Adolf Hitler" for the dash to secure the Meuse bridges. The 2nd SS Panzer Corps with two Panzer Divisions, were held in reserve to reinforce and exploit any success. The 1st SS Panzer Corps was allocated five routes. But each division had permission to deviate from its route as the case warranted. This gave the combat leaders some flexibility with their movement into American Lines towards the Meuse River.

The 1st SS Panzer Division was commanded by General Mohnke. He split his division in two and formed a Kampfgruppe (combat group) which consisted of all of his tanks, a strong element of armored infantry, artillery, engineers and support units. Their task was to capture the bridge at Ombret Rausa on the Meuse River south of Liege. The remainder of the division was to make a dash for Huy.

The Leibstandarte Adolf Hitler, the Premier Division of the 1st SS Panzer Division, was commanded by General Mohnke. The Waffen SS had Colonel Jochen Peiper as the commander of its Kampfgruppe. He had achieved fame and notoriety for his exploits in France and Russia. At 29 he was one of the youngest and most dashing of all the regimental commanders of the German Army and before the war he had been on General Himler's staff. On the 14th of December Peiper learned of his task to spearhead the main thrust from his 1st SS Division Commander, General Mohnke.

He amalgamated two of his strongest companies under the commanding officer of the 1st battalion, Major Poetschke. This gave him 72 tanks, 34 of which were type IV, and 38 type V Panzers. Additionally there were engineer and anti-aircraft companies. Peiper's infantry came from the 3rd Battalion 2nd SS Panzer Grenadier Regiment. This was a mechanized battalion, mounted in medium armored personnel carriers, the Shutzenpanzer wagon, of which there were many variants. Its commanding officer, Major Diefenthal, had four mechanized infantry companies and a regimental assault gun company equipped with six 15 cm assault guns, the "Bison." There were also 12 cm mortars and 7.5 cm anti-tank guns. Artillery support was provided by the second Divisional artillery Regiment with three batteries of 10.5 cm towed light field howitzers.

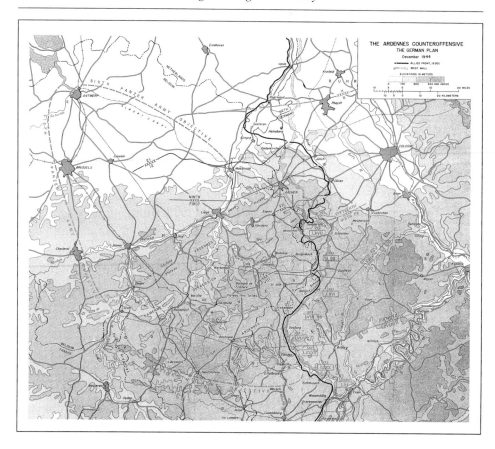

Peiper was provided with an engineer company to clear mines and open up the road net by blowing roadblocks and building bridges. His was the 3rd company of Combat Engineers from the Panzer Engineer Battalion. It was equipped with the engineer variant of the armored infantry truck which carried an assault bridge, mines, and demolitions as well as an armored bulldozer. One of Peiper's glaring mistakes later was his failure to build a bridge at the Lienne River using his engineers.

From outside the Leibstandarte came the 1st SS Panzer Corps' 501st Heavy Tank battalion with 15 type VI Tiger II tanks. The 69 ton monster was armed with an 8.8 cm gun. As a counter to allied air superiority Peiper was given elements of the 84th Luftwaffe flak battalion, equipped with four-barreled 2 cm anti-aircraft guns mounted on a tank chassis, the "Wirbelwind," and also 3.7 cm Flak guns. He also had a sub-unit of the 68th Flak Battalion.

A detachment of the 1st SS Panzer recon battalion was placed under his command on 19 December with several companies, one of which was a mechanized infantry company. There were also Puma eight-wheeled armored cars with 5 cm guns and scout cars. Finally, he acquired the 1st battalion, 9th Parachute Regiment early in the battle and retained one company throughout. In all Peiper had a force of well over 4500 men and 90 tanks. Just as a "spearheading" kampfgruppe in a blitzkrieging main thrust should be, he was equipped with new equipment and fresh forces throughout to mix with his seasoned veterans. When Peiper received his command to lead the main thrust of "Watch on the Rhine", he organized a company of tanks to traverse 50 miles of winding, heavily-forested roads east of the Siegfried line. Having had vast experience in these blitzkrieg forays, he desired to test the capability of his force and equipment to move rapidly in this type of terrain.

Jochen Peiper was born in Berlin January 30, 1915 as the son of Woldemar Peiper and Charlotte Schwartz. Mr. Peiper had served as an officer in the German Army. Peiper completed high school and immediately became part of the Leibstandarte Adolf Hitler, which was the Fuhrer's own guard division. He went to officers training school and graduated as a 2nd Lieutenant. In 1938 he became the adjutant to the Reichsfuhrer SS Heinreich Himmler. Peiper proved to be an outstanding, brilliant person with many leadership capabilities and he became a company commander in the 10th company of the Leibstandarte. His company spearheaded the invasion of Poland and he received the 1st and 2nd Iron crosses for his courageous actions.

This was only the beginning of his rise in the military and his bravery under fire. Peiper was at his very best against the Russians where he became known as "Blowtorch" Peiper for his forays deep behind Stalin's lines that often resulted in the burning of several villages. He commanded the 2nd Panzer Grenadier Regiment's 3rd Battalion. He saved the 320th Infantry Division from encirclement at Charkov and saved 1500 wounded soldiers. On February 14th, 1943 he stopped cold the Russian drive at Charkov, and his regiment smashed forward through the Russian lines, burning villages and killing soldiers and civilians alike. On March 19th, he captured the city of Bjelgorod.

Peiper continued to move up the ladder as he received many German Iron crosses. When the Leibstandarte was sent to France in June of 1944, his division became part of the German forces that were mauled at Caen, Mortain, and Argentan-Falaise following the saturation bombing at the time of the St. Lo breakout from the beachheads of Normandy. This time Peiper was forced to break out of a pocket being closed by the American and British forces at the Falaise gap. The 30th Division had defeated his regiment in the battles at Mortain. It was a full retreat with many losses of men and equipment. The Germans retreated helter-skelter while being bombed by American and British Air forces.

The German engineers laid mines and blew bridges of all types. The delays to the Allies caused by the destructive policy of Hitler's battered Army permitted the likes of Peiper's regiment to get back into the fatherland and become re-equipped and manned for the third time. This time at Euskirken in the Schnee-Eifel region west of the Rhine River.

Unbeknownst to Jochen Peiper, as his regiment became part of the 6th Panzer Army of General Sepp Dietrich in November and December, 1944, he was being equipped for the last time to lead the German Armies in the largest battle of this world-wide war. Nor did he realize that American Combat Engineers would delay his "blitzing" spearhead and finally halt his Panther and Tiger tanks as he was forced to depart with only 800 men on foot. His tanks and armor would be spread over the Belgian Ardennes, never to be used again except here and there as museum pieces.

Hitler conceived two special operations which were designed principally to aid his favorite army commander and compatriot of the early street brawling days of the Nazis party, General Sepp Dietrich and his Sixth SS Panzer Army. The first was the Airborne operation of Lt. Colonel Von der Hydte, a famous German paratroop commander who had participated in the Crete invasion in May of 1941 commanding a paratroop battalion.

Baron Von der Hydte came from a long line of Bavarian Catholics and was related to other great families of Europe. In 1933, at age 26, he was assistant to the professor of law at the University of Berlin. He acquired a Carnegie Foundation scholarship and studied for the next two years in Vienna, Paris, and Italy. He returned to Germany and won a commission in the German Army. He was stationed in the conservative and Catholic city of Paderborn and prior to the war he was anti-Nazi. The Baron's first years of the war showed no real action until he commanded a parachute battalion at Crete, where he won the Knight's Cross for the capture of the village of Canea. He fought in Italy, and commanded the Sixth Parachute Regiment in Normandy during the Allied invasion in 1944. He served with General Erwin Rommel at that time.

The Colonel ran a well-disciplined regiment made up entirely of volunteers to this difficult unit of war. He told his men that they were only ruled by one law, the law of the coordinated unit. The battle is for the very existence of the German nation. In the battle of Normandy von der Hydte's men fought bravely against the paratroopers of the 101st Airborne (The Screaming Eagles) near St. Mere Eglise, Utah beach, and Carentan. After seven weeks of solid combat against a crack American unit, he was forced to pull back his greatly depleted troops through an armored division of the First American Army. More than 3000 men were killed in these vicious battles, but his men gave ground reluctantly as his regiment survived the encirclement at the Falaise Gap. The Americans knew that they had fought against a very worthy and competent opponent.

Colonel Von der Hydte became commandant of the Parachute school at Bergen, Holland when he received orders to report to headquarters and General Student, the overall commander of the German Para-troopers. The General told the Colonel that he was going to go back into action.

"Hitler has informed me that he is going to start a Major offensive against the West," Student advised. "This will be one major battle that will bring the war to a conclusion in favor of the German nation." Von der Hydte was to command this force out of the sky. The offensive was to be a total surprise to the Allies.

The composition of the force to be under the Colonel was to be made up of men from each of the four divisions under Student's command. The "Baron" was excited about leading his men in combat again, and his one hope was that he would have the best men of the four divisions. This would be the first time that he would lead men dropped from the air since 1941.

"You will be sent 1200 men all experienced paratroopers to the training center at Aalten, Holland," Student cited. "You will be able to organize your own battle group, and you must have them ready for the big drop by the 13th of December. Action will take place in the early morning hours of the 14th."

The Baron went to work quickly at the training center in Holland and his men came in from the other training centers. One third of the men had been in his forces in Crete. He formed four parachute companies, a signal section, one company of heavy machine guns, a mortar company, and a company of combat engineers. This entire Kampfgruppe was moved to a German training area close to the transport air force squadron that would drop his forces.

On December 13th Von der Hydte learned that he was to drop north of Malmedy, Belgium and protect the right flank of the spearheading 1st SS Panzer division of General Sepp Dietrich's 6th Panzer Army. He was given a map by General Model showing that his drop zone was ten miles north of the important road junction at Malmedy, Belgium. His mission was to block any or all troop movements of the American forces attacking Colonel Jochen Peiper's armored column as they blitzkrieged east to west. The 1st SS Panzer Corps and the 12th SS Panzer Corps would need flanking protection as they moved through the First American Army's defensive sector. This area included the First Army's fuel and supply dumps, map depot, and other service and supply points, not to mention the headquarters of General Courtney Hodges.

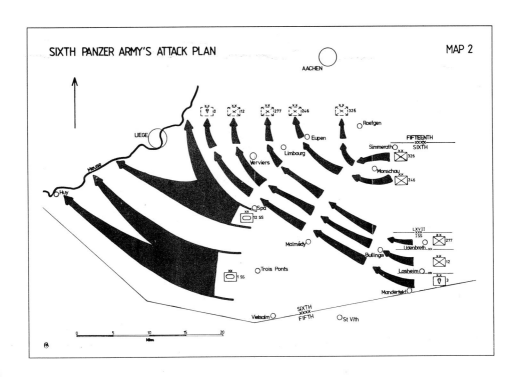

The Baron studied the contour maps of the drop area and found it to be very mountainous rugged country, forested in most areas with some open fields. He learned that the expected weather was overcast skies with drizzles of rain turning to sleet at the early morning hours. There was no snow on the ground and none predicted.

The Baron learned that Colonel Otto Skorzeny, the famous commando who rescued Benito Mussalino, would join the spearheading forces with a regiment of Germans in American uniforms and American equipment and camouflaged tanks. Skorzeny's mission was named "Operation Grief."

Thus Hitler had manned and equipped his main thrust through the center of the First Army with outstanding and experienced leaders, and provided them with the best available equipment. Hitler selected this main thrust to be directed at the very heart of the First Army on a direct line with Malmedy, Spa, Liege and Antwerp. Hitler knew about the vast supply and equipment locations in front of Liege and beyond Malmedy. Especially the fuel dumps with vast quantities of oil and gasoline. Hitler had learned the area of the blitzkrieg was lightly defended with new and some worn out Divisions from the battles in the Huertgen forest. What he didn't know was the count of Engineer combat units who had occupied the area of attack since September. Nor did he have any idea of the fighting capability of these now well-experienced to war Engineer Soldiers. These soldiers had been under fire since the beachhead days and had used all the weapons of war including mines and demolitions, and they had experienced other counter attacks, although nothing of this size.

The plan was to be carried out by Otto Skorzeny, the fanatical Austrian Nazi who had reported directly to Hitler for his part in this offensive. He was one of the leaders who learned in October, 1944 about the great counter-offensive. This gave Skorzeny plenty of time to prepare his men for action, and to acquire the necessary equipment.

The operation was divided into two parts. The main part of his force, nearly 3000 men equipped with tanks, some of which were American, formed the 150th Panzer Brigade. Their task was to move ahead of the Sixth Panzer Army and seize and hold three bridges over the Meuse for the Panzer Divisions that would be following behind. The remainder were to carry out sabotage and cause confusion in the rear areas. For this, Skorzeny formed a small commando unit which contained a few English speaking soldiers to fool the Americans and British.

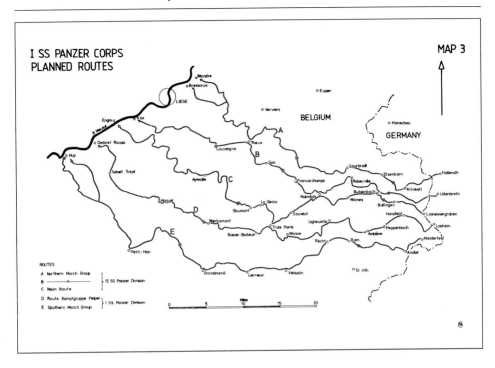

Skorzeny sent teams behind the American lines to capture his equipment and bring the Americans back as prisoners of war. Colonel H.W. Anderson lost his supply officer to this ruse. Anderson was the Engineer Combat Group commander of the 1111th. His Group had been operating with his three battalions in close support of the armor and infantry divisions in front of the First Army headquarters at Spa, Belgium. These units were the 51st, the 291st, and the 296th. The battalions were operating saw mills and were keeping the road net open right up to the Siegfried line since September 1944, as they rebuilt blown bridges, cleared mines, and patrolled the road net.

2

The American Defenses
in the Ardennes

Facing this vast army on the 75-mile Ardennes front, the Americans had slightly less than five divisions, most of them part of Major General Troy Middleton's VIII Corps. Throughout the First US Army, the area had been regarded as a rest camp where the luxuries of hot showers, real beds, and film shows were readily available. Although these comforts had been designed for infantry troops back off of the front lines, these niceties could be used by all the area troops, especially the great baths at Spa, Belgium where General Courtney Hodges had his First Army Headquarters.

Until the middle of November 1944, the front was held by three experienced divisions, but between then and December 15th all three were moved north. In their place came two

Building a timber trestle bridge at Ettel Brück-Luxembourg into Germany September 1944.

Timber trestle bridge at the south end of Trois Ponts in September 1944.

badly under-strength divisions, the 4th and 28th, which had sustained very heavy casualties assaulting the Siegfried line in the Huertgen forest. They had not been fully reinforced. Also, two new divisions recently arrived in Europe, the 99th and the 106th. They had no experience and had been sent to the Ardennes for combat experience along the vaunted Siegfried line.

Bridge blown by the Germans at Melun.

Bailey Bridge across the Seine at Melun, which was built by Gamble's Co. A.

Malmedy Warsh River bridge, built by A Company.

The bridge at Ettlebruck (Timber trestle built by A & C Companies of the 291st).

We in the 291st were spread throughout this area and had become concerned about the wide gaps in the defensive lines from Monshau to Ettlebruck along the dragons teeth and pill boxes of the Siegfried line. We saw them come in and move into positions. Along with many other Engineer Combat Battalions, we had arrived in the area in September, closely supporting the armor and the infantry in the drive into the German border with Belgium and Luxembourg. The German Pioneers (Engineers) had demolished many bridges in their retreat across France and into Belgium and Luxembourg. They were experts in laying waste to lengthy roads as they blew the bridges on the Seine and other rivers and streams in France. They wiped out the bridges on the Meuse in Belgium and followed up by taking away the road net throughout Holland, Belgium and Luxembourg. They laid mines, cratered roads, and established roadblocks to delay the attacking French, English, Canadian and American forces.

The engineer soldiers who had led the assault onto the beaches clearing mines and obstacles for the oncoming infantry were the same engineers who kept the road net open at Carentan, and built the bridges under fire over the Vire River at St. Lo. The road net from St. Lo to Mortain was destroyed by saturation bombing, but these engineer soldiers kept the main supply routes open for the armor and infantry, sometimes under artillery fire.

The retreating and badly beaten Germans were falling back from the Falaise Gap in France towards their fatherland as their Pioneers were taking the delaying actions to prevent it from becoming a route. Thousands of assault bridges and timber trestle river crossings were made by the engineers of the U.S. Army. The Engineers worked long hours for our rapidly moving Armies on the tail of the enemy.

Bridge Marle Sept 11. Built by Company A.

Each division had an organic engineer battalion with corps engineer battalions in close support — army engineers to make the bridges safe for heavy tanks and other heavy loads. In a very mobile war such as the one in Europe, many times the success of whole armies depended on the workability and mobility of its combat engineers, working sometimes as squads, platoons, and companies. As First and Third Army moved across France, into Belgium, and right up to the Siegfried line, the engineers kept pace as there was the Seine, Meuse, Oure, Sure, Ambleve, and Salm rivers and others with many bridges destroyed. Sometimes they had to build the bridges under artillery fire, and do the dangerous job of clearing mines, or deactivating unexploded bombs. At times they fought as infantry, firing bazookas, rifles and machine guns at tanks and the enemy.

September found the Germans driven out of Belgium. As the armored and infantry settled into a period of refueling and preparing to attack into Germany, the combat engineers became very busy. They worked on improving the road net, cutting timber, running sawmills to produce badly needed bridge timber, and aiding the organic division engineers to solidify the defenses of the front-line infantryman. At this time the engineers were establishing telephone lines throughout the area. The squads, platoons, and companies were learning the difficult Ardennes road net and location and tonnage of important bridges.

There were 24 engineer units in the Ardennes area where the Germans directed and executed Hitler's secret war. This one factor proved to be the equalizer in the largest battle in the European war. 200,000 Germans were attacking only five American Divisions. The Germans had 1400 superior tanks and yet were destined to lose the "Battle of The Bulge."

The American divisions along the Siegfried line from Monschou to the Losheim Gap and thence along the line to Lutzkampen were spread rather thinly over a stretch of the

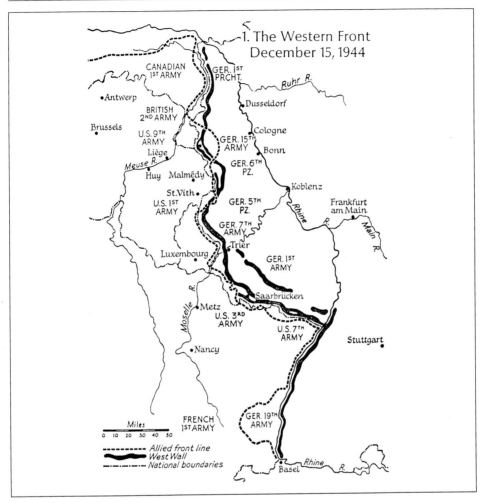

1. The Western Front
December 15, 1944

Ardennes forest with narrow winding roads and many bridges over streams and the Our River. In fact some of the bridges close up to the German west wall had been demolished by the Germans in their retreat and never rebuilt.

The American line of defense included the 99th (Checkerboard Division) to the north with the 14th Cavalry Group on their right flank at the Losheim Gap. On the right flank of the armored cavalry was the 106th (Golden Lion) Division. The organic Combat Engineers of these two divisions were the 324th Engineers of the 99th Division and the 81st Engineers of the 106th Division. In this area there was the 2nd Infantry Division's Combat Engineers near Bullingen and the 254th Engineer Combat Battalion near the village of Lanzerath. Also the 146th Engineers were located near the 99th Division's left flank near Monschau. The 291st and the 168th Engineers had been in this area covering the original clearing of mines, opening up the road net, and building back blown bridges.

The organic engineer units had been blowing pill boxes and destroying dragons teeth in the Siegfried line. The close support engineers had turned to cutting timber and operating saw mills, after having strengthened the Infantry's defensive positions. There would be a tremendous need for bridge timber after entering Germany itself.

On the right flank of the 106th Division came the 28th (Bloody Bucket) Division. This area was known as the skyline drive area and the 28th Infantry were in line from Lutzkampen to Weiler and then south to the Sure River at Wallendorf. A Combat command of the 9th Armored Division would get involved on their right flank. Further south into Luxembourg the 4th Infantry Division had moved into the line from the Huertgen forest.

Each of these divisions had organic Engineer Battalions; with the 28th was the 103rd Engineers, and the 4th Division was supported by the 4th Engineers. The 9th Armored Division had the 9th Armored Engineers. Throughout this whole area where the big battle occurred, there were many more engineer units which had supported the armor and the Infantry with combat engineer tactics across France and Belgium up to the Siegfried line. There was the 44th, 51st, 158th, 159th, 299th, 238th, 35th, 82nd, 296th, 207th, 208th, 164th, and the 510th Light Pontoon Company.

Even though the Divisions were spread out far beyond their capabilities to halt a major counterattack such as Hitler had planned, eventually the use of these engineer forces delayed, and sometimes halted, the advance of the 6th Panzer and 5th Panzer Armies.

The American plan prior to the battle in the Ardennes called for the capture of the Roer River dams in the north and then a drive on to the Rhine by the First Army. The insertion of Divisions into the Huertgen forest was part of this plan, and it had failed miserably with many wounded and killed.

General Patton's Army was to follow up a saturation bombing in the area of the Moselle River with a heavily Armored force and then attack to, and across, the Rhine. Had the higher military authority added more armored units and artillery battalions in this weak line of defense in the Ardennes, there is a chance that the big bulge in the American lines would not have occurred.

Although the five divisions that were involved had four artillery battalions that were organic to the divisions, the Armor within their defenses was insufficient to hold back Hitler's avalanche. For instance the 30th Infantry Division ("Old Hickory") of Major General Leland Hobbs had the 117, 119, and 120 Infantry Regiments. There were the 113, 118, 197, and 230 Field Artillery Battalions, the 105 Engineer Combat Battalion, the 743 Tank Battalion, and the 823rd Tank Destroyer Battalion.

Two of the divisions, the 99th and 106th, had not experienced combat as yet, and had not been able to coordinate the armor and infantry use during battle. The same applied to their engineers and field artillery. Fortunately for the 99th Division, the 291st, the 254th, and the 146th engineers had prepared a solid road net and hardstanding for their artillery emplacements.

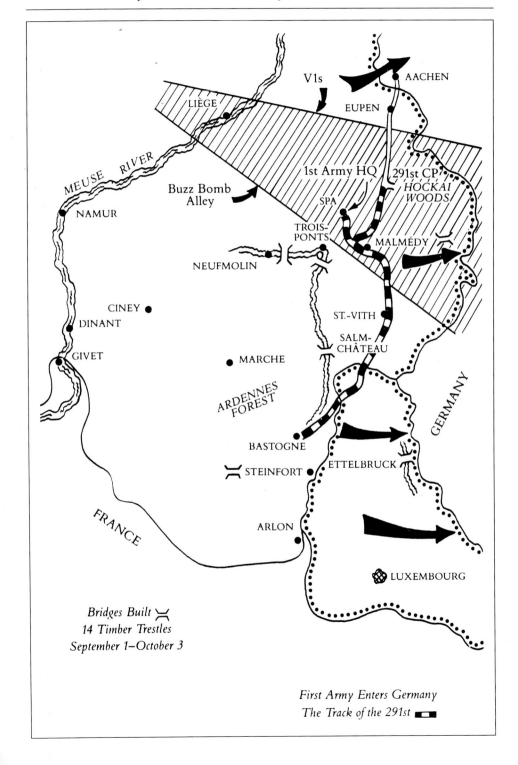

Bridges Built ⋈
14 Timber Trestles
September 1–October 3

First Army Enters Germany
The Track of the 291st ◼◻◼

3

Hitler's Main Thrust

As befitted the force making the main effort, the Sixth Panzer Army was the strongest of the three armies attacking in the Ardennes. Dietrich had three corps Headquarters, five parachute and volksgrenadier divisions, four SS Panzer Divisions, eight hundred tanks and assault guns, and more artillery and nebelwerfers (screaming meemies) than the Fifth Panzer and Seventh Army combined, an awesome 1000 pieces.

The two volkesgrenadier divisions were to attack on each side of Monschau to get into the Hautes Fagnes hills to join the paratroopers of Colonel Von der Heydte. South of Monschau two SS Panzer Divisions of the 1st SS Panzer Corps were to make the main thrust in the vicinity of Krinkhelt-Rockerath and through the northern reaches of the Losheim

28th, Pieper's Armor.

Von Runstadt.

Col. Pieper, commander of Kampfgruppe

Gap. Two more SS Panzer Divisions under another SS Panzer Corps were to constitute a second wave, and most of Skorzeny's Brigade was to operate in support of Dietrich's Sixth Army.

The five roads to be used by the 1st SS Panzer Corps were connected to the Loshiem Gap and wound through the Belgium countryside crossing the high ground north of Malmedy and on to the Meuse River on either side of the city of Liege. The narrow, winding roads were not ideal for the monstrous Tiger and Panther tanks. At either end of the Sixth Panzer Army's jump-off line, there was a calvary recon squadron and the 99th Infantry Division holding a twenty-mile front. Close behind the 99th Division was the well-experienced 2nd Infantry Division. The supposedly crack 6th Panzer Army of General Sepp Dietrich failed in the very beginning when the attack at Monschau was thwarted. Also, von der Heydte's parachute drop north of Malmedy was almost totally unsuccessful when only 400 out of 1200 parachutists landed in the Hautes Fagnes mountain tops.

The opening artillery barrage against the 99th Division was earth shaking and, though it caused many tree bursts and damage to buildings in the area, few riflemen in their fox-holes were wounded or killed.

The three regiments of the 99th division were in place north to south along the Siegfried line from Hofen to Lanzerath for a distance of 21 miles. The three regiments were the 395th, 393rd, and the 394th in that order north to south from Hofen. Each regiment had been assigned an Engineer Combat Company of Lt. Colonel Neale's Combat Engineer Battalion.

Armored infantry.

The Combat Engineers had been with the Riflemen much of the time since the arrival in this area. They cleared mines and built driveways to set up artillery pieces, and at some instances blew pillboxes and demolished dragon's teeth in the Siegfried line. There had been times when they fought as infantry.

The area occupied by the Engineers was always in artillery range and of course they suffered casualties. On the 13th of December the 395th Regimental Combat team assaulted

Seigfried line, near Butgenbach.

the Siegfried line. Company C of the 324th Combat Engineers had men with the team to clear mines, blow up captured pillboxes and cement forts, and seal up those that couldn't be forced to capitulate by bulldozing heaps of soil over the exits.

It was no easy job to demolish these cement forts: each one required several hundred pounds of TNT. In this attack every pound of equipment and supplies had to be carried by hand over a good three miles of trails, over hills and through woods. They found that a fort, once captured, had to be immediately occupied or destroyed. On the 15th of December the never-ceasing artillery pounding paid off. The second battalion, 395th Infantry, with the 324th Engineers captured six pillbox forts and took 15 prisoners.

On the 16th of December, the 395th reached out and, in another attack, captured Arenberg. This marked the very end of the attack into Germany, for on December 16, the 6th and 15th Panzer Armies opened up a thunderous artillery barrage and came crashing through the forests in an all-out attack. The Germans made four main drives, with two against the 99th Division. Volksgrenadier divisions spearheaded the drive to punch a hole in the American line that the panzers could quickly exploit. The Germans made two drives on the front of the 99th Division, one through Hofen and Monschau towards Aachen and one through the Losheim Gap in the middle of the 99th Division sector towards Vervier, Liege, and Antwerp. They did not work as planned! The northern spearhead of the 15th Panzer Army was stopped in the Hofen-Elsenborn area by the center and left flanks of the 99th Division front; the second spearhead from Losheim through Bullingen towards Malmedy, the Meuse River and Antwerp was slightly delayed as Colonel Jochen Peiper's Kampfgruppe blasted through the right flank of the 99th Division and the 14th Cavalry Group. Peiper's combat group was the spearhead of the 1st SS Panzer Corps of the 6th Panzer Army commanded by General Sepp Dietrich.

The 99th Division's right flank caught the full initial onslaught of this Nazi army, stopped it the first day, slowed it down the second day, and added delay in Peiper's time table.

During the evening of December 16, the German thrust was so severe that the 99th had to call off their own attack into the German lines, along with the 2nd Infantry Division to the north. They received a strong enemy attack with infantry and tanks.

The strong enemy attack to the North was repulsed. The infantry was greatly aided in the Hofen area by the 146th Engineers and a platoon of Col. Neale's combat engineers. Mines had been laid, road blocks had been established and bridges prepared for demolition. Throughout the battle of the bulge this small infantry, engineer and artillery force held the Hofen-Alzen area unassisted and without giving an inch of ground.

Near the center of the line the 3rd Battalion 393rd Infantry, which had attacked into the Siegfried line with a platoon of the 324th Engineer Combat Battalion, was struck with repeated heavy attacks. The assaults struck hardest into the right flank and the enemy began pouring into its rear areas. These young Americans kept beating off these assaults as the engineers kept knocking out tanks with bazookas and daisy chain mines right along with the riflemen. Companies kept fighting even though they found themselves surrounded. In

Dietrick.

*Major Diefenthal, German Armored Infantry
Commander.*

the first fanatical German charge, part of Company K, 393rd Infantry, was wiped out, killed
or captured.

Our troops could deal with hostile infantry but found themselves powerless against the
enemy armor, which slipped into the area juggernaut-style and crushed the men in their
foxholes. Our anti-tank guns were of little value, having been immobilized in the wet ground.
The engineers crawled close to those tanks and fired bazookas and placed shape charges on
some. Infantrymen threw mortars against the side of enemy armor as the engineers dug pits
and filled them with gasoline, and set them on fire to delay the enemy tanks. They also
pulled daisy chain mines across the roads.

This battalion was running out of ammunition. It had collected hundreds of prisoners
but in turn was being surrounded. Company I, 394th Infantry of the division reserve battalion, located near the town of Honsfeld on the extreme south flank of the division, was
hurriedly dispatched to it with ammunition and supplies. It fought its way in and joined the
3rd battalion, 393rd Infantry at about 6:00 p.m. This also provided more of Colonel Neale's
men to the battle.

The front of the 3rd Battalion still looked as though it would be penetrated. Regimental
headquarters placed the only reserve it had, the I&R (intel & recon platoon), and the Engineer mine platoon of the Regiment, in position behind the battalion, and about 2500 yards
east of the town of Krinkhelt, to gather in any infiltrating enemy groups. The platoons were
too weak to stop the large size patrols breaking through.

The 3rd Battalion, 23rd Infantry (the 2nd Division's reserve), was released to the 99th Division, and with one company of the 741st Tank Battalion attached, was hurriedly dispatched to the 393rd Infantry. Late that afternoon this battalion of the 23rd Infantry, with a platoon of the 2nd Division organic engineers, established itself on the same line being held by the I&R platoon and the combat engineer platoon. It stopped the large hostile patrols.

Again, the organic engineers of the two divisions played a major role as they knocked out tanks with daisy chain mines as well as bazookas. In some cases they fired their machine guns and rifles.

The artillery battalions, which were in firing positions north and northeast of Rockerath-Krinkhelt, came under intense hostile artillery fire. Starting about 5:00 p.m., the barrage grew in intensity and lasted until about 8:00 p.m. It was large caliber artillery that did the shelling. The enemy had our positions accurately zeroed-in, for every firing battery was bracketed by this fire.

The 1st Battalion, 393rd Infantry, in position along the international highway, received two more heavy attacks. One ferocious assault struck its left flank and overran part of its front line, wiping out part of its Company B. The heroic defense put up by the remnants of the company finally stopped this assault. Rallying around its Company command post, it rushed the engineers, cooks, drivers, and everyone who could fire a rifle, into the fight. It even called its own artillery fire to fall right into its positions. It stopped the onslaught. Another attack struck the right flank of the battalion. Here Company C stopped the assault

The German Pioneers finally build the Bridge at Lanzerath after Peiper is gone.

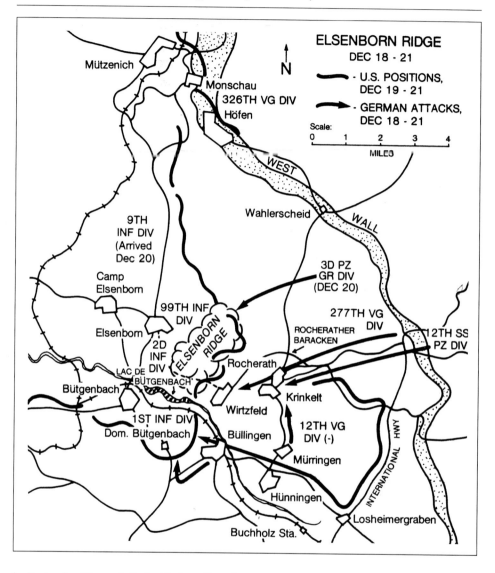

in its tracks. Not satisfied, this battalion then counter-attacked with its Company A and drove the enemy back and out of the area.

Down south, in front of the 394th Infantry, the 1st Battalion, which sat abreast of the Losheim-Bullingen road, was hit simultaneously by a two-pronged attack of infantry and tanks. The tanks attempted to drive straight down the road, but the 324th Engineers had placed mines across the road, destroying the lead tank. It was a relentless attack, consistently reinforced, which during the day practically wiped out Company B. Time and time again these doughboys and engineers fought off the hoards of fanatical SS men. These so-called supermen followed behind their volkesgrenadier soldiers whom they drove ahead, to force the disclosure of the American positions and machine gun locations. Many times they ran into engineer mines. When the situation looked blackest for our side, our staunch defenders would counter-attack to drive the enemy back.

The 1st Battalion, 23rd Infantry of the 2nd Division, with a company of the 741st Tank Battalion and a Company of the 612th Tank Destroyer Battalion, were released at 4:00 p.m. that day to the 99th Division and placed south of the town of Murringen.

On the front of Combat Command 395 in the middle of the 21 mile line, the attack had been called off as they had seized their objectives for the day. They had been fighting offensively on the attack, while all around them, the men of the 99th were beating off assaults by the German armies. They stopped their drive, pulled back, and began to withdraw towards Krinkhelt.

There was only one road south out of the pocket in which the attack had placed the 2nd Division, the Combat Command 395, all of the 99th Division Artillery, and the 324th Engineer Combat Battalion of Colonel Neale. The road had to be held open. The Germans had to be held south and east of Krinkhelt, or all of the troops would be lost. This would be a major job for the Engineers.

The Americans had to hold the enemy out of the Krinkhelt area until the troops in the pocket could pull back and establish a position around Krinkhelt-Rockerath-Wertzfeld. It was a Herculean job, it took courage and guts, which was the crowning glory of the American soldier at this time. Along the 99th Division's right flank, the German attacks came on: they ran into resistance and bounced off, only to come in again, each time probing deeper and deeper westward on the south flank.

The 3rd Battalion, 394th Infantry, located on this southern flank, held off the attacks and by nightfall had driven back the enemy. The 99th and 2nd Infantry Divisions were holding off the breakout of the 6th Panzer Army's main thrust to Liege and Antwerp. The first days of Von Runstedt's attack had expended itself.

The great stance of the 99th's soldiers, riflemen, and engineers was exemplified by Sergeant Murray of Company B, 394th Infantry, whose Company sat astride the Losheim-Bullingen road. When his entire squad was destroyed, Murray seized the weapon of a mortally wounded comrade and charged headlong into the oncoming Germans, firing as he went, forcing the enemy to flee.

1st Sergeant Lyle O. Frank ordered three men with him to take up marching fire and attack into the flank of Germans assaulting his command post. The enemy thought this was an attack in great numbers and quickly withdrew. The route was completed as the men of the 324th Engineers added their weapons to the fight.

The anti-tank guns of the 394th Infantry knocked out a Tiger Tank in this fight, and Staff Sergeant Vernon McGarity received the Congressional Medal of Honor that day for leading his men against enemy infantry and tanks, despite severe wounds. He braved murderous fire as he ran to an advantageous position where he immobilized the enemy's lead tank with a round from a rocket launcher. Fire from his squad drove the attacking infantry back, and three supporting tanks withdrew. He rescued under fire another wounded Ameri-

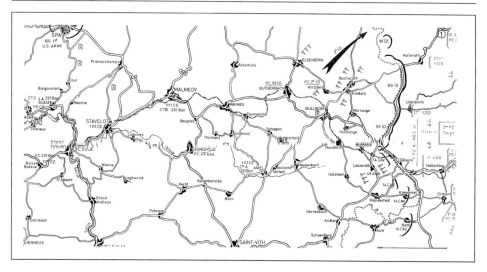

can and then directed fire on a light cannon which had been brought up by the hostile troops to clear resistance from the area. When ammunition began to run low, remembering an old ammunition hole about 100 yards distant, in the general area of the enemy, he braved a concentration of hostile fire to replenish his unit's supply.

By a circuitous route the enemy managed to place a machine gun to the rear and flank of the squad's position, cutting off their only escape route. Unhesitatingly, the gallant soldier took it upon himself to destroy this menace single-handedly. He left cover and, while under steady fire, killed or wounded all of the hostile gunners, and then prevented all attempts by the Germans to man the gun. As the squad ran out of ammunition, the riflemen and engineers were captured.

This was a typical example of the "Hold or Die" along the entire 99th (Checkerboard Division's) front. Despite the lack of front line experience and against overwhelming odds the soldiers of this division were accomplishing a mission well beyond their tour of duty. Little did they realize that they were fighting Hitler's best troops of the vaunted 6th Panzer Army of General Sepp Dietrich. The mix of combat engineers and brave infantry was proving the point.

The Germans had now wasted one day since their artillery barrage began at 5:30 a.m. on December 16th. The attack on the northern shoulder by their supposedly strong Panzer Army had gone nowhere.

Hitler was furious when he heard the bad news. The 17th of December had hardly begun when the guns of the Sixth Panzer Army opened up at 1:00 a.m. Down came a heavy barrage of artillery fire, and every type of mortar round, all along the eastern and southern fronts of the 99th and 2nd Infantry Divisions. The sounds of moving armor could be heard coming from the general direction of Lanzerath and Losheim in the south.

This was the beginning of what became known as the "Battle of The Bulge." This was the beginning of Hitler's greatest effort to smash the Allies in the west in the hope of reach-

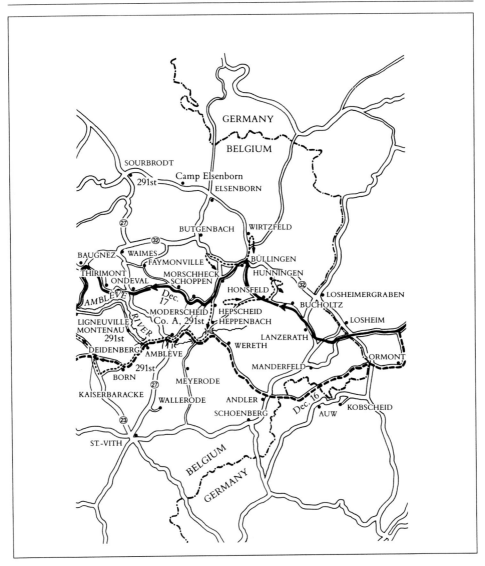

ing a turning point in the war in Europe. His plan called for an attack by two Panzer Armies against five short-handed American divisions and, unbeknownst to him, 24 or so experienced engineer combat battalions. In the end, the Americans handily won, largely due to the efforts of the five divisions and the engineers who set up defensive barrier lines for other American Infantry and armored divisions to form on and defend.

The night of the 16th and the morning of the 17th of December found the actions of the Germans in Hitler's "Secret War" only alerting those along the Siegfried line that something serious was happening in the supposedly quiet but very busy area. All units on the American side were getting ready to assault the German fatherland, especially the Combat

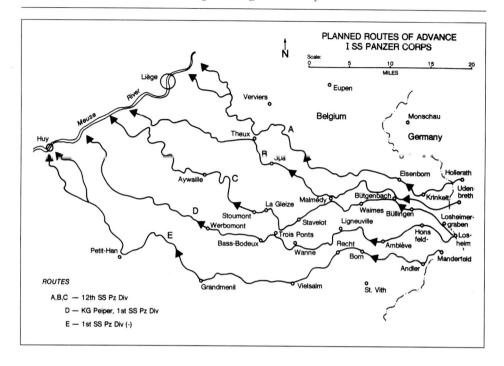

PLANNED ROUTES OF ADVANCE
I SS PANZER CORPS

ROUTES

A,B,C — 12th SS Pz Div

D — KG Peiper, 1st SS Pz Div

E — 1st SS Pz Div (-)

Engineers. Many civilians knew the Germans were up to something, and many soldiers learned about it from civilians. Just like the word of the attack had spread from civilians to American soldiers along the 75 mile front, where the 106th, 28th, and 4th Divisions were in their foxholes, the long range shelling into villages such as Ambleve, Malmedy, and Vervier was an early warning that something was up. The increase in the amount of "Buzz-Bombs" (V-1 Rockets) crashing into Liege, Eupen, near Malmedy, and Salmchateau, as well as First Army Headquarters at Spa, was giving the American soldiers side signals. Those of us who were in the Ardennes since September had always been on the alert for a counter offensive.

Messages from divisions to corps, and corps to army were indicating that the sleeping enemy was coming awake, or not really sleeping at all. But more than messages up the ladder through official channels were occurring at the level of the soldier, the squad, the platoon, the company and the battalion. This was the case in the 291st Engineer Combat Battalion.

The long range shells that fell in Malmedy, Belgium on the 16th of December, 1944 became the initial warning to those of us in the 291st. After the call of Captain John Conlin, our B Company commander in Malmedy, who came to me at my command post in Haute Bodeux about this occurrence, I immediately took off for the village and discovered great damage near the General Hospital along the Avenue of the States. There were medics and civilians killed and wounded. This was high caliber stuff the Germans were using, including a V-1 Rocket that had fallen nearby.

After Conlin had taken over the job of taking care of the wounded and repairing the craters in the road, I left Malmedy and headed to Ambleve where my A Company, commanded by Captain James Gamble, had relocated from Werbomont. Gamble's new mission was to make the move with the 9th Armored Division and remove the mines off the Schwammaneul Dam, upon its capture. Little did I realize when I arrived at his command post in this small Belgian village that I was only six miles from the Losheim Gap where the German Paratroopers had broken into our lines. Nor did I have the faintest idea that the spearhead of the Sixth Panzer Army would come crashing through in the next 24 hours.

Gamble and 1st Sgt. Bill Smith were concerned about the scuttlebutt from the civilians about the build-up of German troops and the firing along the Siegfried line. After a discussion about the mission, I departed from Ambleve and as I passed along the road, the 106th Division check points seemed to be also concerned about a possible attack in their area.

Through the village of Malmedy there were civilians moving towards the west in the late hours of the night. My command car driver, Curtis Ledet, also thought this to be most unusual. At Haute Bodeux, at my command post, I learned that my lines from group had been cut. At 3 a.m. on the 17th of December I got the answer! A call from the Group intelligence officer, Major Dick Carville, revealed that German Paratroopers had been dropped north of Malmedy, Belgium.

The companies of the battalion were all alerted and Captain Conlin sent Lt. Frank Rhea east towards the Siegfried line out of Malmedy. Colonel Anderson, our Group commander, had been in the border war against Pancho Villa with the 28th Division; he also was in WWI with the combat engineers and was highly decorated in that war. His experience in these other wars had made him a very valuable person to Colonel William Carter, the First Army Engineer, and to General Courtney Hodges, First Army Commander. Due to the fact that Anderson had served as the 103rd Engineer Regimental commander when General Omar Bradley commanded the 28th Division, Anderson's 1111th Engineer Combat Group had been involved in many assignments of great importance since the Normandy beach battles.

Here, on December 17th, when Anderson had heard of the parachute drop north of Malmedy from his S-2, Major Carville, he really started to plan some defensive measures. I then relayed a message I had received from Captain Conlin. "Lt. Frank Rhea of our B Company has learned that Germans have an armored column running in the clear near Butgenbach. It has been dive-bombed by American Air forces." This force could only be 10 or 12 miles from Malmedy.

Anderson's reply was not demanding, but suggestive. "Go to Malmedy and see what has to be done. Let me Know." This marked the beginning of the 1111th Engineer combat group's decisive actions in the "Battle of the Bulge" with its two engineer combat battalions, the 291st and the 51st. The 51st was to be commanded by Lt. Colonel Harvey Fraser.

This area had been a busy area for combat engineer battalions since September, but from here on the action would become fast and furious when the engineer soldiers became combat engineers.

4

Kampfgruppe (Combat Group) Peiper's Penetration

The battles at the very tip of the northern shoulder near the village of Hofen had practically been settled on the 16th of December when the Germans were totally defeated as they tried to come through the mine fields and wires laid by the 324th Engineers. Just as the two attacking Volkesgrenadier Divisions hit into the minefields and wired obstacles, the 62nd Armored Field Artillery Battalion opened up along with two Corps artillery battalions that were within easy range. The shells bursting in air above the approaching Germans were terrifying and devastating. The Germans fell back in headlong retreat.

When it was over, at least 100 Germans were dead, and 19 captured. The contrast to American casualties was striking: four killed, four missing, seven wounded. This defeat caused General Dietrich to give up on the attacks on the Monschau-Hofen sector of the northern shoulder and depend entirely on the attack of the 1st SS Panzer Corps. This was being spearheaded by Kampfgruppe Peiper and the 1st SS Panzer Division of General Wilhelm Mohnke. The success of the battle was the result of the efforts of the riflemen, engineers, and particularly the artillery. The latter two branches of the service rarely get credit in the writings of historians.

After the success at Hofen, the V Corps commander, General Gerow sent in the 146th Engineer Combat Battalion, whose men had arrived soon after nightfall and began to dig in before Mutzenich, which was the gateway to Hautes Fagnes, and to Eupen where General Gerow had his headquarters. It was in the area of the Hautes Fagnes where Von der Heydte and his paratroopers had been dropped. It was the mission of the 146th to defend this route.

The southern flank of the 99th Division took an unmerciful pounding from the German artillery on the 16th of December when the 3rd Parachute Division was to lead the attack out of the Losheim Gap in order to open up a hole for Peiper's spearheading regiment of tiger and panther tanks.

The German paratroopers failed to move through the gap due to American fire of riflemen of the 99th Division, mine fields laid by the engineers, a blown bridge, and uncertain foggy weather. Also the slow movement of their supporting armor. This had caused a jam-up on the route taken by Peiper.

Peiper, impatient, hard nosed, and wanting to get on with his mission, forced his way to the head of his column and roughly had horse-drawn artillery shoved off the road. He had some of his tanks move through mines that had not been cleared. The Kampfgruppe finally

Malmedy, Belgium, Dec 16, 1944.

arrived near Lanzerath in the early morning of December 17th only to find that the 9th Parachute Regiment had settled in for the night.

Peiper decided to advance and put one of the 9th Parachute Regiment's Battalions to lead the way as infantry. There was a bridge blown over the railroad near Lanzerath. He led his column down the embankment, over the tracks, and up the embankment on the far side. Thus he avoided the delay of moving up his engineers to rebuild the bridge. This was the beginning of the failure of the Germans to bring their engineers up with the infantry to build the blown bridges to support their armor.

Now Peiper was running free and clear with his eye on the fuel dump at Bullingen. Upon reaching Honsfeld, Peiper sent a half-track to reconnoiter his assigned route leading west. He found that the route would not support his tanks. He thus made the decision to head for the town of Bullingen, refuel his tanks, and for a short distance be on the assigned route of the 12th SS Panzer Division, which was now being tied down by the 2nd and 99th Divisions on this northern shoulder. He now felt that his objective on his assigned route through Werbomont and on to the Meuse River could be had. Little did he know that on this route at this moment were only the 254th, the 324th, the 202nd, and the 291st Engineer Combat Battalions, plus the 1111th Engineer Group. These engineers had no anti-tank guns, and no heavy weapons besides machine guns, bazookas, mines, demolitions, and rifles.

The first contact he would have with the engineers would be with the 254th, who were very busy maintaining the 99th Division supply routes right up to the Siegfried line, where they had also built back the bridges blown by the retreating Germans. The engineers were located in the vicinity of Bullingen, Butgenbach, and near the airfield for the artillery's Piper Cub liaison planes.

The V Corps commander, General Gerow, had advised the commander of the 254th to prepare to defend as combat engineers and infantry if possible against the German breakout.

The 254th with their A, B, and C Companies set up defensive positions along the Honsfeld-Bullingen road along with elements of the 2nd and 99th Divisions. B Company came upon the approach of Peiper's tanks with infantry along the road to Honsfeld. They opened fire on the Germans, who were leading with a half-track, and knocked out the lead vehicle with a bazooka as they fired rifle grenades, rifles and machine guns at the infantry.

When the attackers were repulsed, they came back at B Company two more times and the third time they had tanks in the lead. The men in B Company were overrun as the Germans passed over their foxholes. The men fell back along with the men of the 99th through Honsfeld and on to Butgenbach. They had many casualties, with men captured, and the headquarters company disappeared as some of their men arrived in Bullingen alone or sometimes in pairs. The battalion commander received the Bronze Star from Major General Walter E. Lauer, commanding officer of the 99th Division.

The scattered men of the 254th Engineers were later joined up with the 2nd Engineer Combat Battalion in Bullingen itself. This was where Peiper was aiming to refill his tanks at the fuel dump. Peiper's men were able to capture some of the Engineers as his tanks pulled into town after the Engineers had fired on their tanks.

The after-action reports of the 254th Engineer Combat Battalion for December 1944 reveal the following facts: During the month of December the battalion was assigned to and operated under the 1121 Engineer Group in support of the 2nd and 99th Divisions. From 18 December to 24 December, the Battalion also supported the 1st Infantry Division.

Road patrol and maintenance was continuously carried out except during the period where we were directly assigned to combat operations. These duties included mud and snow removal from main line routes for the upfront infantry, and filling ruts, potholes, and small bomb craters while we were under fire. Seven road barriers, consisting of mines, abatis, and craters were prepared as well as demolitions on the bridges.

Defensive positions consisting of slit trenches, gun emplacements, and 1000 yards of barbed wire concertina were prepared for the 2nd Infantry Division. Gun and radar emplacements were prepared for the 413th and 134th AAA Battalions. A blast wall was prepared for the 1121 Engineer Group Headquarters, and a rock quarry for crushed stone was operated for 12 days, and water points for all units were in operation for the period.

The final statement for the report showed 33 miles of road maintained and three quarters of a mile of road built; gallons of water pumped: 369,470; cubic yards of sand, gravel and shell hauled: 2780.

Combat operation: At approximately midnight December 16th, 1944 a message was received that the 1121 Engineer Group was on a two hour alert as Infantry. The report also directed our commanding officer to report to the G-3 of the 99th Infantry Division at once. At the 99th Division Headquarters the commander was told that the enemy had broken through and was coming up the Honsfeld-Bullingen highway. The G-3 also instructed him that all roads leading into Bullingen were blocked by tank destroyers and light tanks and the

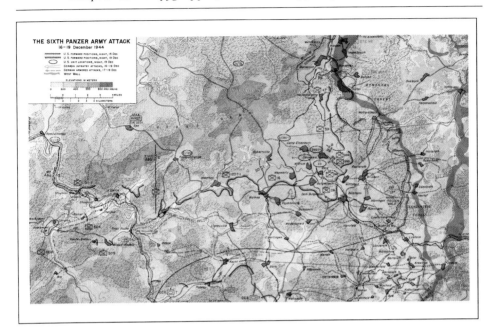

254th was to form a defensive line in front of and south and east of Bullingen, Belgium to protect American tanks.

The commanding officer returned to the battalion and instructed the companies to take up positions on the highway as shown on a map prepared by the S-3. The battalion was formed in two echelons; the forward set up a command post in Bullingen. The companies were to be dug in on the south and the west end of town, and the rear moved to the city of Waimes, Belgium to await further orders.

After setting up the command post in Bullingen, all guards of other units stationed there were notified of the situation. Runners were sent out to locate the positions of the light tanks and tank destroyers. The runners returned and stated that the armor for the road block could not be found. One sergeant of a tank destroyer outfit was brought in by Company B and he stated that he had been captured at Honsfeld, escaped from the Germans, and wanted to report German armor heading towards Bullingen in great strength. He said that he had seen 12 tanks and could hear more coming. A short time later a 1st Lieutenant walked into the command post, stood around to get warm, asked several questions and stated that he had a platoon of armored infantry in half-tracks. His identity was checked and he was satisfactory. When asked where his command post was, he said he was mobile and the Germans were coming and he was leaving. This didn't seem unusual as they normally accompanied tanks, and the tanks had also left.

At approximately 5:00 a.m. flares appeared on our Company B front as tracked-vehicles were coming in our direction. The first positive identification was shouts that were heard in German. The first order was given by Lt. Huff, Company B, who opened fire with rifles, rifle grenades, and machine guns. The German Infantry then piled off of the tanks:

one Panzer tank and six half-tracks; and the vehicles withdrew. The infantry, advancing in partial darkness, got within 15 yards of our positions before being driven back. They pulled back and reorganized, and in about 20 minutes the infantry charged our Company B positions under supporting fire of the tanks. The tanks fired a lot of large caliber shells but most were 20mm high explosive shells and machine guns.

This attack was in greater force and in spite of the tanks and the shouts of the officers, they were driven back after sustaining heavy losses. The next ten minutes gave us time to evacuate wounded but now it was getting quite light. They charged again, but this time the charge was led by tanks. As no American tank fire was encountered, the German tanks spread out and overran B Company positions crushing two machine guns. The brave Engineers stayed in their foxholes and only three men were injured by the tanks passing over them.

The German Infantry were still not able to overrun our positions due to the intensive small arms fire. The German Infantry then withdrew and maneuvered around our flank, which was exposed. In this action one tank was knocked out and two of the 12 damaged. Many of the Germans were left lying on the battlefield.

Having been overrun, the Battalion was instructed to fight a delaying action while falling back on Butgenbach, by G-3, 99th Division. Orders were issued by Battalion for Company C to fight back out of town and northwest along the railroad tracks, Company A towards Wirtfeld, and Company B and Headquarters Company down the Bullingen and Butgenbach road.

Company C fought back through town and took position north of Bullingen. Company A had not been pressed and held. The Battalion took positions to give the appearance of a strongly held line with favorable terrain in front of them. This line could be seen from the town and when their point reorganized, it took the St. Vith road south. The enemy point, on reaching the crossroads of the St. Vith Butgenbach road, was back on Peiper's assigned route. This was the spearheading Kampfgruppe Peiper. He was now on his route running free and clear again. This would not be the only time Peiper would be involved with the American Combat Engineers. The objective of the 254th had temporarily been accomplished: they had added considerable delay to Peiper and his Leibstandarte SS Adolf Hitler.

After the enemy point passed, the support sent tanks towards Wirtzfeld, where the 2nd Division met them with tank destroyers. Now the 12th SS Panzer Division was in action on its road towards Malmedy. The 2nd Division knocked out the first tank of the Germans in this attack, flanking headquarters of the 254th west of town.

At 12:00 noon, two platoons of Company B had worked their way through the woods and joined headquarters west of town and found three anti-tank guns located there. The Germans brought in artillery and shelled the position west of town. At 1:00 p.m. the 254th defensive line dropped back to the crossroads under cover of several light tanks.

At 3:00 p.m. the 26th Infantry of the 2nd Division relieved the courageous engineers and took over their position. Company A was subjected to shelling from our own troops. Because of this the Company Commander ordered the Company to withdraw towards

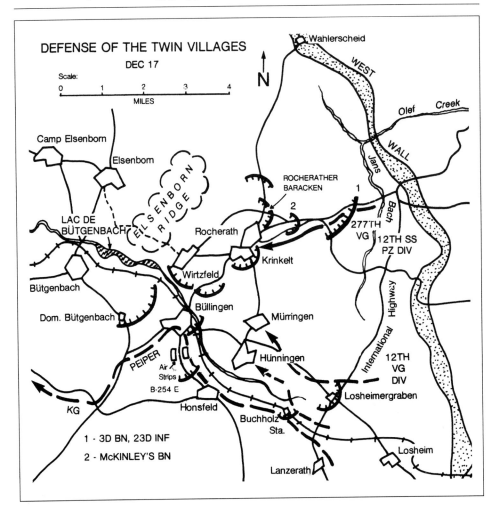

DEFENSE OF THE TWIN VILLAGES
DEC 17

1 - 3D BN, 23D INF

2 - McKINLEY'S BN

Wirtzfield. Enroute the 23rd Infantry was contacted, told of the situation, and they formally relieved Company A of responsibility for their front. After being relieved the Battalion returned to Camp Elsenborn where we reorganized and prepared for our next mission.

On the 17th of December, the first day of the German attack from the American point of view, the most critical situations were the Losheim breakout of Peiper, and the threatened encirclement of the two regiments of the 106th Infantry Division on the Schnee Eifel.

The attack of General Manteuffel's volksgrenadier divisions, to gain St. Vith and open up a road net to the west, was critical to the success of a German broad-based attack. Since the Volksgrenadiers of the 6th Panzer Army and the 12th SS Panzer Division were stopped by the 99th Infantry Division in its sector of the front, it looked like Peiper's breakout was the only event that Hitler had to cheer about.

5

December 17th Movement of Kampfgruppe Peiper

Following the breakout of Peiper's lengthy column at Bullingen his assigned route was to head through the back roads to Ligneville, Wanne, Trois Ponts, Werbomont, and Ombret Rausa on the Meuse River. This was called route D on the 1st SS Panzer Corps attack plan.

During the war trials of Peiper many of the men of the 1st SS Panzer Division made sworn affidavits of the occurrences along Peiper's route of advance. One of these was Siegfried Jaekel. His story is included along with the other actions on this blitzkrieg journey through the Ardennes. The journey began on December 12th, 1944 in the woods near Satzvey, Germany. Jaekel was in the 2nd platoon of the 3rd Panzer Pioneer Company in the Liebstandarte SS Adolf Hitler. He learned that platoon commander Seitz had made a speech, and it was in these words: "We will make a counter-offensive which should develop into something very big. We will have three smoke laying battalions; a battalion of Germans dressed as Americans will make the first thrust and put the enemy on the run. No prisoners of war will be taken. You will remember the German cities which were subject to terror attacks day after day. Our flanks will be protected by Panzer Grenadiers. We will strike the enemy wherever we meet him. Who ever shows himself to be a coward will be shot." Jaekel further stated, "The first prisoners of war that I recall seeing during the offensive were in the outskirts of Honsfeld, as we were leaving this town towards Bullingen. This was between 8 and 9 a.m., 17 December 1944. Just before turning right to go in the direction of Bullingen, I remember passing an American truck which had a machine gun mounted above the cab. As we approached the intersection, I heard machine pistol fire coming from the right and later saw 15 Americans dead along side of the road." Jaekel added that he had seen them surrender with their arms held over the heads.

After the column was bombed from the air and the platoon took cover, the next prisoners of war he remembers seeing were a group of eight who were walking towards the rear on the left side of the road. Jaekel stated, "Our group leader, Sepp Witkowski, ordered us to bump them off! Witkowski fired at them with his machine pistol and Hergeth with a rifle. They were unarmed and held their arms in surrender position. I shot at them with my pistol for two or three rounds.

I remember firing at three prisoner of war groups that we fired on up to Bullingen. The truth of the matter is that I saw and heard of so many American Prisoners of war who had been shot or were being shot during this offensive that I cannot remember every case."

There were 7 American prisoners of war captured in a house in Bullingen that were lined up on a street and shot down after they had surrendered. From Bullingen to Thirimont along a narrow dirt road Jaekel reported that two groups of Americans who had surrendered were shot down. "There were eight men in each group with their hands above the heads. We didn't even stop to examine the bodies. When I fired into each group, I always used my P 38 pistol," Jaekel recalled.

"Between 1:00 and 2:00 p.m. we arrived at a crossroads. This was three to five Kilometers north of Ligneuville (the village of Baugnez). I remember that there was a house and a barn on the right hand side of the road. South of the two buildings there was a hedge row and a pasture. Parked on the right hand side of the road was a panther tank with its cannon pointed at 1:00 o'clock. Just before we reached this tank, I saw approximately 60 to 80 American prisoners of war standing in a pasture.

"In an SPW (Armored car) on the left hand side of the road were men of our unit with pistols in hand. There were also two other SPWs on the right hand side of the road. When we stopped here the Americans were standing in the pasture with their hands clasped above and behind their heads in a sign of surrender. They were unarmed and were not making any attempt to escape.

"Before we came to a halt, I saw some SS officers present and some German soldiers in Panzer uniforms on the tank. As we passed Beutner's SPW we were given the signal to halt, and after we halted he spoke to Witkowski and told him the American prisoners were going to be shot. The men in my SPW loaded their weapons and made ready to fire into the prisoners. This took about three to five minutes before the first shots were fired.

"At this time Hans Toedter and I were trying to get our machine gun ready; Pioneer Hans Stickel and Pioneer Harry Ende were doing the same thing with the rear machine gun. Jochim Hofman and Gustav Neve left our vehicle and stood at the rear SPW, Hofman aiming his machine pistol and Neve his fast firing rifle at the prisoners who were standing in the field. I was serving as loader on the machine gun.

"Witkowski left the PW and stood on the road at the right front corner of our SPW aiming with his machine pistol. Pioneer Hubert Storch stood with the rifle on the back of the SPW. Pioneer Hargeth stood near Storch with a rifle.

"Pioneers Walkowiak and Scholtze, both of whom had rifles, stayed in the SPW. As we were making these preparations, I noticed the men in Losenski's SPW ahead of us were doing the same thing. At their front machine gun was Losenski. His assistant was Aistleitner and on their machine gun was Jirassek assisted by Wasenberger. The other men went to the ground with their rifles."

"In Bode's SPW Kies was at the front machine gun assisted by Mueller. On the rear machine gun was a paratrooper and Horst Hummel. I remember that Bode posted himself in front of his SPW with his driver. Both of them were armed with machine pistols.

"Then came Beutner's order to fire! The first shot was fired from Beutner's SPW. All of these men were firing from their positions into the Americans in the pasture. We fired about 75 rounds from the front machine guns. Then I went to the rear machine gun, loaded it and started shooting into the prisoners.

"As soon as the firing started, all of the American prisoners who were in the field fell to the ground. While I was still in my SPW manning my machine gun, I saw the following additional people shooting into the American prisoners: Neve, Witkowski, Walkowiak, Scholtze, Storch, and Hergeth.

"Then Sprenger's SPW pulled up behind ours and the men in the new arrival began firing into the prisoners. After the firing stopped our SPW was driven further down the road towards Englesdorf (Ligneuville). We stopped beside an American truck. Sprenger's SPW pulled up behind ours. I dismounted from the truck and began walking back towards the pasture. I was walking along the ditch when I saw Gettinger firing in the pasture from his SPW with his machine pistol. When we reached the pasture we entered it and stood for a few minutes to observe the Americans who were still moving or otherwise showing signs of life. As we observed those who were still moving, the three of us chose different targets and went towards them in order to shoot them. I went to a spot where I shot four or five wounded American prisoners with my pistol. I fired one shot into the heart of each wounded man. At the time I fired, my pistol was one meter from the American soldiers at whom I fired. All of these men were moving or showing some sign of life before I fired. After I shot them they didn't move anymore. I am sure I killed every man at whom I fired.

Jaekel, in his testimony, then went on to list the nine Germans who shot up Americans in the southern end of the field, fifteen in the center portion and ten in the north end.

"We stayed in the field 10 or 15 minutes and then returned to our SPW. We mounted and then started down the road towards Englesdorf. After we had moved down the road another 3000 meters another group of eight prisoners came up the road towards the cross-roads. These men were fired on from our SPWS and fell to the ground. We did not stop to examine the bodies.

"I remember upon reaching Engelsdorf the road curved up hill towards the right: I remember seeing another group of prisoners, approximately 50, who were lying in the field on the right hand side of the road. It was my opinion that those men had been bumped off, just like the group in the pasture at the Crossroads. We didn't stop to go among the bodies and examine them.

The two Pioneer platoons spent the night south of Stavelot and, according to Jaekel, near a farmhouse lane there were 18 more American prisoners who had been shot. On the 18th of December, in the afternoon Jaekel's SPW and the others in the Pioneer platoon went on through Stavelot and then were strafed from the air and had to return to the previous position. On the evening of the 18th went through Stavelot again and drove on to Stoumont. Here again Jaekel witnessed the Germans shoot down Americans who had surrendered and gave up their weapons.

The sergeant in charge, Beutner, gave the following order in the heat of the battle at Stoumont, "It is an order that no prisoners will be taken." Jaekel then stated, "We continued up the road in Stoumont and we searched a couple houses and there Witkowski discovered a couple Americans hiding in a chicken coupe. He ordered them out of the chicken house and then told them they would be shot. Witkowski shot them with a machine pistol, Storch with a rifle, and Toedter with a machine gun."

Jaekel then told about Witkowski shooting a civilian and when on the 20th and 21st, he went to a tavern and a castle because of a wound. He heard other Germans shooting prisoners of war in Stoumont, La Gleize, and also near a church.

Thus in addition to the 81 men murdered at the crossroads, the Kampfgruppe Peiper had shot many more men of America who had been captured, gave up their guns, and then were shot down in cold blood. The time, dates and locations of these occurrences check very closely with the after action reports of the 291st, the 30th Division, and the National archives.

6

The Reaction of the Engineers
to Peiper's Breakout

Peiper's column was hit by American air at 7:30 a.m. on December 17th in the vicinity of the Honsfeld-Bullingen area. The attack by the air force planes had been requested by the 99th Division Headquarters at Bullingen. The squadron circled over the 1st SS Panzer Division spearhead, strafed and bombed the Kampfgruppe, and suffered some losses to Peiper's anti-aircraft guns.

This event marked the beginning of Peiper's troubles with the American combat engineers. Lt. Frank Rhea, from the crossroads at Bullingen, sighted the actions of the planes against a free-wheeling German tank column. Corporal Al Schommer, Company A's radio operator, also saw this action from nearby Ambleve.

The reaction of both of these 291st men caused a chain reaction throughout the entire 291st, to the 1111th Engineer Combat Group of Colonel H. Wallis Anderson, to VII Corps and First Army headquarters.

Planting TNT for a road block.

Lt. Frank Rhea notified his company commander, Captain John Conlin, at his B Company Command Post in Malmedy of this most unusual and disturbing situation. Peiper's column of tanks was only about 4 miles from Captain James Gamble's A Company Command post in Ambleve.

The Kamfgruppe was only a few hours away from Malmedy and the First Army's supply and fuel dumps northwest of the village.

In fact, First Army Headquarters of General Courtney Hodges could be overrun in less than six hours unless this main thrust was stopped. The situation along the Siegfried line at this time was such that any penetration by German armored columns through the five American divisions would permit the German armor to reach the Meuse

Pergrin Command Post at Malmedy

River without any opposition from any units except combat engineers. During the months since the Normandy beachhead days, many of the engineer battalions had almost got caught up in a German counterattack, such as the 105th engineers on the river Vire near St. Lo along with the 82nd Engineers.

Several Engineer battalions experienced counterattacks near Mortain, France when the German panzer divisions came back at the 30th Division seven times. The 291st, 296th, and the 105th were there to experience such an occurrence.

There was not much time for Colonel Anderson and I to prepare to defend this vital area in the Ardennes. I had been alert to the facts of this situation since 3:00 a.m. when I received an early call by phone from Captain Conlin in Malmedy. It was now decision making time. Excitedly he advised of Rhea's discovery and he said, "Colonel, we've got a crack at the Krauts. I'll start to set up road blocks in Malmedy."

I advised the Irishman to go ahead and I would bring along some staff and join him. I quickly called Colonel Anderson and advised him of the situation. I told the Colonel that I would take Major Ed Lampp and other staff to Malmedy. Major Lampp was not only my operations officer, but was also serving as my Executive Officer.

Once we had our plan set up in Malmedy, Lampp would return to Trois Ponts with a map of our defenses in Malmedy. After conferring at the Colonel's CP in Trois Ponts, Lamp would set up my rear command post in Haute Bodeux, just on the outskirts of Trois Ponts.

The Abatis (TNT) road block of Lt. Wade Colbeck of "B" Company at Malmedy East. Sgt. Joe Connors, Sgt. Dishaw, CpL. Bob Cresswell, and Cpt. Glen Salsberg were also at the site.

At this time my C Company CP was in the castle Froidcoer, owned by the Georges de Harrene family. Lts. Don Davis and Warren Rombaugh's were located there and their main mission was to operate the saw mill in Trois Ponts (Three Bridges). The third platoon under Lt. John Perkins and Sgt. Ed Keoghan was at Sourbrodt near the Huertgen forest, where they were maintaining the main line of resistance for the 28th Division embattled there.

The battalion motor pool was located in Trois Ponts with the Battalion headquarters personnel located at Basse and Haute Bodeux. Due to the fact that the battalion acted as security guard for the 1111th Group our location was generally near Colonel Anderson's command post since the Normandy days and generally forward of First Army Headqurters.

Captain Gamble's command post was now about to be moving or be overrun by the Germans at Ambleve. He had Lt. Edelstein's platoon with him in this untenable position. Lt. Arch Taylor's A Company platoon was operating a saw mill at Montenau near Born. "Bucky" Walter's platoon was operating a saw mill at Grand Halleux.

Of course, John Conlin had Lt. Frank Rhea's platoon in Malmedy, and Lt. Wade Colbeck's platoon was operating a sawmill in Stavelot and getting ready to have a Christmas party for the neighboring kids in Stavelot.

The staff I took to Malmedy was mainly assistant staff officers for I felt there would have to be top staff people to work with Major Lampp and Colonel Anderson's staff in the nearby command post. I especially took Captain Lloyd Sheetz, my liason officer, to create a liaison with all higher headquarters as need be.

Tom Stack, assistant S-3, Leroy Joehnck, assistant S-2, Warrant Officer Coye R. Selff, assistant supply officer, and Tech-Sergeant Bill Crickenberger, communications, comprised my staff. Little did I realize how well these men would serve me in the most severe combat conditions.

We arrived in Malmedy after a quick trip through Trois Ponts and Stavelot about 11:00 a.m. My first move was to advise Gamble by radio to move back to Trois Ponts and Werbomont and act in battalion reserve and report to Colonel Anderson and Major Lampp upon arrival. The message got through as Gamble was already being pressed by approaching Germans towards Ambleve. Apparently the message arrived when Gamble was loading up to make the tough trip back through heavy traffic and forested roads.

Two of Lt. Arch Taylor's men had been fired on by the men in Peiper's Kampfgruppe but were able to escape and advise their platoon commander of the approach of the German armor. These men were sent to load up gasoline at Bullingen when their truck was demolished by the fire from the German column. They were again able to escape. As it turned out "Arch" was able to load up his men and join Gamble on the way back to Trois Ponts.

When we arrived in Malmedy, John Conlin had set up 13 road blocks and had sent patrols east in jeeps to locate the enemy. Lampp and I had reviewed Conlin's plan and learned that Rhea, Colbeck, and Kirkpatrick had worked out a plan for the defense of Malmedy with their platoons. Colbeck had made a well-organized map of the plan. The use of the men and non-commissioned officers at the road blocks had to be parceled out to include two twelve-hour tricks at each site. This to allow time for sleep.

Lt. Wade Colbeck's road block at the east end of Malmedy. The men are armed with a Bazooka.

"B" Company road block at the bridge in the center of Malmedy. Sgt. Walter Smith is in charge, and the bridge is prepared for demolition.

By 11:30 a.m. Major Lampp was sent back to Trois Ponts to meet with Colonel Anderson to advise him of the plan and tell him we had 150 men in Malmedy. We checked our communications and found that we had phone lines to First Army Engineer Headquarters, the 1111th Engineer Group, and the rear battalion command post at Haute Bodeux. Plus I had the reliable liaison service from the very learned Captain Sheetz.

Conlin had radio and phone contact with his road blocks and the movement by jeep with 1st Sergeant Earl Short. We had combed Malmedy for more troops, but came back empty handed. We knew we were on the wrong side of a two-sided situation. We also knew that Colonel Anderson's experience in his third war would be able to help our situation. He was already talking to Corps headquarters and the Hdqs. of Colonel William Carter, the First Army Engineer, about our plight.

At 11:35 a.m. things began to happen. Major Boyer, battalion commander of the 7th Armored Division's Tank Destroyers, came into town. We halted him in front of the CP and asked him to form on our defenses. He gave us a negative reply when he advised us that his mission was to move to the defense of the 106th Division at St. Vith. Following closely behind Major Boyer came Battery B of the 285th Field Artillery Observation Battalion, the guys who give target designation for our artillery. They were led by two officers and a driver in a jeep. Although this group had nothing but rifles to aid our cause, it could add at least 100 men to the defense.

In the jeep were a Captain Mills and a Lieutenent Virgil Lary. They would not remain in Malmedy as I requested since their mission was also in St. Vith. I now thought we were very fortunate so far, and the 106th Division needed help before we did. It turned out later that Major Boyer was captured at the battle of St. Vith. Mills and Lary followed Boyer out of town on the way to Baugnez, just beyond Sgt. Charles Dishaw's Company B road block, where they were to turn south towards Ligneuville and thence on to St. Vith. They never got to St. Vith!

Sometime in the early afternoon we heard the firing of heavy weapons and what sounded like machine pistols, then there was a pause. A while later more sounds of bigger guns and again what sounded like machine guns and pistols. Just prior to this, one of Captain Conlin's patrols had reported in with the sighting of German tanks in great numbers on the way out of Thirimont.

We now knew that Battery B of the 285th was in trouble and the breakaway Kampfgruppe was at our doorstep. Just before this I had been concerned about their progress towards St. Vith. There was nothing that we could do now but attempt to determine if they had met up with the Germans. I took Sgt. Crickenberger and a jeep out to Dishaw's roadblock and learned from him that the firing had ceased. However, it had not been far away. We continued out to Geromont, parked the jeep, and walked through a pasture towards a line of trees.

Half running, babbling incoherently, disheveled without helmets, came three men. We soon realized they were Americans who turned out to be men of the 285th. We put them in the jeep and brought them to our aid station in Malmedy where I learned that they were Sgt. Kenneth Ahrens, Mike Shiranko, and Albert Valenzi. Once their wounds were treated and they had coffee, they told a clear story of an out and out massacre.

They had surrendered their weapons, were lined up in a field, and were fired upon with machine guns and machine pistols. Most of them had their hands above their heads when fired upon. They had played dead for a while before they could sneak away and escape after some of the Germans had moved on.

We knew we were facing a ruthless enemy who took no prisoners. We also knew if he attacked us we would be badly outnumbered, and if he moved to the south and west we would be surrounded. We now knew that there were German paratroopers north of us. What would 150 men with rifles, machine guns, bazookas, explosives, and demolitions do against a 15 mile long column of armor and infantry?

Our first thoughts were for the men of the 285th. Conlin sent out a weapons carrier with armed men towards Baugnez to pick up some escapees. Lt. Tom Stack brought three of them back in a jeep, and others came to our road blocks. Sgt. Joe Connors brought in Private John Cobbler with six wounds, he died before our Medics could act in his behalf. Some of those who came in later were Ted Paluch, Bill Merriken, Robert Mearig, Harold Billow, Carl Daub, James Mattera, Kenneth Kingston, William Summers, William Reem, George Fox, and Ted Flechsig.

My next act was to check with Captain Sheetz to learn if he had advised Lampp, Anderson, and First Army of the massacre and the location of the German Combat Group (Kampfgruppe). He had!

We were now in trouble! We needed help. We asked Lampp to send Captain Moyer's C Company into Malmedy from Froidville and leave a squad on a roadblock south of Stavelot to protect the bridge over the Ambleve River. Lampp advised that Captain Gamble's A Company had arrived from Ambleve with Arch Taylor's and Alvin Edelstein's platoons. Gamble would send into Malmedy his machine guns and bazookas with men to fire them. Captain Kamen, our Dental Officer, would bring in more Medics.

All of this information was relayed to Colonel Anderson in Trois Ponts where he was counting on C Company of Captain Moyer to prepare the bridges in Trois Ponts for demolition. Anderson and Lampp agreed to use Gamble's Company A in reserve. The Colonel then advised the new battalion commander, Lt. Colonel Harvey Fraser of the 51st Engineer Combat Battalion, to send a company into Trois Ponts. Colonel Anderson had been informing both Corps and First Army of the location of Peiper's column. General Hodges decided to move his headquarters further west as a result.

During the early evening I learned that Anderson had influenced First Army to send me some help into Malmedy. Captain Larry Moyer had arrived and immediately set up Lt. Don Davis' platoon on the west Malmedy defenses. Moyer had left Sgt. Chuck Hensel with his squad to set up a road block on the hill south of the Ambleve River bridge in Stavelot.

Moyer's other platoon under command of Lt. Warren Rombaugh was to stay in Trois Ponts and prepare the bridges there for demolition. Major Ed Lampp was now coordinating the total defenses in the Trois Ponts area with Colonel Anderson. The situation was now becoming clear: the Germans were moving south towards Ligneuville, an additional 45 men had been sent to Malmedy, and the weakest spot in our defense was in Stavelot with only one squad to man the roadblock there.

I soon learned that the 99th Norwegian Infantry Battalion was being sent to Malmedy, along with the 526th Armored Infantry Battalion, and the 825th Tank Destroyer Battalion. I advised Captain Sheetz to contact these units and bring at least a company of armored infantry and some anti-tank guns into Stavelot.

When a unit of the 1st Infantry Division had gone through Malmedy early in the morning, we had learned that the 1st was forming a defensive line somewhere east of us. Now that the 7th Armored Division was moving from the north into Stavelot through Trois Ponts, south to Vielsalm, and then east to the 106th Division at St. Vith, we felt that the reaction of First Army to this German breakout was immediate and decisive. It was only ten hours after Lt. Rhea had sighted Peiper's column near Butgenbach, and action had been taken to defend against a blitzing Kampfgruppe.

We were being shelled in Malmedy and thrusts had been made at our roadblocks. More members of the 295th were being brought in for aid, and then taken to field hospitals near Spa. As I interviewed these victims, they all told the same story. There was no doubt in my mind it was a massacre of surrendered American soldiers.

Captain Gamble sent us ten machine guns and gunners from his position near Trois Ponts, as well as more bazookas for the road blocks.

291st Engineers' Defense Positions in Malmédy
December 17, 18, 1944

1. N-32 roadblock, ¾ mile northwest of Five Points crossroads. Co. B, Lt. Colbeck
2. Chodes-Gdoumont roadblock, Co. B, Lt. Colbeck
3. Co. B on main Eupen–St.-Vith highway
4. Junction roadblock, north of C.P, Lt. Colbeck
5. Inner defense roadblock, Gdoumont Road, Co. B, Lt. Rhea
6. Eupen roadblock, Co. B, Lt. Rhea
7. Co. B sawmill
8. Abatis defense, roadblock, back road to Spa, mixed, Co. B and Co. C
9. Level grade crossing roadblock, Co. C
10. Overpass on Rte. de St.-Vith, Co. C
11. Overpass on Rte. de Falize, Co. C
12. Big viaduct overpass, Stavelot Road, Sgt. McCarty, Co. A and Co. B
13. Wooden bridge roadblock, Warche River, Sgt. McCarty, Co. A
14. 44th Evacuation Field Hospital
15. Paper mill

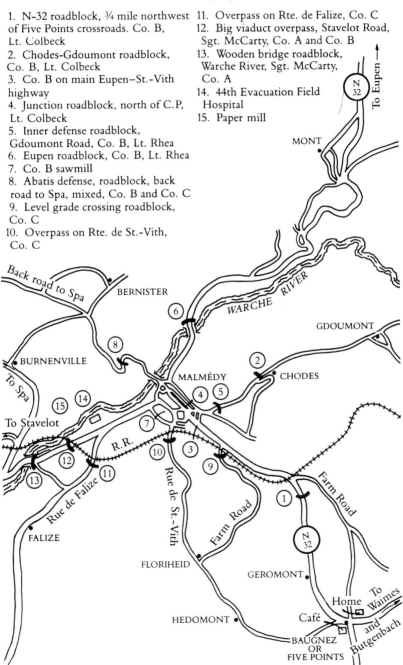

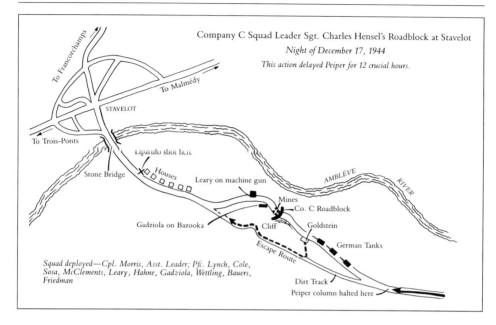

Company C Squad Leader Sgt. Charles Hensel's Roadblock at Stavelot
Night of December 17, 1944
This action delayed Peiper for 12 crucial hours.

To Francorchamps

To Malmédy

STAVELOT

To Trois-Ponts

Liparulo shot here

Stone Bridge

Houses

Leary on machine gun

AMBLÈVE RIVER

Mines

Co. C Roadblock

Gadziola on Bazooka

Cliff

Goldstein

German Tanks

Escape Route

*Squad deployed—Cpl. Morris, Asst. Leader; Pfc. Lynch, Cole,
Sosa, McClements, Leary, Hahne, Gadziola, Wettling, Bauers,
Friedman*

Dirt Track
Peiper column halted here

Shortly after Hensel had set up his roadblock on a narrow, curving road with a high rock cliff on the right, and a 100 foot drop-off on the left, the 13 man squad heard the sound of approaching tanks. In the darkness Private Bernie Goldstein, out on point, yelled "Halt!" with only a rifle in his hand. All hell broke loose! Weapons fired, but the curve in the road protected Hensel and his men. Goldstein managed to escape up over the face of the cliff and head into the woods.

As Hensel moved towards the area where Goldstein had been positioned, the Germans opened up with machine gun fire. Gadziola was able to take a look beyond the curve and saw a large tank cross-ways to the road and almost over the embankment. The darkness didn't prevent the Germans from opening fire.

Gadziola ducked back under cover and told Hensel that he could not see Goldstein. The firing ceased and Hensel and his men heard the German tanks move back up the hill. Hensel discussed the situation with his men, and they decided that they should leave their mines in position and move down the hill to the bridge. They knew that the 7th Armored Division was moving west through Stavelot, and the 13 man squad had been trained to get in, accomplish the engineering mission, and get out—especially in situations like this where their weapons were insufficient to fight tanks and knock out German armor.

Little did Peiper know that at this time the only American unit between his 1st SS spearheading armored column and its objective, the Meuse River, was the C Company squad of the 291st Engineer Combat Battalion.

As they loaded up and moved towards the bridge in Stavelot, they found the engineers of the 202nd Engineer Combat Battalion had just arrived. They had men at a roadblock and men on the Ambleve River bridge. The officer in charge said they had been sent in to relieve

Hensel. He now felt he had done his job and he could move back with his platoon commander, Lt. Warren Rombaugh. He had done his job because Peiper remained back up on the hill and decided to attack at daylight for he felt that Stavelot was heavily defended.

In Malmedy, German shells were falling. We expected an attack from the Germans who learned, at times the hard way, that American troops were defending the village. The Germans had sent some light armor against the roadblocks and suffered loss of men and equipment each time. Peiper knew that Malmedy was on the 12th SS Panzer Division's route and had decided to by-pass it. Around 11:00 p.m. on the 17th word came in to us that the 99th Norwegian Infantry Battalion was on its way into Malmedy. I was overjoyed with the news. I remarked to Captain Conlin, "Colonel Anderson of the 1111th Engineer Group and Colonel William Carter, the First Army Engineer, hadn't let us down."

When Lt. Colonel Harold Hansen came into my CP in Malmedy he was amazed to learn that I only had about 200 men, all on the road blocks. I told him that we now had an Armored Column of German SS strung around south of us. "They have massacred many Americans at a crossroads about two miles southeast of here, and have tested our road blocks."

I then gave the Colonel a copy of our defensive plan and he told me that the 526th Armored Infantry and the 825th Tank Destroyers were also on the way to me. I advised Hansen that I had sent Captain Sheetz towards Spa to lead a task force into Stavelot where we were practically void of troops except for my C Company squad of Sgt. Charles Hensel.

7

More About the Malmedy Massacre

Around midnight on the 17th of December, Lt. Virgil Lary was brought into my CP in Malmedy. Lary was the acting battery commander of the 285th Field Artillery Observation Battalion's Battery B. Virgil had been in the lead jeep that I had stopped as their convoy came through Malmedy earlier in the day.

Captain Kamen and the 291st Medics had taken care of his wounds after the Martin sisters had brought him into Malmedy. The Martin sisters lived on a farm within a half mile of the massacre site. Virgil had survived the massacre when he feigned death under the body of his driver who was one of the first Americans killed by the German machine gun fire that opened up after the surrender.

Standing at the crossroads looking down the road towards Geremont. The first two vehicles are from the Battery B-285th, and the rest are ambulances. These vehicles did not make it past the crossroads. The house on the left is No. 7. (Bill M.)

From a window on the east end of house No. 7. Note the ruins of the café in the background, as well as the tracks running east to west on the Hedemont Road. (Bill M.)

This photo shows the south side of the café (No. 6) ruins. The Massacre Field is to the right of this photo. (Bill M.)

Taken from the crossroads, this photo is west up the Hedemont Rd. towards house No. 7, shown on the left. The roof of my wood shed is in the front portion of the café ruins on the left. The bumper of the jeep marks these men as being with the 30th-117th 2HQ3, and the 21/2 ton was the mess truck of the 285th. (Bill M.)

Lary laid in this spot until darkness when most of the German column had passed on towards Ligneuville. Apparently at the time he crawled out from a pile of bodies, there were no Germans guarding the site, or they had presumed that the remaining men in the field were all dead.

Despite Virgil's serious leg wound he was able to crawl to the Martin Farm where he had fallen into the friendly hands of a Belgian Patriot rather than a German sympathizer. He was given assistance and shelter from the father and daughters of the Martin family. While the daughters tended his wounds, the father came into Malmedy and located our Medics. He was concerned that the Germans would search the homes of the Belgians and would slaughter all who proved to be protecting American soldiers. Lary and I discussed the full story of the German atrocity and also why his column had proceeded on, after my warning of the possible approach of a Nazi column.

I explained to him that shortly after he had departed my CP, one of our patrols had reported the Germans near Thirimont, which was only one mile from the crossroads where the 285th met the column. Lary was calm and gave a clear, concise coverage of the massacre, and after I had this information from him there was little doubt in my mind that the Germans had violated the Geneva convention. I was in touch with Virgil after the war and his life was never a happy one from the time of the war trials until his early death of natural causes. He was a typical American who tried to do his very best at the time of war and like many, many others, suffered because of it.

"When I saw that we had no opportunity to defend ourselves against tanks and machine guns, I raised my hands and yelled at the men of the 285th to surrender. I at that time had stepped up out of the ditch along the side of the road where we were stopped by the German firing. As we surrendered the Germans herded us into the field in rows and removed much of our belongings. Watches, wallets, and in some instances boots and gloves." Virgil seriously stated.

I knew what pain he must have suffered to watch his men be shot down in cold blood after having given up into the hands of the enemy. "The first part of the armored column which consisted of tanks and half-tracks, the men were in SS uniforms, some with skull and cross bones on their caps or helmets." Lary pointed out that when a German Officer came up in a jeep, he jumped out of the jeep and apparently was disturbed because the column was being delayed. He gave some orders and soon the Germans got back into their vehicles and headed down the road. "They left some tanks and men to guard the prisoners and had some of our men drive away with some of our vehicles in their convoy."

"The next part of the convoy arrived with several huge tanks, either panther or tiger giants. One of the tanks stopped and one of the Germans aimed a pistol and fired two shots killing two of our men. We were amazed and startled, because we all felt that they were going to bring up trucks to haul us off to a prisoner of war camp.

"Moments later it became a killing field, as the Germans opened up with machine guns and men were falling in all rows as they were either struck by the machine gun bursts or fell in a defensive effort. I was wounded as I fell when one of the machine guns riddled my driver and one of the shots struck me around the ankle.

"Some of the Germans went through the piles of bodies and checked to see if the men were still alive; those that were received a machine pistol shot through the head. I lost all track of time and I don't remember if I might have passed out, but I do believe that others besides me were able to get away."

I told Lary that I was able to personally rescue Schiranko, Valenzi, and Sgt. Ahrens; all three of them had given precisely the same story of the atrocity. I also told him that we were able to give aid to about 15 others who had escaped from the massacre field at Baugnez. Lary was then transported to a field hospital immediately near Spa.

This photo shows the wood shed where I first took refuge moments after escaping the Massacre Field. I was joined later that night by Chuck Reding. (Bill M.)

This photo was taken from the café grounds looking south in the direction of Lignenville with the Massacre Field in the foreground. The long stretch of tree-lined road is where most of the "B" Battery vehicles stopped when the ambush occurred. (Bill M.)

A scene at the west end of house No. 7, with the attached barn and wood shed at right. A portion of the Malmedy Road with vehicles on it is in the left background, and a portion of the café ruins can be seen above the wood shed. The tagged soldier (#64) was not from the 285th. (Bill M.)

The story of the incident at the Baugnez crossroads as told by the victims all coincided with the description which was given to me by Virgil Lary. Again we informed our own command of the massacre as well as all higher headquarters. This seemed to cause our own forces to do their utmost to perform their duties the best that they possibly could. We found out later that First Army headquarters had advised Bradley, Eisenhower, and many other American units of the atrocity.

Over these many years, I have met annually with the victims who are still alive from this Baugnez incident. Most of them have led wholesome, great American lives but there are a few who have suffered. None of them ever made an issue of what they had experienced during the war.

Lts. Rhea, Davis, Kirkpatrick, Colbeck, and Perkins had all extended their mine fields well beyond the roadblocks. The arrival of more mines and demolitions from 291st battalions supply had aided this type of defense greatly. The trees on all the routes at the outskirts of Malmedy had all been prepared with blocks of TNT connected to detonators in order to close off the roads when the explosions were made.

Lt. Robert Wilson of the 49th AAA Brigade was well stocked with ammunition for his 90-mm anti-aircraft guns. He had been displaced from the area between Honsfeld and Butgenbach very hurriedly when this armored column had broken through. Each of our 15 roadblocks were covered by at least one 50 caliber machine gun and one 30 caliber machine gun provided by the 99th Norwegians. Radio communications had been set-up with each road block and in some instances there were phone cables laid out from the battalion CP.

Standing at the crossroads looking south towards Lignenville. The café ruins (No. 6) are on the right, and the building on the left further down the road (No. 9) was across the road from the Massacre Field. (Bill M.)

All bridges, including both highway and railroad crossings, had been prepared for demolition, and all detonators were set in locations that enabled good visibility for the demolition sergeant.

At 4:00 a.m. Captain Lloyd Sheetz reported in on the situation at Stavelot. We now knew that our enemy was the 1st SS Panzer Division, and we were aware that these were the crack troops of Hitler's military. Sheetz advised that the bridge in Stavelot was in the hands of the 202nd Engineer Combat Battalion and there were anti-tank guns and armored infantry on the defenses. Hensel had been relieved of his roadblock responsibility but one of his men was wounded and one killed.

The Germans were still on the hill south of Stavelot and had been firing on the roads with artillery. Sheetz had met Captain Gamble in Stavelot and Gamble had rescued the wounded man and gone back to the battalion CP in order to serve in reserve when needed.

During the night there had been several incidents at the roadblocks south and east of Malmedy, but these were only feelers for the Germans to test our defenses. There had been sporadic artillery and at times V-1 rockets fired in our direction, but as yet no casualties. There had been some air action, however the overcast skies gave us no identification of this possibility as yet.

Captain John Conlin had made road block assignments to his platoon commanders. Lt. Wade Colbeck had roadblock no. 1, situated on N-32, 3/4 of a mile northwest of five points crossroads. This was the most important one at this time since it was nearest to the location where Peiper's column had massacred the members of 285th's battery B. Lt. Colbeck also had the no. 2 block at the Chodes-Gdoumont road, and no. 4, the junction block north of the command post. Colbeck assigned each of his blocks to a squad leader for 24 hour duty. Each man in the squad was on for 12 hours and slept for 12 hours. Their main duties were to man the machine guns and the detonators for the explosives. They all were equipped with rifles and occasionally sent on patrol.

Lt. John Kirkpatrick set his platoon up on the Abatis defenses near the CP in Malmedy, and on the back road to Spa. Lt. Frank Rhea had the inner defense roadblock, the Gdoumont road, and the road to Eupen.

Lt. Don Davis set up the infantry and machine gun line to cover the two railroad under-passes on the Rue de Falize and the main road to Stavelot. Sergeant Ralph McCarty was assigned to set up these bridges for demolition. Captain Moyer organized the rest of his C Company to set up road blocks at 8,9,10, and 11 defensive positions. Moyer also set up a block on the bridge near Waimes on the farm road.

When Colonel Hansen and his infantry troops came into Malmedy, their company com-manders set up their machine guns and riflemen between our road blocks around the outer perimeter of the village of Malmedy. The railroad offered an excellent position for the riflemen to overlook the fields to the west and southwest of Malmedy.

When the 526th Armored Infantry and the 825th Tank Destroyer Battalions came into town and were solidly inserted into our defenses, we found our situation to defend Malmedy from the attack of any type German forces. This was accomplished by 5:00 a.m. on Decem-ber 18th. I now was able to advise Colonel William Carter, the First Army Engineer; Colo-nel H. Wallis Anderson, the 1111th Group Commander; and Major Lampp of my rear com-mand post, that Malmedy was set up with roadblocks, anti-tank guns, and infantry. It spoke well for the resilience of First Army and es-pecially its chain of command.

The situation at this time favored the Germans. Their spearheading Armored col-umn had penetrated the American lines at the Losheim Gap near Lanzerath.

The armor and infantry of Colonel Jochen Peiper had come through a hole be-tween the right flank of the 99th Infantry Division and the left flank of the 106th Di-vision. They had come over 20 miles of curvy, narrow secondary roads and were now poised on the hill south of the Ambleve River bridge in Stavelot.

When Captain Sheetz came into my CP in Malmedy, he gave us the situation in both

Th e Martin Sisters rescued Lt. Virgil Lary as he crawled to their farm from Baugnez.

Stavelot and Trois Ponts. The defense in Stavelot was now covered by a task force of Major Paul Solis, who was now in charge there of three units: a company of the 526th Armored Infantry, eight anti-tank guns of the 825th Tank Destroyer Battalion, and C Company of the 202nd Engineers. Major Solis had instructed the engineers to remove mines from the bridge in order to set up two anti-tank guns on the other side of the river.

Sheetz had also learned that C Company of the 51st Engineers, Commanded by Captain Sam Scheuber, had arrived in Trois Ponts and was given the mission by Anderson to blow two bridges in Trois Ponts. Also, Sgt. Miller of "Bucky" Walters' platoon had prepared the bridge at the south end of Trois Ponts for demolition. Sheetz advised that Gamble's A Company had two platoons in reserve at Werbomont and Trois Ponts.

As I looked at the map of our defensive positions along the Ambleve River, much depended upon either the blowing of the bridges to take the road net away from the Germans or the possibility of the skies clearing and the American Air forces coming to our rescue. None of this happened. Nor did the 1st SS Panzer Division attack us in Malmedy.

The attack came in Stavelot between 6:00 and 7:00 a.m. as Peiper's men and tanks crashed into Stavelot. After losing several tanks and infantry, he pulled back and reorganized his forces for a renewed attack.

8

The Story of the Valiant 168th
Combat Engineers at St. Vith

William E. Holland Colonel C.E. (Retired), who commanded B Company of the 168th Engineers, sent me some papers he had retained from his experiences in WWII at St. Vith during December, 1944. The papers included a battalion after action report, articles written by Bill for the Veterans of the Battle of the Bulge publication, Bulge Bugle, and a write-up to aid in completing the 168th's Battalion History.

There is no better way to find out what went on in war than to read the information of one who was there during the fighting. Bill Holland brings out quite clearly in these papers the reasons conflict between nations should be settled peaceably. This is the story of the 168th at St. Vith.

During the period 1 December 1944 to 15 December 1944 inclusive, the entire Battalion was in close support of the 106th Infantry Division in VIII Corps operations along the Belgian border and in Germany. We were performing normal engineer tasks of maintaining

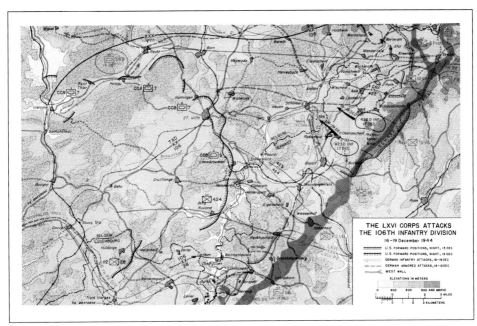

and building bridges right up to the Siegfried line. We were operating saw mills and preparing the wooden material for building the much needed bridges to support heavy tanks. The battalion was working in rock quarries preparing road material for the roads that were failing due to lack of hard surface material in existing roads for tanks and heavy artillery pieces. We also operated water supply points for all American forces in our area.

Much of this work in support of the infantry was performed under intermittent harassing enemy artillery fire and from V-1 buzzbombs. At 1700 hours, 16 December 1944, the 168th Engineer Combat Battalion was relieved of attachment to the 1107th Engineer Combat Group and was attached to the 106th Infantry Division.

At 1715 hours of the same day the 106th Division ordered the 168th Engineers to form a perimeter defense of the town of St. Vith. This was to be done by preparing obstacles on all roads leading into town. These obstacles were to be prepared only and to be made ready for emplacement on short notice. Bridges were to be prepared for demolition, but blown only on order of the Division Engineer, Lt. Colonel Thomas Riggs. All road blocks were to be secured and covered by fire.

Company B of this unit was assigned the sector south of St. Vith, and Company A the sector to the north. Company C was held in reserve in the town of Wallerode.

At 2000 hours, 16 December, preparation of the perimeter defense was complete and security patrols were in position on all roads. The night of December 16-17 passed without incident. At 1030 hours 17 December, the Battalion was relieved of the perimeter defense of St. Vith and was ordered to take up a defensive position in the vicinity of the town of Heuem astride the St. Vith-Shonberg highway. At this time the Battalion Executive officer was instructed to move elements of the Battalion headquarters, Headquarters and Service Company, and elements of the Company Headquarters of the lettered Companies to the vicinity of Vielsalm. Once there they were to contact the 1107th Engineer Combat Group and await further orders. Vielsalm was later evacuated and the rear elements of this Battalion were moved by order of the Engineer Group Commander and without the knowledge of the Executive Officer who at that time was returning to St. Vith to attempt to establish contact with the forward elements of this Battalion.

Reconnaissance patrols learned that Heuem was in the hands of the enemy and that the enemy armor and infantry elements were making rapid progress towards St. Vith. Contact was made with the 32nd Cavalry Recon troop, which was withdrawing to assume positions it had been ordered to take in the vicinity of Meyerode.

On the strength of the information brought in by the recon patrol, the battalion would set up its defensive position on the high ground in the vicinity of Prumerberg where it was met by Lt. Colonel Riggs, who had with him about 40 enlisted men and one officer of the 81st Engineers. Elements of the two units were combined and a line of defense was set up east of St. Vith along a line north and south near Prumerberg. Telephone communications were established with the advanced Command Post of the 106th Division which was located in St. Vith.

At 1205 hours with the men still in the initial phases of digging in, the enemy made contact at two points on the portion of the line being held by the 168th Engineers. There followed a fire fight which lasted about an hour after which the enemy withdrew a short distance.

At 1332 hours it was reported by an outpost of the 168th Engineers that three enemy tanks with accompanying foot elements were east and moving along the highway towards St. Vith.

The leading tank swung into an open field where it came to a standstill and the crew dismounted. The crew was wiped out by the fire of a 50 caliber machine gun of Captain William Holland's B Company of the 168th Engineers. The two remaining tanks continued to move along the highway to within 150 yards of our command post where the lead tank was knocked out with a bazooka. The remaining tank withdrew to cover.

At 1400 hours, 17 December, elements of Troop B of the 87th Cavalry Recon moved up to strengthen our line. The troop, reinforced with one platoon of foot troops, moved into position covering our flanks immediately.

Tanks were again reported to be moving toward our positions. Here the flight of P-47s came into play and the enemy armor withdrew when one of the tanks was set afire by strafing. The tank whose crew had been wiped out earlier was also strafed and burned.

At 1600 hours Col. Rosenbaum, who was in command of CC A of the 7th Armored Division came to the command post to get details on the situation. He conferred with Lt. Colonels Nungesser and Riggs. Captain William Holland, who had moved his B Company in line, had been instructed to "hold at all costs" on the first day of the battle. He stated, "I had one platoon to the left and one platoon to the right of the main road leading into St. Vith from Schonberg. It seemed everyone else had orders to withdraw. The position of these two platoons was immediately adjacent to the company bivouac area that we had occupied since arriving at the Belgian and German border.

"Some Division and Corps Artillery withdrew through our defensive positions. I can remember negotiating with a tank commander of the 14th Armored Cavalry Regiment to hold with us in our positions. He did delay until 1400 hours when he withdrew his tanks through our strong point. He had been receiving more small arms fire than artillery fire on his positions along the hills of the road at Schonberg.

"After the tank company withdrew, and my platoons were digging in I took 1st Sgt. Lennox and we worked our way through the woods adjacent to the main highway leading into St. Vith, toward Schonberg. As we approached the edge of the woods, we met two infantry soldiers who were walking back towards our lines. They had abandoned in place a 50 caliber machine gun, and they were carrying rifles and a bazooka, and were part of the

106th Infantry Division. They asked if I would like to see where the enemy was and we retraced their steps and were soon within 100 yards of the enemy!

"We crawled the last remaining yards to where their machine gun was left. In front of us was a Tiger Tank at a curve in the road. It was 125 yards away and 25 feet higher than our position, because of the topography of the ground. A 105 mm. towed gun was being put into position in front of this tank. After the gun was put into position about eight Germans lined up on both sides of the gun. With the 50 caliber machine gun, I believe I either killed or wounded very seriously all of them. There was a house near this curve where an observer gave fire directions to the Germans.

"The bazooka the Americans had was fired three times and the third round set the Tiger Tank on fire. I received the Silver Star for this action.

"We were afraid the Germans had seen us and had spotted our positions while we were trying to knock out the tank. The Tiger itself had tried to fire on us, however he could not depress his gun low enough. Therefore I moved the machine gun and our crew over to the right 75 yards. We could now see beyond the curve and we could see what heroes we had been. About 300 yards away we could see bumper to bumper for 400 yards was one tank after another. Also another 100 yards was a string of 2 and 1/2 ton dump trucks probably loaded with German Infantry.

"P-47s hit the Germans from the air several times and caused havoc and, as we pumped in our machine gun fire, the Germans were sustaining many casualties. Later, two platoons of C Company of the 168th were brought up in line with our B Company positions. Three hours later, right at dusk, the Germans continued their attack straight down the Schonberg road toward St. Vith and hit our main line of defense. There were four to six Germans in front of each tank and one tank behind the other. The Germans were singing loudly and moved boldly down the highway not firing. I was 20 yards to the right of the road on our main line of defense standing next to my jeep. I was amazed when none of my defensive force opened fire but seemed to be willing for them to go through. I yelled words to the effect-"Get the Bastards" and fired my carbine at point blank range at the German on the extreme left of the first row in front of the lead tank. When this happened the German screamed, dropped, and all hell broke loose! My 50 caliber and 30 caliber machine guns and riflemen opened up with everything we had.

"Unfortunately for us, the gunner in the lead tank, after his tank was hit by a bazooka fired by Sgt. Hill, was very brave. He stayed in his Tiger Tank and fired point blank at us, traversing the gun, firing two or three shots to his right, then back to his left again.

"The platoon of C Company that had reinforced us on the B Company line suffered about 50 to 60 percent casualties. Private Lovejoy, who was the smallest man in C Company and the battalion, was in the edge of the woods and in the ditch. The muzzle of the gun of the Tiger Tank was only 3 feet from him. The next morning when we were removing our dead I examined Private Lovejoy's body and there were no marks on it. He had been killed by the concussion of the 88 mm. gun.

"The fire fight lasted about two hours before the Germans withdrew. Later that night, S\Sgt. Linkus brought his platoon in line with Company B. This was one of C Company's platoons. During the night Captain Ward's A Company also came into line, and we now had a more formidable defense to stack up against the close by Germans.

"The Battalion CP had been promising me tanks for several hours, and finally at 1400 hours two Shermans with 75 mm. guns came up the road behind us, and the 1st Lt. in charge agreed to support my defenses. Shortly, four German Tanks broke through the woods and the Lt. gave his tanks orders to fire. With the first shot from the American Sherman, the 75 mm. gun spun the lead German tank around and set it on fire. Some crew members jumped out and fled. The other German tanks sped back into the woods.

"Things quieted down and we went into the second day with some more support. To our support came an 81 mm. Mortar Section, three mortars on self-propelled mounts in deep defilade behind our hill. They were able to break up the two or three attacks daily thrown at us by the enemy for the next several days. On a number of occasions I called 81 mortar fire on our positions about 50 feet in front to help stop infantry attacks. Not one round fell short."

We were no longer fighting as Combat Engineers, but were purely fighting as infantry against the impossible odds of the combination of both tanks and infantry in vastly superior forces.

At 2100 hours the commanding officer of the 38th Armored Infantry Battalion of the 7th Armored Division and the commanding officer of Company B of the 38th arrived at the Command Post of Lt. Colonel Nungesser. They informed Nungesser that the 38th had been assigned to the defense of St. Vith, and to hold and deny it to the enemy. In view of this fact, the commanding officer of the 38th assumed command of the sector, which we were defending. It was decided that Company B of the 38th would set up a new line of defense a short distance behind the line being held by the Engineer troops. The Engineer Troops were to remain in position until the infantry was dug in, at which time the engineers were to withdraw through the infantry, reorganize, and take up new positions on the right flank of the infantry. This was completed in the morning of the 18th. During the night of the 17th-18th there was sporadic small arms fire, and active aggressive enemy patrolling.

At this time Nungresser was hoping to be assigned to set up road blocks and use their training for Engineer Combat tactics against the enemy, such as lay mines, prepare bridges for demolition, and set up crater charges in the road net. Once the road net should be taken away from the attacking enemy armor, there would be no place for Hitler's forces to go in this heavily wooded area. During the battles for St. Vith, there was very little thought given to having the Engineers do the thing they could do best, and that certainly was not to fight as infantry. On the 3rd day Holland found himself in charge of parts of all the letter companies of the 168th Engineer Combat Battalion.

When the 38th Armored Infantry moved into line, Captain Holland moved the men of the 168th Engineers out of line and had them refreshed and re-supplied with ammunition and more bazookas. While out of line, Holland went back to the CP and discussed the situation with Colonel Nungesser. Again there was indication that more help was coming from General Clark of the 7th Armored Division.

The enemy launched an attack in force at the positions of the 38th Armored Infantry. The line at this point showed definite signs of not being able to hold the attack. Elements of Company "B" of the 168th were employed to bolster the infantry line. After a fire-fight that lasted one hour, the attack was repulsed and the enemy withdrew.

An enemy tank was reported in front of B Company of the 168th, however a tank of the 7th Armored Division moved forward and knocked it out. Under renewed enemy pressure and heavy mortar and artillery fire the portion of the line being held by the 38th Armored Infantry again showed signs of breaking. The combined efforts of the 168th and the 38th served to rally the forces and again Holland's Company B were called upon to bolster the infantry line. This attack was repulsed and the enemy once more was forced to withdraw. The battles seesawed back and forth with many casualties on both sides. During this period additional forces arrived of the 7th Armored Division and by the evening of the 18th, a thin line, but continuous of Infantry, Engineers, and tanks had been established around the town of St. Vith.

On the morning of the 19th of December infantry recon patrols found that the area held by the enemy during the fighting of the previous day had been evacuated. Our entire line had been moved forward into these positions held by the enemy. This necessitated the removal of the enemy dead in order to make the positions habitable for our own troops. Two hundred enemy bodies had been removed and others, which were too far forward of our positions, were left.

At 0505, 19 December, the Command Post of the Battalion was moved back west towards St. Vith. This action was taken because of the excessive amount of artillery fire falling on the old CP. A kitchen was operated by the 168th Engineers in order to serve hot meals and coffee to men on the line and to others brought back for short periods of rest.

The forty-eight hour period commencing at dawn of the 19th was marked by an increase in enemy artillery fire, which fell in the sector of the 168th. Major Boyer's Recon sector was penetrated, and Captain Holland and Major Boyer lead a counter-attack and drove the Germans back.

During the attacks of the 5th and 6th days of the battles, artillery kept increasing and more "screaming meemies" were used. Although the German infantry attacks were frequent they never really penetrated the lines of the 168th. There never was any hand-to-hand fighting, but the close in firing of pistols and carbines was frequent.

"Sometime during the night of the 21st of December we received a message on our infantry 300 radio that the Battalion CP was pulling out and that St. Vith had been taken. Lt. Colonel Riggs of the 81st Engineers came up to our lines and personally gave us the message because he was afraid that we had not heard it. Riggs' plan was for us to withdraw south and west of St. Vith until we reached friendly forces near Vielsalm. It took us several hours to notify all the men on line. During this time the enemy did not attack. As a matter of fact, the Germans launched no major attacks at night during the entire St. Vith offensive.

"As I recall, Col. Riggs and Major Boyer lead the column, and we had doughboys, engineers, and artillerymen in the group. There was an extreme quietness on the battle-field."

At this time it was found that the breakthrough was complete. Orders were issued that small patrols would be formed to attempt to infiltrate through the enemy and back into friendly lines.

On December 22nd a system was devised whereby stragglers and remnants of the 168th would be gathered up and assembled. These were temporarily put under Combat Command B of the 7th Armored Division, located at Vielsalm. The gathering of the unit went on during the 22nd and 23rd of December. On December 23rd CC B withdrew in great disorder through the 82nd Airborne Division, and assembled in Vielsalm. Early on the afternoon of this date, the Combat Command moved to Xhoris, Belgium for reorganization.

9

The 81st and the 168th Engineers on the St. Vith Front

The 81st Engineer Combat Battalion of Lt. Col. Thomas Riggs, organic to the 106th Infantry Division, pulled into the Ardennes on December 8th, 1944. The weather was miserable with a rain and sleet situation. The 106th Division was relieving the 2nd Infantry Division in this area along the Siegfried line. The 2nd Division's mission was to attack the German forces defending the Roer River dams. These dams were obviously in the German formula to be destroyed and flood the Roer River. The 106th Division was being assigned to

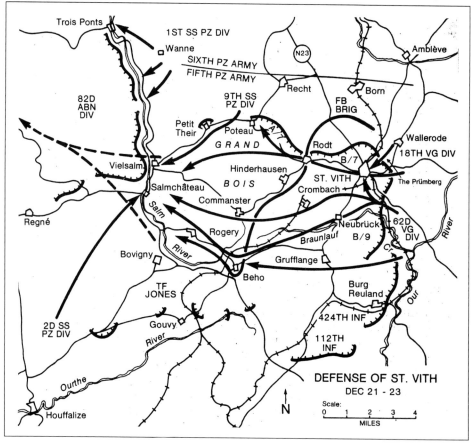

DEFENSE OF ST. VITH
DEC 21 - 23

move into line and occupy the most forward position of the VIII Corps front. This was a 16 mile stretch of pillboxes and dragon's teeth along the Siegfried line, with mines and explosives to prevent the Germans from a sudden breakthrough of the line. The locations of these mine fields were turned over to the 81st Engineers.

Colonel Riggs assigned each of his letter companies to a regiment of the 106th Division. Company A was assigned to the 422nd Infantry, B Company to the 423rd, and Company C to the 424th. Their mission, besides overseeing the mine fields and the preparation of the bridges for demolition, was to maintain and keep open the road net, including the main supply route to the front.

The roadnet beyond the immediate front was maintained by the 168th Engineer Combat Battalion, which was attached to the VII Corps. Their operation was to operate saw mills and maintain the rear road net, including the main supply route to the front.

We in the 291st had watched the 106th Division move through our area in the Ardennes, first with their infantry, then with their artillery, and finally with their supply trains. The 422nd Regiment went into line with the 14th Cavalry on their left flank. The 423rd Regiment was next in line towards the south, and the 424th went into position on the right flank.

This was a large chunk of ground for a division to hold, since the normal amount of line for a division to hold was 6 miles. In fact the entire 85 miles of front, from Monschau to Ecternach in Luxembourg, was entirely too much for five infantry divisions to hold and maintain.

The division on the 106th's right flank was the 28th (Keystoners), who had moved in line from the Huertgen forest. They were mauled badly in the battles there. They had lost over 5000 men, and had moved into the area in November, taking over 25 miles of front.

This frontage was along the Our River, all the way to the junction of the Our and the Sure. On December 7 the veteran 4th Division had taken over the rest of the eastern defense line from Echternach to the boundary of the Third Army of General Patton. The 4th had also suffered great losses in the Huertgen. This was also a thinly held front of 20 miles.

The 9th Armored Division moved into the area in December to assist with the assault of the Roer River dams. Thus on this 85 mile front there was not sufficient infantry or armored Divisions to defend against a major German attack, or blitzkrieg as Hitler called his offensives. Certainly not when there were two largely expanded armies, with 200,000 men, 1400 tanks and 13 Divisions.

How did the American forces stop Hitler's Master Plan? How did the Americans defeat and drive the German's souped-up divisions and armies back into the fatherland with 900 fewer tanks and far less troops? A study of the four shoulders of the Battle of the Bulge—the Northern, the Southern, the Western, and the Eastern—shows how they did it and answers these questions.

The answers are shown quite clearly as one reads of combat engineering units such as the one commanded by Lt. Colonel Thomas Riggs on the Eastern or St. Vith shoulder of the "Bulge Battle." Hitler started the theory that the war is a battle of rapid movement, with tanks, air power, and surprise.

The use of engineers as part of this theory is quite necessary to keep the road nets open for rapid advance. Similarly, the defense against this theory is to take the road net away from the blitzkrieging armies. The winner is that side whose engineers do the job.

In the early morning of December 16th, a heavy artillery barrage echoed at the command post of the 81st Engineer Combat Battalion at Heuem, Belgium. At 8:00 a.m., a messenger arrived from Company A to report considerable activity in the vicinity of the 422nd Infantry, to which the company was then attached. A short time later Lt. Colonel Thomas Riggs, the battalion commander, returned from the Division CP at St. Vith with reports of a concerted German attack along the division front, and orders to assemble the Battalion to be used as infantry.

Riggs soon learned that C and B Companies were already committed to the fire fight within their respective combat teams. A platoon of A Company also was involved in a fire fight with its assigned infantry regiment. The battalion then rushed men to Schonberg to evacuate the bulldozers and heavy equipment. The center of the town was under fire from a 380mm German railroad gun. Most of the equipment was saved and evacuated.

Meanwhile, A Company was in the thick of the fight. The company commander had dispatched his work parties at 8:00 a.m. He then departed for battalion headquarters to report the early morning activity and to attend a scheduled meeting of company commanders. The 1st platoon under Lt. Coughlin commenced work near Regimental Headquarters of the 422nd Infantry. The 3rd platoon under Lt. Woerner was laboring in the area of the 3rd Battalion, and became engaged in a fire fight early. They lost all contact with the Company from that time on. The remainder of the Company located at Auw, Germany, first heard rifle and automatic weapons fire at about 9:30 a.m. Due to the snow suits the enemy was wearing and the foggy conditions, visibility was poor. Elements of the attacking enemy forces had advanced within several hundred yards of Auw and were able to deliver direct rifle fire on members of the company. Immediately, the 2nd platoon was dispersed and sent into previously prepared positions from which they commenced the defense of the town.

Company HQ personnel took up positions in the building which housed the CP and began to return the fire. At this point, the 1st platoon, having heard firing from the direction of Auw, returned through heavy fire. They quickly dashed into the house in which they were billeted and started returning the enemy fire.

At about 11:00, members of the 1st platoon, using tracer ammunition for the purpose, set fire to a barn across the road from their position. While attempting to escape the blaze, ten German infantrymen, who had been firing from the barn, were shot down by the cooks from company headquarters.

Before noon enemy tanks entered Auw with additional infantry support for the attackers, and the three groups of A Company were isolated from each other. In order to avoid complete encirclement, Lt. Purtell's 2nd platoon withdrew up the Ambler road shortly in the PM. The enemy tanks proceeded up the main street with open turrets carrying infantry. The men from the first platoon and Company HQ opened fire on them and inflicted a considerable number of casualties. This action was followed by intense fire from the enemy infantry, while the tanks maneuvered into position to start firing on the houses occupied by the defenders. After the tanks opened fire, Lt. Rutledge found it necessary to withdraw towards Andler with his Company HQ Group. Turning their concentrated fire directly upon the one remaining point of resistance, the German tanks and Infantry laid down a withering storm of steel directed at the house occupied by Lt. Coughlin's platoon. Eight rounds of point blank fire from the tanks burst in the building, and the small arms fire increased in fury.

Realizing his position was untenable, Lt. Coughlin gave the order for withdrawal, which commenced about 3:00 p.m. At this point Tec-5 Edward S. Withee insisted on remaining behind with his M-3 Sub-Machine gun to cover the platoon's withdrawal across the open field behind the house. Even though he knew that death or capture would result.

For this heroic action, Tec-5 Withee (still missing in action) was awarded the Distinguished Service Cross. This platoon joined the unit of the 592nd Field Artillery Battalion and was evacuated to St. Vith, where they made contact with the remainder of the Company the following day. The total casualties at Auw were twenty men. The 3rd platoon, committed with the 422nd Infantry, is assumed to have been surrounded and captured with that Regiment several days later.

At 10:30 a.m. B Company was ordered by the Commanding Officer of the 423rd Regimental Combat team to clear the village of Bleialf, Germany, of an occupying enemy force that had infiltrated that location during the preceding night. Entrucking at Schonberg, the Company moved to a point about one half mile west of Bleialf, from which they continued on foot.

Captain Hynes directed Lt. Gordon to take one platoon into Bleialf to make a recon in force, while the rest of the Company covered their progress from positions overlooking the town from the South. Chief Warrant Officer Carmichael arrived with a truck load of ammunition and accompanied Lt. Gordon and his men on their mission. Upon entering the town, the platoon was met by withering fire from a number of buildings in which the Germans had set up positions designed to hold the town.

The engineer troops immediately deployed into vantage points for firing and began to engage the enemy. Lt. Gordan, displaying a disregard for his own safety and outstanding devotion to duty, continuously moved from building to building, until he had accurately located enemy's positions. Mr. Carmichael then made his way out of the town with this information and made contact with a platoon of tank destroyer guns which were located on the outskirts of town. By directing the fire of these guns on the occupied buildings, Mr. Carmichael enabled them to kill or wound a large percentage of the enemy and render the remaining ineffective, so that Lt. Gordon's platoon could advance and mop up the occupied buildings.

Mr. Carmichael returned to Battalion HQ. This was the last direct contact with Company A, 81st Engineer Combat Battalion.

The drivers who remained with their trucks later reported that the town underwent a terrific shelling by artillery in the afternoon and early evening of 16 December. The shelling was largely directed at the truck bivouac area and continued intermittently all night. Just before dawn the drivers were contacted by an artillery officer who ordered them to the rear. He stated that his unit had been ordered to shell Bleialf and the surrounding area. After telling him of the presence of their Company in Bleialf, and being in positions around it, they moved to Schonberg where they remained until 7:15 a.m. When German tanks approached the village this time, the drivers moved their vehicles to Heuem where the battalion CP was located. They reported the presence of tanks in Schonberg, and that necessitated the movement of the CP from that location. No further contact was ever made with B Company, but the reports of their activities were received from other sources. After retaking the town of Schonberg in January 1945, civilians in the town stated that B Company had made its final stand in and about Schonberg about two days after the action had occurred at Bleialf.

Due to the fact that B Company with its courageous Engineers had been billeted in Schonberg, the civilians were able to identify members of the Company, including Lt. Gordon. Also in a subsequent report of a German Officer, it was revealed that the only place along this section of the front which seemed to have a defense organized in depth was in the vicinity of Blealf. With the exception of a number of drivers, the company clerk, and several men who were on detached service, the entire Company B of the 81st is listed as missing in action. It is assumed that they were surrounded and captured by enemy forces. This was a pure case of Combat Engineers, who were skilled in the use of mines, demolitions, bazookas, machine guns, and rifles, and who were trained for building bridges, blowing pillboxes, opening up road nets, and making assault crossings of rivers, fighting valiantly as infantry.

Headquarters and service company located at Heum, Belgium, was trying to keep abreast of the fast moving situation and to effect the evacuation of heavy equipment of the battalion. The heavy shelling of Schonberg on the morning of the 16th of December, and the shelling of Heuem on the early afternoon of that day, coupled with sabotage by civilians and the infiltrating enemy, effectively destroyed all wire communications with Division Headquarters. Direct radio communications were impossible due to the jamming by the enemy. Radio messages that did come through were late and the battalion became concerned about the correct overall situation.

All of the heavy equipment of the battalion was successfully evacuated except one bulldozer. All evacuations were effected under heavy fire and the last vehicle from C Company in this convoy was trailed up one portion of the Winterspelt-Heckhol-enfeld road by machine gun and mortar fire.

Portions of A Company headquarters under Lt. Rutledge had arrived at the battalion CP in the afternoon of December 16th and were used to reinforce the defensive positions in the vicinity. Captain Harmon returned to the CP at Heuem that night with a dozen men who were survivors of his attempt to fight his way back to Auw on orders from the 422nd Regimental combat team commander. As this group had approached Auw, they were hit by a volley of time fire which burst directly above them. Many casualties were suffered from this action.

Withdrawing units passed through Heuem all through the night of December 16-17. After questioning several units as they passed through, it became apparent that there was nothing between the CP and the enemy but a light screen of mechanized cavalry. At 2:30 Colonel Riggs returned from the Division CP. He had learned that the 7th Armored Division and Combat Command B of the 9th Armored Division were arriving, and an attack would commence at 7:00 a.m. aided by all of the air support necessary. Units of the 7th Armored Division were scheduled to pass the engineer battalion CP just prior to 7:00 a.m. on the morning of the 17th.

Roads were cleared to facilitate these movements, and H. & S. Company consolidated its position at Heuem. In pursuance of this plan, S\Sgt. Moyer and S\Sgt. Deming of the recon section made their way into Schonberg at about 4:00 a.m. to check the condition of the bridge in that town and to gain any indication of enemy infiltration. They reported that the bridge was intact and that the town appeared to be clear.

Shortly after daybreak some enemy small arms fire was directed at personnel dug in on the hills surrounding Heuem. Reinforcing guards were sent out to protect the CP in the belief that the position could be held until the expected attack commenced. At 8:20 a.m., drivers of the B Company trucks arrived at Heuem with the report that enemy tanks had entered Schonberg. At that time orders were received by motor messenger from Division CP to evacuate Heuem and assemble the available units of the battalion at Rodt, several miles west of St. Vith.

The evacuation was accomplished with the loss of a 3/4 ton truck, carrying the SCR 193 radio, which became stuck in a ditch and had to be destroyed. As the last vehicle left Heuem, personnel riding it saw an enemy tank around the corner on an approach road. As a delaying action, a platoon of A Company, 81st Engineer Combat Battalion, was left and was joined by two M-8s of the 14th Cavalry Group. This Group forced deployment and delay of this estimated force of four enemy tanks and a company of infantry.

At 10:00 a.m. on December 17, Lt. Col. Riggs received orders to assemble all available men from the 81st Engineers and the 168th Engineers. The total strength available was slightly more than two Companies, comprising H&S Company and about one third of A Company of the 81st and three companies from the 168th. The original plan to organize this defense about 2 miles east of St. Vith was discarded when it was found that the speed of the armored advance had placed that point within enemy territory. The defensive position was set up along a wooded ridge about one mile east of St. Vith, near Prumerberg. Meanwhile, all heavy equipment was placed under control of Warrant Officer House. It was then moved to a wooded area northeast of Rodt, Belgium.

The enemy morale at that time was very high. The success of their initial attacks and the execution of their breakthrough combined to render the situation extremely difficult for the defending forces. The main enemy thrusts supported by tanks had been effective on the North through Auw, Germany and on the South through Bleialf, Germany. These two prongs joined at Schonberg, Belgium, and the attack continued towards the main communications center of St. Vith, where the 106th Division's CP was located.

This juncture of two attacking salients had cut off the 422nd and 423rd Combat Teams from the remainder of the Division, leaving St. Vith open to a frontal attack by these two enemy elements. The attack was being made by two regiments of the 18th Volkesgrenadier Division supported by the bulk of the Division's artillery and a battalion of forty 75mm assault guns. The Volksgrenadiers were seeking access to the Our River and the road to Schonberg, there to link with their Division's third regiment around the other end of the Schnee Eifel.

The larger picture revealed that deeper penetrations had been made to the immediate North and South of St. Vith. In order for full exploitation of these successes to be effected by the enemy, the capture of St. Vith was mandatory, so as to provide lateral communication between these salients. Thus the defense of the town became extremely important. The sole units initially undertaking that defense were the badly battered remnants of the 81st Engineer Combat Battalion and the available portion of the 168th Engineer Combat Battalion under the command of Lt. Col. Thomas J. Riggs, Jr.

Despite the many difficulties encountered from the lack of adequate clothing, weapons, and entrenching tools, and in the face of the confident attackers that were superior both in numbers and available major fire-power, the morale of the defenders was remarkably good.

All positions were dug in by 4:00 p.m. About an hour before this completion of the defensive positions, four heavy tanks, accompanied by a battalion of infantry, made their appearance at the edge of the woods about 1000 yards East of Riggs and his men. At this point an anti-tank gun sent by the Division CP defense platoon opened fire on them, but the gun was knocked out immediately.

A platoon of the 822nd Tank Destroyer Battalion was initially set up ahead of the first main line of resistance with a platoon of Engineers screening them. These tank destroyers with new guns, received that morning without sights, fired by sighting over the tubes. They forced the advancing tanks to take cover, without casualties to the German tanks. To consolidate the final position on the MLR, these guns were told to proceed at once to the positions in the woods to their immediate rear about 100 yards. The tank destroyers moved north to accomplish this but were never reported again.

After this exchange of fire the enemy tanks turned their 88mm guns on a group of men from the 168th Engineers, who were firing on them from a position on the south side of the road, overlooking the enemy positions, and inflicted severe casualties. Meanwhile a forward observation post about 400 yards in front of the defending positions had been established in the edge of the woods with Lt. Colonel William M. Slayden, Hdqs. VIII Corps, Lt. Lewthwaite, Lt. Sauers, and T\Sgt. Psolka of the 81st Engineers. They were able to pinpoint the position of the German tanks and infantry on the hill at Prumerberg. This information was passed on to Division artillery, but no units were in position to fire the mission.

Therefore, the division air to ground liason officer made contact with an American P-47 aircraft which was in the vicinity, and directed it to the spot. The plane made four passes over the tanks before he located them, and then only one of the tanks had made the mistake of opening fire on the plane. Thereafter, it made seven passes over the tanks, firing at them, and starting a fire. Casualties to the ground troops in the immediate vicinity were considerable. This was revealed by Tec/4 Labes who was laying in the woods nearby while still in the process of infiltrating back to our lines from Heuem.

Shortly thereafter, visibility became so poor that the CP could not operate effectively, and it was removed to the rear. At this time, the men from H. and S. Company, 81st Engineers, who had until that time occupied positions on the North side of the Schonberg-St. Vith Road, were removed and directed to protect the flank of the position on the hill. Their position was filled by elements of B Troop, 87th Recon Squadron, which had arrived together with a platoon of medium tanks.

While H.&S. Company was crossing the open area between the woods, an enemy tank which had worked its way up through a fire break in the woods, supported by infantry, opened fire on the Company from a range of 100 yards. T/5 Fetterman was seriously wounded from the 88mm fire.

Captain Ward of H.& S. Company, 81st Engineers, attempted to get one of the medium tanks to advance and fire on the German tank. The tank by that time had been demobilized by a group of Engineers who had pulled a "daisy chain" of mines across the front of it's advance, and small arms fire had driven off it's supporting infantry. The tank commander refused to expose his tank to the 88mm fire, but after Captain Ward offered to ride behind the turret of the tank to direct it, the tank commander agreed. The two tanks began to exchange volleys. The first round of 88mm fire knocked Captain Ward from the turret of the Sherman tank, but he was uninjured. The third round from the American tank knocked out the enemy tank and our tank withdrew to defilade.

Lt. Col. Riggs established his tank force CP in a basement of the house in the northwest corner of the crossroads at Prumerberg. At about 7:00 p.m. an enemy combat patrol of fifty men armed with automatic weapons penetrated the lines, and the darkness was pierced by an endless stream of tracer ammunition from the firing of both forces. Only about three casualties resulted from this exchange, although one aid man was subsequently shot while attempting to reach one of the wounded men.

The patrol was repulsed, but many of it's members still remained on the ground in the vicinity. During the rest of the night American and Germans were commingled in the front lines.

The only artillery support that was received by these defenders during the first several days of the defense was that afforded by an armored field artillery battalion of the 7th Armored Division, whose liaison Officer, Major Donald Boyer, reported into the task force CP that night. Boyer later arranged for a registering mission at dawn.

Present for the planning that took place in the task force CP were the officers of both engineer battalions, the B Troop of the 87th Recon Squadron of the 38th Armored Infantry, the above mentioned artillery battalion and attached platoon of medium tanks from the 7th Armored Division. At Midnight it was arranged to have Company B of the 38th Armored

Infantry Battalion, 7th Armored Division, relieve the 168th Engineer troops by digging in on the West side of the fire break which was to the rear of existing positions.

Engineer platoon leaders would contact the men and inform them of their relief so they would not fire on the relieving infantry. The engineer officers were then to lead the infantry platoon leaders to their respective areas. After the positions were dug in and organized, the engineers were to withdraw to the rear of the hill to be reorganized and immediately be recommitted on the right flank of the position.

This plan was worked out to separate the Americans from the Germans who were intermingled all along the line. By 3:00 a.m. the relief had been effected. The engineer troops withdrew and reorganized. Reinforced by a platoon of heavy machine guns from Hdqs. Company, 38th Armored Infantry, the engineers moved into the position on the right flank of the hill. The officers and men of the 168 Engineers now measured over two companies, one company having arrived during the night. The provisional platoon of H.& S. Company withdrew to a reserve position behind B Company of the 38th Armored Infantry. Meanwhile the task force CP moved from the top of the hill. Col. Riggs dispatched a member of his staff to contact the company commander of the 23rd Armored Infantry unit on the right to acquaint him with the linking up.

At 9:35 a.m. on December 17th, the commanding officer of the 81st Engineer Battalion, Lt. Colonel T.C. Riggs, was designated as defense commander of St. Vith. Colonel Riggs had available to him two platoons of Company A and his H&S Company of the 81st Engineer Battalion, the 168th Engineer Combat Battalion of Lt. Colonel W.L. Nungesser, one platoon of the 820th Tank Destroyer Battalion (4 towed guns), and the defense platoon of the division headquarters company. Captain Harman had the remainder of his company in St. Vith for the noon meal, and just after noon he received instructions to move out and take up positions east of St. Vith and a short distance south of Prumerberg. The defensive positions were established at about 3:00 p.m. on December 17th.

The men were dug in about five to ten feet apart. At that time the defensive positions were established. Enemy tanks were coming in on both sides of the road to Schlierbach and also the Prumerberg-Setz road. Late in the afternoon of the 17th, three P-47s descended on these tanks and strafed back and forth about five or six times, causing them to disperse into the surrounding woods. Artillery fire delivered at this point assisted in keeping the tanks from advancing further into St. Vith.

The four TD guns were initially dug in several hundred yards behind the engineer positions, but late in the afternoon were sent around to the left flank of the defenses. Only two actually did get around to the left flank of Prumarberg, but one fired effectively to check the westward enemy tank advance.

Colonel Riggs placed one assault gun and one medium tank north of Prumerberg, and wanted two more medium tanks at the Prumerberg road junction. There was a little delay getting the two in at the road junction, until Colonel Riggs issued a direct order. Captain Ward of the H&S Company states: "The tank commander asks me if I was crazy enough to ride the lead tank up to the road junction, and I said I guessed I was. So we did. Just before dark we pulled up by the crossroads and were fired on by the enemy tank coming in our direction. The tank I was riding in fired three rounds, one of which hit the German tank just in front of the left track, forcing its withdrawal."

Just about dark the night of December 17 there was a reshuffling of the defensive lines under the direction of the combat commander of CCB, 7th Armored Division, who had relieved Colonel Riggs of defensive command of St. Vith at 4:25 p.m. on the 17th. The 87th Cavalry Recon Squadron replaced H&S Company, 81st Engineers on the hill north of Prumerberg. Three recon cars, each with three .30 caliber machine guns were dismounted and the guns were distributed along the whole line. A company of the 38th Armored Infantry Battalion replaced the 168th just south of Prumerberg, and the 168th took up positions south of Company A, 81st Engineers.

On the night of the 17th of December, strong enemy patrols attempted to infiltrate the line and probe it out. The patrols drove back one platoon of the 168th Engineer Combat Battalion about 100 yards. No artillery fire accompanied these patrols, but there was some enemy mortar fire.

On the morning of the 18th of December, the defense platoon of division headquarters was relieved and went back to St. Vith, and the H&S Company, 81st Engineers filled in the gap where the defense platoon had been.

Commencing at 9:30 a.m. on December 18, the enemy launched a determined attack on the defense line. No artillery preparation preceded the attack, which was started by an increasing volume of machine gun fire delivered on Company A's positions. An enemy tank pulled beside a house and started firing point blank at the positions of Company A. This was before bazooka ammunition had been brought up to front line positions.

Approximately one company of enemy infantry broke through the Company A positions on the morning of December 18. Lt. Paul E. Rutledge, observing for mortar fire at the point of the penetration, was wounded in the arm and shortly thereafter was killed by a shot in the throat. "He stayed out there in front right up to the end," said Captain Harman, "his silver bar on his helmet shining just a little too bright like a spanked baby's butt, and that's what probably got him."

A total of four separate counterattacks were thrown at the point of Company A lines, and each time Company A was forced to back off and regroup, but the enemy never achieved a clean breakthrough and by 1:00 p.m. the original lines had been restored. The enemy attack was supported by twelve dug in tanks firing stationary from about 300 yards out on both sides of the road. Accurate mortar and artillery fire in front of the defensive line assisted in repelling the attack.

At 3:00 p.m. on the 18th, the enemy launched another counterattack, of greater than company strength. This attack again broke through the Company A positions and the men became panicky and demoralized. Colonel Riggs then personally gathered up some of the stragglers, taking about eighteen men from H&S Company, 81st Engineers, and men of the

168th. They hit the enemy penetration, driving it back. By 4:30 they had restored the original lines. The old gaps were then refilled. The night of the 18th was quiet aside from scattered small-arms fire. The next few days the front was relatively quiet and the enemy did no more than send out a few patrols, with no offensive intentions. A little artillery dropped around the line positions, and more dropped in St. Vith itself during this period.

The final attack, which resulted in the capture of St. Vith, occurred on the 21st of December. This was the same time that Hitler forced his Generals to make an all-out attack to free the entrapped Peiper in the Malmedy-Werbomont corridor. General Sepp Dietrich had ordered his 6th Panzer Army's Divisions to hit the Americans a decisive blow from Monschau to Werbomont, while Skorzeny's Regiment attacked Malmedy.

Commencing at 3:00 p.m. all the front line positions were heavily shelled. The artillery barrages were the heaviest of any the troops had experienced since the start of Hitler's secret war. Just before dark, the enemy brought up a tank and started firing point blank into our lines and knocked out a hole which 25 German infantry came through. Captain Harman tried to organize a group to stem the breakthrough. When six German tanks rounded a corner in the road, they wheeled and backed into firing positions on the edge of the road and commenced to rip the lines further with point-blank fire. Of the four medium tanks in the vicinity, three were destroyed by enemy tank fire, and the fourth escaped. The enemy fired flares from their tank turrets, lighting up the area.

Colonel Riggs attempted to reorganize the broken lines, as he had several days before, again leading the men personally; his fate on this date was unknown. Scattered elements of the broken defense line retreated towards Vielsalm, and the enemy had control of St. Vith shortly after midnight on 21-22 December.

10

The 7th Armored Division
and Clarke of St. Vith

At 2:00 a.m. on December 7th, 1944 Col. Bruce Clarke received a phone call from General Gillem advising him that he had been nominated to become a one-star General. This was exciting to this former engineer officer who had at one time commanded the 24th Engineer Combat Battalion.

The one-star was pinned on Clarke by Major General Robert Hasbrouck, the commander of the U.S. 7th Armored Division. The newly made General Clarke was now the combat commander of Combat Command A of the 7th Armored Division.

At 9:00 p.m. on the night of December 16th Clarke received a phone call from General Hasbrouck advising him that a German counter offensive was going on in the vicinity of the Losheim Gap at the Siegfried Line.

On the afternoon of the 17th of December, Clarke was standing in front of Major General Alan Jones of the overrun 106th Infantry Division looking at a German advanced pa-

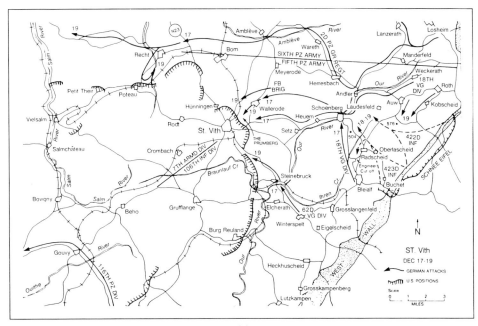

trol. This was in a schoolhouse in St. Vith, Belgium. General Jones said to the newly arrived Clarke, "You take over command!"

"Yes, sir...please give me the troops you have available!"

Clarke, who had driven over 100 miles to get to this schoolhouse, went out to see what force he had. There were somewhat over 200 engineers left from two engineer combat battalions, the 81st and the 168th. These were under the command of a tall and young Lt. Colonel from West Virginia by the name of Tom Riggs. There was also the infantry platoon assigned to protect division headquarters.

Under Lt. Colonel Riggs they were to move to the front, east of St. Vith, until they were stopped, and then they were to dig in and hold. There was the hope that maybe the two surrounded regiments could fight their way back to St. Vith, and the 7th Armored Division would arrive to form on their defenses.

About 3:00 p.m., Riggs' small army of defenders was hit by four German tanks and a battalion of infantry, which showed up 1,000 yards to the front. Fortunately, although this force sprayed the Americans, it did not advance. Clarke learned that Riggs and the men of the two engineer battalions had been attacked many times in the past two days and despite suffering many casualties were able to hold the village of St. Vith against overwhelming odds. Now with another former engineer battalion commander to lend a hand, the men of the 81st and 168th were feeling more relieved.

Clarke had learned that there were three or four German Divisions centered against the 106th Division. The VIII Corps Commander, Maj. General Troy Middleton had passed this word to Clarke. Middleton had pointed this out to Clarke on a map where, on the Schnee Eifel, the 106th Division of General Jones was being overrun. Clarke radioed this message to Hasbrouck and learned that Combat Command B (CCB) had just departed at 0500 hours and would probably arrive in St. Vith by late afternoon. Clarke now knew that the 106th was in serious trouble since they were expecting the 7th Armored to arrive by 7:00 a.m.

During the morning of the 17th of December my command post at the east end of Malmedy witnessed the arrival of an armored column of the 7th Armored Division. Realizing my need for tank support in Malmedy, we stopped the armored column and talked to the Major in the lead vehicle. I asked him for his support on my defenses, but I learned that he was urgently needed at St. Vith and that his name was Donald Boyer. I would learn later that he would arrive at St. Vith and play a major role in the American defenses there.

Around 3:30 p.m. in St. Vith, General Clarke conferred with Lt. Colonel Thomas Riggs and learned that his small army was made up of the headquarters company of the 81st Engineers, the 106th division headquarters defense platoon, the forces of Lt. Col. Nungessor's Battalion, a brace of 57mm. anti-tank guns, and several bazookas.

He had set up on a ridge line facing the Germans: a field to his left, woods to his right. A stray platoon of tank destroyers came by, and Riggs recruited them just in time. Riggs' men had laid mines and made other roadblock defenses to his front against the Germans.

Bruce Clarke paced up and down wondering where his combat command had been delayed. He didn't know that Kamfgruppe Peiper had cut off the route taken by Boyer through Malmedy. Nor did he realize that his CCB was forced to move over the route through Stavelot, Trois Ponts, Vielsalm, thence east to St. Vith—which was much longer—over narrow, winding and more difficult roads for his heavy armored vehicles. He only learned later that part of his forces became engaged with Peiper's Panzers at Stavelot on the morning of December 18th.

But in order to carry out Clarke's urgent orders for all possible speed, they were obliged to fight upstream against a solid mass of wildly fleeing non-combatant vehicles out of St. Vith. The CCB tanks had to struggle to get to the village of St. Vith.

Their desperation was reflected in an account by Major Donald P. Boyer, quoted in John Eisenhower's book, "Bitter Woods." Lt. Colonel Fuller, Corporal Cox, and I took over the job of clearing the path for the tanks, and we started getting vehicles to move over to the sides. Slowly a path was beginning to open and the tanks began to roll at a slow pace with halts every fifty to one hundred paces. Several times we had to wave the lead tank forward at full speed when some vehicle refused to move over. Usually the sight of 30 odd tons of steel roaring down on him was all we needed to get the driver to move over.

"Several times senior officers in command cars attempted to pull out into a space which I was opening up, and each time told them to get back, that I didn't care who they were, nothing was coming through except our tanks and anything else that was headed for the front, and to get out of the way. One company commander, Captain Dudley J. Britton, CCB, 23rd Armored Infantry Battalion said, 'That day I saw the highest ranking traffic cops I have ever seen.'"

Much of this early movement out of the near front line area was similar to the movement out of Malmedy. Among this exodus was mostly supply and medical units along with many civilians. The difficulty it presented to combat units and their desire to get to the aid of the front line troops who were initially being overrun was almost disastrous. Seldom during the battle in the Ardennes was seen the movement of combat troops so completely out of line. This was the desire and courage of the American soldier. He didn't want to let his buddies down.

Rather than wait at the 106 Division headquarters, Clarke decided to go to a crossroads west of St. Vith where he had sent his S-3, Major Woodruff, to guide his troops into a defensive line. Clarke stayed there and bulled any retreating traffic away from the cross roads.

A Lt. Colonel came up to the General and said, "I am Roy Clay, I have a separate Battalion of self-propelled 105's, the 275th Armored Field Artillery. We've got some ammunition left and we're ready to work."

"God bless you, Clay! You're all the artillery we've got. Head out on the ridge east of town, and support those two engineer companies dug in there. Look for a tall engineer Lt. Colonel Riggs." This artillery battalion was to go down in history.

While CCB was still struggling towards the front at nearly 4:00 p.m., Major Woodruff let out a yell. Approaching was the exhausted leading element of Troop B, 87th Cavalry Reconnaissance Squadron, of CCB 7th Armored Division. Captain Stewart reported in to

General Clarke who fell in along on foot. "Keep going right on down on this road. You'll come to a big Lt. Colonel-Riggs. Tell him your attached to him. He'll tell you what to do and be delighted to see you."

B Troop headed on out east of St. Vith to help establish a defensive position. But they had to fight their way to the spot, coming under semi-automatic fire as soon as they had located their chosen ground.

Clarke attached other stray elements as they appeared to his command. Apart from the reconnaissance squadron, only one tank company and one armored infantry company (Company B, 23rd Armored Infantry Battalion) had been able to reach St. Vith by 4:30 p.m. Clarke immediately dispatched them south of St. Vith to establish a defense and to contact the neighboring unit, CCB 9th Armored Division, commanded by Brigadier General Hoge, another former engineer officer.

The tank company (Company A, 31st Tank Battalion) was sent east to reinforce the 106th Division's engineer remnants who were putting up a valiant stand. These companies had to fight their way into their defensive positions.

On the evening of December 17th Clarke received word that two regiments of the 106th Division had been overrun and it was now mandatory that he hold St. Vith at all costs. The mission was now becoming quite clear: that this rail center be held against the heavily attacking divisions of General Manteuffel's 5th Panzer Army. Throughout the night of December 17th the elements of the 7th Armored Division kept rumbling into St. Vith, and all night Clarke kept guiding them into position as he built a large U-shaped defense east of St. Vith. Fortunately, as he built this strong defensive position, Lt. Colonel Thomas J. Riggs Jr. continued to hold back the German forces that were now made up of three enemy divisions.

Joining Riggs were the artillery guns of 275th Artillery Battalion and the tanks of Major Donald Boyer's 38th Armored Infantry Battalion. Riggs' men were holding well against the tank and infantry attacks of the enemy but his ranks were being reduced by casualties. This was a case of well trained combat engineers fighting as infantry.

As CCB headquarters staff moved into the schoolhouse, they were impeded by the 106th Division staff, which moved out after breakfast. One 106th Division Sergeant with bedroll on shoulder advised that the Germans were now shelling St. Vith, and heavy stuff had hit the schoolhouse.

By the night of December 17th, Manteuffel had broken open a hole about 12 miles wide through which he was pouring the 58th and 47th Panzer Corps, three panzer divisions, and two infantry divisions.

During the morning of the 18th of December Clarke continued to build up his U-shaped defense as he emplaced two companies of the 87th Cavalry, two engineering companies of the 7th Armored Division, and parts of the 38th Armored Infantry Battalion. West of St. Vith he placed a reserve—the 31st Tank Battalion, 23rd Armored Infantry, B Company, and 33rd Engineers.

By 4:00 a.m. on the 18th General Bruce Clarke was well prepared to defend St. Vith. Out in front of St. Vith, some of the surrounded and captured men of the 106th division had escaped, and only a few of them had worked their way back to St. Vith. North of St. Vith the Panzer thrust of Peiper had crossed the Ambleve River at Stavelot and was moving beyond Trois Ponts. Also, just north of St. Vith, task force Hansen of the 1st SS Panzer Division had moved through Ambleve, Born, and Recht, with task force Knittel following.

At this time both the defenses of Clarke and Riggs were out on a point with unprotected flanks. Manteuffel's forces turned to a series of probes seeking the weak spot into St. Vith. There was no way for them to know that they were all weak spots because when one probe was made Clarke had his tanks attack and drive off the attacking force. The Germans got the idea that there were several Armored Divisions in St. Vith.

On the German side, General Manteuffel's forces had been delayed three days trying to take St. Vith. General Field Marshall Model ordered Manteuffel to take it on the 19th without fail. Engineer Colonel Riggs had made this all possible with his defenses using the engineers of Lt. Col. Nungressor and his own 81st Engineers. Riggs would continue to hold off the Germans for three days until his forces were entirely overrun on the 21st of December.

The incoming defensive units had to fight their way in before they could join the defensive units beside Riggs—at the end of a frustrating march. One example is described by Lt. Colonel Erlinbusch, commander of the 31st Tank Battalion.

"Company A, 31st Tank Battalion, was ordered to take up a defensive position on the high ground about 2000 yards east of St. Vith. Lt. Dunn, the leading platoon leader, preceded his lead tank in a quarter ton to reconnoiter for positions. About 1500 yards from St. Vith, upon rounding a bend in the road, Lt. Dunn spotted, about 800 yards to his front, three German tanks and about one company of infantry moving in the direction of St. Vith. He turned his vehicle around, issued instructions to his platoon by radio, climbed into his tank, and led his platoon to the point where he saw the enemy approaching. The German force and his first platoon met head on at the bend of the road. The fight was short and at point blank range. We destroyed the enemy tanks and killed or wounded about 50 of the enemy with no loss to our own forces. Company A secured the high ground, blocked the road, and extended its position north from the road along the ridge."

Throughout the night 18-19 December, CCB men could hear large movements of German vehicles arriving in front of St. Vith. Heavy German patrolling was active after midnight, and two substantial night attacks hit CCB's North Flank. All road flanks were hit by 88s and mortars. Both attacks were driven off by the 31st tank Battalion and the 87th Cavalry Recon Squadron. All through the night the Germans hit all sides of the defensive arc as if probing for the weakest spot to hit in the morning.

At the close of the 19th of December the Americans could say that they had completed the first day of their new assignment to hold for three more days. They had been able to establish a large defensive arc bowed out towards the enemy. The center of that arc protecting St. Vith was Clarke's CCB. North of that was the 6th Armored Division between Poteau and Rodt under Col. Dwight Rosebaum. South of Clarke was General Hoge's CCB, 9th Armored Division.

CCB, 7th Armored Division, holding the pivotal sector, was augmented by the 17th Tank Battalion with Company C of the 38th Airborne Infantry battalion, the 434th Armored Field Artillery and two batteries of the 965th. A fire direction center was established for mass firing. Communications were consolidated within and without CCB in preparation for the fourth day of the defense of St. Vith.

General Hasso von Manteuffel was now ready to make his all out attack against St. Vith. He had heard that Peiper had been stopped on his drive to the Meuse River near Werbomont and was being attacked by three American Divisions. His attack must succeed on the morrow at St. Vith.

On the morning of the 20th the defenders were nearly desperate. They had identified the most intimidating collection of Germans confronting them, and it had been rumored that enemy troops had by-passed them and were in possession of towns far behind them such as Ambleve, Ligeneuville, Kaiserbaracke, and nearby Poteau. The Americans were sustaining hundreds of casualties and were losing tanks and equipment.

On the German side, where the attacking force was more vulnerable to casualties and loss of equipment, Manteuffel was three days behind in his schedule and was being pressured to take St. Vith immediately. The forces of the Germans blitzkrieging St. Vith had been the 18th and 62nd Volkesgrenadier Divisions, the 2nd Panzer Grenadier Regiment of the 1st SS Panzer Division, commanded by General Wilhelm Mohnke, plus parts of the 116th Panzer Division.

The St. Vith Americans were now under pressure from two identified regiments of the 560th Volkesgrenadier Division, and parts of the 2nd SS Panzer Division of the 6th Panzer Army of General Sepp Dietrich were going around them to the south.

The flanks of the CCB arc were weak; the open back was totally vulnerable. Therefore, the Americans began moving the wings of the arc backward, changing the arc into a horse-shoe. Casualties were mounting and loss of equipment was heavy, but at the same time the Germans were losing large amounts of attacking troops. St. Vith was the point thrust closest to the enemy.

St. Vith now became an important target for the Germans. Hitler was livid, since Peiper was now entrapped in the Ambleve River valley, and the 99th, 2nd, and 1st U.S. Army Divisions were holding fast on the Elsenborn ridge and the twenty mile front was now secure from Butgenbach through Malmedy.

The target of St. Vith which was now denying them the road net, was seen by the German high command as "the thumb in the throat" of their whole drive at this time. If they didn't bite it off, it would choke them. It was a wedge splitting their 5th and 6th Armies apart. This was the beginning of the time when the German soldiers would be out in the open attacking the American soldiers.

At this point General Hasbrouck sent a message to General William Kean, First Army Chief of Staff. "Am out of touch with VIII Corps, understand XVIII Airborne Corps coming in...my division defending St. Vith, Poteau inclusive...my right flank wide open. I can delay them (the Germans) the rest of today maybe, but will be cut off tomorrow.

"VIII Corps ordered me to hold, and will do so, but need help from the north or Bastogne. Understand the 82nd Airborne coming up on my north, and the north flank not critical."

The answers sweeping through CCB sapped a man's strength: the enemy was rolling up the flank on the southeast; the enemy is at Houffalize, La Roche, and Samree. All behind CCB! The enemy is entrapped to the north at La Gleize in the Northwest.

The atmosphere of a five day-old battlefield becomes pervaded by rumor and the strong odors of fuel, powder and death. Withering fatigue dulls the senses to the most shocking events and threats. Mouths and eyes hang open entranced. Riflemen stare at their squad sergeants, studying. Lieutenants stare at company commanders, probing. It's leadership time on trial.

Later that same night very bad news was received. Unarmed with the night's security password, Lt. Long, a platoon leader in the surrounded 423rd Regiment of the 106th Division infiltrated his way carefully in the dark among the jumpy U.S. outpost pickets. He was heading into the CCB line, leading two other officers and 35 men. When he got deeper into the U.S. lines there was great excitement, and rumor spread that this was the advance patrol of the 422nd and 423rd Infantry Regiments, which would be following.

It turned out that it wasn't as Lt. Long and his men explained that the two regiments had been surrounded and were caused to surrender by their commanders. Thousands of Americans were either shot down or captured and very few were able to escape. Long explained that they were hit from all sides by the Germans, and only a few were able to escape this disastrous situation.

Almost as soon as we were merged in a stadium-shaped valley, they found themselves at the mercy of very short ranged German artillery, and with certainty of being wiped out. The senior regimental commander assembled all the field grade officers and asked for suggestions of a way out. Several were offered. He heard of no plan which would avoid nearly total massacre. He said sadly, "It is my opinion that we should surrender!"

Though their hearts may have disagreed, the senior officer ordered them to return to their units and prepare to destroy weapons. Any men who wanted to could fight their way back to U.S. lines and get a chance to avoid capture. Lt. Long's platoon of 35 were all that he knew of, but he said others could be attempting to infiltrate back.

Clarke established an assembly point in the schoolhouse for all that may make it back. They were given rations, a shower and rest. The following night, December 21-22, they were put back in the defensive line and fought like men possessed.

The 21st of December turned the winter wonderland into an inferno. The Germans wanted St. Vith at any price. They took their time getting ready because it was to be a no-turn-back attack.

Awareness of the impending onslaught somewhat pervaded the whole of CCB. The nervousness was heightened by the fact that Baron von der Heydte's German Paratroopers had been dropped north of Malmedy on the 16th of December. His men were now joining Col. Otto Skorzeny's regiment of Germans in American uniforms for an attack on Malmedy.

At 11:00 a.m. it all happened!

Large formations of German tanks supported the German Infantry and crunched deep into the U.S. lines. They were blasted by direct fire from foxholes and unbelievably forced to withdraw time after time, leaving burning tanks. German infantry was fought hand to hand.

By 1:00 p.m., the entire line of CCB, 7th Armored Division, was aflame with enemy artillery, screaming meemies, tanks and infantry pouring a column of steel at the defenders. Many of these defenders had been under concentrated fire for over 5 days. As the Nazis closed in, they were met in turn by all possible types of fire that could be brought to bear— but still they attacked viciously for Hitler and the fatherland. It was now do or die on both sides.

Major attacks were launched against part of the line held by the 38th Armored Infantry Battalion at 11:00 a.m., 12:30 p.m., 2:00 p.m. and up to 5:30 p.m.; the northern flank, manned by the 31st Tank Battalion and the 87th Cavalry Reconnaissance Squadron, endured attacks from 1:00 p.m. until 6:20 p.m. Killed, wounded and captured were piling up on both sides; however, the attacking German side, which was not under cover, got the worst of it.

Then three heavy assaults were started by the Germans, each directed along the axis of the main roads leading into St. Vith proper; at 4:50 p.m. from the east along the Schonberg road; followed by an attack along the Malmedy road at 6:35 p.m.; with the last starting up the Prum road at 8:00 p.m. Each of these attacks was preceded by intense artillery barrages lasting for as much as 35 minutes. Where the Germans had stored all the guns and ammunition for this major battle was beyond comprehension. This was followed by the attack of infantry and tanks against a defense with far less men, ammunition and weapons.

The Germans were not to be denied, and their relentless pressure since 11:00 a.m. in the morning had left gaps in the line, since there were no replacements for the dead and wounded.

By 8:00 p.m., CCB's lines had been penetrated in at least three points. The battle continued until about 10:00 p.m., when General Clarke, seeing that Lt. Colonel Riggs and his brave men had been overrun and practically wiped out completely, and seeing that his position was no longer tenable, issued the order to withdraw the center of the line to the high ground west of St. Vith. Lt. Colonel Thomas J. Riggs Jr., outstanding football player from the University of Illinois, commissioned in the R.O.T.C., had disappeared from sight. Most of his men had been either killed or captured as they had courageously built up a line of infantry defense long before General Clarke and the 7th Armored Division had arrived in St. Vith. Lt. Colonel Nungessor had added two companies of his 168th Engineers to this defense that had saved St. Vith from capture for 48 hours before the arrival of any infantry or armor.

Those elements which were cut off east of town were ordered to attack through town or north of it to join the forces which were establishing a new defensive line. Officers were established west of town to collect stragglers and to place units in defensive positions as they got back within the friendly screen.

During the time this concerted drive was being made on the front, the troops on the north flank were not heavily engaged, although there was a definite threat in the Ober-Emmmels-Neider-Emmels area. It was planned to anchor a defense west of St. Vith on this still substantial north flank and hold there. The center of the defensive line (from Hunningen to the St. Vith-Wallerrode road was to swing back to the west of St. Vith and establish a line for elements east of the town to fall back through. With great difficulty this was accomplished, and most of the troops were brought out as units.

All through the night of 21-22 December, stragglers were coming back from the troops which had been overrun east of St. Vith. Officer control posts had been set up on all roads to intercept these men and send them to the Hinderhausen area. This was done and by early forenoon of December 22nd about 150 stragglers had been brought up.

The attack along the east front defended by the 38th Armored Infantry Battalion, with attachments, received perhaps the heaviest assault late in the day. Col. Fuller was in charge; the durable, exhausted Tom Riggs had served as executive officer, but now he had evidently been captured. The command post was a stone house a half mile behind the line.

This late attack was so ferocious that in task force Boyer all guns were on swinging traverse, piling up German bodies in the ditches. But every 15 or 20 minutes there would be a cloud of smoke as a German got close enough to lob a grenade into the gun crews. One 50 caliber squad that had been holding off waves of Germans was hit by a Panzerfaust. The gunner fell over the gun, half his face gone; the loader lost his arm.

A new crew moved in immediately to man each gun as crews were knocked out. The German waves were so insistent, Americans called their own artillery down right in front of their own lines. Yet the Germans came—wave after wave. At 6:50 p.m. Major Boyer reported to Col. Fuller that he could hold through the night. But at 7:00 p.m. the earth opened up on him under artillery that he knew would be followed by tanks and then infantry. He called Fuller for help, but the command post was blown up and Fuller was wounded.

Boyer was losing gun crews every 15 minutes. He ordered that no more gun crews crawl out of foxholes to man exposed guns. His gun crews were being manned by the wounded. Heavy snow fell, landing on the men and turning red.

Orders came explaining that German tanks had broken through into St. Vith. Boyer, like Riggs, had no chance to withdraw to the new defense line behind St. Vith. Boyer had no chance to pull out as a unit. He ordered his men to split up into small groups in the dark and try to infiltrate back, practically in step with the advancing Germans. They were overrun and all wounded, killed or captured.

Clarke had artillery gunners repairing a possible road out of St. Vith to the west working along with remnants of three Engineering Combat Battalions: the 168th, the 81st, and the organic Engineer Battalion of the 7th Armored Division. This was to be a pull out to the west as soon as they could stem the attack enough to disengage. St. Vith had been held as requested by all higher headquarters, from the Corps, to 1st Army of General Hodges, General Montgomery and Eisenhower.

St. Vith had depleted many of the men and much of the equipment on the American side of the battle but this sacrifice paid for five days of delay to the German armies of Adolf Hitler, whose goal to be at the Meuse River in 48 hours had at this point been long gone and his crack troops were being badly mauled.

At St. Vith his 5th Panzer Army had been held for five days from December 17th. On the Elsenborn ridge the 99th and 2nd Infantry Divisions had held up the 6th Panzer Army except for the escaping and blitzkrieging Kampfgruppe Peiper. By this time, however, Peiper had been stopped by the combat engineers and was being wiped out by the attacking 3rd Armored Division, the 30th Infantry Division, and the 82nd Airborne Division of Major General James Gavin. The movement of these divisions into the First Army defenses against the main thrust of the German Armies had been meteoric.

The battle of the Ardennes thus far was a tremendous shock to all of those on both sides. There were signs on the American side of a total collapse. However, on the German side there was total disappointment at the failure of the actions of Colonel Von der Heydte and his parachute drop north of Malmedy, and the failure of Colonel Otto Skorzeny to capture the bridges over the Meuse River for the now defeated Colonel Jochen Peiper and his combat group.

Hitler's Generals were now willing to pull their armies back into the fatherland and to again prepare a defense to the west of the Rhine River. Their loss in men, equipment, and

General Bruce Clarke presenting a copy of his book to Chairman of the Veterans of the Battle of the Bulge, former Col. Clyde Boden.

material was beyond belief. They were now concerned about further losses from the Allied Air forces, which soon would have the type of weather to attack the long columns now vulnerable throughout the Ardennes.

Hitler overruled his Generals at this time and decided to continue to pursue the armored attacks against the First Army in the north and move in to surround and capture Bastogne. The plan was to use Armored forces north and south of Bastogne, attacking northwest towards the Meuse River and thence to mop up the village with infantry or Volkestorm troops. This type of decision-making only caused further deformation of Hitler's fast depleting forces and eventually permitted the Allies to win the war.

11

Kampfgruppe Peiper and the Attack from Baugnez to Stavelot

When Colonel Jochen Peiper completed his instructions to his forces at Baugnez—to move on and not waste any time with prisoners—they became organized and followed him in an American jeep towards Ligneuville. He had informed the men that their objective was the Meuse River and they should not waste their time with delays of this type. The column then moved on as the prisoners remained in the field with Nazi guards and a few tanks to hold the prisoners at bay.

Peiper at this time had no infantry or armored forces of the Americans to impede his progress on his assigned route. At Ligneuville there was General Timberlake, the commander of the 49th Anti-Aircraft Brigade with some of his forces with their guns to defend the village. There was also some supply forces of the 9th Armored Division under the command of Captain Seymour Green.

Earlier a large convoy of the 7th Armored Division had stopped in the village to close up the column, but had then moved on. Many of the civilians had then moved west fearing the arrival of German troops as reported by stragglers moving through the village. The owner of the Hotel du Moulin, Herr Rupp and his wife, had decided to stay even though about 2:00 p.m. there was heavy firing heard from the Baugnez-Thirimont area. Shortly thereafter an American bulldozer entered the village and stopped at the hotel long enough for the operator to announce that there had been German fire at Baugnez from tanks.

Seymour Green and his 1st Sergeant jumped in a jeep and headed in the direction of Baugnez to check it out. General Timberlake and his forces immediately pulled out heading for Vielsalm. Captain Green swung around a bend in the road and ran upon a jeep leading a German armored column and was forced to surrender. As the German column approached Ligneuville they were fired upon by a Sherman tank belonging to the 14th Tank Battalion in the village. Green's service company had been working on two Shermans when Peiper's column approached.

The lead vehicle in Peiper's column was a Panther tank commanded by Peiper's adjutant, 1st Lt. Arndt Fischer. When Green's men sighted the German tank, they fired a round of 76 mm. and set it on fire. As a half-track approached with Peiper in it, his driver took cover behind a house. Peiper jumped down and went to the aid of Lt. Fischer, who was badly burned. The German tanks then proceeded to destroy the remainder of the American armor in Ligneuville as well as the assault guns.

The SS Panzer grenadiers of Major Joseph Diefenthal then proceeded to round up the remainder of the American troops in the village. Peiper went into the Hotel du Moulin and refreshed himself with food. At this time he didn't realize that he had cut off the route of the 7th Armored Division's move to St. Vith in support of the 106th Infantry Division. As he studied his map he learned that he could drive on to Stavelot by way of Beaumont and Vaux Richard. This would place his attacking forces back on his assigned route through Trois Ponts and Werbomont.

Peiper's main concern was the bridges over the Ambleve and Salm Rivers. He was also concerned about the forces now known to be in Malmedy as reported by his patrols and his intelligence officer. He knew that Malmedy was on the 12th SS Panzer Division's route of attack. If he could get beyond Werbomont, he would be out of the defiles provided by the Ardennes forest, with its narrow winding roads, which were difficult for his heavy tanks. He was now behind schedule and he was anxious to shove on to Stavelot. The Meuse River was only 25 miles from Werbomont, about three tank hours from the center of Trois Ponts.

Peiper left Ligneuville with the head end of his long steel-ribboned, snake-like column spread 15 miles behind him. Madame Marie Lochem, a nearby Belgian farmer's wife, looked out from her barn and saw twenty American soldiers marching up the street. A German sergeant, Paul Ochmann, pulled eight of them aside to dig graves for two German soldiers. Madame Lochen looked on in horror as the sergeant shot all eight of the Americans through

Site of Sgt. Charles Hensel's road block south of Sravelot.

the head. Seven of the men were killed, but one of the men played dead, Corporal Joseph Mass. He escaped, but later was recaptured.

Peter Rupp was sixty-nine and had witnessed the executions. He was concerned about Captain Green and the fourteen other Americans in the hotel under guard. The Germans did decide to kill them all until Peter Rupp furnished the German soldiers with wine and cognac. The Nazis then forgot about murdering the prisoners.

At this time Peiper, who is pushing on towards Stavelot, is unaware that his men have massacred 81 Americans at Baugnez crossroads and now 7 men at Ligneuville. Both of these locations now have monuments commemorating these men who sacrificed their lives. The monuments were placed by the Belgian people.

Peiper is also unaware of the fact that after dark on a cold night, Sergeant Charles Hensel, a squad leader of the 2nd platoon of C Company, 291st Engineer Combat Battalion, was setting up a road block on a hill south of the Ambleve River Bridge. The block was well selected because it was located just north of a wide sweeping curve with a high rock cliff on the western side of the almost one-lane minor road. The east side was even more hazardous with a sudden drop down to the river in the valley below. It would be most difficult for a Tiger or Panzer tank to negotiate this curve even without a road block in place. One little slip by the tank operator would cause the tank to go down the steep embankment. Especially since the tank driver had 180 degree or night vision. The grade of the road was steep and downhill which made matters worse.

The platoon commander of Hensel's squad was Lt. Warren Rombaugh. They had been operating the night shift at the saw mill in Trois Ponts when Rombaugh told Hensel that his job would be to set up the road block. Lt. Rombaugh warned him that the next unit to approach Stavelot from Ligneuville could very well be German.

Hensel alerted his men. The detail loaded up the squad truck with mines, wiring, demolitions, a 30 caliber machine gun, a bazooka and ammunition. The men were Corpoal Eugene Morris, assistant squad leader, Private First Class John Leary, Francis Lynch, John McClements, Gadziola, Cole, Hahne, Wettling, Sosa, Bauers, Friedman, who drove the truck, and Private Bernie Goldstein. The detail left the castle Froidcouer at dusk.

They made good time until they ran into heavy 7th Armored Division traffic in the railroad viaducts leading into Trois Ponts. They finally got a break in traffic and proceeded to the village of Stavelot; it was 6:30 p.m. when they arrived and the village was lit up by the heavy movement of tanks going west. Hensel's little convoy crossed the Ambleve River bridge, and ascended the long winding hill up to the heights. When he came suddenly to a curve and saw the dangerous solid-rock cliff using his beam light, Hensel halted the movement and made this his roadblock.

While at the rear battalion command post at Haute Bodeux, Major Ed Lampp learned of Hensel's mission to set up the roadblock south of the bridge at Stavelot. He sent Lt. Cliff Wilson to Stavelot to check the location of Hensel's road block. Wilson was able to meet Hensel at the bridge and see the selected location for the block. Wilson reported to Lampp that the block was ideally suited for the purpose and it was beyond any houses near the top of the hill. The rocky cliff also made it a blind curve where the road had narrowed considerably.

Private First Class John Leary tore down some reflector lights that would have helped the Germans to see the dangerous curve. Other men placed a row of thirteen mines across the road just below the curve in such position that any vehicle rounding the curve could not see them until it was on top of them. Hensel gave Private Golstein, who spoke excellent German, the detail out on the point. Corporal Eugene Morris took Goldstein out beyond the curve and positioned him beyond a small white cement building. Neither man could know that at that very moment and not far away, the Germans were talking together about probing towards the Stavelot bridge that Peiper was concerned about. When Morris returned from positioning Goldstein, Hensel put him and Gadziola about thirty yards below the mines, with a bazooka. Then, below the bazooka team, about the same distance, he placed a 30 caliber machine gun with Privates First Class John Leary and Francis Lynch in charge.

By now it was nearing 7:30 p.m. on December 17th and Hensel decided to send Jack Bauers up with Goldstein on the point. Bauers didn't know the location so Hensel went with Bauers towards the curve in the road.

Peiper had decided to send three tanks, and some reconnaissance half-tracks down the road towards the bridge. The armored vehicles had parachute infantry men riding the decks.

Beside his little cement building, Goldstein, entirely alone with only his M-1 rifle, kept watch. He has said it was pitch dark. Shortly he heard the armored vehicles approaching, going very slowly, almost creeping, as if they were feeling their way in the dark. They were traveling so hesitatingly and so quietly that, just beyond his position, Goldstein could hear the men on the decks talking in German. He had been born in and grew up in Austria so he recognized the language.

At about the same time, Hensel and Bauers rounded the rock-faced curve and approached Goldstein's position. They both heard the motors at the same time when they were within thirty feet of the building behind which Goldstein was standing. The Armored vehicle motors were very low, barely turning, as though they were barely moving or halted. Hensel and Bauers stopped and within seconds, hardly believing their ears, they heard Goldstein challenge the Germans with a loud commanding "Halt!" It was funny, it was wild, it was incomprehensible to them. But nonetheless, alone and with only a rifle, Goldstein had demanded that the tanks halt!

When Goldstein yelled halt, the Germans on the decks scrambled to the ground and opened fire with their rifles. But the machine guns on the tanks opened fire and they beat a hasty retreat back around the rock cliff. Then one of the big guns, a 75mm. gun, fired.

Goldstein, who passed away in Brooklyn in 1994, has said that when this gun went off the shell went right over his head. He was blinded by the flame and thunder, and when the earth shook under his feet he decided that this was no place for a boy from Brooklyn and he took off up over the hill.

Below the curve, the men of Hensel's squad became considerably confused. Morris and Gadziola tried to fire the bazooka. Leary and Lynch did not fire the machine gun. There

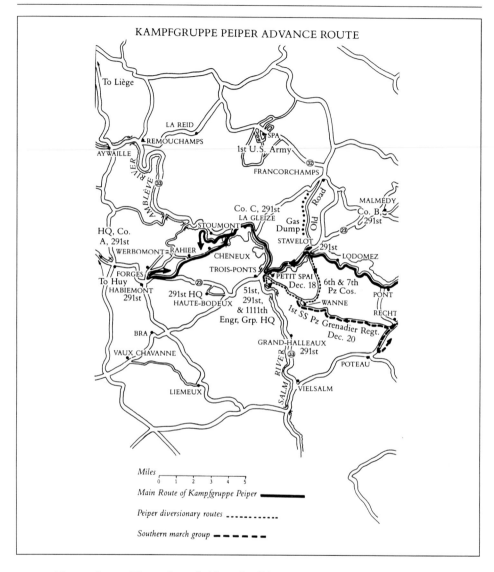

KAMPFGRUPPE PEIPER ADVANCE ROUTE

To Liège

LA REID
REMOUCHAMPS
SPA
AYWAILLE   1st U.S. Army
                            FRANCORCHAMPS
RIVER   32

AMBLÈVE 33   MALMÉDY
                    Co. C, 291st   Old Road Co. B,
                    LA GLEÍZE   291st
              STOUMONT   Gas
HQ, Co.   Dump   23
A, 291st   STAVELOT
WERBOMONT RAHIER   291st
              CHENEUX   LODOMEZ
         TROIS-PONTS
FORGES   PETIT SPAI   PONT
To Huy   Dec. 18   6th & 7th
HABIEMONT   23   Pz Cos.
291st   RECHT
         291st HQ   51st,   1st SS Pz — WANNE
HAUTE-BODEUX 291st,
BRA   & 111th Grenadier Regt.
         Engr, Grp. HQ   Dec. 20
VAUX CHAVANNE   GRAND-HALLEAUX
                 33 291st
                              POTEAU
         RIVER
         SALM
LIEMEUX   VIELSALM

Miles
        0   1   2   3   4   5
Main Route of Kampfgruppe Peiper ━━━━━

Peiper diversionary routes ....

Southern march group ▬ ▬ ▬ ▬ ▬

was nothing to fire at. The tanks or half-tracks did not come around the curve. Up ahead of Leary and Lynch were only their own men, and a lot of noise around the bend. Some of the men came back to them and said they were going to fall back to the bridge. But the men on the road block were worried about Goldstein. He had not returned and they thought he might be laying around the curve with wounds. They didn't want him to be left on top of that hill. As the firing died down a little, Bauers pled to be allowed to go get him since they had shared the same pup-tent together. Hensel said O.K. and Bauers crept around the cliff, but he was greeted by machine gun fire and had to withdraw.

The men moved up the machine gun to the point of the curve just short of the row of mines. Some of the men had fired their rifles, which probably indicated to the Germans that this defense had much fire power. Everything became still for about twenty minutes. Then there were sounds of receding vehicles back up the hill. Now Gadziola asked permission to go around the curve to find Goldstein. Hensel gave his approval and Gadziola crept around the curve. He immediately saw the slight shape of a vehicle slide across the road as if it had lost a track, or one of the treads slipped. It was close to going over the embankment and down into the valley below. Gadziola did not tempt its machine gun fire. He returned to the squad and reported the presence of what he thought was a tank in the utter darkness.

He saw no evidence of either Goldstein or the Germans.

They waited for a while and then Hensel thought it wise to go back to the bridge and report the location of the German column. This information might prove to be of value to the battalion's defensive positions. They decided to leave the mines in place and moved to the truck. They took the machine gun and the bazooka and coasted downhill towards the bridge. As they approached the bridge they met Lt. Cliff Wilson whose driver in the jeep was Private First Class Lorenzo Liparulo. Hensel advised Wilson about the attack of the Germans at the roadblock. Hensel stated that there were no casualties but Goldstein, however, was missing in action.

Wilson had been sent by Major Lampp, the 291st operations officer, to find out how the roadblock was doing. Wilson told Hensel that the bridge was to be prepared for demolition by the 202nd engineers and there would be some armored infantry troops and tank destroyer guns brought into Stavelot to defend against the German column. Hensel was advised by Wilson to return to his platoon commander.

There were engineers on the bridge at this time and Hensel thought they were preparing the bridge for demolition. The officer on the bridge told Hensel that he had been told to relieve him from the roadblock on the hill. Hensel then departed back to join his platoon.

The men on the bridge were from Company C of the 202nd Engineers. Their commander was Lt. Joe Chinland whose company had been in Stavelot most of the day removing the First Army maps from the depot. When they saw the movement of the 7th Armored Division through Stavelot and heard the rumors of the German breakthrough, Chinland had moved his company back to Trois Ponts.

We had been very busy in Malmedy during the time Peiper's Kampfgruppe had accomplished the move from Ligneuville to meet up with Hensel's roadblock on the hill south of Stavelot. There had been several survivors of the massacre who came into Malmedy. I ordered the Medics at Haute Bodeux to come to Malmedy because the casualties were building up from both the massacre as well as from sporadic artillery fire.

I had contacted Lampp and asked for A Company's machine guns and gunners and told him to hold Captain Jim Gamble's A Company in reserve, which I had discussed with Colonel Anderson earlier. He informed me that all headquarters were aware of my situation and the armor and infantry forces were on the way for my use.

I informed Lampp that Lt. Tom Stack would be taking wounded men from the massacre to the field hospital near Spa and would report our situation to Colonel Carter's engineer headquarters. I told Lampp of the dangerous situation in Stavelot, where I could very well be surrounded by midnight without help.

At 7:50 p.m. we heard from the 526th Armored Infantry and the 825th Tank-Destroyer Battalions, and their movement was in our direction. I advised them of our immediate need for a task force from both units to move into Stavelot and set up a defense there. We also advised them that we would send Captain Lloyd Sheetz to meet the task force enroute at a given point and Sheetz could lead them into Stavelot. The agreed upon spot was at the junctions of N-23 and N-32 near the small town of Meiz.

The 1111th Engineer Group journal revealed the above facts as Sheetz phoned the information to the Group Executive Officer, Lt. Colonel Kirkland. Kirkland verified our request to use the armored infantry and tank destroyers as we needed them.

I advised Sheetz to head for Stavelot to check the situation there and then head for Group before heading on to meet the task force for Stavelot's defense.

At 8:10 p.m. Colonel Anderson notified the Corps and First Army command posts that contact had been made between the 291st and the task force. The 291st would prepare defenses in Stavelot and Malmedy. We had learned from Colonel Anderson that the 30th Division of General Leland Hobbs would move to the Malmedy, Stavelot, Werbomont line to establish a northern shoulder of the breakthrough. The "Old Hickory" Division would be enroute from the Aachen area. At this time part of the 1st Infantry Division "Big Red One" had gone through Malmedy and was setting up defensive positions to form a solid northern shoulder from Waimes to Butgenbach. When this defensive situation was developed, and the 291st roadblocks in Malmedy were fully established, there would be a solid defense against the spearheading main thrust of Hitler's large scale counter-offensive. The 1st Division would close on the 2nd Infantry and the 99th Infantry Division to form a solid barrier line from Werbomont to the Siegfried line and the Elsenborn Ridge. Ahead of this infantry line would be a solid Engineer barrier line with mine fields, Abatis, bridges, and craters prepared for demolition, as well as the Combat Engineer weapons: bazookas, rifles and machine guns. Each division would have four Artillery Battalions, two tank destroyer battalions, and complete coordinated fire. The Germans would have a tough time penetrating this First Army defense.

We also learned that the 82nd Airborne Division was on its way from Rheims, France to form on the "Malmedy shoulder line," as General Bradley would later call it in his writings. I didn't realize at the time the very important part that Colonel Anderson was playing in this quick and decisive action to this major crisis. Colonel Anderson's experience in the Mexican border war and WWI, as a combat engineer commander, was serving us well in this period of conflict. The "Colonel" had been commander of the 103rd Engineer Regiment of the 28th Division when it was commanded by General Omar Bradley.

Colonel Anderson's expertise and calm response to my needs have always been uppermost in my mind as I continue to write and research, for history's sake, the full story of our Engineers in the European Theater of operations in WWII.

Shortly after 8:00 p.m. Warrant Officer Coye R. Self arrived in Malmedy with a truck load of ammunitions, mines, and demolitions that we had ordered from Battalion supply. The supplies were quickly funneled out to the men on the various road blocks. Especially strengthened was Sergeant Ralph McCarty, who now had two very important roadblocks on the main road to Stavelot at the west end of town.

He had one at the wooden bridges over the Warche River, and another at the big railroad viaduct. Mines and demolitions were sent to McCarty and Lt. Frank Rhea to wire the two bridges for demolition.

At 8:30 p.m. Captain Paul Kamen, the Battalion Dental officer, came in with a weapons carrier full of medics and medical supplies. Kamen explained that the Medical Officer, Captain Walter Kaplita, was away when the message came in for the need for medical help. Paul Kamen also advised that the road from Stavelot to Malmedy was under some artillery fire. The medics were set up in the vacated field hospital facilities.

This proceeded to be a very busy evening in our command post at the east end of Malmedy. This would go on into the night with the infrequent sound of German artillery. The next visitor was Mike Popp, Major Ed Lampp's command car driver who came in with a look of disaster on his face. The first bit of news he had was that Captain Gambles's A Company had arrived back at Haute Bodeux from Ambleve. "They must've had a very rough trip through the forest roads to get there. Major Lampp wanted me to advise you that Gamble had two platoons with him: Lt. Taylor's and Lt. Edelstein's. Gamble was instructed to send you some machine guns and gunners. Colonel Anderson knows that Gamble is back and that he can serve in reserve when needed."

Mike then spit it out quickly, "Colonel, there are some enemy tanks on the hill south of Stavelot and they have fired on Hensel's roadblock!" This information had been given to Popp by Captain Lloyd Sheetz. Popp had no other details, but now we were in real trouble and without any infantry or armored guns. The possibility of being surrounded in Malmedy was very much in the picture.

Popp departed from the CP to head back to our command post in Haute Bodeux with a message for both Anderson and Lampp. "Demolish the bridge over the Ambleve River at Stavelot without fail." To make certain that the message got back to Lampp and Anderson, we quickly phoned the words to both Group and battalion.

The next visitor was one of B Company's patrols who brought in the greatest news we had that day. The patrol on the back road to Spa had met with the advance elements of the Norwegian infantry Battalion who had been sent by First Army to reinforce my defenses at Malmedy. A Lt. Colonel was with them, the runner said. The Colonel wanted to know how to get in to Malmedy, for he thought that it might be in enemy hands. "Tell him to come in on the back road to Malmedy. Avoid the main road."

At 10:00 p.m. Colonel Harold D. Hansen and his executive officer, Major Bjornstadt, arrived and as they shook hands we quickly laid out a map of the area showing not only our defenses in Malmedy and Stavelot, but the overall plan from Malmedy to Werbomont. I showed Colonel Hansen the location of the 1111th Group headquarters, First Army at Spa, and my rear command post at Haute Bodeux near Trois Ponts.

Private Bernard Goldstein, the hero who said "Halt" to the approaching German tanks at the road block south of Stavelot.

I told Hansen that the high railroad embankment surrounding Malmedy offered an excellent defense for riflemen and machine guns. This would cause the Germans to attack up hill should they come through our mine fields. There were excellent locations for anti-tank guns, as well as artillery positions in the hills north of Malmedy.

I told Col. Hansen that I had 180 men on the road blocks. He promptly replied. "One hundred and eighty! How come you stayed here? My God man, why didn't you run like hell?" I also told him about the massacre of the men of B Battery of the 285 Field Artillery Observation Battalion.

Colonel Hansen advised me that we would have a battalion of armored infantry and a battalion of tank destroyers to reinforce our over-all defense. I told him that there was a German Armored column on the hill south of the Stavelot bridge, and my Captain Sheetz was to meet a task force and lead them into Stavelot. I also told him that we had requested our Group headquarters to blow the Ambleve River bridge to prevent us from being surrounded.

Hansen and Bjornstadt then moved out to set up their CP nearby in Malmedy. Hansen said he would line up the armored infantry and the tank destroyer battalion.

Shortly thereafter, the 526th Armored Infantry and the 825th Tank-Destroyer Battalions rolled in and immediately started to set up their guns to support the roadblocks at the most vital points of our perimeter defense. There had been some confusion and delays, but by sending Captain Sheetz to meet the convoys at a specific point we straightened out the situation. We were able to enhance our defenses in both Stavelot and Malmedy during the evening of the 17th and the morning of the 18th.

Our patrols indicated that the German armored column was possibly over ten miles long. Hearing this news, I was impressed to realize that within less than 24 hours Colonel Anderson and Colonel William Carter had provided such action to my defenses. I was puzzled with the action of the German column when I learned that the roadblock of Sergeant Hensel had caused them to hold off on their attack.

12

Kampfgruppe Peiper's
First Battle at Stavelot

After his first attempt to send an advance unit of his column into Stavelot, Peiper chose to close up his column, fuel his tanks and rest his men. The frequent movement of lights through the village of Stavelot concerned Peiper. He believed the village was heavily defended. Hensel's roadblock convinced him of this fact.

Little did he know that the trouble was the 7th Armored Division on its way to St. Vith by way of Trois Ponts and Vielsalm. His only opposition was a thirteen-man engineer squad. During the night, Peiper's artillery shelled the American traffic as the Kampfgruppe prepared to attack in the morning. Even if he could not reach the Meuse, he might at least break into territory more useful for his monster Tiger and Panther tanks.

The Ambleve River bridge at Stavelot.

Dead German soldier in the first battle at Stavelot.

But Peiper's delay cost him 16 hours, hours precious to the American First Army defense. That night Goldstein finally worked his way down from the hill. He arrived at the bridge and met Lt. Cliff Wilson, of the 291st motor pool, and the 202nd engineers. Goldstein told Wilson of his escape, and he wanted to return to the hill to locate Hensel. Wilson's driver, Lorenzo Liparulo, drove as the two soldiers checked for Hensel's squad at the roadblock.

They stopped at the Vieux Chateau near the junction of Somagne road. Suddenly, machine gun fire broke the stillness. Liparulo slumped over, wounded in the head and the leg. Goldstein, wounded in the hip, staggered back to the bridge where the engineers took him to a first aid station. These Germans were foot soldiers and part of a patrol.

At the same time, C Company of the 202nd Engineers was at the bridge with orders from Colonel Anderson to blow it. There was no reason to keep the bridge intact but Lt. Chinland, the company commander, instructed his men to put anti-tank mines on the bridge instead of preparing it for demolition. The engineers then positioned a 50 caliber machine gun to cover the bridge. Lt. Chinland left one platoon to guard the bridge and two platoons to defend the town square.

Captain Charles A. Mitchell, commander of Company A, 526th Armored Infantry Battalion, was there. Serge Fontaine, a Belgian historian, will combine his efforts with Captain Mitchell. Here is their account: "On the 17th of December 1944 we were billeted in Chateau Grimonster which is south of Liege, Belgium. On the afternoon of that day I was called to battalion headquarters at Harze for an urgent meeting. Lt. Colonel Carlisle B. Irwin,

Peiper's tank doesn't make it into battle at Stavelot.

battalion commander, informed us that the Germans had started an offensive in our area. The 526th was to be sent to secure the first line of defense. My company was to move out within the hour."

"We joined the rest of the battalion on the road near Aywaille. We proceeded into Spa where we had another meeting with the battalion executive officer, Major Paul Solis. Our mission was with a task force under Solis to head to Stavelot with a company of the 825th Tank Destroyer Battalion. We were to meet with Captain Lloyd Sheetz of the 291st Engineer Combat Battalion near the small town of Meiz. Sheetz would lead us into Stavelot where we would soon learn there was a German Column stopped on a hill south of Stavelot, but ready to attack. Our mission was to establish roadblocks east and southeast of Stavelot.

"Once we arrived at the bridge over the Ambleve, Major Solis ordered me to place roadblocks south of the bridge and north of the river. I therefore placed the first platoon under the command of Lt. Charles Beardslee, on the north side of the river and north of the street Rue Devalove. Lt. Harry A. Willyard and the second platoon [were placed] on the north side of the river and south of the street Rue Devalove. The third platoon commanded by Lt. James J. Evans remained in reserve at the square. One gun of the anti-tank platoon, commanded by Lt. Maynard Rogers, was placed near the bridge, and the third gun in reserve near the square. The tank destroyer platoon of the 825th was under the command of Lt. Jack Doherty.

"Two squads, with their two half-tracks from Lt. Willyard's 2nd platoon were sent across the river to establish a roadblock. I was not informed nor was I aware that the bridge was to be prepared for demolition by the 202nd Engineers. The pitch black night and the unfamiliar terrain in a strange town made strategy and communications extremely difficult. We had been very fortunate to have Captain Sheetz of the 291st Engineers to lead us into Stavelot and show us a map of the area. He also advised us of the Germans on the hill to the south.

"Two squads crossed the river as ordered and proceeded up the hill about one half mile. At that point they stopped and radioed that movement could be heard in the distance, which they believed to be tanks and other vehicles. I therefore ordered them to return to the bridge. I was unaware that any other units had been sent across the bridge.

"Shortly after the arrival of Major Solis in Stavelot, Captain Jim Gamble, Company A commander of the 291st Engineer Combat Battalion, arrived at the bridge with his 3rd platoon, commanded by Lt. Arch Taylor. Captain Gamble had been sent into Stavelot to check out the situation on the bridge and to locate Private Goldstein who had been reported missing. Gamble found the bridge covered by the 202nd Engineers of Lt. Chinland and Captain Mitchell setting up the defenses. He learned that there were anti-tank guns to defend the bridge."

Once Gamble found the bridge in the hands of the 202nd Engineers and the village of Stavelot in the hands of Task Force Solis, he crossed the bridge and went up the Vieux Chateau road and located the badly wounded Liparulo.

Gamble then returned to the battalion command post at Haute Bodeux and immediately took Liparulo to the medics, where he passed away from his wounds. Goldstein had been hospitalized for his wounded hip.

Gamble gave the full story of the defenses in Stavelot to Major Lampp and in turn all information was phoned to Colonel Anderson's command post a short distance away in Trois Ponts. Fortunately, Gamble was still available for his standby in the reserve, for the situation was becoming more fluid by the hour.

"One of my half-tracks returned safely to the bridge and crossed over. I had learned later that Germans had occupied the houses on the south side of the river before our arrival and wrecked the second by stretching a cable across the road. When we first arrived in Stavelot and met with Lt. Chinland, Captain Sheetz and Major Solis, there were three rows of mines on the bridge placed there by Lt. Chinland's men. Major Solis ordered Chinland to remove the mines from the bridge and set up his three platoons in defensive reserve. Solis told Chinland that he was going to move armor and infantry across the bridge to set up road blocks south of the bridge. He now ordered me to defend the bridge.

"Shortly after we heard the noises of the Germans preparing to attack down the hill as they fired mortars, artillery, and rifle fire into the village."

Serge Fontaine picks up the story: "This battle of Stavelot was crucial, maybe the longest and surely most prominent for the civilian population who found themselves suddenly in the horrors of war.

"My main motive for telling this factual story is the visit of the first defenders of the town and along with the 291st Engineers and the 117th Regiment of the 30th Division. I have written these lines in their honor.

"The day of the 17th is marked by an intense military traffic. Stavelot is jammed by the transit of the powerful 7th Armored Division, which is moving towards Trois Ponts and Vielsalm to occupy defensive positions in St. Vith. Also worth mentioning is Colonel David Pergrin of the 291st Engineer Combat Battalion, who set up defensive positions in Malmedy.

"At 0530 hours on December 18th Peiper prepares his forces for the attack. He sends his Grenadiers (3rd Battalion of Major Diefenthal's 11th Company) to cover the whole hill of Stockau. He commandeers two inhabitants of the hamlet: E. Glaude and J. Califice to serve as guides and forces them on the hoods of two U.S. Army jeeps. The jeeps are at the head of the column. The jeeps come up on the mines laid by Sgt. Hensel's squad of the 291st Engineers near Corniche road. When the jeeps hit the mines the Germans were thrown clear and Glaude and Califice escape down the road to the old Guard Post of the Belgian Army of 1940. They then went by the old way to Lodomez lower down.

"Meanwhile, two half-tracks from Company A 526th, one towing a 57 mm gun, sent up a patrol to Hensel's roadblock at Corniche. They arrived at the Vieux Chateau road and watched for the approach of the enemy. Sgt. D. Lowe inspected the surroundings. Suddenly rifle shots are ringing out. Immediately, the half-tracks turned back under the heavy fire. The 526th half-tracks sped down hill to the Ambleve bridge, but the lead vehicle hit a cable stretched across the road and crashed. The men crawled from the second half-track after they crossed the bridge.

"Two other half-tracks of the 825th TD, each towing a 75mm gun, drove up the foot of the Vieux Chateau road. The SS men erupted with fire. The half-tracks are knocked out. The first crew of the 825th managed to run, but a mortar round killed the second crew. The vehicle burned, its six occupants dead. Anthony Calvanese, hit in the leg, bounded from the burning vehicle and escaped into the Simonis house.

"At 0600 hours both platoons are now engaged with the 11th Company of the Panzergrenadiers, and they are forced to pull back and retreat across the bridge under heavy small arms, machine gun, and mortar fire. The Germans take advantage of the retreating Americans and advance towards the bridge, but they are repulsed by the badly outnumbered Americans. The Germans have heavy losses as do the Americans including their company commander who is wounded.

"The machine gun squad of Staff Sergeant Jack Ellery of 3rd Platoon stays on the south side of the bridge and, as the Germans rush, Ellery is killed by a machine gun burst near the bridge on the bank. His men cross the Ambleve River bridge with difficulty.

"Several of the 526th men re-cross the bridge. Lt. Jim Evans, who commands 3rd platoon is killed by shrapnel in front of the bridge on the right bank while he is trying to assemble his men."

Captain Mitchell had ordered Lt. Willyard of 2nd platoon to mine the bridge and to prepare the bridge for demolition and place a wire. He had already placed the explosives and the wire, but he does not succeed in blowing the bridge when he received the order. This was just at dawn, however the line to the detonator was not long enough. This is Serge Fontaine's story of the bridge that was not demolished. The story of Captain Mitchell of the blowing of the bridge is somewhat different than Serge Fontaine's. However, the bridge was never blown and the combatants on the American side would have had much better odds in this battle if they had successfully demolished the bridge.

Serge Fontaine continues the order of events; "At that time, the firing line becomes stabilized along the river, but the heavy German armor is coming near. About 7:00 a.m., [we finish] removing the remaining mines from Sgt. Hensel's road block at the Corniche road, where the knocked out jeeps were blocking the road. The German column advances rapidly down the Vieux Chateau road, firing as it approaches and pounds the bridge and the town.

"Both 75 mm guns of the 825th have taken up positions on the Allee Verte, which is two blocks north of the bridge. They are firing relentlessly at the juggernauts of the SS. These guns were under control of Sgt. Celanto and Sgt. Hauser. These two pieces are responsible for knocking out four German tanks. Dale Nelson is also on the Allee Verte with his half track mounted with a .50 mm caliber machine gun; he is killed in the action there. Suddenly, a violent cross fire erupted as the 203rd Anti-Aircraft Battalion of the 7th Armored Division entered Stavelot. Its Battery D stops at 0800 hours on the side of the Allee Verte to protect its convoy. It opens its fire with a quadruple mount [of] .50 caliber machine guns and its 37 mm guns for about an hour. Its rapid fire proves effective, but it loses three vehicles and counts five wounded before moving on to join the battalion. The long detour over Francorchamps hill becomes necessary because the movement on the main route through Stavelot has become near impossible.

Panther tank fails to make the grade to the bridge at Stavelot.

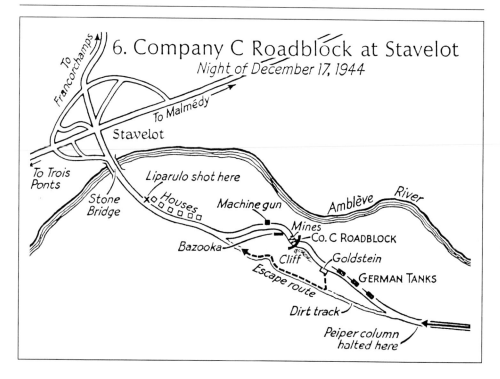

6. Company C Roadblock at Stavelot
Night of December 17, 1944

"Had Peiper attacked through Hensel's roadblock on the evening of December 17th, the 7th Armored Division would have not been able to get to St. Vith to help the unfortunate 106th Infantry Division.

"The German tanks soon advance under the cover of houses of the Vieux Chateau road. The stables of the farm Rennsonet and farm Lejeune are burning. House Dizier is ablaze in turn. Buildings collapse.

"German snipers take cover in the houses of the left bank from where they literally riddle the houses on the west bank with bullets. The U.S. mortar platoon tries to dislodge them with heavy fire, but with little success. At 0830 hours, the German tanks approached the bridge. It is the 1st Tank Company that leads the fight under command of SS Kremser; when he is wounded, he leaves his command to German Hennecke. The tank No. 111 loses its tracks near the bridge and a second Panther is hit.

"A U.S. 57mm anti-tank gun is positioned at the foot of the bridge under the command of Staff Sgt. Carl Smith. This gun fires at the first Panther which is approaching. The shells bounce off of the heavy armor. The German tank that cannot lower its muzzle then rushes on the smaller American gun. Sgt. Smith and his men flee as the heavy tank crushes their gun. A second 57 mm gun is knocked out in this battle.

"At 0900 hours, the SS tanks cross the bridge and move onto Gustave Dewalque street, isolating the second and third platoon of the 526th Armored Infantry. These tanks opened fire with their machine guns, killing Pauline Liver and Marcel Tombeau at point blank range. The Panzers then move on the Rivage, avoiding Chatelet street, which was being raked by American machine gun fire.

"The Panzergrenadiers of Major Diefenthal are progressing behind the tanks. They infiltrate the town and a fight develops from house to house. Captain Charles Mitchell's infantrymen courageously defend against overwhelming odds but they cannot contain the German advance supported by tanks. At this point Captain Mitchell wished that the bridge had been blown. He wondered why Major Solis had given the job to him rather than Lt. Chinland of the 202nd Engineers.

"The command post at Rivage moved back to the market place as men of the 202nd Engineers fired rifles and machine guns to support to the 526th; however, their original mission was to defend the bridge as engineers. They were to fight as infantry as a last resort.

"At 0930 hours, the enemy pushed up the Haute Rivage street. The column turned at the corner of Henri-Massange street and onto Neuve street where there were no Americans. A 75 mm gun of the 825th is removed from the Allee Verte to the corner of Basse-Cour, and [it] fired 15 shells at the tanks on Henri-Massange street. The resistance became useless as the Germans, through sheer weight of numbers, pounded the meager American forces. Peiper's infantry numbered in the thousands; only 100 Americans defended Stavelot.

"Captain Mitchell soon gives orders to retreat up the hill over old Francorchamps road. As he attempts to advise all of his platoons to make this move, a German mortar barrage adds to the futility of fighting on. The 75 mm gun positioned near the Basse-Cour lane is spiked by a Gammon Grenade since it is impossible to bring about a half-track to remove it. The other gun is withdrawn with part of the tank platoon of the 526th towards Malmedy by way of N-28 road. The first and second platoons miss the old Francorchamps road and go

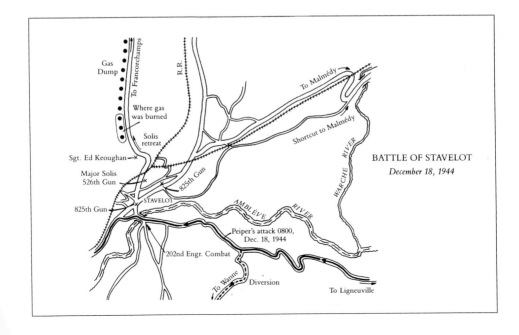

the way of the Combes and Malmedy. The 202nd Engineers go by way of the Haute Leves road around noon. They leave several machine guns and trailers. Major Solis, Captain Mitchell and Lt. Wheelwright, with 27 men of the 3rd platoon and the only rescued gun of the anti-tank platoon, also head up towards Francorchamps. Several soldiers of the 3rd platoon are still straggling about in town near the tanneries."

The losses for the 526th amount to: killed in action, J. Evans, D. Nelson, J. Ellory, and L. Fisher; 15 wounded in action, and 26 missing in action. The platoon of the 825th has lost six killed in action: John Armstrong, Frank Richesin, Douglas Newman, Bernard Gallagher, C. Leach, and F. Williams; and several wounded in action. Among the missing are prisoners of war.

Kampfgruppe Peiper drove on with about 70 armored vehicles. His delays began when Sgt. Hensel's squad blocked his route at the narrow rock cliff. Here at Stavelot, he lost 16 hours on his dash to the Meuse. Peiper had not faced any American armored or Infantry divisions. Peiper had 48 hours to reach the Meuse River. By the time he left Stavelot, he already had lost that 48 hours.

Skorzeny's 150th Brigade failed to capture the bridges over the Meuse that would facilitate Peiper's drive to Antwerp, Hitler's ultimate prize.

Captain Mitchell now receives orders from battalion headquarters to evacuate Stavelot and defend the high ground near the road to Spa. Mitchell again describes the action: "I began to gather my troops for departure. The confusion was tremendous; we were under constant shelling. I ran all over the area as I tried to get information to all units by radio or by word of mouth that we were to leave Stavelot and proceed to Spa.

"Those men who could returned to their half-tracks and proceeded to retreat as ordered. However, many of the vehicles missed the road to Spa and proceeded instead to Malmedy. Two half-tracks, one of which was an anti-tank, and their men, including Wheelwright, and I in my jeep, driven by Sgt. Jack Mocnik, proceeded towards Spa up the Francorchamps road.

"We had progressed about a mile when we came to a huge gasoline dump. Realizing the gasoline would be a boon to the German troops, Lt. Wheelwright and I decided to destroy it by igniting it. Since we had been followed by Germans out of town who we heard laboring up the hill behind us, we needed to take immediate action. About this time Sgt. Ed Keoghan with a squad of men from the 291st Engineer Combat Battalion joined us. At first we tried to stack cans of gasoline in a pile and fire our machine guns into the stack; however, this attempt failed. Keoghan then took a can of gasoline and spilled it over the cans and then ran a spill of gas out about 40 feet. We lit the spilled gas; there was a huge column of smoke and flame. There were no more sounds of moving tanks below our position.

"Sometime later, hearing activity in the woods behind us, we feared we were surrounded by German troops. Frantically, we tried to change our position until one of our men shouted 'American troops!' It was the 1st Battalion of the 30th Division's 117th Regiment. As the commander, Lt. Colonel Robert E. Frankland approached, he said, 'Now men you can put out the fire.' Major Solis accompanied these troops.

"Since I was there, I knew that my A Company had conducted themselves in a fearless manner against overwhelming odds. I feel that the men's attention to orders was exemplary. These men performed above and beyond the call of duty. They dismissed the risk of injury or death in order to accomplish their mission. For those who died, we can only say to their families they died in a most courageous way. To those who lived to tell the tale, I would like to express my great admiration for the individual and collective courage of each man of this organization, which was baptized under fire and emerged victorious."

The Stavelot Bridge over the Ambleve River.

13

The History of the Battles of the Ardennes

A natural route into France from Germany was by way of Aachen and the Belgian plain, just north of the Ardennes. In 1870 the Germans used this route, and then again in 1914 and 1940. In 1944 they were repeating history once more. The Allies failed to use history for training and thus did not detect the build-up of two massive armies in the very area where the Germans had been successful in the past century.

Geographically speaking, the Ardennes is a plateau, but it is so deeply cut by small streams, that it appears almost mountainous. A heavy patchwork of deciduous and coniferous forests provides additional wrinkles.

Despite these formidable features, the region has a surprisingly extensive network of roads. In most cases they follow the winding stream valleys and thus could be easily blocked. At every crossroads or road junction, a small collection of stone farm houses add additional obstacles to advancing military units.

The Germans had demolished all bridges in this entire area as they made their retreat back into Germany behind the Siegfried line in September 1944. Little did either side realize the advantage this would later become for the Americans in the "Battle of The Bulge." The German engineers had aided the German Infantry and armor as they delayed the attacking American Divisions and forced them to build assault bridges. The combat commands were forced to cross many rivers and streams in assault boats until combat engineer units and bridge companies replaced the blown bridges with Bailey bridges, floating pontoon bridges, and in many cases timber trestle bridges. The combat engineers that were organic to the divisions were generally assigned to clear mines, knock down road blocks, and blow pillboxes.

The American attack through the Ardennes and into the Siegfried line in September of 1944 required the use of over 100 engineer Combat Battalions. They built back the blown bridges from the Meuse River to the Siegfried line and from the Huertgen forest to Echternach in Luxembourg along the German border.

This effort went on for almost two months as each engineer battalion built as many as 50 bridges in this two month period. Bridges good for tanks were built at almost all the cities and villages that were battered during the fighting in the "Bulge Battle."

One result of the massive effort to open up the road net for our attacking divisions was that the engineers learned all about the road net in the area. They also knew the tank carry-

Smoke bomb for cover to build a bridge.

ing capacity for virtually every bridge crossing. This allowed them to blow every bridge that could carry a tank, for example. It also allowed them to leave standing a bridge or crossing that may have appeared strong enough to support a tank, in the hope that an unsuspecting German driver would try to cross it and find himself disabled on a collapsed bridge.

The main thrust of Hitler's plan was not aimed at Bastogne as most historians had assumed and had penned heavily in their script. The Sixth Panzer Army of General Sepp Dietrich had this assignment: to aim at Malmedy, Spa, Liege, and Antwerp. The 1st SS Panzer Corps was to lead the attack and feed on the fuel and supplies of First U.S. Army, and to cross the Meuse on each side of Liege. The three "Colonels" of the special forces picked by Hitler were to make all of this possible. Paratroopers led by Von der Heydte were to act as a blocking force north of the village of Malmedy, Peiper was to spearhead the attack, and Skorzeny was to interrupt the American forces and capture the bridges over the Meuse.

The success of this venture called for surprise and the rapid movement of not only Peiper and the 1st SS Division but of the 12th SS Panzer Division's breakout through Malmedy and north thereof. It was pertinent that these two crack German armored columns get to the bridges in this area before they were blown by American Engineers.

Prior history of the German battles through the Ardennes show they had been very successful with armored spearheads. They never had to bring their engineers forward to build the bridges blown by the French or Belgians.

This time it was an entirely different story. American engineer units had to rebuild bridges that were destroyed by retreating Germans at Malmedy, Stavelot, Trois Ponts, and Habiemont. Thus our forces could pursue and attack in their quest to stop Hitler. But those bridges would have to be blown again, sometimes by the same American engineer units that had rebuilt them, to stop Peiper and the 1st SS Division. A review of the entire "Battle of the Bulge" proved it to be an engineer's battle. It was a struggle for mobility on a road net not really designed for monster tanks. A battle where the winner would be determined in part by who took away the road net at the proper time.

This was especially true in the area of the main thrust where the American Engineers detected the breakout of Kampfgruppe Peiper and quickly reacted as combat engineers in order to prepare roadblocks at key locations. As a result, they took away the road net of the spearheading 1st SS Panzer Corps of Hitler's beefed up 6th Panzer Army.

The true untold story of the "Battle of The Bulge" is the full accounting of the courageous actions of these well-trained and experienced combat engineer units in the most massive battle in U.S. History. The tale has been approached by Charles MacDonald in his outstanding book, "A Time For Trumpets." Robert Merriam briefed the subject in his "Dark December" as did a few others. Most historians, however, focused much of their writing on Patton and Bastogne, which, although important in the final victory, really only played a minor part in the overall battle.

There were 114 engineer combat battalions, each with 650 men and officers. These units were highly trained in the use of combat weapons and demolitions, the laying and

103rd Engineers attacking a pillbox on the Siegfried Line.

clearing of mines, and the building of all types of assault bridges. They were expected to work under all conditions including at night or under enemy fire.

Many of these units were in close support of the armored and infantry divisions in the drive across France and Belgium, and into the German Siegfried line. Many had been involved in German counter attacks, and had reacted to this kind of situation. Many had fought at times as infantry, when there would be no other choice. There were also instances when division corps commanders unwittingly threw the engineers in as infantry when engineering tactics may have been more effective in halting the enemy. Where they were used as combat engineers in the "Battle of The Bulge", they proved to be most successful.

The amazing story of the German Army's efforts in the battle was the failure of the German engineers to move up front and build assault bridges for the fast moving armored columns. For example, in Peiper's drive to the Meuse he failed to rebuild the bridge at Habiemont that was blown by A" Company of the 291st Engineer Combat Battalion on December 18th. There were 4 hours and 30 minutes between the time of the blowing of the bridge and the arrival of the 30th Division. This was plenty of time for the German Engineers to build an 180 ft. assault bridge.

103rd Engineers using TNT to demolish Dragons' Teeth at the Siegfried Line.

The key battles in the Ardennes were fought on the northern shoulder by the 99th and 2nd Infantry in front of the Elsenborn ridge. This prevented the 12th SS Panzer Division from breaking through Malmedy, Spa, and Liege. The battle at St. Vith prevented the German Panzer Divisions from getting to the Meuse River south of Liege.

A third key battle was the fighting at Stavelot, Trois Ponts and Stoumont, Belgium whereby the 30th Division, the 3rd Armored Division and the 82nd Airborne Division wiped out the 1st SS Panzer Division.

A fourth very important battle occurred on the morning of the 21st of December. Hitler's favorite commando tactician led his 150th regiment of Armor and Infantry, disguised as an American Combat team, to capture Malmedy and free the badly beaten and entrapped 1st SS Panzer Division of General Wilhelm Mohnke, led by Colonel Jochen Peiper. This was the mission of Colonel Otto Skorzeny, who had failed to capture the bridges over the Meuse River. The Sixth Panzer Army of General Sepp Dietrich was also ordered to make an all out attack with his full Army in this major battle against the forces of the First Army of General Courtney Hodges. Dietrich's effort was to coincide with Skorzeny's attempt to take Malmedy, which was defended by the 30th Division, the 99th Norwegians, the 52th Armored Infantry Battalion, the 825th Tank Destroyer Battalion and the 291st Engineer Combat Battalion.

The American forces on the defenses from the Siegfried line near the Elsenborn Ridge were the 99th Infantry, the 2nd Infantry, the 1st Infantry, the 30th Infantry, the 82nd Airborne, and the 3rd Armored Divisions. These divisions each had an organic combat engineer battalion assigned directly to the division. These combat engineer battalions were the 324th, the 2nd, the 1st, the 105th, the 23rd Armored Engineers, and the 307th Airborne Engineer Combat Battalion.

Also in this battle along the Northern shoulder on the 21st of December, 1944, were the 146th Engineer combat battalion in close support of the 99th Infantry Division, the 254th Engineer Combat Battalion with the 2nd Infantry Division, and one company of the 51st Engineers in Trois Ponts along with the 291st Engineers.

14

The Serious Situation on the Northern Shoulder

On the night of December 17th the Hitler-concocted battle in the Ardennes was starting to cause panic in the higher headquarters of the American command. Peiper was on the hill south of Stavelot, Belgium with 237 armored war machines and 8000 armored infantry. Headquarters personnel began to realize that this awesome force was only 8 miles from General Hodges' command post at Spa.

The only troops within miles of the First Army CP were the 291st Engineer Combat Battalion's 150 men and 15 road blocks in Malmedy. These were the men of Company B commanded by Captain John Conlin. In Stavelot a 13-man squad under Sgt. Charles Hensel had set up a roadblock that caused Peiper to halt his column. The 291st headquarters company, three platoons of Captain Moyer's Company C, and three platoons of Captain Gamble's Company A were in the Trois Ponts-Haute Bodeux-Werbomont Area.

The 1111th Engineer Combat Group headquarters of Colonel H. Wallis Anderson was also in Trois Ponts. There had been a parachute drop by the men of Colonel von der Heydte about five miles north of Malmedy. Peiper's column was known to be about 15 miles long and could be strung out along the route as far back as Thirimont.

Enroute from the Aachen area and headed for St. Vith was the 7th Armored Division. They were to reinforce the 106th Infantry, which was being attacked by 4 divisions of the 66th German Corps. Two American Divisions, the 99th and the 2nd Infantry, were being attacked by the 12th SS Panzer, the 277th Volksgrenadier, the 12th Volksgrenadier, and the 9th Parachute Divisions. The defenses of the 99th and 2nd Divisions had been violently attacked, however they had set up a solid line from Rocherath, Krinkelt, through Bullingen, and Butgenbach. The 1st American Infantry was enroute towards Butgenbach and Waimes to set up on the right flank of the 99th Division.

Of greatest concern to Hodges was the threat of Kampfgroupe Peiper, so he ordered his headquarters to move west to Chaudfontaine, Belgium. Working with VIII Corps and Colonel H. W. Anderson, he started some forces in the direction of the 291st in Malmedy. Orders were given to the 99th Norwegian Battalion to head for Malmedy along with the 526th Armored Infantry Battalion, and the 825th Tank Destroyer Battalion.

Hodges had conferred with General Simpson of the American 9th Army and was able to have him dispatch the 30th Division of General Leland Hobbs to the Malmedy, Trois Ponts, and Werbomont area. Major General James M. Gavin was dispatched by SHAEF to meet with Hodges at Chaudfontaine and move his 82nd Airborne Division from France to meet the needs of General Hodges.

It appeared from the meager information available that the Germans in Stavelot were in great force. If Colonel Anderson and the Engineer units at Trois Ponts could not halt Peiper by blowing the bridges at Trois Ponts, he could well be on his way to the Meuse River in open tank country. During the evening of the 17th and early morning of the 18th of December, many changes occurred in Malmedy, Stavelot and Trois Ponts.

Captain Jim Gamble arrived in Trois Ponts with two platoons after a very rough trip from Ambleve. He reported to Anderson at his command post and advised the Colonel that he had the 2nd platoon of Lt. Alvin Edelstien and the 3rd platoon of Lt. "Arch" Taylor with him. Anderson advised Gamble to report to the rear CP of the 291st at nearby Haute Bodeux. Gamble was advised by Anderson to report to Major Lampp, who was in charge of my rear operations center.

Anderson advised Gamble that his company was to prepare the bridge at the South end of Trois Ponts for demolition. Then his platoons would act in reserve to take care of any change in the original plans. Gamble also learned that Captain Moyer had been sent to Malmedy with Lt. Davis' platoon of C Company, and the 51st Engineers had been ordered to send a company into Trois Ponts from Marche. Originally the plan called for Captain Moyer's Company C to prepare the three bridges in Trois Ponts for demolition; however,

Captain John Conlin and 1st Sgt. Earl Short of "B" Company.

Captain Lloyd Sheetz, Liaison Officer.

Captain Kamen and the Medics in Malmedy.

when I requested more help in Malmedy, the overall plan to blow the bridges had to be changed.

Many of the Headquarters and Service personnel were located in the Haute Bodeux-Trois Ponts Area. The battalion motor pool maintenance was located in the village and C Company was operating a saw mill in Trois Ponts.

When Gamble reported to Lampp, he was advised to send machine guns and crews, bazookas, and ammunition into Malmedy. He was also told that his men under Sgt. J.B. Miller were preparing the bridge at the south end of Trois Ponts for demolition. Lampp then advised Gamble that his two platoons would remain available for action at any time due to the very fluid situation and word that the Germans had dropped paratroops in the area. It didn't take long for Gamble and his men to become very active during the night of the 17th and in particular around 3 A.M. on the morning of the 18th.

Gamble learned that Peiper had been stopped on the hill South of Stavelot. He also heard about Goldstein's yelling "Halt" at the approaching German Tanks. He learned from Lampp that Goldstein and Liparulo had not returned. About 2:30 A.M. Lampp gave Gamble instructions to take a platoon and go into Stavelot and check three things: the whereabouts of Goldstein, the defenses being set up in Stavelot, and the condition of the bridge being handled by the 202nd Engineers.

During the evening of the 17th of December we were being shelled in Malmedy and our road blocks had been tested by the Germans. Following the arrival of Moyer and our machine guns from Gamble, Captain Lloyd Sheetz, my liaison officer, arrived with great news. Help was on the way in the form of infantry, armored infantry, and anti-tank guns. The 99th Norwegian Infantry Battalion, the 526th Armored Infantry Battalion, and the 825th Tank Destroyer Battalion had been assigned to move into Malmedy and form on our defenses. Due to the urgings of Colonels Anderson and William Carter (the First Army Engineer), the First Army Operations officer, Major General Kean, ordered each of these three battalions to head quickly to Malmedy.

Sheetz and I decided to send a company from the 825th and the 526th into Stavelot to protect our position in Malmedy from being surrounded should the German Armored Column attack through Stavelot. We both realized that the blowing of the bridge over the Ambleve River was mandatory. Colonel Anderson's office in Trois Ponts was notified of this need when Sheetz went into Trois Ponts while on his way to lead the Armored Infantry and Tank Destroyers into Stavelot.

Major Lampp responded to my request for medics in Malmedy by sending Captain Paul Kamen. The battalion Dental officer received this assignment in the absence of the battalion Medical officer, Captain Walter Kaplita. Little did Kamen realize that the number of American soldiers, civilians, and even German soldiers requiring aid greatly exceeded the capabilities of his five-man medical staff. He would first treat the victims of the massacre.

Such was the case of 1st Lt. Virgil Lary, who was brought into our CP shortly after midnight by the Martin sisters. The Martins owned a dairy farm very close to the massacre site at Baugnez. Lary had been able to crawl away from the site under the cover of darkness. The Martins found him on their doorstep. Once Kamen's medics took care of his wounds, Lary described the massacre. His story coincided with all the other victims' accounts. The one difference was that he saw the German who fired the first shot.

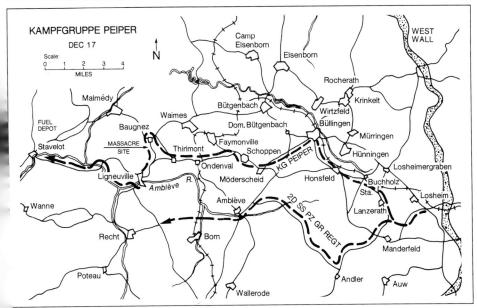

15

The Death of the Golden Lion

By dusk on December 8, the green troops of the 106th infantry division were hunkered down in the dense, snow-covered forest of the Schnee Eifel waiting to move to the front. We of the 291st watched them come in and form on the defenses vacated by the 2nd Infantry Division.

Four days later, the Golden Lion Division was in place along the Siegfried line. They occupied the quietest sector of the 85-mile-long "Ghost Front."

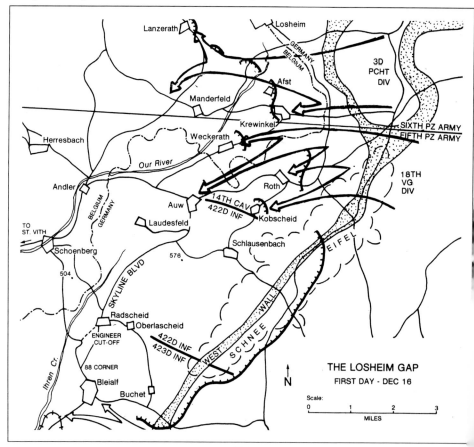

THE LOSHEIM GAP

FIRST DAY - DEC 16

By dawn on December 16th, the "Battle of the Bulge" began with the German military arrow pointed straight at the 106th's heart.

By dusk on December 22, six days later, the Golden Lion was dead. Nearly 12,000 of the division's 16,000 men were dead, wounded, or prisoners. One depleted regiment and a handful of men from the divisional units survived to fight on. In those seven freezing days of misery in the worst European winter of the century, 16,000 individual stories of bravery, panic, and fear took place.

History now credits the 106th GIs as a major force in blunting Hitler's last offensive. Those young men who went into their front line positions for the first time disrupted von Rundstedt's immaculate timetable. The German drive failed. The European war ended a little more than four months later.

Hitler took the route the experts said was impossible to traverse: the Ardennes. He did it in weather that negated Allied air power, and he tried to split the Allied armies in two by driving his forces to the rail center of Liege. To succeed, his blitzing forces had to break through road centers such as St. Vith, Malmedy, and Eupen.

Facing the Germans were three Regiments of the 106th: the 423rd, 424th, and 422nd; four battalions of artillery: the 589th through the 592nd; and the 81st Engineer Combat Battalion. At different periods of time, the division enjoyed the support of the 14th Cavalry Group, the 275th Armored Field Artillery Battalion, the 820th Tank Destroyer Battalion, the 634th Anti-Aircraft Battalion, the 112th Infantry Regiment of the 28th Division, and the 168th Engineer Combat Battalion.

The thinly spread GIs of the 106th would be hit by the 18th Volksgrenadier Division, the 62nd Volksgrenadier Division, and the 116th Panzer Division. The 423rd, 424th, and 422nd defended this area.

At 0530 on December 16, 2000 German guns bellowed into action along the 85-mile Ardennes front. The Germans opened up with their big railroad guns and saturated the area in front of St. Vith where the 106th was in position. Up to this point, the soldiers of the 106th had not experienced an artillery barrage of any type.

In the Losheim gap, the Germans punched a tremendous hole in the American lines. Volksgrenadiers and paratroopers crashed through the 14th Cavalry Group and the 99th Division, all on the left flank of the 106th's 422nd Regiment. By 0830, the Germans were in Roth and pushing to the rear of the 422nd.

The GIs of the 14th Cavalry and the 422nd fought off the attacking German Infantry, finally forcing the Germans to fall back with many casualties. But the overwhelming numbers of the Germans with tank and artillery support prevailed.

On the first day, the 18th Volksgrenadier Division closed on Roth, Auw, and Kobscheid, behind the 422nd Regiment. The Volksgrenadiers attacked Roth with strong support from their assault guns. The Germans sought access to the Our valle and the road to Schoenberg.

The 422nd Regiment's front stretched for more than four miles along a crest on the eastern slope of the Schnee Eifel. In the center, the 423rd held five miles, with one battalion curving around the extreme southern end of the Schnee Eifel in front of Bleialf. The Alf

River valley separated the 423rd from the division's other regiment, the 424th, which was deployed south of the division on a six-mile front.

The situation seemed most untenable. The Our River was behind the 424th. Many gaps existed between strong points along the three-regiment front. Attacking forces could easily slip by both ends of the Schnee Eifel and meet at Schoenberg, trapping the entire division.

In addition to the natural vulnerability of the 106th's positions, the routes around the Schnee Eifel were only lightly held. Only one regiment of the 14th Cavalry Group guarded the Losheim gap. The 14th was a small recon outfit equipped only to alert others in case of an attack. If the Germans attacked, the 106th would get no help from either flank.

Major General Alan W. Jones, the commanding officer, understood that the Schnee Eifel had to hold, but his worst fears were realized on the first day of the German offensive. Two Volksgrenadier regiments poured through the Losheim Gap, brushing past the 14th Cavalry Group. By midmorning, the Germans were on the road to Auw, only 12 miles from St. Vith. They were already three miles behind the northern flank of the 422nd Regiment. The garrison in Auw, a company of combat engineers of the 81st Engineer Combat Battalion, opened fire on the Germans. The German tanks soon took Auw and overran the engineers. The Germans now controlled the road to St. Vith.

Stan Wojtusik, a rifleman in the 422nd, tells his story of events on the Schnee Eifel: "At the southern end of the Schnee Eifel, a regiment of Volksgrenadiers surged up the valley of the Alf River overrunning the position of the 423rd Regiment's anti-tank company and capturing most of the village of Bleialf. A force of the 81st Engineers recaptured the village but couldn't hold it, but they had staved off disaster only briefly.

"The 423rd had used up most of its ammunition and the German advance of two regiments with Tiger tank support threatened the two American regiments from both the north and the south. Only five miles separated the northern and southern arms of the rapidly closing German pincers.

"By nightfall on the first day the 106th Division was in grave peril. The 424th was being driven back to the Our River and the two regiments on the Schnee Eifel were threatened with entrapment. We had difficulty digging our foxholes in the snow-encrusted ground and were being slowly forced back by the German infantry, who followed up an artillery barrage with a charge at our lines through the woods. We drove them back several times; however, they came at us with tank support. When we counter-attacked, we found dead Germans left in the fields.

"During the night, we could hear the Germans bringing up reinforcements, and we knew we were running low on ammunition and food and expected an all out attack in the morning. We heard that the 7th Armored Division was on the way to support us. The conditions were miserable at best and to fire and fall back was making it difficult to prepare so many foxholes.

"At 6 a.m. on the 17th, the Germans renewed their two-pronged attack and closed the gap when they converged from the north and south and linked up at Schoenberg. The trap had snapped shut.

Around noon we could feel the increase in the incoming artillery and mortar fire, and we learned that the regiment was trapped and there was a possibility of retreating off of the ridge. There followed a heavy bombardment of heavy stuff as we fell back further to the west. The weather became quite cold during the night of the 17th. News came down from the commander of the 422nd Regiment, Colonel George L Descheneaux, at 4 a.m. on the 18th instructing the 422nd to attack enemy tank concentrations along the Schonberg and St. Vith road and also to set up a defense protecting St. Vith. The men by this time were running out of food and ammunition but were still willing to make the attack against the heavily armed Germans.

The regiment moved out, leaving the wounded behind with medics. Despite rain and fog, they slugged their way to within striking distance of Schonberg and dug in for the night. Descheneaux's regiment moved into a wooded area and were lined up to receive an airdrop of ammunition and supplies. This effort was a failure, and this battered and hungry group moved towards the Bleialf-Auw road where they were pounded by machine guns and heavy fire. They were quickly surrounded by the Germans with panzers. Descheneaux had no other choice but to surrender. His men were hemmed in on all sides and being raked by German machine gun fire.

We were rounded up by the Germans and marched in groups into Germany. We remained active for four days and some of us still refused to surrender but were later captured. Being a prisoner of war was worse than being in battle. Food was scarce and not anything but thin soup. On a train moving back into Germany, we were fired on by our own Air Force, and many of our men were wounded or killed. We ended up in a Stalag and were later freed by the Russians at the end of the war. The Russians treated us well."

Colonel Charles Cavender's 423rd Regiment suffered the same fate. On December 19th, while preparing to attack towards Schonberg, they were heavily shelled by German artillery. The German infantry overran their field artillery positions. The three battalions of the regiment were soon pinned down, but they continued to fight. Ultimately they were overwhelmed and forced to surrender.

Thus, though the men of the 106th fought as all American soldiers do, they were defeated by vastly greater numbers of men and war material. Thus, we lost two-thirds of the 106th (Golden Lion) Division early in Hitler's counter-offensive.

16

The Blowing of the Bridges at Trois Points

While Peiper lay on the hill south of Stavelot on the night of December 17th, he refueled his armored equipment from his mobile fuel trucks and contemplated the difficulties that lay ahead of him. His patrols had indicated that there were enemy troops on the Ambleve River bridge at Stavelot, and his map indicated that there were three bridges to cross in Trois Ponts. If the enemy blew the two bridges at the northern end of Trois Ponts over the Ambleve and the Salm Rivers, he might be able to cross the Salm at the South end of the village. Early in the morning he sent a task force of armored infantry and tanks down the narrow-winding road towards Wanne. The mission of this task force was to capture the lower Salm bridge.

Although Peiper had lost 12 hours laying on the hill, he felt he might make up time if he could get through Trois Ponts and back on his assigned route. This delay and the ensuing delay involved in the first battle at Stavelot would cause him to lose his effort to get to the Meuse River. The delay gave Col. Anderson time to prepare the bridges in Trois Ponts for demolition.

The original plan worked out by Anderson and Major Lampp of the 291st called for C Company of the 291st to prepare and blow the bridges in Trois Ponts. However, when Captain Larry Moyer took his C Company platoon into Malmedy, Anderson ordered Company C of the 51st to do the two northern bridges and a squad of A Company of the 291st to prepare the lower Salm bridge for demolition. On the early morning of the 18th of December, Anderson and Lampp had Captain Gamble's complete company in Trois Ponts and 20 men from Lt. Rombaugh's C Company, 291st, assigned to the defenses. In addition the 291st motor pool was located in Trois Ponts.

Anderson had also been able to set up a .57 mm. anti-tank gun from the 526th Armored Infantry at the 51st Engineer's road block in front of the railroad viaduct on the Stavelot road. The 51st had brought mines, primacord, and TNT in great supply and were only too glad to add the .57 mm. gun to the defense.

The bridges were prepared for demolition by 9:00 a.m. Anderson then advised Lampp, the 291st Executive Officer, to set up an overall defense to guard the bridges. Earlier Anderson and Lampp had agreed to hold Captain Gamble's 2nd and 3rd platoons in reserve for any quickly developing emergency in this most critical and ever changing time.

Lampp assigned Walters to set up a defensive line along the Salm River with mines, machine guns, and bazookas from the south end of the bridge northward. Captain Sam Scheuber established a similar line of defense from the northern end of Trois Ponts to the south. When this defense seemed to be lacking in numbers, Sgt. Paul Hinkel's squad was assigned to fill in on Walter's left flank. Hinkle's squad had been on duty as guarding the 1111th Group's Headquarters. Lt. Rombaugh's 20 men were assigned to the defensive positions of Captain Sam Scheuber.

The sounds of the battle could be heard by the engineers in Trois Ponts and by 10:45 A.M. Peiper's column was seen coming from Stavelot. The lead tanks approached the road block out in front of the .57 mm. anti-tank gun. The gun crew from the 526th Armored Infantry, reinforced by six men of the 51st Engineers, promptly opened fire.

The lead tank, a Panther, was hit and it flung about in such a way that it blocked the road temporarily. The next Panther in line fired on the roadblock. Shortly the .57 mm. was knocked out and all four members of the gun crew were killed. They were McCollum, Hollenbeck, Buchanan, and Higgins. A 51st man, Pvt. Audrus Salazar, was slightly wounded by fragments in the leg.

Salazar hurried back across the Ambleve bridge, and the order to blow the bridge was given. The other five men of the 51st on the roadblock fled through the viaduct and had to make their escape up the La Gleize road since they were cut off from Trois Ponts.

Col. Anderson had witnessed the blowing of the bridge and then was dismayed to see Peiper's men massacre in cold blood an old couple who lived on the other side of the Ambleve River. This would be only the first of many civilians that would suffer a similar fate.

Peiper's Panther was knocked out by American Air at the Chenaux Bridge.

Peiper's Panther knocked out by American Air at Cheneux, December 18th.

When the Ambleve bridge went up with a thundering explosion and every color of the rainbow, Peiper heard it and observed the debris flying in all directions. It angered him, for he correctly judged that there was little strength in Trois Ponts, but they had blocked him and now were adding more delay to his effort to get to the Meuse River. He was hoping to get there on this date.

But his nemesis was catching up to him. The overnight delay at Stavelot had given the 51st Engineers (Company C) time to reach Trois Ponts and wire the bridges, while the 291st fronted roadblocks. One 291st roadblock (Sgt. "Cuck" Hensel's) had tilted the scale that caused the delay.

Peiper studied his map and saw that the only thing for him to do now was to swing north to La Gleize. There was a bridge over the Ambleve there that would support his heavy tanks in the hamlet of Cheneux. Maybe the bridge would still be intact. Maybe he could beat the engineers to it.

Across the river Col. Anderson had his field telephone hooked up to the line with the Headquarters of Col. William Carter, the First Army Engineer. Anderson was counting the Armored vehicles in Peiper's column as they headed into the Ambleve River valley towards La Gleize. Again the engineers were notifying the staff of First Army and Corps Headquarters of the location of the spearheading armored column of the main thrust of Hitler's "Secret War."

Unseen to Anderson, Peiper's men also swarmed into another house near the 291st motor pool and killed ten people, among them a young lad and a pregnant woman. These Belgians were also known to the men of the 291st.

As Peiper's column swung northward towards La Gleize, Colonel Anderson sent a message to First Army headquarters at Spa, for this movement menaced the Army Headquarters itself.

In addition to their defensive positions along the west bank of the Salm River, Captain Scheuber's Company had set up a roadblock across the Salm River, on the heights, on the road that approached from Wanne. At about noon the roadblock saw about three German tanks coming up this road. The men of the 51st opened fire with an AT rocket launcher (bazooka) in order to stop the tanks but they were unsuccessful. The tanks came on. They were, of course, the lead tanks of the company of Mark IVs that Peiper had sent down by way of the secondary road south of the Ambleve River, which led to Wanne. Their goal was to capture the bridge over the Salm at the south end of Trois Ponts, which Bucky Walter's platoon of A Company of the 291st had prepared to blow.

All three tanks opened fire on the men of the 51st and they had to get out in a hurry. The men on the road block crossed the Salm without losing any men.

South of Trois Ponts at the lower Salm bridge, Miller saw the enemy tanks on the hill. He watched them as they maneuvered around. But he knew they had nothing to fear from the tanks at that moment. There was no road down off the hill in their direction. In order to reach the bridge the tanks would have to turn around, go south, come down off of the hill and approach the bridge from the south.

The appearance of the column on the heights caused Anderson to become worried about the bridge over the Salm inside of Trois Ponts. At 1:00 P.M. he gave the order to

Small pockets of resistance were wiped out by the Wirbelwind and the German Armored forces.

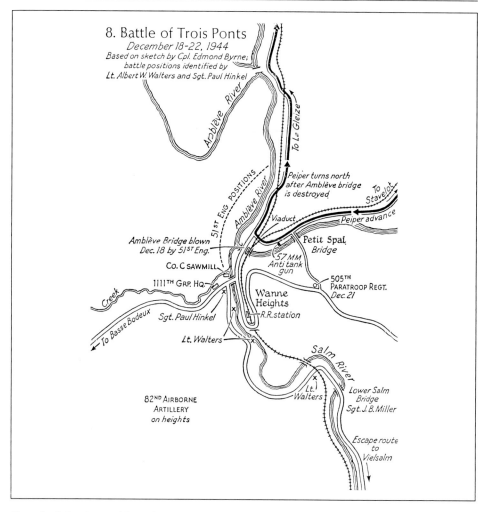

8. Battle of Trois Ponts
December 18-22, 1944
Based on sketch by Cpl. Edmond Byrne;
battle positions identified by
Lt. Albert W. Walters and Sgt. Paul Hinkel

Ambléve River

To La Gleize

51ST ENG. POSITIONS

Ambléve River

Peiper turns north
after Ambléve bridge
is destroyed

To Stavelot

Viaduct

Peiper advance

Ambléve Bridge blown
Dec. 18 by 51ST Eng.

Petit Spai Bridge

Co. C SAWMILL

57 MM Anti tank gun

1111TH GRP. HQ

505TH PARATROOP REGT. *Dec. 21*

Creek

Wanne Heights

To Basse Bodeux

Sgt. Paul Hinkel

R.R. station

Lt. Walters

Salm River

Lt. Walters

Lower Salm Bridge
Sgt. J. B. Miller

82ND AIRBORNE ARTILLERY
on heights

Escape route
to
Vielsalm

Captain Scheuber to blow the bridge. It was a great blow and as the debris went skyward, the column of German tanks did not bother to come down off of the hill.

However, when Sgt. Miller heard the explosion to the north, he and his men saw the Germans sliding down the hill on foot to get to the bridge. He turned the detonator key and watched the bridge move in small pieces towards the sky.

When all three bridges had been blown there was no way for Peiper to get into or through Trois Ponts. Anderson now realized that the next bridge of importance on Peiper's route would be at Cheneux, which would get his column back on the main route to Werbomont. Anderson met with Walters around 1:30 p.m. and advised him to set up a defensive line along the Salm River and tie in with Captain Scheuber. Also Anderson advised Sgt. Paul Hinkel of the 291st to set up his men, and the men of Lt. Rombaugh of the 291st, on this defensive line and to coordinate the line with Captain Scheuber.

At about 2:00 P.M. Major "Bull" Yates, the executive officer of the 51st Engineers, reported to Anderson and was quickly advised of the overall critical situation in Trois Ponts: a long column of Germans headed towards Liege or the Meuse River. Anderson also told Yates of his new mission: move his headquarters to Modave and set up a barrier line of engineer units east of the Meuse River. The defense of Trois Ponts was turned over to Yates who would have over 300 men from the 51st and 291st.

Anderson then moved his headquarters to Haute Bodeux for two reasons: the Germans were now shelling his command post in Trois Ponts, and final plans had to be made with Lampp and the 291st to solve the problem of the free running German column.

When Anderson arrived at the 291st rear CP at Haute Bodeux, Major Lampp had a roomful of staff and company officers. The first question was put on the table by Lampp. "Which bridge do we blow next? " A quick look at the map indicated that when Peiper got across the Cheneux bridge he would have to cross the bridge at Habiemont over the Lienne River. Both Anderson and Lampp looked at Gamble, whose company had done great service here since their arrival on the 17th from Ambleve. He had two platoons available in reserve and pointed to Lt. Edelstein. "Al, you have the honor!"

Kampfgruppe Peiper was soon in beautiful, open tank country; there were no defenders between his 237 armored vehicles and 8000 armored infantry. He had a good chance of getting to the Meuse River on this day, December 18th, provided he could successfully cross the bridge at Cheneux and then move west on N-23. He would thus rejoin his regularly assigned attack route to the Meuse.

The bridge at Cheneux where Peiper's column was bombed by American Airforce.

17

The Stopping of Kampfgruppe Peiper at the Lienne

On the night of December 17th, the situation all along the First Army front looked desperate to General Courtney Hodges. There was a rather lengthy German Panzer column on the hill south of the First Army Headquarters only 10 miles from Spa. Hodges had made the decision to move his Command center west to Chaudfontaine. At this time there was only the 291st Engineer Combat Battalion to the front with some First Army security forces on the way to assist the 291st.

From Malmedy east to the Siegfried line was the 1st Infantry Division, the 2nd Infantry Division, and the 99th Infantry Division attempting to hold the line against the entire 6th Panzer Army of General Sepp Dietrich.

General Hodges telephoned General Bradley and asked for SHEAF's only reserve units, the 82nd and the 101st Airborne Divisions located near Reims, France. The most critical point was at Stavelot. The 82nd Airborne was advised to head to Werbomont and the 101st to Bastogne.

Major General James Gavin was in command of the 82nd Airborne Division and he decided to go to Spa and meet with Hodges where he found out that Peiper had crossed the Ambleve River at Stavelot. Now First Army headquarters, all the big supply installations,

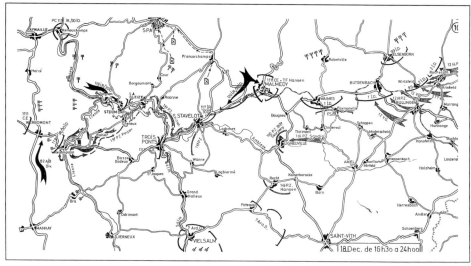

and everything north of the Ambleve was threatened. Hodges ordered Gavin to take the 82nd to Werbomont. Gavin had just left to make a personal reconnaissance at Werbomont and set up an assembly area, when General Leland Hobbs arrived at the General Hodges' headquarters. Hobbs reported that his 30th Division was in an assembly point for the night at Eupen.

Hobb's 119th Regiment was only 5 miles North of Spa. As he conferred with Hodges, the messages had come in from Colonel Anderson of the 1111th Engineer Group that Peiper was now at Trois Ponts and the Ambleve River bridge had been destroyed. Peiper had turned north in the direction of Stoumont. At this point General Hobbs was ordered to send his 19th Regiment in the direction of Stoumont. Little did the top brass know that at this

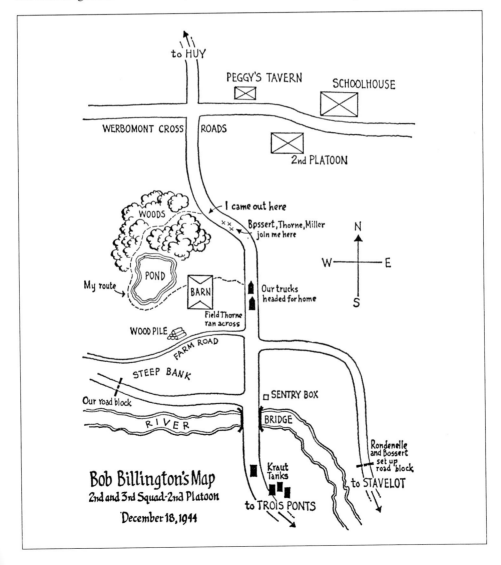

to HUY

PEGGY'S TAVERN   SCHOOLHOUSE

WERBOMONT CROSS | ROADS

2nd PLATOON

WOODS

I came out here

Bossert, Thorne, Miller
join me here

N
W——E
S

POND

My route

BARN

Our trucks
headed for home

Field Thorne
ran across

WOOD PILE

FARM ROAD

STEEP BANK

Our road block

SENTRY BOX

BRIDGE

RIVER

Rondenelle
and Bossert
set up
road block

to STAVELOT

Bob Billington's Map
2nd and 3rd Squad-2nd Platoon
December 18, 1944

Kraut
Tanks

to TROIS PONTS

time all that was in front of the German armored column and the Meusse river was Lt. Alvin Edelstein's Platoon, A Company, 291st Engineer Combat Battalion. He had orders to blow the bridge at the Lienne River on N 23.

About 1:00 p.m. General Pete Quesada, commander of the 9th tactical air force, sent word that this long, snaking German column had been spotted by reconnaissance planes and that its head was located in the vicinity of La Gleize.

This was disastrous news! Without knowing the intention of the enemy, Hodges tried to second guess him. Peiper could proceed on down the Amblève and cut the First Army's rear installations, or he could turn westward at La Gleize and go to Werbomont. There he would most certainly prevent the 82nd Airborne from assembling and he could then reach the Meuse River. Hodges therefore ordered Hobbs to send his 119th Regiment to cover both Stoumont and Werbomont. Hobbs immediately managed to get his regiment over to Remouchamps. The battalion of Major Hal McCown was sent to Werbomont.

General Quesada's message about the finding of the long column caused some small planes to be sent up. They found by flying low that the column stretched back from the Cheneux bridge for 15 miles to a point just south of Malmedy. Thunderbolts, Mustangs, and British planes took advantage of the break in the clouds and swept down on the German column as it passed through Stavelot.

The men of the 51st and the 291st saw from their defensive positions in Trois Ponts, Malmedy and Werbomont this heavy action from the air and felt some relief for the first time; however, the clouds quickly closed over as they watched some American planes get shot down by German Anti-aircraft fire.

Peiper lost some tanks and suffered casualties in his column but he reorganized and headed on across the Cheneux bridge towards N 23 route.

The story of the blowing of the bridge over the Lienne River at Neuf-Moulin near Habiemont has been told by many writers including Charles MacDonald in "A Time For Trumpets", Janice Holt Giles in " The Damned Engineers ", and Jean Paul Palude in "Battle of The Bulge Then and Now." Pallud's book is a British writing which was well researched and loaded with photographs which show the "Battle" both then and now.

When Captain Gamble gave the assignment of blowing the bridge at Habiemont over the Lienne to Lt. Edelstein's platoon, a radio message was sent from the rear command post at Haute Bodeux to Sgt. Edwin Pigg at Werbomont. He was ordered to wire and guard the bridge at Habiemont. Pigg was not only a platoon sergeant but a demolition expert as well. The message was urgent and sent in the clear.

Edwin Pigg then rounded up a strong detail, mostly third squad of the 2nd platoon, whose squad leader was Sgt. R.C. Billington. This was part of the detail that Lampp and Anderson was holding in reserve for such action.

The men loaded up the platoon truck with mines, prima cord, TNT, and dynamite and set off for the schoolhouse at 1:30 p.m. These were the only line troops left in the Company A headquarters in Werbomont. The others were either on the defenses in Trois Ponts or on the recent mission hunting down reported enemy paratroops in the Trois Ponts area.

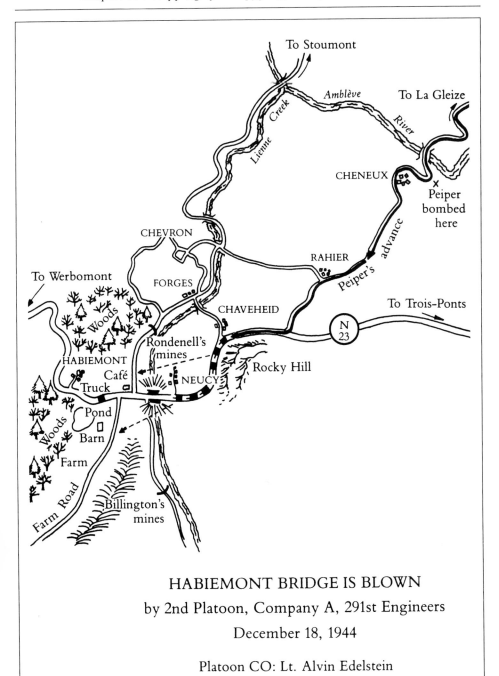

HABIEMONT BRIDGE IS BLOWN
by 2nd Platoon, Company A, 291st Engineers
December 18, 1944

Platoon CO: Lt. Alvin Edelstein

They loaded their equipment and men into the platoon two-and-a-half ton dump truck with "Hooks" Kovacs as the driver and headed through the heavy traffic of retreating civilians from Trois Ponts. They became aware that the civilians were fleeing the Germans. Little did they know the impact of their mission.

The roads were jammed and Sgt. Pigg had to move slowly towards the bridge where he arrived at 3:00 p.m. He immediately started to wire the bridge, advising the men to move back to the truck when the bridge was blown.

The following men were in the detail and they had much experience in the use of explosives, mines, and unexploded bombs from the beachhead days and the drive across France and into Belgium. They were now ready to face the most important action of World War II!

> S/Sgt. Edwin Pigg 2nd Platoon Sergeant
> Sgt. R.C. Billington 3rd squad leader
> Cpl. Fred R. Chapin Asst. 3rd squad leader
> Cpl. Harry Bossert Asst. 2nd squad leader
> Pfc. Abraham Miller 3rd squad
> Pfc. Shorty Nickell 3rd squad
> Pfc. Harry Sansbury 3rd squad
> Pfc. Robert Thorne 3rd squad
> T/4 Edward Lufsey 3rd squad
> T/4 Louis Kovacs Platoon truck driver
> Pvt. Johnny Rondenell 2nd squad

Sansbury and Lufsey were sent across the bridge to serve as security. Sgt. Billington and Cpl. Fred Chapin were under the bridge with the men and set to work with the wiring. Sgt. Pigg stayed on top. Chapin was the demolition expert of the squad, having excelled in training. He had completed many, many demolition jobs. Billington calculated the type of blow that was needed, the amount of TNT, and the kind of wiring to be done. The men knew that a German armored column was not far away and at this time there were no American infantry or armored divisions within miles of the bridge.

Dynamite charges were wired to all the piers, connected with primacord, then wires were run from both sides of the bridge to be hooked to the detonator. It was not an easy job, nor one that could be hurried, although the men worked rapidly. Around 4:00 p.m., the convoy of the 291st headquarters and the headquarters of the 1111th Engineer Group arrived at the bridge. They had orders from First Army to move to Modave and set up an engineer barrier line in front of the Meuse River. With this group was Lt. Alvin Edelstein, their platoon commander. Edelstein dropped off at the bridge to be with his men and direct the blowing of the bridge. Shortly after the arrival of Edelstein, Major General James Gavin arrived at the bridge. Gavin had just come from First Army and was moving his 82nd Airborne Division into the area from Reims, France. Edelstein told Gavin of the situation and of his assignment to blow the bridge. Gavin asked Edelstein about a location to set up his command post and assemble his troops. He was told that Werbomont was the ideal place.

The men who took care of Kampfgruppe Peiper at Hablemont by blowing the bridge (Clockwise from top left): Corporal Fred Chapin, Sgt. Bob Billington, Sgt. Paul Hinkel, and Sgt, Edwin Pigg.

When the armored column of Colonel Joachim Peiper was thwarted at Trois Ponts by the blowing of the three bridges there by C Company of the 51st Engineers, commanded by Captain Scheuber and the platoon of Lt. "Bucky" Walters of A Company of the 291st, he turned his 1st SS Panzer spearhead north onto the winding road down the canyon of the Ambleve River valley towards La Gleize. He now had some Tiger Royal Tanks of the 501st Tank Battalion in the column. He had failed to get through Trois Ponts onto his assigned route and he was running far behind his time schedule to reach the Meuse. The 12 hour delay at Stavelot was costly. He now aimed his lengthy column through the village of La Gleize heading towards Cheneux where he hoped to find the bridge intact over the Ambleve River. Just beyond Cheneux he would arrive on his assigned route to the Meuse River. At the same moment that Peiper's 15 mile column arrived near La Gleize, Sgt. Pigg was wiring the Lienne River bridge.

Peiper found the Cheneux bridge intact and as his lead tanks crossed and started to make the curve south of the bridge he was hit by General Quesada's planes of the American Air Force. They bombed his column between 3:30 and 4:00 p.m. Peiper had to hide his tanks off the road as much as possible and sweat out the bombing period. Not until fog covered the area and he removed his disabled tanks from the bombed roads, was he able to get his column moving. Then he proceeded as rapidly as possible toward the main highway which led to Huy, the destination on which his eyes were fixed for a long time.

Back at the bridge, Sgt. Pigg had witnessed the American bombers blast something on the ground just after two Belgians, Rene Simonet, a resident of Trois Ponts, and his brother-in-law, a local farmer, had ran across country to tell them in perfect English where Peiper's vanguards were located. Simonet stressed the awesome size of his tank column.

The timing of the lifting of the fog, the bombing of the column, and the preparation of the Lienne bridge was as close to being a miracle as possible. Peiper's column with a Tiger Royal in the lead forged ahead to the N-23 route and turned towards the Neuf-Moulin bridge by way of Neucy. Somewhere near Neucy they ran into a pair of jeeps manned by a

Bridge over the Lienne which was blown on December 18th by Lt. Edelstein's platoon!

pair of 1111th Engineer Group staff officers and their drivers, who happened to be on the way from Spa towards Trois Ponts. The Germans spotted and fired on the lead jeep, killing the Group's motor transport officer and his driver. The second jeep with the operations officer got away and avoided the German tanks. The dead American officer was carrying the documents outlining the defensive engineer barrier line for the Meuse River.

At 4:45 p.m. about midway into the evening's period of dusk, Corporal Chapin spotted the first German tank as it nosed out of the gloom about 200 yards east of the demolition prepared bridge.

The Engineers were ready, even with a second charge should the first charge fail. So were the Germans. The gunner of the lead Tiger Royal saw activity on the bridge and opened fire with his main gun. The engineers ducked in every direction. The detonator left in the open was grabbed by corporal Chapin who looked for a signal from Edelstein, and as the platoon commander waved his arms, Chapin let her go. 2500 pounds of TNT sent the timber trestle flying in bits and pieces in all directions!

In complete dismay, Colonel Peiper shouted "Those Damned Engineers. Those Damned Engineers!" All of this in the din of the explosion of the bridge. Peiper now saw the dream of reaching the Meuse River disappearing in front of him. The leading Tiger Royals approached the bridge and opened fire with their machine guns at the engineers as they raced for their truck. Corporal Chapin, who was nearest to the machine gun fire, was the last to make the truck but all of the "Damned Engineers" made it safely. They were able to stay overnight with the advance party of the 82nd Airborne at Wermomont and return to their company headquarters on the morning of the 19th of December.

One of the unsung heroes of the "Stopping of Peiper" was Private Johnny Rondenell. He was assigned by Pigg to set up a daisy-chain mine road block on the west side of the Lienne River about 300 yards north of the blown bridge along the road to Forges. This set-up was made to stop any German vehicles that could cross the bridge at Forges. John had walked to the point where he chose to set up the block. The spot was ideal at the end of a curve in the road and with trees and dense woods on each side of the road.

John hooked up eight mines on the chain and pulled them across and perpendicular to the road and quietly waited at the edge of the woods. It was now 5:30 p.m. and darkness had set in.

Peiper at this moment realized that he was in a real quandary. He knew his tanks were too heavy to ford the marshlands and river without becoming bogged down. He looked at his map and failed to find a bridge over the Lienne that would support his tanks. He made the mistake of failing to move up his engineers to build a bridge at the Habiemont location. The American forces could successfully build a Bailey bridge 180 feet long at this sight in less than 4 hours.

Peiper now decided to send out light reconnaissance vehicles to explore the road net for possible answers to his overall problem of being stopped again by American Engineers. One recon team went back to Cheneux and worked its way to the Forges bridge and crossed over to go south in the direction of Habiemont. It was about 7:00 p.m. and very dark. Johnny

Another view of the 180 foot long bridge.

Sgt. Joe Geary in September, 1994, standing at the site where Johnny Rondenelle pulled Daisy Chain mines across the road near Habiemont.

Rondenell retold the circumstances surrounding this incident at the 291st reunion at West Point in 1994.

"I heard the sound of approaching vehicles that sounded like half tracks and I felt that the daisy chain mines would do the job. However the first half track passed through the mines and nothing happened. Soon a 2nd light half track did the same. At this time I felt concerned that these German vehicles were on there way into American defenses.

"I then pulled the mines to the west about 2 feet and didn't have long to wait. I moved back further into the woods and soon heard a loud explosion as the recon vehicle flipped completely over. I then made a hurried retreat back into the woods. I then started to head back toward Habiemont, but found myself lost in the deep woods. I don't know how long I was lost but a few hours later I found the site where we blew the bridge. There were two knocked out German recon vehicles there and a number of dead German soldiers. I worked my way back to Werbomont and found the 82nd Airborne troops arriving."

Somewhere around 9:00 or 9:30 p.m., Major Hal McCown, commander of the 2nd Battalion of the 119th Infantry Regiment, 30th Division, had posted some tank destroyer guns at the bridge site. As the two German half tracks approached, the American guns knocked out the German recons.

The blowing of the bridge and the arrival of the 30th and 82nd Airborne Divisions marked the sealing off of the spearheading 1st SS Panzer Division. It also stopped the main thrust of Hitler's counter attack to the Meuse River and Antwerp. The timing of the blowing of the bridge prevented Kampfgruppe Peiper from moving on to the Meuse River unopposed. This event caused the German generals to think that Hitler's plan would fail.

The furthest advance that Peiper's armored giant would make during the battle was made by his recons at Habiemont. The odd part of the action is that he was stopped by a single American engineer, Johnny Rondenell.

This was a case whereby the combat engineers had accomplished their purpose using engineer tactics and were able to escape without anyone killed, captured, or wounded. The well trained men of Captain Gamble's company and Lt. Edelstein's platoon would live to continue their combat engineering skills on the Roer, the Rhine and the Danube Rivers. In his book "Dark December", written in 1947, Robert Merriam told the story of Edelstein and his men in this manner. "An engineer company of the 51st Engineer Combat Battalion had been ordered to Trois Ponts, and had arrived there about midnight on December 17th, the night that Peiper arrived in Stavelot. Their orders were to blow the bridges at Trois Ponts if the enemy approached. This small group along with two platoons of A Company of the

The monument erected by the Belgian people led by Emil Lacroix and his jeep team in 1982. It is dedicated to the men of the 291st Engineer Combat Battalion!

291st Engineer Combat Battalion blew the bridges and set up a defense of Trois Ponts. Peiper then turned north, into the steep valley of the Ambleve River as it turned north towards Liege. And this was his undoing. Once again Peiper attempted to burst out into the open as he found a crossing of the Ambleve River North of Trois Ponts, and sent his main body along a new road towards Werbomont. Once again a squad of engineers, this time from the 291st Engineer Combat Battalion, blew a bridge in his face, this one only four miles from Werbomont; and again Peiper, without adequate bridging equipment, and with orders to avoid all resistance, turned north deeper into the Ambleve River Valley, where he was fully entrapped and later wiped out by the 30th Division, the 82nd Airborne, and the 3rd Armored Division.

"Here was a case where the case of Divisions and Armies rested for a few brief moments on the shoulders of a handful of men: first, at the town of Trois Ponts, and then, only hours later, with another, smaller, handful of men at the bridge just east of Werbomont. Had either of these groups failed in their job (and the temptation to run away must have been very great), the probability that Peiper would have got to the Meuse River the next morning, behind Skorzeny's "Trojan Horse", would have been very high."

Robert Merriam was the on-the-ground historian for the 7th Armored Division.

18

General James Gavin
and his 82nd Airborne Division

No account of the battle in the Ardennes in the winter of 1944 would be complete without General "Slim Jim" Gavin's story of the actions of his courageous paratroopers against the main thrust of Hitler's massive counter-offensive.

"Early on the evening of December 17, as I was dressing for dinner, I listened to the evening news on the radio. It sounded ominous. Serious German penetrations had been made in the Ardennes area. Knowing our thinness in that area and the paucity of our reserves, I was quite concerned. A few minutes later, at our house in Sissone, France, I received a call from the Chief of Staff of the XVIII Corps. He told me that I was the Corps Commander, that General Ridgeway was in England.

He told me that SHAEF considered the situation in the Ardennes as critical, and I was to notify the 82nd and 101st Airborne Divisions to prepare to move in that direction. As Corps Commander I was to report to General Courtney Hodges, commanding the U.S. First Army, without delay. He was in Spa, Belgium.

We began to prepare our movement orders. Troopers had to be recalled. It appeared the best time to move was after daylight, and we would arrive in the battle area just after dark. We were to head to Bastogne with the 101st Airborne following afterward. After I had issued these orders, at 11:30 p.m., I headed for Spa. I took with me two staff officers. It was a very miserable night with a steady light rain and fog, and several bridges were knocked out due to the war. I reported to General Hodges in person at 9:00 a.m.

We went directly to the war room, where the Chief of Staff, General William Kean, was present with other staff members. Hodges seemed a bit weary, having been through a trying 48 hours.

General Hodges First Army rested its left flank on the city of Aachen, twenty miles to the north. He had three corps in line—the VII on the left, the V in the center, and the VIII on the right. A frontage of about 100 miles. The situation on the left was quite stable, although the troops were heavily engaged. The situation on the right appeared to be wide open, how wide open we did not know. We began our discussion with General Kean talking about two regiments of the 106th Division that had been cut-off by the German attack. They were in heavily forested, mountainous area.

We then went on to discuss the employment of the XVIII Corps. Looking over the map, Kean pointed out Bastogne and Werbomont for each of the two divisions until Hodges

The church at Chenaux remained standing with civilians in the basement during the battle with Peiper.

received a message from Stavelot that the Germans were across the Ambleve River. Stavelot was only 8 miles away from Hodges headquarters. It was then decided that I would move the 82nd Airborne to Werbomont and the 101st would go the Bastogne.

In the meantime the 1st SS Panzer Division would pass through Stavelot after a battle there in the direction of Werbomont. It was almost as close to Werbomont as I was at the time and much closer than the 82nd Airborne Division, which was rolling across Belgium in trucks on what was essentially an administrative move. In our state of mind at the moment, it was difficult for us to conceive of the Wermacht, having been so badly beaten and having lost all its tanks and trucks a few months before, now being capable of mounting another offensive. Especially since we now had complete control of the air.

No factory and no industry had escaped the overwhelming effect of our air power. Many believed this fact, but the German military establishment survived—indeed was in far better shape than any of us realized—and once again the 82nd was engaged with the Wehrmacht, this time under heavy odds and difficult circumstances.

Here I sat in Spa realizing that this German effort which I learned later was the main thrust of the Sixth Panzer commanded by Lt. General Sepp Dietrich, a political crony of Hitler's. It consisted of the 1st SS Panzer Corps and the 2nd Panzer Corps. It was to attack on a twenty mile front with the 1st Panzer Corps in the assault, followed in column with the 2nd Panzer Corps. The assault corps, the 1st, consisted of the 1st SS Panzer Division; the 12th SS Panzer Division; and three infantry divisions: the 3rd Parachute, the 12th Volksgrenadier, and the 277th Volksgrenadier. The following Corps, the 2nd, had but two divisions, the 2nd Panzer and the 9th SS Panzer. It was a very powerful force attacking on a very narrow front.

It was equipped with 500 tanks and armored assault guns, including 90 Tiger tanks. It was like a monstrous steamroller with five divisions, including two Panzers, in a huge front roller, and two Panzer Divisions in the smaller rear roller. There had been some discussion in the German General staff about the old problem of whether to lead the assault with the

Chenaux following American bombing on Peiper during the 18th.

Panzer formations or to use the infantry divisions for the breakout and then turn the Panzers loose in the open country. Field Marshall Model ruled in favor of the latter.

Hitler had counted on a complete breakthrough for the armor in the first 24 hours, followed by a race to the crossings over the Meuse River which were to be reached on the third day.

The column which had just crossed the Ambleve River in Stavelot was the 1st SS Panzer Division, the Leibstandarte Adolf Hitler (Hitler's body guard) was picked for the key assault role. Its leading battle group was commanded by a 28 year old Lt. Col. Jochen Peiper, a tough, ruthless, daring commander who had made quite a reputation for himself on the eastern front.

When I learned later of his trip through Belgium and the massacre at Baughnez, the most interesting part to me was his sudden stop at the top of the hill south of Stavelot. Peiper's arrival immediately south of Stavelot brought him, for the first time, before a force that would prove to be as effective as a good combat division. They were the engineer troops of the U.S. First Army, the 291st, the 51st, combat engineers of the 1111th Engineer group.

B Company of the 291st had established 15 road blocks in Malmedy, which forced Peiper to avoid that village and proceed on to the west. Most of the engineers had been based in the vicinity of Trois Ponts and Werbomont.

On December 17th an engineer squad from the 291st was detailed to establish a road block south of Stavelot. The traffic between the two towns was heavy and they had difficulty making their way. They arrived at Stavelot about 6:30 p.m., well after dark. They crossed the bridge and ascended the hill on the south side. The squad was under the command of Sgt. Charles Hensel. They came to a point near the top of the hill where the road made a sharp turn to the right around a rock cliff. Sgt. Hensel decided that that would be a good place for a road block. They strung their mines across the road. He sent Private Goldstein ahead to give the alarm on the approach of the Germans. Behind the mines, as a covering force, he placed a bazooka team and a 30 cal. machine gun.

It was now nearing 7:30 p.m. Goldstein concealed himself behind a cement building when he heard the approach of tanks. They were moving very slowly, and he could hear the German soldiers talking. Hensel was approaching Goldstein with Corporal Bowers when he heard Goldstein, in good GI fashion, challenge the tanks with a loud commanding, "Halt!" The Germans reacted instantly, spraying the area with small arms fire and firing their tank guns at the challenge. Incredibly, Goldstein escaped and finally made his way back to the squad which at that time was assembled near the bridge at 9:00 p.m.

There was considerable confusion about the bridge, and no one was exactly sure who was responsible for what happened. Explosives were placed, but the bridge was not blown. Among the Engineers at the bridge site was a company from the 202nd Engineers.

At this point Gavin cited Janice Holt Giles in her superb book, "The Damned Engineers."

Gavin then goes on to tell the story of the blowing of the bridges in Trois Ponts by the 51st and 291st engineers and the final stopping of Peiper at Habiemont as Lt. Edelstein of A Company of the 291st blew the bridge that stopped Peiper's progress to the Meuse River.

Gavin stated, "The work of the Engineers had been superb. They were courageous and resourceful."

Gavin now picks up his story as he prepares to leave General Hodges and his staff at Spa: Immediately following the conference with Hodges and his staff, in Spa, I hurried by jeep and drove to Werbomont, to place the 82nd in a blocking position as soon as it arrived. The 101st Airborne were advised to head for Bastogne. I arrived in mid afternoon at Werbomont and began immediately to make a reconnaissance of the entire area. It offered excellent defense possibilities. In the course of my recon, I went down to the foot of the hill to the town of Habiemont. There I met a lieutenant with a detachment of engineers. They had prepared the heavy masonry bridge over the Lienne River for demolition. Quite a few civilians carrying bundles of clothing and bedding were coming down the hill from the direction of Trois Ponts. They were excited, and all stated that the Germans had passed Trois Ponts and were coming this way. I drove along Lienne creek in the direction of the Ambleve River and encountered no signs of the enemy. However, I did find a small bridge intact at the town of Forges. It was about a quarter of a mile from the bridge at Habiemont; I asked the Lieutenant about it. He said that he needed all the explosives that he had to blow the Habiemont Bridge. It did not appear strong enough to take heavy tanks. I then drove down to Bastogne to issue the orders to General McAuliffe of the 101st.

A knocked out Peiper tank found on the La Gleize to Cheneux road.

It took me an hour to drive down to Bastogne, and there met with General Troy Middleton, the Corps Commander. He had no solid information except that the situation was quite fluid and that they were leaving. The 28th Division had been overrun, and they were uncertain about what had happened to it. I talked to some of the 28th Division officers and they were quite depressed and disturbed, not knowing the whereabouts of their division.

About this time General McAuliffe arrived. I gave him instructions to put the 101st Airborne in Bastogne and to prepare an all around defense and stay there until further orders, reporting to the commander of the XVIII Corps. I left driving through Houffalize shortly after dark. I arrived at Werbomont at 8:00 p.m., just as the first vehicles of the 82nd began to arrive.

While I was at Bastogne, Peiper's column had moved across the bridge at Cheneux over the Ambleve river. It was well after sun down when he went through the small town of Rahier, halfway to Habiemont. If he could get the bridge at Habiemont, he would then be clearly in the open for a fast run to the Meuse during the night. The Engineers had put together a demolition team commanded by Lieutenant Alvin Edelstein. They hastily prepared the bridge with explosives. They then located the detonator a short distance away, where the man in charge, corporal Fred R. Chapin, would be able to see the signal from Lt. Edelstein. So the Engineers watched closely and carefully in the early dusk for the approaching Panzers.

Finally, the form of a long, slow moving column of tanks began to take shape. As it got nearer the Panzers fired an 88 as a warning to those near the bridge to leave. The psychological experience of being on the receiving end of an 88 is devastating. The projectile has an extremely high velocity, and on impact fragments fly in all directions. Corporal Chapin ducked and stayed, watching for the signal from the Lieutenant. Finally, Edelstein frantically signaled for him to blow the bridge. He depressed the plunger and then saw a streak of blue lights and a heaving blast of dust and debris. The bridge was blown! The Germans opened up with all of their weapons from the far side, but by then it was too late. They turned back in the direction of Rahier. At this time Peiper would have had time to bring up a bridge and his engineers to move across the 180 foot wide creek well before the arrival of American armor or infantry.

Following this encounter, around 9:30 p.m., an infantry battalion of the 30th Division deployed along Lienne Creek to secure the arrival of the 82nd Airborne Division. They were able to knock out with their anti-tank guns some recon vehicles of Peiper's at the bridge (These were the recons that had crossed over the daisy chain mines of Johnny Rondenell of A Company of the 291st Engineers).

The 30th Divisions deployment was generally toward the north and the Ambleve River, where the remainder of the 30th Division was closing in on Peiper and the 1st SS Panzer Division. They left a platoon at the site of the Habiemont bridge. The platoon leader put several men in foxholes near the road covering the bridge site. The rest of the platoon went to the upper story of a nearby house. In the middle of the night they heard the sound of tracks and the approaching of Panzers. Evidently, although the main bridge at Habiemont had been destroyed, the Germans found that they could cross the smaller bridge at Forges to the north with lighter vehicles. They now moved cautiously towards the main road to Werbomont.

As they neared the roadblock, a soldier from the upper story of the house saw them and fired a bazooka into the lead vehicle. I talked to him about it later. Evidently the back blast from the bazooka was a tremendous shock to those in the room from which he was firing. Nevertheless, the combination of the firing from the house and the small-arms fire from the road had caused the Germans to make a hurried withdrawal, abandoning their vehicles. However, they did take some of the Americans with them as prisoners.

When I arrived in Werbomont earlier in the evening, I established a command post in a farmhouse a few hundred yards off of the main road. As the 82nd troopers arrived, they were deployed around Werbomont into combat positions. Trucks continued to arrive all during the night. The last before daylight during the 19th of December. My G-3, Colonel John Norton advised the only action during the night was at the Habiemont bridge. The Engineers had done their job there and now it was our responsibility to make this a jump off point against the likes of Col. Jochen Peiper.

The Arena in which the 82nd was to join the 1st SS in battle and the German 9th SS, the German 2nd SS, and the 62nd Volksgrenadier Division in turn, in a huge square 10 miles on a side. It begins with Werbomont in the northwest corner. From Werbomont moving to the east mountains fall off sharply to the small town of Habiemont, which is on Lienne Creek, three miles away. From Habiemont a good paved road moves over a high mountain to the

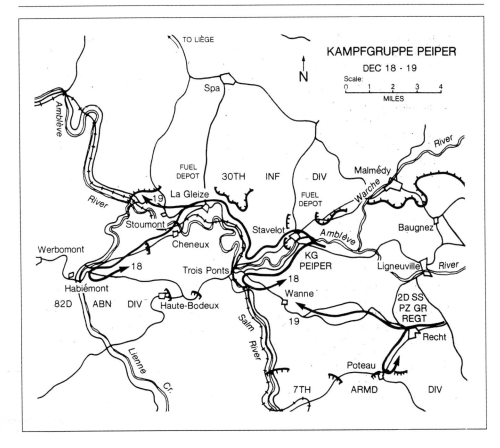

key town of Trois Ponts about seven miles away. From Trois Ponts to La Gleize the Ambleve River meanders through high forested hills northward. From Trois Ponts southward flows the Salm river, all the way to Vielsalm, a key city diagonally across the 100 square mile area from Werbomont. One and a third miles to the southwest of Vielsalm is a dominating terrain feature, Thier Dumont. This mountain dominates the area for many miles. Along its southern side was a paved road all the way to the Division's area of responsibility, and the towns of Fraiture and Manhay. This was an excellent position for defense.

The snow began to fall a few days after we moved into the locality. This made the mountain areas almost impassable, although the infantry fought through them throughout the battle. The entire area began to go under snow just before Christmas, and before the battle for control of the area ended early in January, the high hills were waist deep in snow.

It was an extremely challenging prospect, from a tactical point of view, for the division to be pitted against the best of the German divisions leading the main effort toward the Meuse in this snow blanketed and difficult terrain. On December 19th, full of confidence, we were advancing rapidly to attack.

The XVIII Airborne Corps opened its headquarters just north of the 82nd's on December 19th. We immediately became under the command of that Corps. I was delighted to see General Matthew Ridgeway and his Corps back in action.

Ridgeway's orders were for the 82nd to deploy in the direction of Trois Ponts, Vielsalm, and to open up communications with the U.S. 7th Armored Division at St. Vith.

I assembled the battalion and regimental commanders for the issuance of orders. The 504th would be deployed from Cheneux near the Ambleve River to Trois Ponts. There the 505th was to take up a front south to Grand Halleux. The 508th was to pick up at Vielsalm, occupy Thier Dumont, and protect its flank towards the west. The remaining of the 325th were kept in division reserve. On December 19th the 325 Glider Infantry sent troops out 13 miles to the west and also Grand Menil and Manhay, ten miles to the south. The 505th sent troops out to Habiemont and then Basse Bodeux and Trois Ponts. The 504th moved in the direction of Rahier. The 325th Glider Infantry, minus a battalion, was kept in Werbomont in Division reserve.

We were aware that a Panzer column was bottled up in La Gleize, and that the 7th Armored Division was fighting a brilliant delaying action around St. Vith, nine miles beyond Vielsalm. The moves made on December 19th were prudent and designed to get information and gain contact with the enemy, all under such conditions that we kept the initiative and maintained control of all the division, even though it was being scattered over 100 square miles.

Shortly after daylight on December 20th, I met Colonel Reuben Tucker, commanding the 504th, in the small town of Rahier. He told me that he had learned from civilians that approximately 125 vehicles including 30 tanks, had moved through the town the day before, going in the direction of Cheneux. Obviously, this was one of the armored columns of the 1st SS that had attempted to cross at Lienne Creek near Habiemont and then had to turn back when the men of Lt. Edelstein blew the bridge. Tucker was anxious to go after them without delay. Any ordinary infantry regiment would want at least a battalion of tanks before it attacked, but Tucker's idea was to go after the Germans and take their armor away from them. Besides, he had been carrying with him about a truck load of panzerfausts he had captured from the Germans in Holland. They would prove to be the paratroops' best antitank weapon.

So, with the German panzerfausts and his superb infantry, Tucker moved at once to attack the German forces in Cheneux. We particularly wanted to capture the bridge over the Ambleve River at Cheneux. Initial contact was made with the Germans at the western exit by a patrol that had been sent by the 1st battalion of the 504th. They fired on a German motorcyclist who was accompanied by a small foot patrol. This was followed by a company of Germans moving along both sides of the road. Heavy fighting took place, in fact it lasted all day long. I was present during the attack and the German fire power was impressive. They were using a great many 20 mm. flak weapons that infantry find most uncomfortable to face.

Major General Jame Gavin, commander of the 82nd Airborne Division.

Colonel Tucker had employed the 1st battalion of the 504th against the Germans trying to exit from Cheneux. It was a hard fight, and as darkness descended on the battlefield, companies B and C were under tremendous fire from the village. Not to be daunted, Colonel Tucker ordered the battalion commander, Lieutenant Colonel William E. Harrison, to make a night attack. Harrison had parachuted with me in Normandy, and he was a very courageous soldier. They now had two tank destroyers, which made them to feel equal to almost anything they met. As they pushed towards Cheneux, they came across well organized defenses surrounded by barbed wire. The force opposing them turned out to be the 2nd SS Panzer Grenadier Regiment. Heavily reinforced with mobile flak pieces, mortars, machine guns, and assault artillery.

To breast this fire and rush the 400 yards of open terrain, the two companies attacked in four waves at intervals of fifty yards. The moment the American assault waves could be discerned, the enemy opened an intense accurate fire. Twice the attackers were beaten back, both times with gaping ranks. The first two waves were almost completely shot down. Company C ran into the wire, and having no wire cutters available, was stalled momentarily. Finally the two tank destroyers worked their way to the front and began to shell the German guns. With their support a third wave was thrown against the village. This time a few men lived to reach the outlying houses. In a brief engagement at close quarters the Americans silenced some of the flak and machine guns, then set up a defense to guard this slight toehold until reinforcements could arrive.

The battalion commander set up his command post in a house close to the edge of town. During the night Tucker decided to make a wide envelopment of town, using his 3rd battalion, commanded by Lt. Colonel Julian Cook. They made a very wide flanking movement over very rough ground; the move took six hours, but by late afternoon they were overlooking the bridge across the Ambleve. They cut off the Germans in the town and completely destroyed their command. Tucker had lost 225 dead and wounded, mostly from the two assault companies. Company B had 18 men left and no officers. Company C had 38 men and three officers. Few Germans were captured. The rear guard fought to the end, but most of the Cheneux garrison still living escaped during the night.

Tucker captured fourteen flak wagons and a battery of 105 howitzers as well as many vehicles. The 504th was proud of the battle. The troopers had actually jumped aboard the flak wagons and in hand to hand combat had taken them over. When I went over the battlefield the next day, they pointed out to me that they were now the 504th Parachute Armored Regiment. It had been costly, the Germans were well equipped and gave us a good fight.

19

Major "Bull" Yates
and the Defenses of Trois Ponts

Colonel Anderson learned that all three bridges in Trois Ponts had been blown. He moved to Modave to establish a barrier line of engineer units in the east of the Meuse River. He then turned the defense of Trois Ponts over to Major Yates of the 51st Engineer Combat Battalion. Yates had came into Trois Ponts around 2:00 p.m. on the 18th of December. On a map Anderson pointed out to Yates the locations of the three bridges that had been blown, two by Sam Sheuber's platoon, and one at the south end of Trois Ponts over the Salm River by Lt. Walters platoon of the 291st Engineer Combat Battalion.

Anderson explained to Yates that the German armored column had moved north up the Ambleve River valley. He showed him on the map where he had set up a defensive line of combat engineers made up of Walter's platoon from the 291st, Lt. Rombaugh's platoon, C Company, 291st, his security squad under Sgt. Paul Hinkel of the 291st, and Captain Sam Scheuber's C Company of the 51st, less 20 men.

Anderson explained to Yates that Captain Gamble of the 291st had two of his platoons in the area, which he had been using on special occasions and in reserve. He told Yates that he would use one of these platoons to blow the bridge at Habiemont to prevent the armored column from heading west. The two platoons of the 291st and the rear command post of the 291st, under the command of Major Lampp, would also move back to Modave. They would become part of the Meuse River barrier line. Colonel Anderson would take over a large portion of the barrier line from Werbomont to Marche and on to Bastogne. The blowing of the bridge at Habiemont could possibly cause Yates a problem communicating by vehicle to the outside.

When Yates drove his jeep to inspect his defensive line along the Ambleve and the Salm rivers, he found that Sgt. Paul Hinkel of the 291st had been meshed in with 20 men from Lt. Warren Rombaugh's platoon and in turn with the company of Captain Scheuber of the 51st. Sgt. Hinkel recalls that Major Yates approached his gun emplacement shortly after the thundering blaze of German fire had hit the area.

Major Yates then sent a detail to find out what was the cause. He soon learned that it was a freak. The shells were coming from a destroyed M-7 tank. The heat from the burning tank had caused the 105mm. shells to simmer. When they got hot enough they started to detonate and fly off in all directions. They were just sizzling out into space and not exploding. The men hoped that the Germans would think that the town was much more heavily

Bronze Star Medalists, Lt. Arch Taylor and Lt. "Bucky" Walters (Upper and lower left).

defended than it actually was. It is also said that Major Yates got another idea from this false show of strength.

He took about eight trucks and ran them up and down a hill all night, up the hill in the dark, down the hill with full lights on, in the hope that the enemy would believe that reinforcements were arriving all night. The entire strength in the town consisted of C Company of the 51st Engineers (minus 27 men), Lt. Walter's platoon of Company A of the 291st Engineers, 20 engineers of Lt. Rombaugh's C Company of the 291st, who had been operating the saw mill in Trois Ponts, and the 13 man squad of Sergeant Paul Himkel from Company A of the 291st, who had the security guard detail in Trois Ponts for the 1111th Group Headquarters. With other stragglers who had moved into Trois Ponts, Yates at best had around 300 men in Trois Ponts, all equipped with rifles, machine guns, bazookas, mines and demolitions. The northern shoulder, starting with the blown bridge on the Ambleve River, was under the supervision of Captain Scheuber. The remainder of the defense showed Sgt. Paul Hinkel's men in the center near the saw mill, with "Bucky" Walters' defense along the Salm River, south to and including the blown bridge at the lower end of Trois Ponts.

When the Germans shelled the former headquarters of Col. Anderson, Yates had already moved his command post to a more fortified position, more in the center of his defensive line. He was a tall, very aggressive and fearless man who was determined to hold this position at all cost, and he inspired the men of both engineer battalions.

Walters advised Yates that after the Salm River bridge had been blown by Sgt. Miller he had lost about five of his men. Yates ordered Walters to make sure and cover the blown bridge with his forces. Walters also told Yates that they could see German foot soldiers on the hill above the bridge.

Trois Ponts was entirely cut off now. Major Yates had no communications with any-body, anywhere. Anderson had departed and took his command post and the rear command post of the 291st with him to Modave. Yates did get word back from civilians that the bridge at Lienne Creek had been blown. He also figured at this time that his defense was the front line and he and the men of the two battalions were practically surrounded.

Yates' battalion commander had his own plate full with the rest of the battalion around Hotton. Walters, in his post-war review of the situation, said it was quite scary but they were behind the blown bridges and they had good positions guarding the river bank. The men were in good spirits. They had no doubt they could hold until reinforced, and Major Yates intended to let somebody know they needed reinforcing. He kept patrols constantly prob-ing: if an outfit with any strength came along, Yates meant to know about it.

Soon after Yates had checked his defenses and established that his positions had good fields of fire for the machine guns and bazookas, an enemy tank arrived and reached the junction of N23 and N33, where its crew dismounted. At that point Sgt. Evers Gossard's 50 caliber Machine gun crew from Company C fired on the Germans. Five of the German's six-man crew were hit, and three were killed, but the sixth man jumped into the tank and turned its gun towards the machine gun. Gossard and his crew retired at that point. But the tank stayed the rest of the day, firing at targets of opportunity.

Group and Battalion Commanders of Col. H.W. Anderson (Front, center).

Major "Bull" Yates gets a Silver Star.

Captain James Gamble receiving a Bronze Star for his bravery at Trois Ponts and Werboment.

Anderson and Lampp left from the 291st command post at Haute Bodeux. Anderson told Captain Gamble to blow the bridge at Lienne Creek, and to move his platoons (commanded by Lts.' Taylor and Edelstein) to Modave, where they would become part of the barrier line of engineer units. Edelstein was to blow the bridge at Lienne Creek using the men from Werbomont.

Gamble and his company had done much after his arrival back in Trois Ponts from Ambleve on the night of December 17th. He had furnished the defense of Malmedy with machine guns and gunners as well as bazookas. He had gone into Stavelot around 3:00 a.m. on the morning of December 18 along with Lt. Arch Taylor and rescued Pvt. Goldstein and Corp. Liperula, who were wounded by Peipers men in Stavelot. He then returned to Trois Ponts and advised Major Lampp and Col. Anderson that the defenses in Stavelot were now complete with the 526th Armored Infantry and the guns of the 825th Tank Destroyer Battalion in place. He also advised that C Company of the 202nd Engineers were at the bridge over the Ambleve River. Now he had the important job of blowing the bridge that would stop Peiper.

When Peiper attacked off the hill in Stavelot, he sent a task force of tanks and armored infantry down the back road from south of Stavelot through Wanne and on to Vielsalm.

He had studied his map and felt that he could capture the bridge over the Salm River at the south end of Trois Ponts. This could get him back on his assigned route to Werbomont and then the Meuse River. When the task force tried to capture the bridge with infantry, Sgt. Miller blew the bridge. Now the task force battled briefly with the men in Yates' defensive line, but could not cross the rivers at any spot and were forced to head back to Stavelot and then join Peiper enroute to Werbomont through La Gleize.

These were the same troops that Sergeants Gossards and Hinkel battled at the junction of N23 and N33. They had 1st SS patches on their uniforms. The men of the 291st and the 51st kept sniping at the Germans across the river, but the enemy response indicated a decided German advantage. Yates drew in the engineers defensive lines around 5:00 p.m. to tighten the perimeter and give all around protection to the town. He made certain that all of the blown bridge sites were covered to prevent the German engineers from building assault bridges.

On the afternoon of December 18th Yates and Scheubers' men witnessed the American Air force bombing and strafing Peiper's column on the ground. P-47s came in and knocked out four or five tanks on the Stavelot road. When Lt. Green's platoon returned to Trois Ponts and Lt. Nabor's platoon withdrew into town, the three platoons were consolidated into two. One group covered the river north of town, and Green, along with Milgram's 3rd platoon, covered the noreast side of town including the bridge over the Ambleve River. The remainder of the defensive line was covered by Lt. Rombaughs' engineers, Paul Hinkel's squad, and "Bucky" Walters' platoon all of the 291st, whom Anderson and Lampp had set up on the original defensive positions. The men of the 291st had a rather extensive line which covered the bridge at the south end of Trois Ponts. Listening posts established 500-600 yards out from the main line of resistance (MLR) during the day were pulled into a tight perimeter during the night.

At 9:00 a.m. on the 19th Lt. Green and T\Sgt. Mathew R. Carlyle went out on reconnaissance. They crossed the river and headed up the Stavelot road toward the knocked out 57-mm. gun. No enemy was found in the railroad underpasses, but up the road four men in American uniforms were crowded around the 57 mm. gun. They turned out to be Germans who fired at the two Americans. Green and Carlyle withdrew without further incident.

In another action just south of the Aisomont road, four or five men of Lt. Nabors platoon engaged the enemy on a hill just south of the Aisomont road. The enemy replied with

Colonel Anderson's bombed and shelled Headquarters in Trois Ponts.

The 82nd Airborne and 505th Parachute Airborne Regiment attack uphill at Trois Ponts.

both small arms and artillery. No casualties resulted, but it taught the engineers to keep better hidden and change positions frequently in order to avoid artillery concentration.

In another instance Major Yates watched a Belgian boy of about 12 running toward the river, followed by a German rifleman firing at him. Four or five other German soldiers stood close by laughingly watching the incident. In anger, Yates fired several shots at the spectators, dropping one of them before they dispersed. The boy and his tormentor disappeared behind the buildings.

In light of this incident, Yates redeployed Walter's men. He ordered one squad to guard the lower Salm bridge, and he put the rest of Walter's men into two positions west of the river bank. Yates already had Sergeant Paul Hinkel's guard detail, with some 51st men, at that upper Salm bridge site. Walters put his first detail just below that point and positioned the others as ordered. They were concerned that Peiper might try to use his engineers to bridge the rivers and get into Trois Ponts. Thus far Peiper had tried to capture the bridges intact and had failed miserably except at Stavelot.

Trois Ponts was entirely cut off. Major Yates had no communications of any kind with anybody but the civilians who told him that the Americans had blown the bridge at Habiemont over Lienne Creek. This meant that at any time he and his men could be attacked from the rear.

At about 9:00 P.M. that night a patrol sent out by Major Yates met a patrol from the 82nd Airborne's Reconnaissance Squadron. This was a unit of Colonel William Ekman's 505th Parachute Regiment. Ekman's men had now pushed into Haute Bodeux, Basse Bodeux, and the hills behind Trois Ponts. But they thought that Trois Ponts was in enemy hands.

Receiving Bronze Stars from Col. David E. Pergrin for Malmedy, Stavelot, and Trois Ponts defenses are (from left to right): 1st Lt. John Brenna, Capt. Bill Mckinsey, and Major Ed Thampp.

They thought that they would have to fight to capture the town. Instead when the patrols met, it was learned that the engineers of the 51st and the 291st were very much in command of the whole west bank.

Well, things were looking up for both the engineers and paratroopers. Ekman was able to advise the grinning Yates that at this time Peiper had been stopped cold by the blowing of the bridge at Lienne Creek and was being attacked by the 30th Division of General Leland Hobbs and the 82nd Airborne of General James Gavin. The Engineer Group of Colonel H. Wallis Anderson and his two battalions, the 291st and 51st, had sacked the leading column of Hitler's main thrust.

Near Trois Ponts in the predawn hours of December 21, the day after the 1st SS had made an attempt to cross the Ambleve River at Petite Spa, Major Yates led a patrol across the Salm to see what the Germans were up to. Not far from the river, Yate's engineers discovered German engineers, the first any of us had seen in the bulge, attempting to install an assault bridge. This could be designed to take the place of a structure that had collapsed earlier under the weight of a German self propelled tank-destroyer.

Yate's patrol was itself discovered as it attempted to withdraw, and a bullet fire struck Major Yates in the arm. He escaped only after plunging into the swift waters and swimming to the far bank while Sgt. Paul Hinkel's squad sprayed the Germans from its nearby road-block position. As he had his wound treated, Yates made his report to Colonel William Ekman, the commander of the 505th Parachute Infantry. Ekman ordered the area around the new bridge bombarded by the 82nd Airborne parachute artillery battalion that was deployed on the heights overlooking Trois Ponts. The German engineers were dispersed by the devastating gunnery and the bridge-building effort floundered. The German engineers were assigned to the 1st SS Panzer Division of General Wilhelm Mohnke.

The evening before, late on December 20, Company E of the 505th parachute Infantry's 2nd battalion had crossed the Salm footbridge below Trois Ponts and advanced to the village of Wanne to establish a blocking position astride a potential route of advance. By 11:00 p.m. December 21, Company E found the hilltop position surrounded by Germans advancing directly towards the Salm footbridge. An eight-man outpost opened fire on the assault guns with Bazookas, and all of the German vehicles were destroyed or disabled. However, the German infantry launched an immediate counter-attack, and all eight American paratroopers were killed or captured.

Within minutes, the main body of Company E reported the sighting of German tanks and more infantry maneuvering off the road, also in the direction of the Salm. Lt. Col. Vandervoort, the 2nd battalion commander, placed an immediate call for artillery to support Company E. He also sent Company F across the footbridge to support Company E on the Wanne Hill. Members of Company C, 51st Engineers, had strengthened the footbridge somewhat, so a jeep towing a 57mm anti-tank gun was able to cross over and link up with the parachute company.

The anti-tank gun knocked out several late arriving German tanks, but the lieutenant commanding it was killed by the German counter fire. The German and American soldiers were locked in a mutual death grip when Colonel Ekman ordered all of Vandervoorts' troopers to pull back across the Salm.

As the paratroopers began the very dangerous daylight withdrawal, all the available engineers of the 51st and the 291st were ordered to cover them from various defensive positions along the west bank of the Salm. Holding an enfilade position north of the footbridge, overlooking the blown railroad bridge, was part of Bucky Walters' platoon of Company A, 291st. Bucky assumed, correctly, that the Germans would be right on the heels of the retreating paratroopers and would use their momentum to try to force their way across the Salm footbridge.

The Company A engineers were ready by the time the paratroopers began pouring down the steep slope of the ridge on the east bank of the Salm. As expected the Germans were right behind them. Handfuls of hard-pressed Americans jumped from high up the slope directly into the swift ice-cold water, while others rushed towards the footbridge. It was clear to the Engineers that their country men were routed. Many German soldiers stopped on the heights to open fire on the swimmers, but many of them followed the paratroopers right over the cliff.

For the longest time, the engineers, armed with .30 caliber machine guns, were unable to fire on the Germans for fear of hitting their friends. At length a knot of Germans amounting to about two platoons raced out onto the footbridge. Bucky ordered all his machine guns to fire. At the same time, Paul Hinkel's squad opened fire from the west end of the footbridge itself, and so did many engineers from the 51st Combat Engineers. The main body of

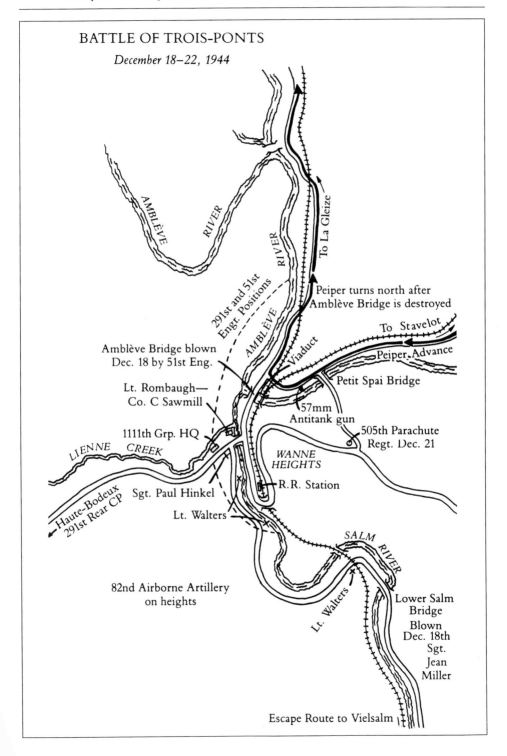

BATTLE OF TROIS-PONTS

December 18–22, 1944

AMBLÈVE RIVER

AMBLÈVE RIVER

To La Gleize

291st and 51st Engr. Positions

Peiper turns north after Amblève Bridge is destroyed

To Stavelot

Viaduct

Amblève Bridge blown Dec. 18 by 51st Eng.

Peiper Advance

Petit Spai Bridge

Lt. Rombaugh— Co. C Sawmill

57mm Antitank gun

1111th Grp. HQ

505th Parachute Regt. Dec. 21

LIENNE CREEK

WANNE HEIGHTS

Haute-Bodeux 291st Rear CP

Sgt. Paul Hinkel

R.R. Station

Lt. Walters

SALM RIVER

82nd Airborne Artillery on heights

Lt. Walters

Lower Salm Bridge Blown Dec. 18th Sgt. Jean Miller

Escape Route to Vielsalm

the Germans was stopped with extremely heavy casualties, but a handful surged all the way across the bridge and ran smack into Hinkel's squad. These Germans were thrown back in fierce hand to hand combat, and the bridge was swept clear within several minutes. Some Germans made for the blown railroad bridge but failed as well. At about 3:00 p.m. as the battle of the bridges raged to a bloody conclusion, Colonel H. Wallis Anderson called the wounded Major Yates to order all of the 1111th Group Engineers in Trois Ponts to turn their responsibilities over to the paratroop engineers and withdraw immediately to the new Meuse offensive barrier. "Bull" told the Colonel about the fight that was then raging and assured him that he would sort things out if the battle ended on terms favorable to our side.

At 4:30 p.m., Major Yates called Bucky Walters to his command post and told him of Colonel Anderson's order. "Bull" detached all of the 291st engineers from his makeshift engineer task force and advised Bucky to locate the main body of our battalion. The Group that belonged to the 51st rejoined Lt. Colonel Harvey Fraser and their main body in Marche.

Shortly thereafter, Yates blew the Salm footbridge and left town with Company C of the 51st Engineers. Bucky had a difficult task moving his platoon back from Trois Ponts to the Company A command post of Captain James Gamble near Modave. He was checked at many road blocks as though he and his men were Germans in American uniforms, particularly since he was coming from the area where the enemy was firing big guns.

There were many American heroes in Trois Ponts: Yates, Scheuber, Walters, Hinkel, Gamble, and Lampp. But the calm and confident veteran of three wars, Colonel H. Wallis Anderson, stood out. He summed it all up when he was asked by the Belgian civilians, "Why did you and your Engineers stay and defend against such overwhelming odds?" His answer was right to the point, "We didn't come thousands of miles in your defense to turn and run at the sight of the Germans."

Engineers usually don't receive many medals, as do the Infantry. The rare award to a unit of any type is the Presidential Citation. The odds of two Engineer Battalions in an Engineer Group receiving the President Roosevelt Honors is one in a million—but the 51st and the 291st in Colonel Anderson's Group did it!

20

The 30th (Old Hickory) Division Comes Aboard

The First Army headquarters was electrified by the news of a strong enemy column as far west as Malmedy, Belgium. General Hodges had been proceeding on the theory that St. Vith and Bastogne, in the VIII Corps sector, were the biggest threats to the First Army. He thought General Gerow's V Corps, with the 2nd and 99th Infantry Divisions, had not yet been deeply penetrated. But he had rushed the 1st (Big Red One) Infantry Division to bolster them east of Malmedy. Col. Anderson had advised the First Army Engineer, Col. William Carter, of this situation.

General Omar Bradley had transferred the 30th Division, which was in line in the Aachen area, from General Simpson's Ninth U. S. Army to Hodges in order to bolster the northern shoulder. But now the critical situation was only 10 miles south of First Army where only one Engineer Combat Battalion, the 291st, was between the First Army headquarters and the German Armored Column.

Major General Leland Hobbs.

The collapsed bridge at Petite Spa by an overload of a Panther tank.

Here was a frightening penetration all at once. What concerned the higher commanders was that Malmedy was a strategic goal for the enemy. Its capture would open up the roads to Eupen and Vervier to the north, and to Franchorchamps, Spa, and Liege, northwestward. Its capture would, in fact, lay bare the heart not only of First Army, but of the entire northern allied effort. Liege was the biggest supply dump on the continent and was furnishing most of the supplies for the British as well as the U.S. Armies. Malmedy must not be captured, therefore it must be reinforced, and quickly.

The 291st had become familiar with the 30th Division in Normandy, and in particular the efforts of Lt. Colonel Carrol H. Dunn and his 105th Engineer Combat Battalion on the St. Lo breakout. We were also in close support with the 30th Division in the drive to Mortain.

Early in the afternoon on December 17th, Hodges ordered the 30th to move southward from its position back of Aachen. Its destination was Eupen to become part of V Corps. It took the division only four and one half hours to get ready to take off, an incredibly short time. At 4:30 p.m., Major General Leland Hobbs, the division commander, reported he was moving out. This probably meant that he wouldn't get his men to Malmedy until morning.

To the 30th Infantry Division, sitting quietly behind the Roer River slightly North of Aachen, the events of Dec. 16—two corps south—seemed remote. The G-2 report showed the action to the south to be only a heavy shelling.

The trip south was a nightmare in both planning and execution. Refugees and civilians were clogging the highways as they seemed to want to escape the area. During the night the Luftwaffe was active over the column, but mostly flares and not bombs.

The 119th regiment had detrucked for the night, and the 117th were routed through with instructions to seize and defend Stavelot and Malmedy. The 119th paused at Hauset, just south of Aachen, the first night and then proceeded south on the afternoon of the 18th.

Most of the troops had little idea of what they were to do. The division had been called the "Workhorse" Division by the Americans and "Roosevelt's SS Troops" by the Germans. The 117th Regiment, in the lead, was butting its way through streams of withdrawing vehicles in and around Eupen and Spa, where 1st Army headquarters was moving out towards the west. By dawn of the 18th the regiment had reached an assembly area near Malmedy and, preceded by the intelligence and reconnaissance platoon, was headed for its objective: Malmedy. The 118th Field Artillery Battalion pulled away from the Infantry protection and went into positions on the high ground ahead of the doughboys, about a kilometer north of Malmedy.

Malmedy, nestled at the foot of hills protecting Spa, had been reported to be in the hands of enemy paratroopers. The 117th was surprised to find it in the hands of friendly Americans. Not only that, they found a solid all-around defense had been set up by the 291st Engineer Combat Battalion. The defense consisted of 15 roadblocks. The 99th Norwegian Infantry Battalion formed between the road blocks with infantrymen dug in around the village and particularly positioned on the railroad embankment.

Company B of the 526th Armored Infantry Battalion was positioned as Infantry at the west end of Malmedy to protect the bridges. The guns of the 825th Tank Destroyer Battalion were placed in positions to protect the road blocks of the 291st around the perimeter of the entire defensive position. The 3rd battalion of the 117th set up on roadblocks and prepared for business, gratefully picking up the troops that were on hand and ready to fight.

Germans attempt to cross the Ambleve River in assault boats near Stavelot.

Peiper's tanks hit by artillery near Stoumont.

The 1st battalion moved down through Franchorchamps and detrucked two miles north of Stavelot at 8:30 in the morning. At 10:30 Captain Mitchell of A Company, 526th Armored Infantry Battalion, reported that his company had been ejected from Stavelot by a large number of enemy tanks. They knocked out three of the German monsters, though.

The GIs set the fuel dump on fire. Some civilians later stated that the Germans had started up the hill but changed their minds when the dump was set on fire. The 2nd battalion, reinforced by the 291st Engineers, took up positions along the road and railroad line, which ran along the hills from Malmedy to Stavelot. They set up roadblocks and patrolled to the Ambleve River, which ran west towards Stavelot. Footbridges over the Ambleve River were already blown. Two underpasses where the railroad crossed were also prepared for demolition, and minefields were laid.

At 11:00 a.m. friendly forces were reported on the edge of Stavelot, but fighting there raged during the afternoon. The square in Stavelot was like a no-man's land. At 2:55 p.m. ten enemy tanks with infantry surged forward to attack the 1st battalion. The fighting was still bitter when American fighter bombers appeared on the scene an hour later to strafe and bomb an estimated 40 tanks south of the river. The battalion drove on to take the town of Stavelot northwest of the Ambleve River. The second battalion knocked out three enemy tanks in counterattacks against its position on the flank.

At 6:00 p.m., soon after dark, the Division Command Post was being set up in a small hotel in Franchorchamps. This town was blocking the enemy approach to Spa and Verviers. Thanks to wire left by First Army Signal Corps, and the assistance of V Corps wire teams, 30th Division Signal Corps swiftly put in telephone communications to the regiments that had arrived in the battle area. Most of the Division troops were still on the move, but unity of control had been established.

The 119th Regiment had resumed its march south during the afternoon, circling through Verviers and Remouchamps, on the north bank of the Ambleve River. There, under instructions from General Hobbs, the 2nd battalion circled further west to Aywaille before continuing south to Werbomont and then east.

The rest of the regiment, led by the 3rd battalion, moved east towards Trois Ponts along the road skirting the north side of the river. Time-space factors indicated that the enemy columns could thus be intercepted at Stoumont and Habiemont, where the 291st Engineers had blown the bridge.

Identifications made during the day to the east indicated that the 1st SS Panzer Corps, controlling the 1st SS and 12th SS Panzer Divisions, was operating in the Malmedy-Stoumont area.

The original Hitler plan showed that his main thrust was to be led by the 1st SS Panzer Corps with five distinct routes or Rolbohns. These routes on the map were lettered A,B,C,D, and E. The Northern March Group, the 12th SS Panzer Division, was to use routes A, B, and C. The main march group was to include the spearheading Kampfgruppe Peiper and the 1st SS Panzer Division attacking on routes D and E.

The paratroopers of von Der Heyde had failed in its mission to drop north of Malmedy and set up a blocking position in the mountains and forests of the region called Hochai woods. Hitler had rested his highest hopes on the Sixth Panzer Army, and Dietrich had pinned his on the crack 1st SS Panzer Corps. It had been beefed up until it was the strongest Corps in the entire offensive.

The 1st SS Panzer Corps was commanded by SS General Hermann Priess, and all of his armored troops were SS. There were 4 Armored Divisions, but two, the 2nd and 9th, would remain in reserve to be committed in the second wave. In the top sector of the 1st SS Panzer Corps, the leading armored division was the 12th SS Panzer Division (HitlerJugend).

This was the leader of three Panthers into Stoumont.

In the bottom sector, it was the elite 1st SS Panzer Division (Liebstandarte Adolf Hitler) commanded by SS General Wilhelm Mohnke. Hitler made certain that these forces were well equipped and staffed with high quality personnel.

The sector assigned to the 1st SS Panzer Corps was narrow in order to make an all out initial breakout. It lay roughly just north of Hollerath along a northwest angle to cross the Meuse just above Liege, to the seam with the Fifth Panzer Army in the south, which roughly followed the St. Vith-Vielsalm-Menil highway.

Five roads in this sector were assigned to the advance, the three more northern roads to the 12th SS Panzer Division (Hitler Jugend) and the central and southern roads to the 1st SS Panzer Division (Liebstandarte). The past history of the successful "Blitzkriegs" of the German armies in Poland, France, and Russia had been made with these same units and people who were leading this counterattack.

The top road, route A, debauched across the border between Hollerath and Undenbreth, swung northwest through Sourbrodt, angled up through Sart, Pepminster (on the fringe of Verviers), on to Nessonvaux, then up to cross the Meuse at Bressoux and Wandre.

Route B, just below route A, crossed the border south of Undenbreth, swung northwest before reaching Loshiemergraben, went through Robertsville, Beverce, Franchorchamps, Spa, Theux, and on to cross the Meuse in the suburb of Seraing and at Irox. Both routes A and B were to be used by the 12th SS Panzer Division's Armored Infantry and reconnaissance battalion.

Route C, which was to be used by the 12th SS Panzer Division's Armored column, moved from Losheimergraben up through Bullingen, on to Malmedy, thence to Stavelot, touched Trois Ponts but turned north to La Gleize, followed the bends and turns of the Ambleve River through Remouchamps and Aywaille and crossed the Meusse at Engis.

Route D, assigned to the armored column of the 1st SS Panzer Division, debauched from Losheim, and went through Lanzerath through Honsfeld. Then it moved on to

Stavelot Bridge over the Ambleve River blown by Lt. Cofer of the 105th Engineers. Replaced by 105th engineers for the attack.

December 18th, a dead German in the square during the battle at Stavelot.

Heppenbach, to Ambleve and up to Ligneville. At Ligneville it was to take a very bad secondary road across country to Wanne. It was to cross the Salm by the lower bridge south of Trois Ponts and pick up highway N-23, which it would then follow to a crossing of the Meuse at Huy and at Ombret Rausa.

Route E, which crossed the front near Manderfield, ran through Andler, up to Wallerode, through Born, Recht and Poteau to Vielsalm. Thence it ran through Lierneux, Menil, and swung up through Modave and Barse for a Meuse crossing at Huy. Route E was assigned to the southern march group of the 1st SS Panzer Division, a reinforced infantry regiment and the division's recon battalion.

This period of the big battle of the bulge finds the First Army Headquarters moving west for the second time out of Chaudfontaine. The reason for this is again the spearheading Kampfgruppe Peiper, who is known to have been stopped at Habiemont by the engineer squad of Lt. Edelstein, Company A, 291st Engineer Combat Battalion. General Hodges now knows that the 82nd Airborne of General Gavin, and the 30th Infantry Division of General Leland Hobbs are ready to attack the trapped Peiper. Hodges realizes that he can't take a chance and have his headquarters overrun.

Despite the constant displacement of the First Army Command Post, communications were being well maintained between the staffs of First Army and the Corps Headquarters. Also, from Colonel H. Wallis Anderson's Command Post and staff with First Army and Corps Engineer staffs. This had been complete since the discovery of Peiper's column at Butgenbach by Lt. Frank Rhea of the 291st. Anderson had sent Staff members repeatedly to First Army headquarters to relay the position and movement of Peiper's column to Col.

Fran Currey, Medal of Honor winner on the 50th Anniversary return to Malmedy.

William Carter's Engineer Command Post at First Army. In fact, Captain Lundberg and his driver were killed by Peiper's men near Cheneux, when Lundberg was returning to 111th Group from a mission to Col. Carter's headquarters at Spa. Anderson, though, still maintained excellent phone communications with both Corps and First Army.

Hodges and his staff had done an amazing job of reinforcing the area of the breakout in such a short period of time. On the 99th Division's front, General Walter E. Lauer and General Walter M. Robertson of the 2nd Infantry Division had been able to hold off the attacks of the 277th Volksgrenadier Division, the 12th SS Panzer Division and the 12th Volksgrenadier Division in the battles at the Elsenborn ridge. The two divisions were greatly aided by the 146th, 324th, 254th, and the organic engineers of the 2nd Infantry Division as the Infantry fought and fell back to their final defensive positions on the Elsenborn ridge. The engineers laid mines, blew bridges and in general were the last to leave the former defensive positions.

One of the very important actions of the 99th and 2nd Infantry Divisions was to prevent the 12th SS Panzer Division from breaking through their lines onto routes A, B, and C. This crack Division was to attack directly through the Butgenbach, Malmedy, Spa, and Liege routes and cross the Meuse north and south of Liege. After three days of fighting, the 12th SS was mired down and had suffered loss of tanks and infantry. This also left Peiper with no protection on either of his flanks.

Fortunately Hodges had the 1st Division, which was moved from the north on December 18, form a solid defense from Waimes to Butgenbach on the right flank of the 2nd Infantry Division. Thus in 48 hours the First Army had a solid defense from the Siegfried line through Butgenbach, Malmedy and Stavelot. The organic engineers of the 30th, 2nd, 1st, and 99th were now in position to lay mines, prepare bridges for demolition, and develop other defensive road blocks. At this time the 291st, 254th, and the 146th engineers were also well integrated into this strong defensive line.

The 120th Infantry's reconnaissance elements reached Malmedy on December 18. The main body, arriving that night, prepared to take over Malmedy from the 3rd Battalion, 117th Infantry, which was needed further west. The 823rd Tank Destroyer Battalion, the 743rd

Tank Battalion, and the light field artillery battalions of the 30th Division traveled in combat team attachments.

The 119th made contact with the enemy at 9:45 p.m. in Stoumont. A patrol sent east to locate the enemy reported about 30 tanks parked nearby. Later in the evening an enemy half-track blew up in one of the 105th Engineer's mine fields that Colonel Dunn had cleverly laid to protect the infantry from sudden attack. This and patrol reports alerted the Germans to the presence of the 2nd Battalion of Major Hal McCown.

The German situation had now become very uncertain, with its spearheading 1st SS Panzer Division trapped in the Ambleve River Valley. Peiper's flanks were left unprotected, and he was now in the throws of an all out battle with the 30th and 82nd Airborne Divisions.

Fighting still raged in Stavelot. At 9:15 p.m., fresh enemy infantry in American trucks and half-tracks approached. Three fully loaded armored personnel carriers were knocked out. The fighting remained bitter. The bridge at Stavelot still boasted a defense by the 1st Battalion, 119th Regiment, dug in about a mile behind the Stoumont position.

Another enemy spearhead that had crossed the Ambleve River east of Stoumont stumbled into the 2nd Battalion's position. It was the same task force that had hit Private Johnny Rondonell's daisy chain mines. About 9:30 p.m. these enemy half-tracks, carrying troops of the 2nd SS Panzer Grenadier Regiment, got past the first friendly position after firing two rounds into a house occupied by most of the men of the detachment. Then, forty yards from the nearest tank destroyer gun, the leading tank made the mistake of flashing on its running lights. Private First Class Mason Armstrong of Company F saw the lights, found a bazooka and a machine gunner, and knocked out two more half-tracks from a position in a nearby building. Three others were abandoned as the enemy withdrew back towards the main body near Stoumont. This action was near the site where Edelstein and his men had blown the Lienne Creek Bridge.

A short time later, the 119th Regiment closed on the left flank of General James Gavin's 82nd Airborne Division. They were assigned to General Mathew Ridgeway's XVIII Airborne Corps. This would complete the First Army defensive line on the northern shoulder of the big bulge battle. This entire defensive position of the First Army had resulted from the actions of Colonel H. Wallis Anderson's Group. They had established the key road blocks at Malmedy, Stavelot, Trois Ponts and Habiemont.

The key road blocks and the blowing of the bridges in Trois Ponts and Habiemont had forced the 1st SS Panzer Division into a trap. This caused the combat group of Colonel Jochen Peiper to end up fighting for its very existence in the battles at Stavelot, Trois Ponts, La Glieze and Stoumont.

Daybreak of December 19th found "Old Hickory" spread over 17 miles of battle line. The fog of battle obscured much of what was going on, and blotted out almost completely the events in more distant parts of the Ardennes battlefield. Paratroopers and sabotage agents were reported everywhere. The troops in Stavelot had uncovered evidence of the atrocities committed by SS troops against both civilians and captured American soldiers. The atmo-

The civilians massacred near Trois Ponts were buried in a mass grave.

sphere was charged with uncertainty and fear, which in time might affect even the spirited "Old Hickory" men coming into the battle.

General Hobbs requested artillery support from First Army. The 740th Tank Battalion, fresh from the States, raided an ordinance depot and returned with a collection of tanks, tank destroyers, self-propelled guns, and half-tracks.

In its first action near Stoumont on the afternoon of December 19th, the 740th was to knock out three Panther tanks with 4 shots and kill 70 of the enemy in 10 blazing minutes. At the same time another tank was smashing up two Panthers 150 yards away and a Tiger at 1200 yards. The 105th Engineers of Colonel Dunn drew 15,400 mines, distributed two thirds of them to the regiments, and started laying the rest in front of the German attack.

Contact had been made with the German spearheads on the 18th. Tactically, the next job was to drive them back so that a coherent defense could be organized. 30th Recon troop patrols linked the Division's left flank with the 1st Infantry Division, which held an east-west line to the east of Malmedy. The obvious line to defend was from Malmedy to Stavelot, then west along the Ambleve River to Stoumont, until the 82nd Airborne Division, taking positions immediately south of the river, could tie in with the 30th. They could then advance to the north-south line of the Salm River up to Trois Ponts, where it joined the Ambleve River. Thus the first efforts of the division would be bent on cleaning out the river line.

The German target was clearly Liege, a vast supply center for the First and Ninth Armies. The shortest route there was from the Malmedy-Stavelot sector, where good roads arched over the ridge line of the Hohes Venne rolling hills to Spa and then Liege. This fact obsessed Division, Corps, and Army. How much of the German Army had been committed and how much remained in reserve was unknown.

The threat of a new enemy attack to the northwest was frightening. The 30th Division had to keep an eye on Malmedy. At Stoumont on December 18th, the paybook of a dead German revealed the presence of the 1st SS Panzer Division Leibstandarte Adolf Hitler. Actually, the whole of that division was stretched out across the Old Hickory's front.

When the first division elements contacted the enemy at Stavelot on December 18th, the 1st SS Panzer Division was rolling westward in two columns, with the main force of Peiper to the north. The stronger column was using the route Bullengen-Ligneuville-Stavelot-La Gleize-Aywaille. The southern column traveled abreast via Ponts-Trois Ponts-Werbomont. Its companion in the 1st SS Panzer Corps was the 12th SS Panzer Division (Hitler Jugend), attacking on the right. The 99th Infantry Division had stopped the 12th SS on the Bullingen-Butgenbach corner of the breakthrough area. Had the 12th SS Panzer Division broken through Malmedy on December 17th the Germans could have well succeeded in making the Meuse River that day. The spearhead of the northern column was already through Stavelot when the doughboys of the 117th Infantry put in an appearance there. At Stavelot, Peiper's column was engaged by the 526th Armored Infantry, the 825th Tank Destroyers, and the 202nd Engineers. A squad from the 291st Engineer Battalion's Company C had stopped the column south of Stavelot on the evening of December 17. Peiper's whole column stretched back to the village of Ligneuville. Thus, while the American commanders were primarily concerned with a drive to the Malmedy area, the 1st SS Panzer Division was worried about progressing west and the threat to their flank at Stavelot.

Peiper's panzers struck at Stoumont at 7:00 a.m. on December 19. The American forces were overrun by a strong attack. The 3rd Battalion held after two infantry attacks but finally fell to an all-out German infantry assault. The 3rd Battalion accounted for a dozen German tanks and three half-tracks but, out of ammunition and overwhelmed, they surrendered. During the battle, they lost all but 10 men out of 447 who entered the fight.

The enemy's control of Stoumont created a new menace for a secondary road led over a ridge and connected up with the Spa-Verviers road, in the rear of all division installations. Captain Carlton E. Stewart eliminated that problem by leading a company of the 3rd Battalion and blocking the enemy from breaking through.

In Stavelot, the Germans held one third of the town. They again attacked with 10 tanks and two companies of infantry, but this attack failed thanks to the 1st Battalion, 117th Regiment who moved slowly through the town. By noon, the 117th rolled but the last houses north of the river.

Early in the afternoon, ten panzers tried to cross the Ambleve River bridge but were driven back with heavy losses, dispute fire support received from the far shore. By now, Von Rundstedt, Model, and even Dietrich had given up on reaching Antwerp and were now considering a withdrawal into Germany due to their great loss of manpower and equipment.

Peiper contacted Mohnke by radio at Wanne and asked for support. Mohnke had moved up his headquarters from Ligneuville to Wanne and was busy attempting to force the remainder of his 1st SS Division across the bridge at Petite Spa west of Stavelot. After General Mohnke had moved to Wanne he learned that the 1st SS Panzer's Task Force Sandig had crossed the Petite Spa bridge and joined Peiper's forces north of the Ambleve. Task Force Knittel had moved along the southern side of the Ambleve and prepared to attack Stavelot. At this point Stavelot had become key to German success in the north.

The third Task Force of the 1st SS Panzer Division, commanded by Colonel Max Hansen had moved into Wanne preparing to support the attack with tanks and Panzer Grenadiers. The Germans were anxious for the entire 1st SS Panzer Division to break out of their encirclement in the Ambleve River Valley. Hansen's regiment had broken out of the Losheim Gap following Peiper's attack and quickly moved west through Ambleve, Born, Kaiserbaracke, and into the Stavelot-Wanne area. The village of Ambleve was where Captain James Gamble's A Company, 291st, first became aware of the German breakthrough. The Germans in this Task Force had faced little opposition and now had the mission of aiding the endangered Kampfgruppe Peiper. Dietrich and his 6th Panzer Army staff were now making plans to move the 12th SS Panzer Division south of St. Vith and send this battered Hitler Jugend force Northwest to outflank the First Army's forces on the northern shoulder.

General Mathew Ridgeway, the commander of the XVIII Airborne Corps, who had been in England when the German offensive opened, arrived in Werbomont on the 19th of December with his entire staff. He took charge of the entire American front from Malmedy through Stavelot, Trois Ponts and Stoumont, including La Gleize. His command would soon be enlarged until he commanded 9 Divisions and his front would extend for 65 miles.

Ridgeway now had under his command the 82nd Airborne Division, the 30th Division and the retreating 7th Armored Division. He also had the 1111th Engineer Combat Group of Colonel H. Wallis Anderson, the entire 291st Engineer Combat Battalion, and one company of the 51st Engineers.

The battle coming up looked like an all-out attempt by the German task forces to rescue Peiper, or to reinforce him and have him continue on to the Meuse River. Should the 12th SS Panzer Division (Hitler Jugend), be able to go south of St. Vith and attack through the retreating 7th Armored Division, and drive on northwest to the Trois Ponts sector, the German counter-offensive might succeed. General Hermann Preiss, commander of the 1st SS Panzer Corps, had heard from Mohnke and was told that the forces of Peiper had captured Cheneux, La Gleize and Stoumont, but he could go no further unless Peiper was reinforced.

After a see-saw battle in Stavelot on the 18th, General Leland Hobbs, commander of the 30th Infantry Division, poured reinforcements into the town which was now under artillery fire.

Two battalions were sent in from the 117th Regiment out of Malmedy, the 743rd Battalion, and a platoon of the 823rd Tank Destroyer Battalion. The tank destroyers were set up on the night of the 18th so as to cover the bridge crossing. From the time they took their

The Stavelot Bridge before Lt. Cofer blew one span.

positions no more German Divisions could cross. Across the river the entire pocket bounded by the Highway N-32, the Ambleve and the Salm, was now in the hands of General Mohnke's troops from the 1st SS Panzer Division. The rear march order of the 1st SS had crossed the Ambleve River at two places, one over the Bridge at Stavelot and across the river in rubber boats at or near the Petite Spa bridge. The 1st SS Division's Task Force Knittel had closed on Peiper's rear at La Gleize. Task Force Hansen was located at Recht with orders to close on the Stavelot area, and Task Force Sandig was now at Ligneuville to close on the south bank of the Ambleve at Stavelot.

On the morning of the 19th of December the situation of Hitler's main thrust looks like this. The 2nd Infantry Division has stabilized the line at Rockerath to Wirtzfeld and the 99th Division has formed a solid defense on the Elsenborn ridge. The 1st Infantry Division has built a formidable line of defense from Butgenbach through Waimes to tie into the 291st and 99th Norwegian Battalion at Malmedy where the 120th Regiment of the 30th Division is now moving in to position.

The 117th and 119th Regiments of the 30th Division have now formed a line of defense from Malmedy to Stoumont and Werbomont where the 82nd Airborne is now in line with three Regiments in the Trois Ponts-Vielslm-Manhay sector.

The 19th of December marks the beginning of the greatest single battle of the entire battle of the Ardennes. It is an attempt by the Germans to free their spearheading 1st SS Panzer Division's Kampfgruppe Peiper and break out to the Meuse River. Hitler has be-

The collapsed bridge at Petite Spa.

come livid resulting in the failure of his heavily built up 6th Panzer Army equipped with new and improved armor, arms and troops. It will involve the entire Sixth Panzer Army, half of the Fifth Panzer Army against the reinforced and stable First U.S. Army of General Courtney Hodges.

At the first light of December 19th Peiper's tanks and infantry had overwhelmed the 3rd Battalion of the 119th Infantry and the battalion had lost over 300 men. This was the beginning of the effort of Peiper to break out of the entrapment caused by the engineers at Habiemont. Intensely frustrated, Peiper was seeking ways and means to break out of his boxed-in situation. He contacted the commander of the 1st SS Recon Battalion, Gustav Knittel and asked him to attacked towards the east and recapture the village of Stavelot. Knittel turned his column and attacked towards Stavelot in order to drive out the 117th Regiment of the 30th Division.

Repeatedly the 1st SS units tried to capture the Ambleve River bridge at Stavelot, but they had been unsuccessful. By the evening of the 18th of December, the bridge was in the hands of the 117th Infantry and A Company of the 105th Engineers of Lt. Colonel Dunn. He was given the order by General Leland Hobbs to blow the bridge in the face of the Germans to prevent them from again attacking from the south.

It was the only bridge available for several miles, a bridge the Germans needed to continue their bold offensive towards Liege. If they could capture the Stavelot bridge intact, and hold it, their heavy panzers and supply vehicles could cross and support every opportunity. Use of the bridge would enhance their options towards taking Liege and Antwerp.

It was about noon on the 19th, when Lt. Leland Cofer received orders to go to Stavelot and blow the bridge. A Combat Reconnaissance of the bridge area and base had to be done. Cofer and his driver, Tech/5 Barone, jeeped as close as they dared, then continued on foot. This was the "frozen front line" occupied by the 117th Infantry, who had secured the houses and cellars facing the river.

The enemy held all of the high ground south of the river with at least one tank and a number of their infantry with other weapons, covering the bridge. The snow encrusted bridge was in no-man's land.

In daylight it would have been instant suicide to approach the bridge from any direction out in the open. Lt. Cofer had to get a better view to determine where to place his explosives, and how much to use.

By crawling from one house to the next, he was able to arrive at an upper floor window that gave him an excellent view of the bridge. By standing well to the rear, in the shadows of the room, he found an oblique view and remained unseen by the enemy. He sketched a rough drawing, estimating the length and width of the bridge, and the thickness of its deck. There was a GI jeep wrecked and an American soldier sprawled near the friendly side of the river.

While standing near the window making his sketch, Lt. Cofer was a witness to a duel between an American 823rd tank destroyer and a German panzer south of the river. After some maneuvering by both mechanized combatants, the TD put a couple of accurate rounds into the side of the enemy's tank, which resulted in a heavy billowing smoke, followed by its surviving panzer crewmen bailing out and running for cover. Their retreat was so quick that nearby American infantrymen could not get in a shot at them.

Returning to his jeep, Lt. Cofer sought his 105th Engineer A Company command post to draw up a plan and organize a demolition crew. Cofer estimated an excessive amount of TNT to be certain of the bridge's total destruction. His decision was nothing near an Engineer School solution. They could not easily place the demolition under the bridge-they would have only a brief and limited opportunity to place them on the top decking. He chose 1000 pounds of TNT with caps placed randomly in various boxes to ensure it would all explode.

TNT is super stable and needs quite a shock to set it off. They also fabricated three slow burning fuses, long enough to burn one minute, with detonators and fuse lighters. That was two more than necessary, but it was his insurance to guarantee complete detonation.

Lt. Cofer planned to approach the bridge well after dark, but not delay too long for fear that the Germans might be planning an assault of their own to recapture it that very night. He arranged through the 117th Regimental Headquarters for high explosive artillery fire at a regular rate on the enemy side of the river, mixing a few smoke shells to camouflage not only his intentions, but also the source of the noise he and his men would undoubtedly make carrying heavy boxes of demolition down a street strewn with broken glass.

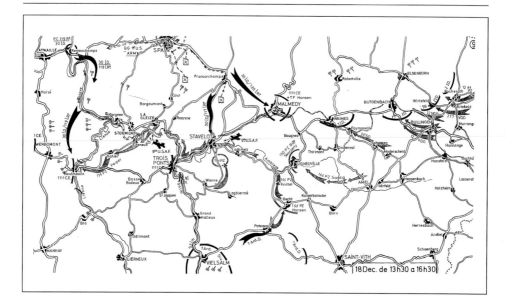

Stavelot had been under heavy enemy fire and the streets were lined with broken glass and debris lying among the cobble stones. Friendly artillery cover would begin at a predetermined time. But first, they instructed a French-speaking GI to go from house to house and warn all civilians to clear the area. Two 6x6 trucks hauled the demolition down the hill as near as possible. When the artillery started, his crew unloaded, and each man, carrying a box of TNT, headed through the debris for the bridge site a long four blocks away.

Staff Sergeant McKeon (who was killed a month later), Staff Sergeant Lowell Richardson, and Sgt. Ray Scott accompanied Cofer, with the remainder of the crew following along behind. They quickly set all of the demolition boxes directly on the thinnest part of the deck atop the first span. The men delivered their boxes and hastily withdrew.

On a signal, McKeon, Richardson and Cofer pulled all three fuse lighters simultaneously, then took off on a dead run, disregarding any possible noise their departure might make. A couple of short blocks away......KAAABOOOM!! It was a terrific explosion. Stone masonry houses next to the bridge just collapsed.

It must have been quite a shock to the Krauts in their outposts exposed to the elements on the other side of the river. The 117th artillery suddenly stopped, but an enemy machine gun began firing blindly up the street through the dust and smoke from the south side. Cofer and his crew jumped into a nearby doorway. Sgt. Ray Scott (Big Springs, Texas), 3rd squad leader of the 3rd Platoon of Company A, was severely wounded during this action and was evacuated to a nearby field hospital for treatment of his wounds. It was necessary for Lt. Cofer to perform a return recon mission in order to determine the results of the night's task.

Sergeant Richardson, who later received a battlefield commission, and Lt. Cofer stole back to the north bank of the Ambleve River and peeked over the rubble in the street to confirm that a huge hole had indeed been blown through the bridge decking. The first span had just disappeared. Captain James Rice, A Company Commander, Los Angeles, California, commented later to Hal Boyle, an AP War correspondent, "No damned German tank can jump that!"

The blowing of this bridge sealed in Peiper's entire regiment and other supporting 1st SS Panzer units. The 1st SS Panzer Commander, General Wilhelm Mohnke, was now livid with rage as he tried to force the troops of his division to wade the river at both Stavelot and Petite Spa. His purpose was to drive the men of the 30th Division back from the river's edge, regroup, rebuild both the bridge at Petite Spa and Stavelot, and go to the rescue of the forces of Peiper.

Generals Preiss and Dietrich were pounding on Mohnke to get on with the blitz to the Meuse River, which was rapidly fading out of the picture. The river soon ran red with German blood. American battlefield courage had again won the day. The Germans had truly failed.

Lt. Cofer's ingenuity and leadership again stalled the advance of a formidable enemy panzer column and hostile infantry attack. A few days later, A Company was ordered to other hot spots in the Stavelot-Trois Ponts area and continued to fight valiantly with their mines, demolitions and bazookas.

Lt. Cofer was promoted to Captain and received several battlefield citations. But more than that, Leland Cofer had earned the respect and admiration of his men from the very first day on Normandy's Omaha Beach in June 1944. Cofer's concern for his men's welfare had always been a high priority.

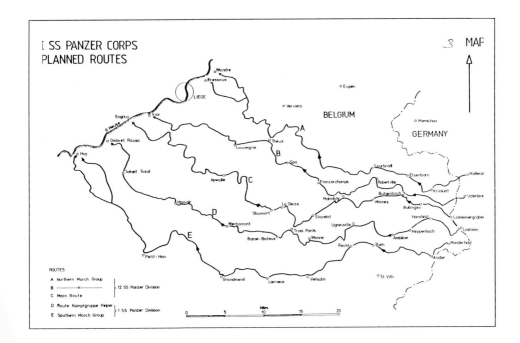

21

The Decisive Battle on the Northern Shoulder (Dec. 21)

The situation along the Northern shoulder on the early morning of December 21, 1944 was one of a solid defense established by the American forces from Monschau, Butgenbach, Waimes, and Malmedy. East of Malmedy, Sepp Dietrich had assigned his 3rd Paratroop Division to attack the U.S. 1st Infantry Division from Waimes to Butgenbach. Also his 12th Volksgrenadier Infantry Division along with the Armor of the 12th SS Panzer Division. The 2nd U.S. Infantry was being attacked by the 12th and 277th Volksgrenadier Divisions as the 99th U.S. Infantry was holding the Germans at bay on the Elsenborn Ridge with the 9th Infantry Division on their left flank.

The German high brass and Hitler were deeply concerned about the entrapment of Kampfgruppe Peiper and the generals knew that if this battle on the 21st failed, their chances of getting to the Meusse River were nil. They had already given up on getting to Antwerp when Peiper and the 1st SS Panzer Corps had failed to get to the Meusse in 48 hours.

On the American side, the combat engineers had set up and manned road blocks, and prepared bridges for demolition at all key locations. Deep mine fields had been laid in front of the infantry, and the defensive positions of the infantry and artillery had been strengthened with roads and infantry shelters to protect against enemy artillery and mortar fire. The artillery positions were set up with 2-inch crushed rock as a hard surface road material and hard standings for artillery gun positions in the very wet areas of the forests. The engineer combat battalions had developed a solid defensive barrier line in front of the Infantry and artillery from Monschau to the Elsenborn Ridge, through Butgenbach to Waimes, and through Malmedy, Stavelot and Trois Ponts. This barrier line included engineers with bazookas and Daisey-chain mines, and trees with blocks of TNT to explode the trees across the roads. Fortunately on the Northern shoulder, the Engineers had been in line long enough to prepare this barrier line combined with the artillery and the infantry.

By December 21, American troops opposing the northern prong of the German offensive had "knocked a part of Hitler's personal operational plan into a cocked hat." The Division commanders, the Corps commanders, Dietrich, Model, von Runstadt, and eventually Hitler himself, had to face the fact that the Sixth Panzer Army and Hitler's beloved SS troops had failed to do the job Hitler had asked of them.

Three of the divisions opposing the Sixth Panzer Army were the crack 2nd, 1st, and 9th Infantry Divisions who had rapidly moved almost overnight into line with the newly arrived 99th. This made a solid defense when the 30th and 82nd Airborne were added to the line in the west end. The rapidity in which First Army had reacted to the German offensive was most formidable.

This solid shoulder were determined to prevent any further expansion of the German offensive. The Germans were now at the point of do-or-die with the entire counter-offensive of Adolf Hitler. At General Sepp Dietrich's order, General Mohnke on December 21 was to employ every available resource to break through to Peiper. He was also advised by even Hitler to use Otto Skorzeny's 150th Panzer Brigade. General Model had also insisted in an all-out attack by Dietrich's Sixth Army all of the way from the Siegfried Line through Malmedy and on to Stoumont and Werbomont.

Ever since the 16th of December when the Germans had opened up their violent opening barrage of artillery and long range rockets, the Americans in the strongpoints of the Elsenborn Ridge and the villages of Butgenbach, Waimes, Malmedy and points west were expecting such an all out offensive. In Malmedy we saw the 30th Division's morning intelligence report which indicated the presence of Skorzeny's forces, the 1st SS Panzer Division and troops of the 3rd Parachute Division. The report indicated the potential of the German attack on the morning of the 21st.

Part of the rational in attacking Malmedy was that early in the offensive one of Skorzeny's operatives on entering Malmedy had reported finding it lightly held by the 291st Engineers.

Unbeknownst to Skorzeny, that had markedly changed. At this time we in the 291st had about 200 of our men from B and C companies. The other two thirds of our battalion were involved at Trois Ponts and other barrier line positions.

German tank knocked out in Malmedy by Pfc. Frank Currey of the 30th Division on Dec. 21st. As previously noted, Frank would later receive the Medal of Honor.

Warsh River Bridge in Malmedy, blown down to stop Skorzeny's forces by Lt. Frank Rhea's men.

We had been strengthened by the 99th Infantry Battalion of Lt. Colonel Hansen, the 526th Armored Infantry Battalion, the 825th Tank Destroyer Battalion and all of the 120th Regiment of Col. Banner Purdue and the 30th Division. Amid the hills and valleys behind the town there were six artillery battalions and Dec. 21st was the day when American artillery was free—as authorized by the war department at General Eisenhower's request—to use the VT or POZIT fuse on its shells.

All along the line the 1st, 2nd, 99th, and 9th Infantry Divisions were all backed up by at least four Artillery Battalions all equipped with the air bursting artillery shells which could wipe out platoon sized enemy troops with one exploding shell. To add to the hazards of battle, it started to snow on the early morning hours of the 21st of December and it had become bitterly cold. Since the time that Kampfgruppe Peiper had broken out at Butgenbach and was seen by Lt. Frank Rhea of the 291st at 8:30 a.m. on the morning of the 17th, First Army of General Courtney Hodges had done an astounding shift in Divisions to move out of combat lines and travel 30 to 40 miles. Then to form on lines established by engineer units in less than 48 hours and be able to confront a heavy armored and Infantry attack under overcast skies with little or no help from the air force, was almost a miracle.

Probably the most thankful of all the units in Malmedy at the time was the men in the 291st and their commander. Despite being at one time almost surrounded in Malmedy by Peiper and some paratroopers of von Der Heydte, and discovering the massacre of the men of the 285th Field Artillery Observation Battalion, we now felt that this German breakthrough could be defeated. The most unusual occurrence of the 20th of December was for us in the 291st to be advised to turn over our road blocks in Malmedy to the men of the 30th

Skorzeny tank knocked out at Malmedy by John Noland with Daisy Chain mines.

Division and move to Modave, Belgium and become part of a large engineer barrier line east of the Meusse River. Already on the evening of the 18th of December, Col. Anderson and the 1111th Group headquarters had been advised to move out of Trois Ponts and begin to develop this barrier line with other engineer combat battalions.

Colonel William Carter, the First Army Engineer had been given this responsibility by General Hodges, and in turn had passed part of this Engineer barrier line on to Colonel Anderson. The higher authority had now become quite concerned that should the Germans reach the Meusse, and Peiper was almost there, it may take a lengthy time and strong divisions to stop them.

We had moved a small contingent into Spa on the evening of the 20th, prepared to take on a new mission when I received word from General Leland Hobbs, the commander of the 30th Division, that he had been able to rescind our orders from First Army, and that we were needed on our roadblock defenses in Malmedy.

As we moved into Malmedy around 5:00 A.M. on the morning of the 21st, we saw flares shooting up as we swung around the curve beyond the Warsh River bridge. Skorzeny had opened up his attack and his approaching infantry had hit the trip wires in front of our deeply laid mine fields.

Using the 150th Panzer Brigade as a regular ground force was the idea of Peiper himself, who had become convinced as early as the second day of the offensive that his brigade would be unable to accomplish its mission of seizing the bridges over the Meusse. As Mike Popp, my command car driver raced the car towards and over the bridge, we started to hear artillery fire, and we realized we were in the middle between our own forces and the enemy.

Just ahead of the railroad viaduct and the entrance to Malmedy an American soldier of some size stepped out in front of the car and yelled halt; he had a rifle. It was Sgt. John Noland, who was in charge of a roadblock with daisy chain mines. These were five or six mines strung together about two feet apart on a chain or rope. The purpose of this engineer weapon of war was to pull the chain across the road in front of a tank or other enemy conveyance.

I learned from John that the enemy was starting an attack here at the west end of Malmedy, and he advised me and Mike Popp to quickly proceed on into Malmedy. We headed into the town square and parked in front of Lt. Col. Howard Greer's battalion command post. Greer commanded the 1st Battalion of the 120th Regiment of the 30th Division. With Col. Greer was Captain Richard Trauth, liaison officer of the 230th Field Artillery Battalion. They both informed me that their patrols had observed the German build-up to attack Malmedy and captured prisoners had revealed that this attack was being made by Skorzeny's Brigade.

I headed immediately to my command Post at eastern Malmedy. I learned from Captain John Conlin that he was busily setting up the 15 road blocks that we were starting to turn over to the 30th Division, and all indications seemed to show that the Germans were preparing to attack the forces in Malmedy.

Captain Kamen, the 291st Dental officer who was in charge of the medics told us about the 17 men of the 285th Field Artillery Observation Battalion who had survived the massacre at Baugnez. One had died of seven wounds shortly after he was brought to the medical building. All of these men had been treated for their wounds and taken to the Field Hospital near Spa. There were names on the list such as Merrikan, Mattera, Willows, Lary, Rheam,

Peiper tank knocked out at La Gleize.

and others. Captain Kamen stated, "Thank goodness! We held Malmedy or these men would not have survived like the others who were killed in the field."

We were now beginning to hear the sounds of battle with more outgoing fire than the occasional incoming heavy stuff. There was the crash of artillery against the buildings in the town and on one occasion the loud crash of a V-1 missile. The most annoying was the weird sound of the German "screaming meemie." Word soon came by radio that the west end of Malmedy was being heavily attacked by tanks. This was Lt. Frank Rhea's and Master Sergeant Ralph McCarty's area of defense.

I left the command post and headed on foot in the direction of the west end of Malmedy. After I had gone towards the paper mill one of the men of the 291st came running towards me. It was T/5 Vincent Consiglio and he was practically exhausted as he blurted out the story of the battle at the Warche River bridge and the nearby paper mill. The men who were assigned to blow the bridge were the men of "K" company of the 30th Division when Sgt McCarty had been relieved of this responsibility on the night of the 20th. Now in the morning of the 21st when we learned that the Germans were attacking in this area, Sgt. McCarty had assigned Consiglio, Pvt. William Mitchell, and Pvt. Joseph Spires to seek out the Detonator from the Infantry and take over the blowing of the bridge should it become necessary.

Consiglio told me about the events at the paper mill. "Colonel, before we could get to the bridge and find the detonator, the sky became lighted up with flares, and firing of mortars and artillery from both sides became active and made it impossible for us to get to the bridge, so we crashed into a nearby building and took cover.

"The house was the command post of the 823rd Tank Destroyer Battalion, who had several three-inch towed guns positioned behind it, and several 50 caliber machine guns also dug in behind the house. A Captain was in charge and he immediately got the TD men on their guns and began firing in the direction of the fields to the west.

"Soon the infantrymen of Company K came into the house for shelter and we were organized to fire back at the enemy from the windows of the house, with the medics set up in the basement. I took a position at the kitchen window and the captain asked me to give target destination of the enemy for his gun crews. Soon the enemy infantry and tanks were beginning to swarm up into the area near the house. Consiglio ran down into the basement. He found a window over a coal bin and he moved up and began to fire out the window. Sometime later the enemy infantry were swarming all over the yard and started to toss hand grenades into the basement. The infantry was thrown back by some of the men of Company K led by P.F.C. Francis Currey, A BAR man who was firing his own weapon with vigor. Then he found a bazooka, but it had no rockets. Curry dashed across the road and returned with them and loaded them for another K Company man who blasted the turret off of the tank and knocked it out."

Seven or eight tanks were maneuvering around the house below the bridge. Currey went out with a bazooka alone and fired into the tanks. He then dashed across the street again and found some rifle grenades in the TD half-track. From the flank position he fired all the grenades at the enemy.

Col. Otto Skorzeny.

When Consiglio peered out the window and saw the huge tank turning its gun towards the window, he fled upstairs. There he found Spires of the 291st firing his rifle in the direction of the bridge. Consiglio took a position beside Spires and they both fired their rifles out the window at the attacking Germans.

His grenades gone, Currey went out and started firing the 50 caliber machine-gun mounted on the half-track. He later abandoned it and grabbed a 30 caliber machine-gun and started firing it at the Germans below the bridge. The fight around the paper-mill and the bridge went on and on, very hot and fierce; it also swirled around the house in which the TD men, a handful of Company K Infantrymen, and engineers Consiglio and Spires were trapped.

Two tanks then approached the road and crossed the bridge and came on, guns blazing towards the house. They joined others which had came across the field, and all of the tanks started maneuvering about the house. Then the larger tank approached the road and crossed the bridge and came on, guns blazing, towards the house. It took a position whereby it could fire directly at the house and paper mill. Almost immediately it began to shell the house with its big 75 mm gun. One of the shells hit the kitchen of the house. Consiglio ran down to see if he could find Private William Mitchell of the 291st.

When Consiglio ran into the kitchen he found all the men had been killed, including the D Captain. He ran into the first floor and found Mitchell. He helped Mitchell put on a bazooka vest and Mitchell went to the front window to fire the bazooka; as he raised the window the Germans fired their machine guns and killed him.

Everywhere Consiglio went he found dead Americans. He then grabbed a machine gun and began spraying the enemy with heavy fire. A tank nosed around the house and he had to abandon the machine gun. He then ran up the stairs and joined Spires at the south window. At sometime during the morning Spires yelled out that he had been hit. Consiglio then aided Spires to move to the basement where the medics were taking care of the wounded. About that time the gunners on the three-inch guns outside came running into the basement. They had found Skorzeny's men all over the place and couldn't seem to stop them. Pvt. Currey seemed to rally them and they went out and tried again. Some of them were killed; however, Currey fought on and was able to wipe out many of the Germans in American uniforms.

The artillery in the hills north of Malmedy found the range and began plastering the area with the air-bursting shells of the POZIT fuse. Soon thereafter the bodies of the attacking Germans started to pile up in front of the railroad embankment, and the all-out efforts of the men of Skorzeny came to waste.

After Consiglio's description of the battle at the Warche River bridge and the paper mill, I sent Consiglio to the B Company command post of Captain Conlin and hurried to the command post of Lt. Col. Howard Greer in order to learn the status of the over-all battle on this 21st of December as the snow continued to fall.

I was very much concerned about the status of the troops of Lt. Don Davis and those of Lt. Frank Rhea. Both of these units of the 291st were located at the west end of Malmedy where this all out attack was taking place. Rhea's men had the demolitions on the bridges and the railroad viaduct, and Lt. Davis' men were on line as infantry with bazookas, machine guns, and rifles after having laid mines out in front of the embankment. Davis had the infantrymen of the 99th Norwegians on his left flank and Rhea had the men of company K of the 120th Regiment on his right flank.

When I arrived in Col. Greer's Command Post Captain Trauthe, the artillery Liason officer, was present and they were both excited about the success that the artillery was having against the Germans in this all-out attack. Greer indicated that his men up front were reporting that the Germans effort was being stopped and many of his tanks were being knocked out.

Greer also gave credit to B Company of the 526th Armored Infantry and the 825th Tank Destroyer Battalion with their guns and action at the railroad embankment near the viaduct. I now felt relieved to know that our efforts to hold Malmedy was now a reality.

I went back to the battalion command post and met with Conlin and my liaison officer, Captain Sheetz. They said that the bridges had not been blown at the west end of Malmedy but the report from Master Sergeant Ralph McCarty indicated that the Germans had failed to penetrate at the viaduct; however, the battle at the paper mill and the Warche River

Lt. Tintari, Lt. Walters, and Captain Conlin locate mines near the approaches to Malmedy.

Bridge was still going on with much action. McCarty advised that many of the German foot troops had been wiped out in the mine fields, and especially by the American artillery fire.

Sheetz had obtained some information on the big picture from General Hobbs' headquarters. We knew that Peiper had been entrapped between Stoumont and Stavelot and was now being pounded by the 119th, and 117th Regiments of the 30th Division. Also the 82nd Airborne of General Gavin was now aiding in the wipe out of his forces and the remainder of the 1st SS Panzer Division of General Wilhelm Mohnke in the vicinity of Trois Ponts and Wanne.

The information Sheetz received from General Hobbs' Headquarters also included facts about an all out attack from the Siegfried line to Malmedy along the northern shoulder where the 9th, 99th, 2nd, and 1st Infantry Divisions were defending. The nine German Infantry and armored divisions opened up a massive offensive coordinated in time with Skorzeny's brigade attack on Malmedy.

At this point we in the 291st command post knew that this was a last ditch effort of Hitler's Nazis and Volkestorm troops. We had become aware of the dropping of Von der Heydte's paratroopers north of Malmedy, for three of them had surrendered to our roadblock at the east end and Sgt. Martin of C Company had brought them in to the CP. We had learned that we were being attacked by Peiper because one of his scouting squads had hit one of our roadblocks. And now we had become very much aware of the noted commando spy; Colonel Otto Skorzeny was attacking us with camouflaged men and equipment. One of his jeep patrols had hit the roadblock of mines south of Malmedy, and B Company's 1st Sgt. Short had identified the dead clothed in American uniforms except for their German boots.

Of his two attacks, Skorzeny's left wing attack was the strongest of his units. They had moved in column up the Rue de Falize from the vicinity of Bellevaux. Abreast of the wooden bridge, one section of the column had taken a farm road that crossed the field over to the paper mill. The rest of the column had continued up the Rue de Falize. The column that followed the farm road had tripped the flares as I approached from the north in my command car on the early morning. This opened the battle prematurely for Skorzeny on the flank. The tanks on the Rue de Falize now had guns blazing, and the Company B of the Norwegians on top of the railroad embankment and Sgt. John Noland at the railroad viaduct with daisy chain mines and a rifle opened up with all they had. Through the portholes of the railroad over passes, the anti-tank guns of the 526th Armored Infantry and the three inch guns of the 825th Tank-Destroyer Battalion added all their fire power.

About that time the lead tank struck the minefield out ahead of the railroad overpass and was set on fire. The other tanks maneuvered around it, and the infantry poured past it. The Germans in American uniforms then attacked toward the railroad embankment. Again and again they charged, screaming, "Surrender or die!" Their fanatic charges reached clear to the foot of the embankment. Again and again they tried to set up their machine guns, and paid a dreadful price for their efforts. The Norwegians, along with the men of Lt. Don

Skorzeny Panther tank knocked out in the field near Geromont by Lt. Colbeck's mines.

Davis, were firing point blank into the Germans with both rifles and the machine guns as the bodies piled up in the field.

The Artillery guns of the 230th Field Artillery Battalion opened up again with its air-bursting shells, which exploded in the air in the vicinity of the target. Some flung down their guns and raced for the embankment to surrender. Skorzeny's men were too tough to panic long and hundreds died in the futile effort made against the railroad embankment.

Private Bernard Koenig, B Company 291st had just left the 3rd platoon command post to take his turn at the gun emplacement manned by the 3rd platoon when the attack began. He was still some distance from the position. He hit the dirt and laid there for thirty minutes, sheltered to some extent by the lee side of the embankment. When the intensity of the artillery fire died down a little, he ran for the foxhole at the gun position. From there he watched the German tank burning in the predawn darkness like a Roman candle, a torch of light sending off sparks.

The roadblock at the big railroad viaduct was defended by Sgt. McCarty's men who reacted promptly as the tanks and infantry rolled nearer. It was impossible to know the strength of the enemy, but occasionally, in the flare of the artillery fire, or in the light of the burning tank, the infantry could be seen charging. The engineers fired everything that they had: rifles, machine guns, bazookas.

At another position, Corporal Isaac. McDonald suddenly remembered that the safety catches on the daisy chain of mines across the road had not been thrown. He dashed out to throw them, and earned a Bronze Star for his effort.

At still another gun emplacement, near one of the 526th's anti-tank guns, a mortar shell landed and killed an infantryman and knocked down Sgt. John Noland, a bulldozer operator serving as an infantryman. He bounced back up, and fearful that the tanks would reach the overpass, ran out to drag the daisy chain across the road. The tank was blown up and caught on fire. This effort earned Noland a Silver Star.

In the middle of the fight at the railroad embankment, another mortar shell hit in some trees near the position of Sgt. McCarty's men. A tree splintered and sent its fragments in all directions. Pfc. Wiley Holbrook was hit and died instantly. The back of his head was literally sheared off. He was a big, good-humored man of A Company 291st, who had been at the roadblock since the 17th of December.

The men of B Company 526th Armored Infantry had also been at this roadblock since the late evening of the 17th and had served well in the face of this mortar and machine gun fire from the men of Skorzeny. There were approximately 30 of them on this occasion. Pfc. Richard Ferris was one of them, firing directly at the approaching tanks. The men of the 526th had relieved the men of K Company of the 30th Division. Many of them were wounded and one killed.

The men of the 526th went further up into the hills to protect the gun emplacements of the 825th Tank-Destroyers. Fran Currey of the 30th Division later would receive the Congressional Medal of Honor for his heroic action in this battle and Consiglio would receive a Bronze Star. Consiglio decided to run for help as the battle here was winding down. As he was able to escape and head towards the command post, I was able to meet up with him and hear first hand about the battle at the Warche River bridge and the paper mill.

Pfc. Richard Ferris of B Company of the 526th Armored Infantry Battalion described the battle at the bridge and viaduct. "About 10:00 A.M. the Sgt. hollered that the Germans would make a left hand turn and come up the hill. This meant we were facing the wrong way and immediately dug more holes to meet the oncoming Germans. Some of us went part way down the hill to watch the battle and the tank-destroyer with their 4-inch gun. The

Skorzeny Jeep with four Germans in American uniforms hit the road block south of Malmedy.

Blowing of the Malmedy Railroad Viaduct on December 22nd.

Germans were attacking with one Tiger Royale and 5 tanks disguised to look like American Sherman tanks. Our TDs were firing but didn't have the range. Suddenly the Tiger Royale turned, stopped and fired a shell which landed only about 30 feet in front of the gun emplacement, blowing the four men onto the ground. I thought they would run. They jumped back on their gun and the German soldiers following the tanks were knocked out by the American fire.

"Our tank-destroyers put three holes in the Sherman tanks and bounced shells off of the Tiger Royale. The Tiger did not fire again. It was abandoned with its motor running. It idled there with its motor running until it ran out of gas. It got stuck in the muddy-snowy ground.

"On the hill looking into the valley city of Malmedy, Sgt. Arthur Mann, Sgt. Leo Day, and Lt. Milton Bernstein had patrolled to a dirt road at the bottom side of the hill. Charlie Simmons and I were talking with the tank-destroyers when a lot of small arm German firing rang out at the bottom of the hill. We watched the tank destroyers grab weapons and spread out at the bottom of the hill. We watched and did the same thing, working our way from tree to tree, until we were with our men. Sgt. Arthur Mann was wounded, but dropped to his knees and fired point blank into a German, killing him and then another. When we arrived the Germans ran off. Lt. Berstein had captured a German and we then moved back up the hill. On the way back we stopped at a bridge with a house nearby and found an American Captain dead inside with other American dead."

"Outside there was a German tank that was burned out. I was told that the dead Captain had thrown a five gallon can of gasoline and then shot at it to set it on fire. As he tried to run

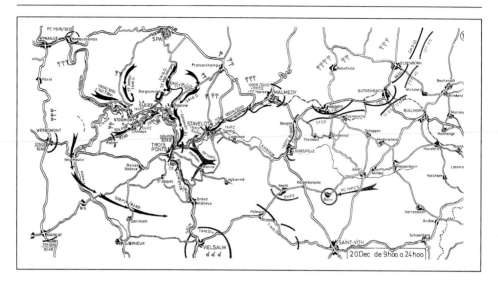

back, he was killed. Some soldiers said, 'This ain't nothing. Up a little ways the dead are stacked up like cord wood.' I did not take time to look."

During the battle Sgt. Lee White and Pfc. Gutowski of B Company of the 291st were dug in on the hill above the bridge and were heavily shelled by mortar fire and both were wounded and evacuated, but survived.

Lt. Davis and his C Company men of the 291st were also dug in on the railroad embankment south of the railroad viaduct and, along with the men of Colonel Hansen's Norwegians, constantly were exchanging machine gun and rifle fire with Skorzeny's men as these Nazis in American uniforms tried to approach the railroad embankment. Sgt. Mort Tuftadol had gone out on patrol for the Norwegians shortly before the German attack and brought in prisoners, and the men of Norway had learned about the oncoming attack. They had passed the word on to Lt. Davis. This permitted Sgt. Albert Melton, the platoon leader of the 291st men, to get the machine guns ready for firing.

The battle around the paper mill and the wooden trestle bridge slowly subsided toward the middle of the afternoon. Our artillery had really turned the tide. The guns of the 230th Field Artillery Battalion had plastered the fields south of Malmedy with over 3000 rounds of fire. The guns of the 825 Tank-Destroyer Battalion had blasted away at Skorzeny's disguised tanks. Skorzeny threw in the towel, after a long and desperate try, disengaged his men and slowly pulled them back along a six mile ridge line south and west of Malmedy.

The two prong attack, one up the Rue de Falize to move through the underpass and into the village of Malmedy, had came to a conclusion just short of the underpass when the lead tank was knocked out by the daisy chain mines of the 291st Engineers. A combination of the artillery, machine gun, and the rifle fire of the Norwegians and the men of Lt. Don Davis had taken care of hundreds of the attacking men of Skorzeny. This was accomplished with hardly any serious casualties to the Norwegians or the Americans who fought well side by side.

The left flank attack at the Warche River bridge and the paper mill lasted much longer and both sides had killed and wounded men. Skorzeny's attack at the east end of Malmedy also was a miserable failure as both of the roadblocks of the 291st held throughout. These were the defensive positions of Lt. Wadr Colbeck and Lt. John Perkins of B Company and C Company of the 291st Engineers. These positions were well supported by C Company of the 120th Regiment of the 30th Division, the artillery of the 230th Field Artillery Battalion, the guns of the 825th Tank Destroyer Battalion, and the 90 MM. anti-aircraft guns of Lt. Robert Wilson.

This was quite a change since December 17th when the only force in this particular area was the 13 man squad of Lt. Colbeck with mines, machine guns, bazookas and rifles. In less than four days the response of Colonel Anderson of the 1111th Engineer Combat Group was like a miracle to the men of the 291st who were in line against unbelievable odds.

Skorzeny's all out movement down the road from Baugnez and through the fields of Geromont with both infantry and tanks was quickly discovered by all concerned as the American forces opened up with a barrage with mortar, artillery, and machine gun fire as the approaching Germans were being literally wiped out before they could get to the road-blocks of the 291st. The battle was over before it had hardly been started. Hundreds of

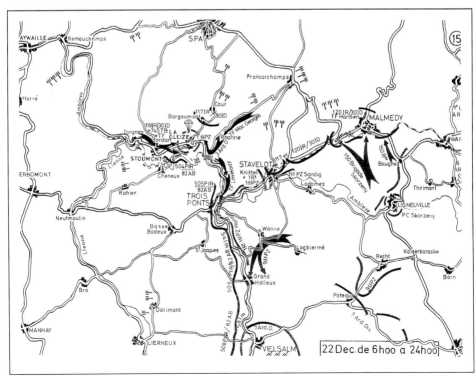

Germans were captured or killed with all of their tanks destroyed or knocked out in the mine fields.

Captain Murray S. Pulver commanded Company C of the 120th Regiment and his men had held its position on the left flank of the 30th Division and were in contact with the 1st Division on the left of the 30th at Waimes. There were casualties on both sides; however, the Germans left the field of battle with very few men left to fight again. Many of the captured Germans had all or parts of the uniforms of the American soldier.

Lt. John Perkins and Sgt. Peter Piar of the 291st went into the field near Geromont to check out a knocked out German tank. The engineers were required to do this. The Germans often planted booby-traps on knocked out equipment.

Skorzeny wrote a book entitled "Skorzeny's Special Missions" in which he describes the battles in Malmedy on the 21st of December 1944. "Just when I heard the attack begin, I heard heavy gun fire from the north. The right wing of the attack had run into a violent barrage and was being held up. I ordered the right wing to hold fast and form prepared for a counter attack to permit the left flank to move ahead into Malmedy.

"In any case, the right wing must stand fast if the left wing were to succeed. For a long time I had no news of the latter and the only evidence of what was going on was the sound of battle and vehicles bringing back the wounded. When it was light, I went ahead on a ridge from which I could see, not the whole of Malmedy, but a substantial portion of the road net on the western side. I had a good view of six of our tanks engaged in a hopeless

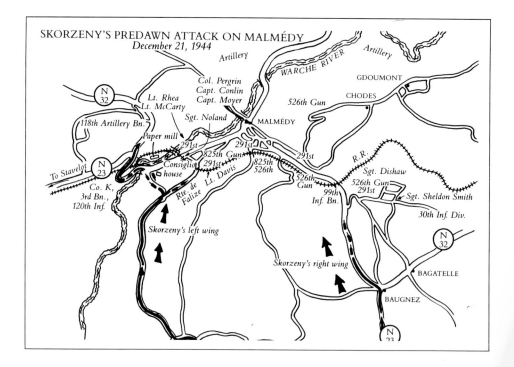

SKORZENY'S PREDAWN ATTACK ON MALMÉDY
December 21, 1944

Skorzeny tank disguised as American knocked out by P.F.C. Fran Currey of the 35th Division.

struggle with a superior force of the enemy while trying to protect the left flank of the attack.

"Soon afterwards the first infantry arrived, and I had learned that they had run up against well held and strong defenses, which could not be overrun without artillery support. Our tanks were fighting a hopeless action in order to cover the retreat. I gave orders that the unit should reform behind the crest with a view towards counter attack. By the afternoon we had established a frail defense about 10 kilometers long. Our heaviest weapons were medium mortars. To deceive the enemy as to our strength, I had ordered several reconnaissance's to be carried out. The American artillery fire had greatly increased and was concentrated upon the valley, the village of Engeldorf and the roads leading to it.

"Towards evening I went to Division headquarters to report. This was General Mohnke's CP in Lingneuville, where he had parked his wheeled office to control the actions of his 1st SS Panzer Division. I had not reached the entrance when a familiar sound made me take a flying leap into the house. The ensuing bang was eloquent enough. From the truck, which had received a direct hit, we pulled the wounded driver, who had received a splinter the size of a pencil out of his back.

"We waited for the next salvo and jumped into our armored car. It was pitch dark, and we could hardly see anything in the murk. So we groped along, keeping towards the middle of the road. We had just passed the bridge when three shells landed quite near. I felt a blow on the forehead and jumped out of the car into the ditch. A truck came rumbling along and ran into my car, which was not showing any lights.

"Then I felt something running down my face and got a terrible shock when I put up my hand and discovered a bleeding piece of flesh hanging down over my right eye. After a few minutes we were back at division headquarters. Then I also found that I had two holes in my trousers and bruises on my shoulders, I realized how lucky I had been. My wounds were dressed and I returned to duty."

Skorzeny would no longer use his brigade in the Ardennes and this marked the end of two of the special forces by Hitler and the German high command. The paratroops of Von der Heydte had failed and now operation "Grief" had come to an abrupt halt. Soon the forces of Kampfgruppe Peiper was destined to meet its end.

The attempt to free the entrapped Peiper using Skorzeny to open up the hole at Malmedy had no success whatsoever. Also along the entire northern shoulder where General Sepp Dietrich had forced his Sixth Panzer Army through the First Army Divisions from Monschau to Werbomont had also been a miserable failure. The 9th Infantry, 99th, and 2nd Divisions supported by at least 12 battalions of artillery and at least six Engineer Combat Battalions had pounded the German Panzer and Volkesstorm Divisions with heavy artillery and tank-destroyer fire. As the Infantry attacked in waves through the minefields the Engineers used their machine guns and rifles. If some tanks broke through, the engineers used bazookas and daisy chain mines to stop them. At no time along this defensive shoulder of First Army were there any breakthroughs made against this stalwart defense made up of the infantry, artillery, tank destroyers, and especially engineers. All of these units were working as a team against the so-called crack troops of Hitler's best Panzer and Volkestorm Divisions. The 9th, 99th, the 2nd and 1st Divisions had used its coordinated artillery to wipe out thousands of infantry and tanks of the 277th Volkesgrenadier, 12th SS Panzer, 12th Volkesgrenadier, and the 3rd Parachute Division along the line from the Elsenborn Ridge to Waimes. At the end of the day of December 21st the 6th Panzer Army of General Sepp Dietrich had received such a pounding along this line that many of their panther and tiger tanks had been wiped out in the minefields of the American Engineers and by bazooks in the close-in fighting. All bridges had been prepared for demolition and in no instant was it possible for the Germans to break out at these engineer roadblocks.

The engineer combat battalions engaged in this major battle of December 21st were the 1st, 2nd, 146th, 254th, 9th and 324th. The number of instances where the engineers pulled daisy chain mines in front of tanks were numerous. There were casualties among the Engineers and infantry on the American side but not nearly the high numbers of the attacking enemy. This was a case whereby the Americans had succeeded in preparing proper defenses in this very mobile war.

West of Waimes where Skorzeny's tanks and infantry were spread all over the terrain the attack on Malmedy had reached its end, but farther west the Germans were attempting to free the entrapped Peiper and his still fighting forces. As part of the renewed effort to break through, the battalion of the 2nd SS Panzergrenadier Regiment that tried to cross the

A German Tiger knocked out at La Gleize.

Ambleve River at Stavelot tried again on the morning of the 21st. Again the Germans tried to wade the heavy stream, their weapons held high above their heads; they displayed considerable less spirit than the day before, and they had no tank support. The attack quickly collapsed. Although a few men of the battalion were able later to get across the river at an undefended sector between Stavelot and Trois Ponts, the presence of task force Lovelady prevented them from reaching Peiper. All they could do was augment Knittel's recon troops in the hamlets overlooking Stavelot. They were eventually mopped up along with Knittel's troops by the 117th Infantry supported by Lovelady's tanks of the 3rd Armored Division which joined the American forces in the Stavelot-La Gleize area.

The 1st SS Panzergrenadier Regiment, which had seen little fighting except for a brief encounter at the forming American line behind St. Vith, made Mohnke's main effort supported by tank destroyers and tanks transferred from support of the other Panzergrenadier Regiment. The troops were to get across the Salm River at Trois Ponts and further up stream.

By that time, a company of the 82nd Airborne Division's 505th Parachute Infantry had established a small bridgehead beyond the Salm, along the heights around the railroad station that is across from Trois Ponts, and the rest of the regiment had dug in at likely crossing sites upstream. At the hamlets of La Neuville and Grand Halleux, the paratrooper's engineers wired two bridges for demolition, but delayed blowing them in anticipation of the drive on St. Vith.

The bridgehead that had been formed by the paratroops was soon overcome by the Germans and the men of the 82nd Airborne were forced to retreat back across the Salm, and Major Yates and his men of the 51st and 291st were forced to blow the rebuilt bridge. At Stoumont on December 21, Peiper tried to force his way out of entrapment and head for

Belgian civilians massacred by the men of the 1st SS Panzer Division near Stavelot.

Targnon, but this action failed. On the 20th of December General Hodges had been able to obtain the 3rd Armored Division of General Maurice Rose to send a combat team into the battle of Trois Ponts, La Gleize, and Stoumont. Task force McGeorges went towards La Gleize by way of Cour, and Task Force Lovelady towards Trois Ponts.

At the Sanitarium of Stoumont, Peiper had been holding out with his tanks and infantry. Two of the infantry battalions of the 119th Regiment had battled with Peiper and were defeated, and the battalion commander, Major Hal McCown had been captured. The battles here were causing the civilian population in this area many hardships. The sanitarium basement was the cover for many of these wonderful people.

During the afternoon of the 20th of December and the full day of the 21st, Task Force Lovelady of the 3rd Armored Division had fully separated Peiper's forces from those of SS Pazer Knittel and 1st SS Regiment Hansen. Knittel and Hensen forces were being suddenly reduced by the combined infantry and tanks of the Americans. Just before this period the Petite Spa bridge has gone down as a result of overloading with an armored vehicle much in excess of the bridge's 3-ton capacity. The Germans were now in trouble since the blowing of the Stavelot bridge by Lt. Cofer of the 105th Engineers, and no other bridges on the Salm or Ambleve Rivers were intact. It would now be only a short time before the 117th Regiment, the 82nd Airborne, and the 3rd Armored Division, would wipe out the forces of Knittel and Hansen. And so they did by the night of the 22nd of December.

All that was left to wipe out by Task Force Jordan at Stoumont and Task Force McGeorges at Cheneux, La Gleize, and the village of Roanne was the remaining dwindling forces of Peiper and Sandig, both of Mohnke's 1st SS Panzer Division. The 117th Regiment, the 504th Airborne, and the 119th Infantry, along with the engineers of the 105th all were able to eliminate the bulk of the Peiper armor and troops by the evening of the 21st of December. He became entirely surrounded and all that he had left were foot soldiers and they were in the castle Froidcouer.

The battle at the Sanitarium at Stoumont was greatly aided by the American 740th Tank Battalion which fired about 50 of its 155 mm. self propelled artillery shells into the German defenses at the sanitarium. The 105 Engineers built a corduroy road over a wet spot from the snow to get the tanks of the 740th into position. The job was completed by midnight and four tanks headed for the sanitarium. They fired their guns point blank into the windows and routed the German Infantry and tanks with great loss to the enemy.

To Father Hanlet and the civilians in the basement, the silence that followed was eerie, almost as terrifying as the incessant explosion of shells they had so long endured. One shell had even penetrated a wall in the basement and had lodged among one of the supporting arches, but in a large chorus of rosaries it had failed to explode.

Father Hanlet rushed upstairs. The Germans had gone! He was confident the Americans would arrive soon, and Merci Dieu, not one of his charges, had been hurt. Furthermore the seriously wounded American to whom the Priest had performed last rites was still alive and holding his own. Stepping across the stiff bodies of fallen Americans and Germans, Father Hanlet paused to say a prayer for the dead. This was the beginning of many years of warm relationships between the Belgian citizens of the area and the Americans who came to free their country.

It was close to mid-morning when General Harrison, the deputy commander of the 30th Division, noticed the absence of German activity in the sanitarium and directed his forces to attack towards Stoumont; however, they soon learned that Peiper was now concentrating his forces at La Gleize. At noon on the 21st of December, Peiper had called his commanders to his headquarters at the farm house near the Chateau de Froidcouer and told them his plan.

Another of Skoreny's tanks is knocked out during the battle of December 21st.

Since the Americans had already demonstrated that they could cut the highway connecting La Gleize and Stoumont, and the American paratroops of General Gavin on the other side of the Ambleve might cut the dirt road linking the two places, he intended to avoid the risk of having his force split by falling back on La Gleize. There he would await reinforcements from the rest of the 1st SS Panzer Division. Or, if that failed, attempt to return to German lines.

In preparation for the withdrawal, Peiper ordered all American prisoners of war and German walking wounded to move from the Chateau-de-Froid-Couer to the cellars in La Gleize. Seriously wounded Americans and Germans were left in charge of a German Medical Sergeant and two American aid men. Also left behind on a whitewashed wall in one of the basement rooms was a charcoal drawing of Christ with thorns on his head and tears on his cheeks—whether drawn by a German or an American no one will ever know.

Froid-Couer is the home of the Georges de Harenne family, and I have had the pleasure of visiting at their home along with British General Mike Reynolds many times.

In September 1944 on the occasion of the 50th anniversary of the freeing of the Belgians from the Nazis reign of terror, I again looked on this folly. The 99th "Checkerboard" Division had been magnificent in holding back three attacking divisions of the 6th Panzer Army from the very outset with excellent support of the Combat Engineers of Lt. Col. Neale, the 324th, the 254th, and the 146th. They also had support of four Field Artillery Battalions, the 370th, 371st, 372nd, and the 924th. The field artillery had pounded the Germans with over 8000 rounds of crashing shells.

The 2nd Infantry Division "The Indianhead" had pulled back from their attack towards the Roer River Dams to closely support the 99th Division as they were about to be overrun at Krinkheld and Rockerath. The experienced men of Major General Walter M. Robertson also had four Field Artillery Battalions and the 2nd Engineer Combat Battalion established a solid engineer barrier line at the Elsenborn Ridge and thence west through Bullingen. The Germans never penetrated their defenses.

The 1st Division "The Big Red One" of Brig. General Clift Andrus had formed on the defensive line at the right flank of the 2nd Division and had established Engineer roadblocks that were never penetrated from Butgenbach to Waimes. Their four field artillery battalions were the 5th, 7th, 32nd, and 33rd. The 1st Division artillery had coordinated with the 12th, 15th, 37th, and 38th Field Artillery units of the 2nd Infantry Division.

The coordination between these three divisions during the period from the 17th to the 21st of December made it so that many attempts of the Volkestorm and Panzer Divisions ended up in total failure with great loss of men and tanks. The 12th SS Panzer Division was one of General Dietrich's crack Divisions and it had lost many men and tanks in their efforts to break out through Waimes, Malmedy and Spa which was their assigned route of advance to the Meuse River. Theirs was the assignment of the northern routes of the 1st SS Panzer spearheading Corps to the Meuse River.

22

The Defeat of the 1st SS Panzer Division and Peiper's End

On the 21st of December, Peiper found himself hopelessly surrounded by the forces of the 30th Division who had battered his troops in Stoumont. The 3rd Armored Division, with two task forces, were cutting into his lines with tanks and tank destroyers. The 82nd Airborne was gradually wiping out his armor and infantry as he is forced to withdraw what is left of the unit into the village of La Gleize. On the eastern fringe of La Gleize, where his last headquarters existed, Peiper was conscious of the terrible pounding his men, and his wounded, were taking.

The battle proved disastrous for not only Peiper's men, but for the civilians and the Americans alike. Homes, churches, and even sanitariums had been smashed by crashing artillery and bombing from the air strikes. Knocked out tanks and military equipment of all types were left where the battles ended. To describe the battles and the heroism of the American soldiers can best be stated in one word—courageous.

Wreckage of Combat Group Peiper in La Gleize.

Panther knocked out in the center of La Gleize village.

Peiper's attack into Stoumont.

Colonel Jochen Peiper, Commander of Kampfgruppe (Combat Group) Peiper.

On the 22nd of December, Peiper asked for permission by radio to break out. He stated that he could do it on foot, without vehicles or wounded. He was told he could break out if he brought his wounded and tanks. By December 23rd, Colonel Jochen Peiper, up at La Gleize, was almost out of supplies. Mohnke and Dietrich had tried everything in the book, including air drops and floating supplies down the Ambleve to him. Nothing succeeded in the attempt to get additional troops in to him. There was no bridge available to get tanks and armor across the Salm or the Ambleve. Engineers tried to build a bridge at Petite Spa but were shelled heavily by 30th Division artillery and were unsuccessful. Peiper had failed to bring his bridge company up with him on the 18th, a miscalculation which had a disastrous effect on his operation.

The final battle at La Gleize did this!

The 3rd Armored Division Combat Command B sent a task force down into the Ambleve pocket near Trois Ponts. They were reinforced by the 117th Regiment of the 30th Division in Stavelot. The 30th Division's 120th Regiment's reserve battalion from Malmedy made the final attack against General Mohnke's troops and prevented them from reaching Peiper.

Peiper decided to escape his own way. He had an important prisoner, Major Hal McCown, commander of the 2nd Battalion 119th Regiment. Now Peiper sent for McCown and wanted to make a deal with him. He would release all American prisoners he had taken except McCown, if McCown would sign an agreement that when German wounded were sufficiently recovered, they would be released. If Peiper's men were returned to him, he would release McCown.

McCown told him that he had no authority to sign such an agreement and if he did it

Major Harold McCown was captured by Peiper and later escaped.

Another tank destroyed in La Gleize

Yet another Peiper loss at La Gleize.

would probably not be honored by American Commanders. Nevertheless Peiper insisted. McCown signed a document saying he had heard Peiper make this offer.

Peiper produced another American officer and both he and McCown signed the agreement. At 1:00 A.M. the following morning Peiper led what was left of his great Kampfgruppe, which had so arrogantly and so proudly ridden roughshod over so many. Eight hundred of Peiper's weary men, led by the Belgian farmer Paul Frolich, crossed the Ambleve River near La Vienne and hid under the cover of the forest.

Just before Peiper's decision to leave La Gleize and the castle Froid-Couer, the American command launched a heavy artillery barrage at his force in La Gleize. This was just before midnight and set the village ablaze. Pursuing their mission in the morning his remaining forces of the 1st SS Regiment made their last attack towards Coo, but in vain. The bridge at Coo was blown up by the 105th Engineers of Lt. Colonel Dunn, and this was the last way out for any of the remaining 1st SS forces.

Left behind was an unbelievable destruction of the family lives of these very kind and thoughtful Belgian people who had now suffered the pangs of German occupation for the third time since 1940. They experienced the sadness of death to loved ones. They bore witness first hand to the terrible use of tanks, artillery, and bombing from the air. Theirs was a situation whereby the very homes, farmlands and streets of their villages were the battleground. The destruction in the village of La Gleize could only be defined as "total." Even the church where the Sisters of Notre Dame de Namur had prayed were demolished, but with walls standing. There was much evidence of the massacre of Belgian citizens and

American soldiers in these villages as was revealed in the book written by Gerard Gregoire entitled "Fire, Fire, Fire" and positively disclosed in the war trials.

Peiper sent a soldier ahead to make sure that his group could make it safely across route N-23 and then head for the Salm River. After a short wait, the trooper returned and his group headed across N-23 and then headed for the Salm River. N-23 was the route Peiper needed badly through this area to get to the Meuse River, and it was denied to him at Habiemont. The weary battered column crossed N-23 just east of Basse and Haute Bodeux and the 291st Engineer Combat Battalion's headquarters. When the large group were crossing the highway, they were fired on by a small convoy of General Gavin's 82nd Airborne Division.

They then crossed the highway near St. Jacques and again there was a skirmish between Peiper's men and the 82nd Airborne which was adjusting its defensive line along the Salm River from Trois Ponts to Vielsalm. During this skirmish, Major Hal McCown escaped and was able to work his way back to the 119th Regiment. Peiper was then able to proceed on to the Salm River. The location was north of the bridge blown by Lt. "Bucky" Walters of A Company of the 291st Engineers. There were many of the troopers who failed to make it in the cold and snowy waters of the Salm. There was never a real count of those who drowned there, or of the numbers of those who were able to climb the heights into Wanne where the headquarters of General Wilhelm Mohnke of the 1st SS Panzer Division had been established.

German s try to get into the entrapped Peiper, but the bridge fails to be built due to the 30th Division artillery.

The 82nd Airborne moves into Tois Ponts.

During the retreat from La Gleize the SS column had just passed through the 505th Regiment of the 82nd Airborne. The amazing escape of Peiper also occurred when the 7th and 9th Armored Divisions were arriving at Vielsalm from their strategic withdrawal from St. Vith.

With the demise of Peiper and the wipe out of Skorzeny at Malmedy, we learned in Malmedy that Col. Von der Heydte, the noted paratroop leader of the German armed forces had surrendered to the 99th Division at the Elsenborn Ridge. He had a few of his men with him and had suffered a broken arm during his drop north of Malmedy on the 16th of December. At this point in time, on the entire northern segment of the "Battle of The Bulge", the First Army had come through with a great victory. The best troops of Hitler's armies had been soundly defeated and the German Generals knew that the possibility of reaching the Meuse River was gone. They had given up reaching Antwerp when Peiper was stopped.

Looking at the maps of Hitler's massive counter-offensive and overall plan it appears that the main offensive thrust was aimed through Malmedy: Spa, Liege, and thence on to Antwerp. Hitler had assigned this main thrust to his favorite commander, General Sepp Dietrich. A secondary thrust was assigned to Baron von Manteuffel, General of the 5th Panzer Army. Manteuffel's divisions were not considered as strong or well-equipped as those of Dietrich's.

Now is the time to take a good look at the actions on the 5th Army front of General Manteuffel.

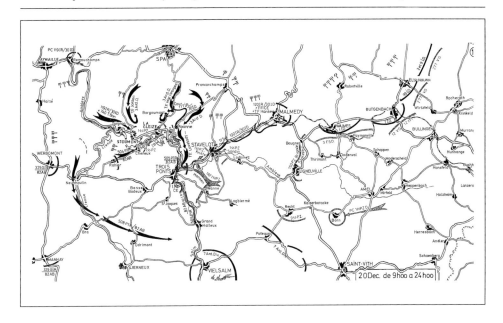

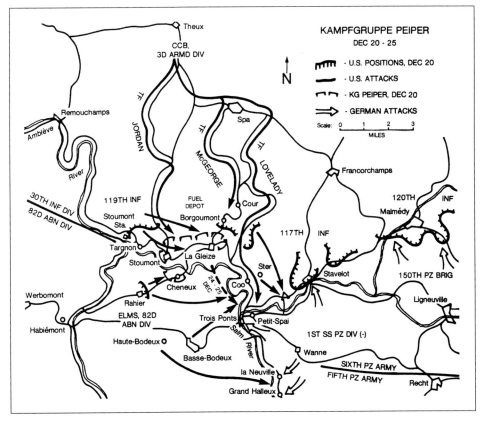

23

The Assault of the 5th Panzer Army

The Operational plan for the 5th Panzer Army of Hitler's "Wacht Am Rhein" shows two Corps attacking side by side with a direct thrust to cross the Meuse River on each side of Namur. The northern wing of the 5th Army was to drive through the Losheim Gap and the southern wing about 25 miles south. The 7th Army was to be in a blocking position on the left flank. The plan shows Bastogne in the 7th Army Zone.

The XLVII Panzer Corps consisted of the 7th Panzer Division, Panzer Lehr Division, and the 26th Volksgrenadier Division, all reinforced by one volkes mortar brigade, one volks artillery corps, and the 600th Engineer battalion for bridging purposes. According to intelligence information on the American side, none of the German divisions were up to strength since the losses during the retreat out of France and the effort to shore up the 6th Panzer Army for the main thrust.

The German losses at the beaches and the saturation bombing for the St. Lo breakout had reduced the divisions of the 5th Army as much as 30 percent. The 2nd Panzer Division had been in the rear area for four weeks to rest and refit.

The Panzer Lehr Division had just returned from the Saar area. It had 60 percent of its troops, 40 percent of its tanks and tank destroyers, 60 percent of its guns, and 40 percent of other weapons. One tank battalion had no tanks due to previous losses; the 26th Volksgrenadier Division was without one regiment, the remainder of the division was at full strength and had several senior commanders. Many subordinate commanders were without combat experience, and the division had not been trained in offensive operations, particularly the platoon and squad leaders existing. During the battles the casualty rate to lieutenants compared to company and battalion officers.

On the American side, the three divisions facing the 5th Panzer Army were not in any better shape in experience for several reasons. The 106th "Golden Lion" Infantry were new in line and still bringing up supplies of all types and were really not combat ready. They were just finding out how to go on patrol and coordinate the artillery and tank destroyers with the infantry. They did have time to learn about the terrain and river crossings which were somewhat foreign to the Germans. One advantage that the 106th had over the Germans was the well trained combat engineer battalion, the 81st, and corps engineer battalions such as the 168th that had excellent knowledge of the bridge locations and capacities.

The 28th and the 4th division had been in the battle of the Huertgen forest which was called by the GIs "the Death Factory." If ever there was a major mistake in the war in Europe by the top American brass, this battle along the dark forests of the Roer River and the Belgian-German border was it.

American infantry battalions were fed into the forest against the well dug-in Nazis of Field Marshall Walter Model. This was in an area where the 291st were maintaining the mainline of resistance into the forest itself. This was a platoon of C Company commanded by Lt. John Perkins and the platoon Sergeant was Ed Keoghan. The headquarters was at Sourbrodt where they also operated a saw mill. When I visited the platoon and learned about this attempt to capture the Roer River dams through the Huertgen and started down the skyline drive into the forest, I quickly realized what Perkins and Keoghan had advised. Its no place for man or animal.

Here was fifty square miles of rugged, hilly woods lying on the German-Belgian border below the city of Aachen. From September 1944 to February 1945, a new American division of infantry was fed into those dark green somber woods. It was not tank country; however, Model had set up a solid defense of infantry, artillery, mortars, tanks, and tank destroyers.

A couple of weeks later another division was sent into the forests to relieve the previous troopers. The shocked, exhausted survivors would be pulled out, with great gaps in their battered ranks. Comrades around them had died by the hundreds. The Germans had the upper hand throughout. The 9th, the 4th, and the 28th infantry divisions had all been

A 5th Panzer Army goal—the Meuse River Bridge at Hiey.

subjected to this most dangerous phase of the war in Europe. By the end, 30,000 Americans died or were wounded there and many thousand more cracked and went down with combat exhaustion. Now here on the German-Belgian border were two of those divisions being refitted and many positions being refilled by new men from squads up to battalion level. Organizations later assigned to the German XLVII Corps in operations around Bastogne would arrive in poor condition, with strengths ranging from 50 to 70 percent. These included the 9th and 116th Panzer Divisions, the 3rd and 115th Panzergrenadier Divisions and the Fuhrer Begleit (Escort) Brigade.

The one glaring difference in the German unit structure when on the attack was the failure to have engineers (Pioneers) come forward and quickly rebuild blown bridges while their bridge sites were under artillery fire. Their pioneers were very efficient in blowing the bridges and laying mines when their troops were retreating as was the case across France and into Belgium, Holland, and Luxembourg. The blitzing armored spearheads like Peiper's depended on the capture of the bridges in the attack as was the case at Stavelot, Trois Ponts and Habiemont.

For the 5th Panzer Army's effort, General Manteuffel planned to have his two Panzer Corps attack abreast. The 58th Panzer Corps, commanded by General Walter Kruger, was to attack on either side of the border village of Duren, on the Our River 10 miles south of St. Vith. It would then cross the northern reaches of the ridge line the Americans knew as the Skyline Drive and jump the Meuse River, just down the bend from Namur.

The 47th Panzer Corps, commanded by the General of the Panzertroops, Heinrich von Luttwitz, was to cross the Our River a few miles further south, jump the Skyline Drive, take the road center at Bastogne 19 miles beyond the German frontier, and seize the crossings of the Meuse upstream from Namur.

Each Panzer Corps had two divisions and the 5th Panzer Army had two Panzer Divisions acting as reserve when needed. Originally a part of the Pennsylvania National Guard, the 28th Division had been fighting since Normandy and had occurred such losses in the Huertgen that people had been calling its red shaped keystone patch "The Bloody Bucket." The division was holding such an elongated defensive front, that each of the Panzer Corps were destined to strike little more than a regiment.

In the north Kruger's 58th Panzer Corps faced a little more than 3000 or so of the men of the 112th Infantry Regiment, while von Luttwitz's 47th Panzer Corps faced the 110th Infantry Regiment. The Division's third Regiment, the 109th, was to become involved with the supporting attack of the 7th German Army.

On the Skyline Drive giving the engineer support to the 110th Infantry Regiment of the 28th Division was B Company of the 103rd Engineer Combat Battalion, with its command post located in Hosingen, Belgium. C Company with the 103rd was assigned to the 112th Regimental Combat Command. A Company was in support of the 109th Infantry Regiment.

These three companies had suffered many casualties in the battles of the Huertgen forest where they cleared mines under fire, blew pillboxes throughout the forests and fought at times as infantry. On this 16th day of December they had been heavily involved in keep-

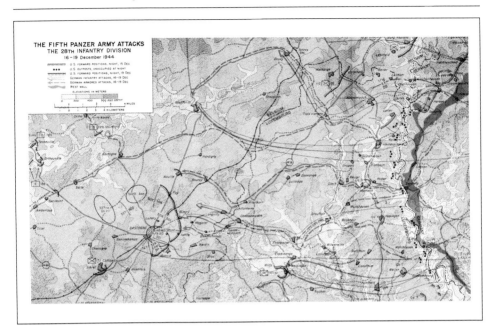

ing the road net open and clear of snow and ice. The roads were muddy trails with no hard surface.

They had also carried demolitions to the pillboxes along the Siegfried line and were subjected to small arms fire when they prepared to destroy the dangerous obstacles. Fortunately, they had received new recruits to fill in the vacancies caused by losses of engineers in the Huertgen. One of the difficulties of defending the 28th Division area was the location of the Our and the Clerve rivers, where the Germans had blown the bridges in their retreat into their homeland. The American engineers had built back many of them since their arrival in the area.

When the attack came the 112th Infantry were defending where Manteuffel had advised his divisions to attack without an opening salvo, so that the leading infantry could go up the draws between the widely spaced strong points. Like in the Huergen, the German soldier could move behind our lines in the wide gaps and attack the Americans from the rear. Their own patrols had learned after their arrival that there were no gaps in the Germans lines.

The 28th had kept a watchful vigilance in its "Quiet Sector" in the Ardennes. Their experience in the bloody forests of the Huertgen had taught them that. Foxholes were next to sleeping dugouts, patrols probing. The Germans with three armies massed on a 90 mile front and tried for a break through at the point they felt most thinly held: The Keystone Sector.

The mighty furor broke loose and the "Battle of The Bulge" began! The German mighty thrust hit the 110th Infantry Regimental Team in the center of the 28th Division sector.

Company "B" of the 103rd Engineer Combat Battalion bore the brunt of that exploding German counter-offensive. Company K of the 110th Infantry Regiment and Company B of the 103rd were encircled at Hosingen. Fighting their way out, the majority of the men of B Company were captured, wounded or killed. They had destroyed their equipment and inflicted many casualties on the enemy. Here and elsewhere on the 80 mile front, the Germans were throwing what looks like a Sunday punch at the American forces: battalions of Tiger Tanks, rocket artillery, Panzer, Volkgrenadier, and Parachute Divisions.

In the 112th Regiment sector across the Our River, heavy artillery fire was followed by strong armed forces and infantry in waves. By daylight on December 17th, enemy tanks and infantry from northeast and southeast penetrated the 1st Battalion area to support positions, kitchens, and command post. Company C engineers became fighting engineers as infantry to repel the enemy, joining forces with a composite company formed from the regimental training area. The counter attack slowed the enemy advance and the engineers later cleaned up enemy pockets. The Combat Team won the Presidential Citation for the gallant action.

The 109th team with Company A of the engineers held to its position for three days in the face of the powerful enemy onslaught. When darkness fell on December 18th, the 109th pulled back on high ground at Diekirch when the 9th withdrew, leaving both flanks exposed. The next afternoon, after repulsing a heavy attack that left 300 enemy dead and 80 prisoners captured, the 109th Combat Team was attached to the 9th Armored Division since contact with the 28th Division was cut off. This later placed them at the southern hinge of the bulge. Company "A" of the 103rd Engineers was given the assignment of blowing the bridges, creating craters, and laying mines to stall the advance.

In pressing the attack to the enemy, the 109th Combat Team coordinated their action and wiped out an estimated two battalions of enemy infantry and a battalion of field artillery. Just how long it would be before General von Luttwitz and his 47th Panzer Corps could get across the little Clerve River and begin traversing the 15 remaining miles to Bastogne depended primarily on the 28th Division's 110th Infantry, sorely pressed but holding at the end of the first days fighting along the Skyline Drive. It also depended to a lesser degree on what happened to the divisions other two regiments.

Whether the 109th Infantry could provide help to the central regiment depended in turn on the advance of the 5th Parachute Division of the Germans, the northernmost unit of the 7th Army. Once past the tier of small villages behind the Our River the Paratroopers were to aim for Wiltz, where the 28th Division's commander, General Dutch Cota, had his headquarters only 12 miles from Bastogne. That advance would take place along the seam between the two American regiments and at the seam, in the village of Hoschied atop the Skyline Drive. There was only a small American force: a section of the 110th Infantry's Anti-Tank Company with three Shermans and the 707th Tank Battalion's assault gun platoon, six Shermans mounting 105 mm. howitzers.

At 2:30 a.m. of December 17th, General Cota notified the 109th Infantry Commander, Colonel Rudder, in Ettlebruck, that earlier in the night several German assault guns had

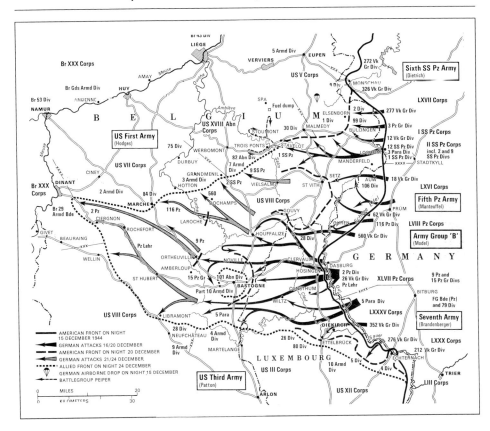

crossed the Our on a weir at Vienden, and with a Parachute battalion had moved up a winding road toward the Skyline Drive and Hoschied. That looked to Cota like the Germans intended taking Hoschied, and then to cut off Rudder's Regiment. Cota instructed Rudder to send a platoon each of infantry and tanks to reinforce Hoschied.

The tanks and soldiers riding on them failed to make it, for the Germans had already cut the Skyline Drive south of the village. The tanks, assault guns, and men of the anti-tank company fought as infantry and held throughout the day but at nightfall, almost out of ammunition, the foot troops climbed aboard vehicles and fell back to Wiltz with the 687th Field Artillery Battalion. The stand at Hoschied had delayed the Parachute Division for a day, but at that point the Paratroopers had split the two American Regiments. From then on the 109th Regiment would be totally involved in trying to prevent the Germans from expanding the southern shoulder of their penetration.

At the other end of the Skyline Drive, where the 112th Infantry was on the German side of the Our River, and where the Germans had failed on the first day to get a bridge over the river at Ouren, the Americans through the night could hear the noise of German tanks. The German Engineers had caused a full days delay when it took them more than 24 hours to build a bridge. Here also was a case where the Germans failed to capture a bridge before the

American engineers had blown it. In many cases the German heavy tanks would arrive at the bridge site and they would have to stop and search for a bridge location that would carry their 45 and 60 ton tanks. Failing to use their combat engineers was obvious from the very beginning of their major offensive. Delays were caused by trying to relocate their route of advance, and it took ten hours to break up the jammed columns and move an engineer company from the rear. A quick reconnaissance would have revealed in advance the condition of the bridge.

A battalion of the 116th Panzer Division was moving into the village of Lutzkampen for renewed attack before daylight on the 17th. Through much of the night searchlights played against the clouds, keeping the American line in a kind of twilight and helping volksgrenadiers and panzergrenadiers to move into attack positions.

Continuing the battle of the 17th, von Manteuffel's 5th Panzer Army was joined by the tanks of the 2nd Panzer Division, which after crushing American resistance in Marnach were pushing on to west of the town of Clervaux. The Americans who barred their way west was the 110th Regiment and its engineers.

By now the 110th Regiment had been repeatedly penetrated and greatly out-numbered, and was surrounded and under continuous assault. As darkness fell, German tanks thrust through the Americans in the ancient castled town of Clervaux, and seized the bridge over the Clerve River.

Just to the south, the 26th Volkesgrenadier Division was still waging a war of position against stubborn U.S. defenders just west of the Our River. Although the Grenadiers could not force their way into the road intersection at Hosingen, they did manage to seize a bridgehead across the Clerf River at Drauffelt. The American garrison did not give up until the following day. Amid a terrible traffic bottleneck at the recently completed Gemund bridge—one of the few the German engineers were able to build under fire—the Panzer Lehr Division wormed across the river with its recon battalion.

On the other side Kampfgruppe Kaufmann, the combined elements of the left hand regiment of the 26th and Lehr recon battalion, engaged the American company bravely defending the villages of Holzthum and Consthum. Ownership of the villages was vital to the German cause, controlling the roads as they did leading into the Skyline Drive. On the American side, the commander of the VIII Corps, General Troy Middleton, agreed with General Cota to withdraw the 110th Infantry behind the Clerve with the idea of forming a new delaying line west of the river. But that approval was too late. Col. Hurley Fuller, the commander, and almost all of the regiment except Colonel Strickler and the remnants of the 3rd battalion in Consthum, plus uncommitted Company G were about all the 110th Infantry could still contribute as an organized force to further delay the onrushing Germans. All that Middleton had to throw into the fight were three engineer combat battalions, a separate armored field artillery battalion, and the 9th Armored Division's Combat Command Reserve.

It was precious little with which to delay three German divisions, including two Panzer divisions, long enough to allow the 10th Armored Division's Combat Command B and the

101st Airborne Division to get to Bastogne. Not until late afternoon on the 18th would Middleton know if the Combat Team would reach the town, and it might be well into the night before the first airborne troops arrived, which meant only the next day could he get any of the airborne troops into the line of defense.

Middleton sent one of the engineer combat battalions (The 44th) to help Cota at Wiltz, and the other two (The 35th and the 158th) to form a barrier line of road blocks in villages just beyond the eastern periphery of Bastogne. Earlier assigned to the general support of the 28th Division, the 58th Armored Field Artillery battalion was to support all units in front of Bastogne. Having also ordered the 9th Armored Division's CCR from Trois Vierges to an assembly area closer to Bastogne, Middleton, with his Corps Hdqs. in Bastogne, told Colonel Joseph H. Gilbreth, the commander of 9th Armored, to establish road blocks in front of Bastogne in order to stay the onrushing Germans.

As yet not tested in battle the 9th Armored's CCR had the usual components of a combat command: a battalion each of armored infantry, medium tanks, and armored field artillery. They had a company each of self-propelled tank destroyers, armored engineers, and aircraft artillery. Yet the fighting had already drawn off a portion of Colonel Gilbreth's command, a platoon of tank destroyers to help the 112th Infantry in Ouren, another to help the 110th Infantry at Clervaux, and a company of medium tanks appropriated by General Cota to help the 110th, of which only three survived.

The courageous actions of the combat engineers involved in the defense of Bastogne were not the only highlights of the battle of Bastogne, so were the delays and the stopping at times of the 5th Panzer Army from the Siegfried line to Bastogne itself.

The 103rd Engineers were a battalion assigned and organic to the 28th National Guard Division, and at one time part of three battalions making up the 103rd Engineer Regiment of the 28th Division. When the Regiment was part of the Division under General Omar Bradley, Colonel H. Wallis Anderson was the Regimental Commander. They had been trained under Anderson.

The battalion had a unique history, having fought in World War I and now in World War II; it had been decorated highly in each of its war experiences and one of the companies had received the Presidential Citation.

The actions of the engineers of all three companies had been told at a reunion in 1986. The incidents that members of each company describe cover actions in the Huertgen as well as the battles against Hitler's attacking Panzer and Volkestorm Divisions.

Much of the action in the Huertgen was in the attack whereby the engineers were requested by the tank commanders and Infantry commanders to spearhead the attack with mine detectors and open up the heavily mined roads. Ted Behuiak, "A" Company, John Gilmore, "B" Company, and Dick Minton, "C" Company described this action in this manner: "We were always concerned to be out in front of the infantry on these occasions of leading the attack with mine detectors and wire probes to remove the buried mines. Many of the mines were prepared to include booby traps attached to certain mines. The Germans would then line up snipers to fire on the men in the attack.

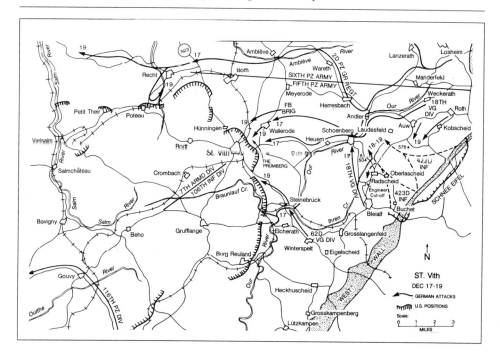

"Without rifles or any weapons we had to depend on the infantry to give us covering fire. We suffered many casualties during this mine clearing detail. It was much safer when clearing the roadway for tanks, because when fired on by the enemy we were able to take cover behind the tanks. In the Huertgen this was the most difficult either way because of the dense forest and the hiding place for snipers."

Elmer Schneider of A Company describes an incident whereby the Germans had left a small damaged German vehicle out on a road in a mined area. The squad leader for Company A tried to move it off the road with his shoulder; however, the Germans had placed a mine hidden under a front wheel. "The explosion killed our Sergeant."

Frank Morrisey, C Company, describes the actions of a detail to blow heavy concrete pill boxes and dragons teeth along the Siegfried line. "The battalion commander, Lt. Colonel Seig of the 103rd, would receive instructions to send a detail up to the line just beyond the dragon's teeth and get rid of a pill box used by the Germans to fire on the 28th Divisions dug-in infantry. A ten-man team would each carry fifty pounds of TNT in a sack and two men would take reels of wire, primacord, and an explosive cap. The movement was always up hill to the boxes overlooking the enemy. This made the trip not only dangerous, but tiresome. The operation was always done under cover of darkness.

"On an extremely cold night our unit was given this task to perform. As we moved slowly up the road wet with fine snow, we were fired on by Germans within 30 yards of the pillbox by rifle fire. One of our men was struck on the shoulder, but fortunately we were able to rollover in the ditch and lay quiet for 30 minutes. We then quickly moved up and placed our TNT, hooked up the primacord, inserted a six inch cap, and pulled the plug. This gave us 15 seconds to move back. The explosion was loud and clear as we escaped with one wounded man."

Thus in the race to Bastogne, the 110th Regiment and its company of the 103rd engineers, against ten to one odds, had delayed, thwarted, and despaired the movement of a full German Corps. The individual soldiers of the 110th broke up in small groups and walked many hazardous miles to the west towards Bastogne. Many were captured, some were killed and wounded, some just disappeared, never to be heard from. Unfortunately, there was no medal that could apply to these American soldiers.

24

The 44th Engineer Combat Battalion
and the Defense of Wiltz

On October 1, 1944 the 44th Engineer Combat Battalion arrived at Houf-falize, Belgium and established Battalion and Company Headquarters in the forest a few miles outside the city. From this time on the battalion received many missions in the support of infantry divisions located in the area of Malmedy, Bastogne, Marche, Grandmenil, and Vielsalm.

On October 14th, the Battalion Commander, his staff, and all Company commanders were called to 2nd Division Headquarters at St. Vith, and the battalion was given a new mission by Major General Robertson. The monumental tasks was to prepare fortifications for the 23rd Regiment of the 2nd Infantry Division. The task required construction of:

1. 41 machine gun emplacements
2. 34 Tobruk shelters-covered and enclosed
3. 58 squad shelters- covered and enclosed
4. 1375 feet of trenches
5. 7 company command posts- covered and enclosed
6. 6 company kitchens
7. 2 battalion command posts
8. 9000 yards of tactical barbed wire and 8925 feet of mine fields.

The line companies moved their hdqs. near the mission site and began preparing for the mission ahead. Many difficulties were encountered before the mission was completed. Weather and material procurement was least difficult — but doing this work at times under fire and it made it necessary to do the work at night. The men received very little sleep due to the great need to protect the on line infantry.

A deadline was set for this mission for 1 November, 1944, and it was completed 2 days before the deadline. The battalion after receiving a commendation from General Robertson then moved their battalion CP in the area around Vielsalm, Belgium and continued its operations throughout its engineer assigned area.

Much of this work took them into Luxembourg and locations along the American defensive lines. This included the positions of the 28th, 4th, and 2nd Infantry along the Siegfried line. This included fortifications for the 23rd Infantry of the 2nd Division in November. During the early part of December the American Armies came to a sudden halt. At this time is when the 44th saw the build up of the 4 Divisions along the Siegfried line.

At noon on 17 December 1944 the battalion was relieved of assignment to the 1107th Engineer Combat Group and assigned directly to the 28th Division. The battalion was assigned directly to the town of Wiltz, Luxembourg. This was due to the situation on the 28th Division's front along the great German wall.

General Norman D. Cota's three regiments along the Siegfried line had been attacked on the morning of December 16th. The 110th Infantry had formed a defensive line in depth with strong points of company strength at Marnach, Clervaux, the Regimental Hdqs., Weiler,

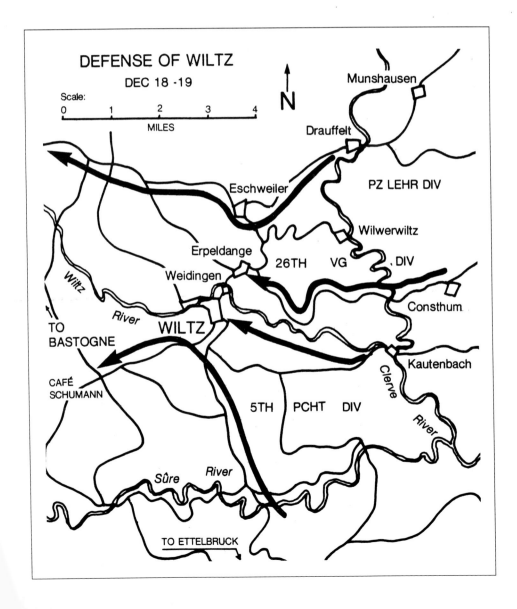

Hosingen, and Conthsum. The Regiment also had some other defensives held in platoon or squad strength along the front and at crossroads and bridges. Artillery of the 28th Division's 110th Regiment was located on high ground in order to give support to the main strong points.

The fighting was bitter when the units of the Fifth Panzer Army attacked into the center of the 110th Regiment of the 28th " Bloody Bucket " Division. and only a few strong points had been taken by the vastly superior numbers of men and tanks on the German side. The men of the 110th Regiment fought throughout the day with determination, but yielded ground only when they had been overrun. At the end of the first day, the 15th of December, the Americans held but time was running out.

On Friday night on December 15th, the 44th Engineers bedded down in their sleeping bags after completing another day of duties in their assigned area. No one dreaming that something was due to happen. The general topic of conversation at that time was planning for some type of Christmas celebration or the pulling out of the line of the veteran 2nd Infantry Division. The 44th had worked closely with the 2nd which was being replaced in the line by the 106th Golden Lion Division.

At about 10:00 A.M. on December 16th orders were received from VIII Corps placing the 44th Engineers on a two hour alert and converting them from engineers to infantry. At 11:30 A. M. several men from the 106th Division reported that they had been overrun east of St. Vith and they were the only ones who had escaped. They had occupied a part of the defensive positions constructed by the 44th Engineers for the 23rd Infantry, 2nd Division.

At 2:00 P.M. the 44th was taken off the two hour alert and placed on a six hour alert and the 44th was to operate as engineers and infantry. During Saturday night there was an increased amount of troop movement through Vielsalm. This was the 7th Armored Division enroute to the aid of the 106th Division at St. Vith.

On Sunday December 17th at 10:00 A.M., Lt. Col. Clarion J. Kjeldseth, received orders to move out, destination, Bastogne. The mission of the 44th was to form a semi-circle around Bastogne along with two other engineer battalions.

About 12:50 the advance party moves out. At 2:00 P.M. The rest of the Battalion moved out, destination Bastogne. Before the 44th reached Noville, a messenger from VIII Corps contacted Col. Kjeldseth and changed the mission of the 44th. The orders were — Move to the Clerf River: join up with the 707th Tank Battalion Artillery supporting the 28th Division and secure the west end of the bridge at Drauffelt. Before the 44th could move out, Col. Winslow, VIII Corps Engineer, contacted the Battalion Commander, and again changes the mission of the 44th.

The reasons for this change was that the bridges at Drauffelt and Clervaux had been captured by the Germans and tanks and troops were already on the banks of the Clerf River in force. The 44th Engineer Combat Battalion along with the 707th Tank Battalion along with 6 tanks, five self-propelled assault guns, and four towed three-inch anti-tank guns, were ordered to Wiltz.

The battles along the Siegfried line from Monschau to Echternach now appeared to be changing minute by minute and was developing to be the largest battle in the war in Europe in an area where the Germans had crashed into Belgium four other times.

About 5:30 P.M. on the 17th of December the 44th Engineers closed on Wiltz, and Lt. Col. Kjeldseth and Major Goodloe R. Stuck reported to Major General Norman D. Cota, Commanding Officer, 28th Division. General Cota assigned the following troops to the 44th; One provisional company (made up of band members, cooks and clerks) which was attached to the 3rd platoon, Company C, Lt. Bruck, commanding. platoon of riflemen, and additional troops that had been assigned by Col. Winslow.

At about 6:30 P.M., Lt Col. Hoban handed over to Lt. Col. Kjeldseth the defense of the City of Wiltz. All of the troops which were in the city came under his command. At this time all of the information on friendly or enemy troops to the east were non-existent.

Col. Kjeldseth called his staff together to draw up a plan for the defense of Wiltz!

Company A commanded by Captain Donald McConnell, will form a defensive line north and northeast of the City, with 1st and 2nd lines of defense. Company C, commanded by Captain Charles Lachman, will form 1st and 2nd lines of defense east and Northeast joining with Company A. Company B, commanded by Captain Thomas P. Johnson, will be held in reserve and only be released On orders of the battalion commander. Food and ammunition was to be distributed by the S-4, Captain Maurice R. Smith. Communications was to be established by all units of the battalion and to higher headquarters. The bridge across the Wiltz River was to be blown when necessary. This bridge was blown by Company A on Tuesday afternoon.

Captain Smith, S-4 delivered food and ammunition to the companies on Sunday evening. The rest of the night was spent on improving defensive positions, and the companies sent out some patrols. Three German soldiers were captured.

When these prisoners were interviewed by Major Goodloe Stuck and Sgt. Willeseh. It was learned that the 26th Volkesgrenadier Division, one regiment of armored recon from Panzer Lehr Division and supported infantry were in front of the engineers to the east and northeast of Wiltz. At this time the 5th Parachute Division had not been identified on the intelligence maps.

When the 44th Engineers closed on Wiltz and were in place a provisional battalion hastily was formed from the 28th Division headquarters, about 200 men were withdrawn from Wiltz. Backing up the 44th Engineers were six crippled tanks and 5 assault guns from the battered 707th Tank Battalion, which had been fighting in Wilerwiltz. Here were six three inch towed tank destroyers from the 630th tank destroyer battalion and one battery of artillery from the 687th Field Artillery Battalion, consisting of three guns.

On Monday, with the capture of Consthum and the capitulation of the strong point at Hosingen, the threat of the Panzer Lehr Division main supply route was removed. One of the Panzer Lehr Divisions Recon Regiments, the 902nd, advancing by way of Munshausen now cleared of American troops, at the crossroads east of Eschweiler, the 902nd turned left and bore down on Wiltz.

German field artillery now west of the Clerf River opened fire on Wiltz at noon. About two hours later tanks and self-propelled guns struck the 44th Engineers. Just prior to this attack Company B was committed to the line. The few tanks, three to be exact, supporting the engineers were quickly overrun by the mobile German tanks. The engineers held their fire for the German infantry following the tanks. The deadly fire from the rifles and machine guns of the engineers along with American Howitzers south of Wiltz slowed the German advance. At dusk the weight of the German Armor was too great to be held in check and the engineers were ordered to fall back behind the Wiltz River. For some reason the pressure on the 44th eased briefly as the 902nd Recon Regiment turned north and joined its division. Infantry of the 26th Volksgrenadier Division took over the attack.

Wiltz lay on the boundary line which divided the attack zones of the 47th Panzer Corps and the 85th Corps, the 5th Parachute Division had lost control and instead of by-passing Wiltz on the 19th attacked Wiltz from the south. It would seem that this was a planned attack along with the 26th Volksgrenadier Division that would attack Wiltz on the 19th of December from the north and east. The two divisions attacking Wiltz at the same time was not planned. But it did happen !!!

On the morning of the 19th, the headquarters of the 28th Division moved from Wiltz to Sibret, Southwest of Bastogne. As the 26th Grenadiers began their flanking move to the North, the engineers were not concerned because they were expecting help from the tanks of the 10th Armored Division, a combat command on the American side. The 10th never arrived !!! This was a severe blow to the defenders of Wiltz.

The Germans on the north side of town moved in on the attack, and at 2:00 P.M. they attacked and drove the provisional troops left by the 28th, to stand with the Engineers, off the ridge. Company A of the 44th had their left flank exposed as a result. A Cavalry unit also on Company A's left flank pulled out also.

The 44th was hit from the east and northeast by infantry armed with machine pistols charging in alongside tanks. As the riflemen and gunners cut down the German assault teams, they saw their own ranks thinning. According to Captain Leo F. Miller, 44th engineers, the important road junction at Erpeldange changed hands four times in less than four hours. Captain Miller recalled later, "They would bring tanks right up to the road junction and drive us back and then we would regroup and drive them out. They all seemed to be equipped with machine pistols, but they seemed to fear our 50 caliber machine gun fire. I saw some Germans that it just tore up."

At the same time the 26th Volksgrenadiers were attacking from the north and northeast, the 5th Parachute began to attack from the south and southeast. The bitter fighting during the afternoon and evening of the 19th was as General Cota described in his commendation to the 44th. "Due to the nature of the actions, these operations were the most difficult known to warfare."

When darkness finally came the 44th withdrew, with the remaining assault guns into the city of Wiltz. The 44th Engineer Combat Battalion had lost 4 officers and 150 men

44th Engineers building an infantry shelter along the Siegried Line for the 2nd Infantry Division.

during the afternoon action. When the 44th moved back the bridge was blown by Company A on orders from Captain Donald H. McConnell. The assault guns were left to cover the wrecked bridge. Their fate is unknown!

By dark the perimeter had been broken in several spots and the defenders pushed back into Wiltz. The tanks and assault guns were no longer usable. The tank crews and assault gun crews joined the 44th as riflemen. Ammunition was down to a few rounds per man and radio communications had completely broken down. The 44th engineers and men that had stood when their ammunition was down to their last rounds and at this hour Wiltz was surrounded with German infantry and mobile equipment.

An attempt was made by the 28th Division at Sibret to send help to Wiltz, but it never made it as it was totally destroyed at a road block about six miles from Wiltz. The account of this can be found in the Memoirs of Captain Smith, Lt. McCleod, Lt. Black and others.

Col. Strickler, an infantry battalion commander of the 28th Division would write in his book about the 44th Engineer Combat Battalion. "They sacrificed their lives doing the impossible for other Americans."

The 44th Engineers would hold in place and fight the rear guard action while the other personnel moved out. Those that attempted to use vehicles, in their attempt to leave Wiltz never made it. Many vehicles exploded when they hit the mines laid by the Germans in front of the road blocks. The 44th Combat Engineers the rear guard unit in Wiltz, probably suffered the most. The Germans accounting for 18 officers and 160 men, killed, wounded or captured during the withdrawal.

The rear guard action fought by the 44th on the night of the 19th was bitter with no quarters asked and none given by either the Americans or the Germans. These defenders after firing their last rounds broke up into small groups and attempted to reach the Allied lines cross country, mostly moving at night. Many of the 44th did succeed in reaching American lines.

The defense of Wiltz is but one example of many that took place along the front and behind the front during the Battle of The Bulge. The time bought by the Americans at Wiltz was costly. The 110th Regiment virtually destroyed, the men and fighting vehicles of 5 tank companies lost, the equivalent of three engineer companies killed or missing. Tank destroyer, artillery, and miscellaneous units wiped out in the action.

The Germans paid just as dearly if not more during this action. It is a certain fact that the attacking force receives many more casualties than the defensive force in their prepared fortifications. The defenders in this case fought with all they had until they had nothing left at all, in this small sector of the largest battle in American times.

25

The Battle on the Southern Shoulder and the 7th German Army

General Erich Brandenberger and his 7th Army were overlooked by Hitler when he passed out the new equipment and beefed up the 6th Panzer Army of General Sepp Dietrich. He was given nothing compared to the 5th Panzer Army of Hasso von Manteuffel. He had no Panzer Divisions under his command, and instead of it representing an army it could have represented a light German Corps. Brandenberger would be attacking with the 5th Parachute Division, the 352nd Volksgrenadier Division, the 276th Volksgrenadier Division, and the 212th VG Division.

These divisions were very much understaffed and had lost many of their troops in the mad dash across France and Belgium when they had many of their officers and men fall to the American and British Air Forces. Their retreating columns lost much of their equipment which Hitler failed to replace.

Facing the Germans was the 4th Infantry Division, the 9th Armored Division's Combat Command of Major General John W. Leonard, and the 109th Regiment of the 28th Division. Both of the divisions had been severely mauled in the battles in the Huertgen forest and were short of rifle strength and the replacements lacked combat experience. The 12th Infantry Regiment of the 4th Division had been burnt out. It had lost 1600 men in five days of combat in the Huertgen, which was half of its strength. The same day the 12th Infantry was withdrawn, 33 men of the 28th Division's 109th Infantry slipped exhausted into their own lines. They were the last survivors of a company that had been surrounded for five bitter days, without food or drink, and with only the ammunition they carried on their person. In snow and sleet, fighting from foxholes knee deep in mud, they had battled against everything the Germans threw against them. They were the last men of the shattered 28th Division to see combat in the Huertgen.

One part of the Huertgen battle was the second attack on the village of Schmidt which became the most costly division-strength attack in the whole of WWII. In one regiment alone, the 112th Infantry, there had been 232 men captured, 431 missing, 719 wounded, 167 killed and 544 non-battle casualties, making a total of 2093 out of the original 3000 men who had gone into action two weeks before. Many of these men were combat engineers.

Now, here on the south shoulder of the German counter-offensive the same divisions were in line against four German Divisions. Fortunately the American side had some armor and the Germans had all infantry.

One unfortunate part of the bulge battle was that Hitler had successfully moved two Panzer Armies into the area facing the Belgian Ardennes and the border of Luxembourg. There had been a complete breakdown of intelligence, and the divisions placed in line were the least experienced or physically equipped to withstand the onslaught of two Panzer Armies. The Germans had become aware of this situation both north and south of the American 85 mile front of the Siegfried line where the 99th, the 106th, the 28th, and the 4th Infantry Divisions were in a stretched out line. The German intelligence could easily send Germans in American uniforms behind the lines and seek out the location and strengths of the American units. In fact, Colonel Otto Skorzeny was able to send his forces under cover to points along the Skyline Drive and capture men and equipment. Tom Williams, the 1111th Engineer Group's supply officer was captured there along with his jeep. Later he was found at a prisoner of war camp at Wolfsburg, Germany. This was where Skorzeny had obtained the jeeps for his German-in-American-uniform patrols, who had worked their way behind American lines.

Most of the Americans who had spent time in the Ardennes since September wondered why we didn't attack before the Germans found this big hole in our lines. This would have been a much more feasible area than the Huertgen, or Patton's area of attack south of Luxembourg.

On the southern shoulder of the German offensive, among the frontier villages, forests, and rolling hills between the southern reaches of the Skyline Drive and the Our River and below the confluence of the Our and the Sure, on either side of the Ernz Noire, the Americans were having their difficulties at the start of the second day of the big battle. Yet they were better off than their colleagues elsewhere, primarily because they were facing no German armor. The German Divisions were having problems throwing bridges across the Our and the Sure in order to bring forward such fire support as they did possess: horse-drawn division artillery and the under strength battalion of self-propelled assault guns.

The 103rd Combat Engineers and the 4th Division Engineers had blown the bridges before the arrival of the Germans. The German Pioneers (Engineers) had failed to move up with the infantry to replace the blown bridges. Also there were mines to clear and blown craters which were delaying the attacking Germans.

Although the 109th Infantry's Commander, Colonel Rudder had committed his reserved infantry battalion to rescue the entrapped Company E that was surrounded in Fouhren, he still had medium tanks of the 707th Tank Battalion to add weight to the renewal of that effort. During the night the 60th Armored Infantry Battalion, in line to gain the battle experience, had reverted to its parent command, the 9th Armored's CCA, and the bulk of the commands tanks and self-propelled destroyers were to enter the fight.

On the high plateau east of the Ernz Noire, generally along the highway linking the Echternach and Luxembourg city, the 12th Infantry's commander Colonel Chance had committed the rest of his reserve battalion; but the commander of the 4th Division, Tubby Barton, had arranged to borrow a company of medium tanks from the 9th Armored's CCA, which at daybreak on December 17th began moving to Luxembourg from the section of 3rd Army in northeastern France. The combat command was to become available at the start of the 3rd day, December 18th.

American commanders intended on the second day, December 17th, to use their local reserves to rescue surrounded units, strengthen threatened units, and block exits from the gorge of the Ernz Noire leading into the rear of units on each side. Rudder and the 109th Infantry was to rescue Company E in Fourhen; Collins of the 60th Armored Infantry was to block roads leading into his rear from the Ernz Noire and maintain contact with his line companies on the wooded heights overlooking the Sure River; and Chance of the 12th Infantry was to rescue the men of Company F in the Parc Hotel outside of Berdorf and the men of Company E in Echternach. They were also to reinforce the hard pressed men of the 3rd Battalion southeast of Echternach in Osweiler and Dickweiler.

In the northern part of the 109th Infantry's sector, the commander of the 85th Corps, General Kneiss, was trying to break the 5th Parachute Division loose in order to lean on the advance of the adjacent Panzer Lehr Division. The Germans were content to bypass most isolated defensive positions in favor of pushing on to the Skyline Drive. Yet if they were to open the road for their drive to the west, they had to have Hoscheid on the Skyline Drive. That's what had led to the day-long fight for the village, ending after nightfall with the American withdrawal. A road westward at last available, the 5th Parachute Division became in effect an adjunct for the 5th Panzer Army's drive to the Muese River.

The situation for the 5th Parachute Division at Hoscheid was similar to that of the 352nd Volksgrenadier Division at Fouhren. The Volksgrenadiers needed the village in order to gain access to the valley of the Sure River at Diekirch and their assigned road leading west; but without support from assault guns it was difficult to force the 109th Infantry's Company E from Fouhren.

103rd Engineers planting mines after blowing the bridge.

Because of American artillery fire, it was late in the night of December 17th before a bridge was in place to allow assault guns to cross the Our River. Trying to rebuild the bridge under fire, which had been blown by Company A of the 103rd Engineer Combat Battalion, the German engineers had not come up soon enough to get the job done. Even though the two American companies trying to gain Fouhren had help from a platoon of medium tanks, the Volksgrenadiers managed to prevent them from breaking through to the village.

When company E radioed in some desperation requests for food and ammunition, Colonel Rudder ordered a patrol to get through after nightfall. But again Fouhren remained out of reach. The last word from Company E came by radio one hour after midnight. When a patrol from the I&R platoon, accompanied by a tank, got within 200 yards of the village at daylight the men saw that the house that had served as the company command post had burned to the ground. Company E, 109th Infantry had ceased to exist.

The collapse at Fouhren meant increased pressure on the 109th's 3rd Battalion close by, in the angle formed by the confluence of the Our and the Sure Rivers, for it left that battalion's left flank exposed. Eliminating that battalion was critical to the German advance, for it was forward observers who were directing the shelling of the 352nd's bridge site. This was delaying the Hitler minnion's advance. At dawn on December 18th, a German regiment hit the 3rd Battalions North flank and surrounded and captured a platoon of Company K, but the Battalion held. Despite that stand the positions of the 109th Infantry of Colonel Rudder were fast becoming untenable, for there was no way to halt the German movement between the widely spaced American positions. By midday of December 18th, German forces the size of companies and even battalions were moving with impunity behind the American held villages.

Here and there they overwhelmed outposts trying to fill the gaps between villages: a brace of 57 mm. anti-tank guns, a few men from C Company fighting as infantry, and a squad of A Company of the 103rd Engineers guarding a well prepared road block crater. As early as the pre-dawn hours of December 17th a battery of 105 MM. howitzers of the 107th Field Artillery Battalion just behind the southern reaches of the Skyline Drive came under small arms fire from German patrols; and in the early evening of the 18th an entire battalion of the Volksgrenadiers attacked the battery, also a battery of 155 mm. howitzers of the 108th Field Artillery Battalion. While neighboring batteries took the Germans under fire, two half-tracks from the 447th Anti-Aircraft artillery Battalion raced up the Skyline Drive, their quad-50's blazing, and chased the Germans off the road. From the north a platoon of tanks sent a break through to Hoscheid and returned to drive the Germans away. The artillery pieces were for the moment safe, but it was obvious that all the artillery in support of the 109th would have to displace.

By that time, Companies F and G had fallen back on the 2nd Battalion's headquarters village of Bastendorf, and remnants of Companies A and B, having failed to reach Fouhren, fell back under fire to a road junction following the Sure River into Diekirch. If the men of the 3rd Battalion were to withdraw they would also need that road. Early that same afternoon, two assault guns supporting a battalion of Volksgrenadiers hit the road junction. With the first rounds the German guns knocked out six 57 MM. antitank guns and one of the three medium tanks still fighting with Company A. For a moment it looked like a breakthrough, but with the help of two surviving tanks the U.S. infantry held. The American soldier hung in tough, regardless of the branch of service.

To the Regimental Commander, Lt. Colonel James Rudder, the near disaster at the road junction underscored the need to pull his regiment back and consolidate along a new line. Colonel Rudder moved to the high ground above Diekirch, where on the 19th his regiment was attacked by the 352nd VGs, but they were badly defeated and then Rudder fell back along the Ettlebruck-Bastogne highway and joined the rest of the 28th Division. Under protective artillery fire most of the troops left Diekirch before midnight along the road to Ettlebruck, and before daylight the following day were digging in on the high ground south and west of Ettlebruck. From these positions they could cover the Ettlebruck-Bastogne highway and the principal highway leading south from Ettlebruck to Luxembourg city. A Company of the 103rd Engineer Combat Battalion blew bridges both at Ettlebruck and Diekirch.

For the 60th Armored Infantry Battalion along the Sure River and the gorge of the Ernz Noire, the basic concern was likely the German movement up the undefended gorge and egress along one of the three roads leading into the rear of the American positions. There was also the possibility of envelopment from the north, where the first day the Germans had eliminated a small outpost which the armored infantry battalion commander, Colonel Collins, had positioned to give the alarm.

During the night of December 16th, the commander of the battalion's parent unit, Colonel Thomas Harrold of the 9th Armored Divisions CCA, took steps towards blocking those possibilities. He sent the 19th Tank Battalion's company of light tanks to screen the northern flank; attached a troop of 89th Cavalry Recon Squadron to Collins to patrol the road from Ernz Noire into Collins Hdqs, the town of Beaufort; and sent another troop plus the 76 MM. self-propelled guns of Company B, 811 Tank Destroyer Battalion, to block the other two roads up from the gorge.

Those were timely steps and an example of using all types of units to get the job done, but they were insufficient to prevent German infiltration. During the night of the 16th, troops of the 276th VGs Division worked southward through some woods in the rear of Collins Companies. Although a counter-attack by the attached Cavalry cleared the ridge line, the Germans in the woods remained, which meant that the line of Companies of the 60th Armored Infantry Battalion were cut off.

At the same time a regiment of VGs moved unopposed up the gorge of the Ernz Noire to the settlement of Mullerthal, where the road along the bottom of the gorge met another bisecting the gorge, an intersection that became known to the American troops as the "T". From Mullerthal, the Germans threatened the village of Waldbillig, not far from firing positions of 3rd Armored Field Artillery Battalion.

As night came on the 17th, Volksgrenadiers at the other end of the Gorge poured into Beaufort. Colonel Collins ordered his headquarters troops to withdraw while the attached

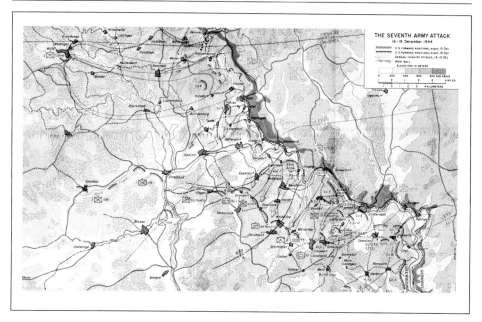

troop of Cavalry under Captain Victor Leiker fought a rear guard action. Leiker's troop managed to hold about two hours, just long enough for self-propelled pieces of the 3rd Armored Field Artillery Battalion near the next village to displace.

During the night the commander of CCA, Colonel Harrold, was assembling a force to attack early the next morning to relieve the men of the 60th Armored Infantry, and drive the enemy into the river. It was an impressive force; two companies of mediums of the 90th Tank Battalion, a company of the 9th Armored Engineer Combat Battalion mounted in half-tracks to fight as infantry, and clear mines laid by the defending Germans. There was also a troop of the 89th Cavalry Recon Squadron, and the 60th Armored Infantry's I.& R. platoon. The attack was to begin from what was fast becoming CCA's new offensive line, extending from Waldbillig northward along a ridge line through a village of Savelborn, and on to screening positions of the light tanks in Ermsdorf.

At the same time on the German side, the commander of the 276th Volksgrenadier Division, General Kurt Mohring, was preparing to attack the center of the line at Savelborn, from which Harrold's attack was to debouch. Mohring had a battalion of VGs and an anti-tank company with 54 panzerfausts.

Unknown to General Mohring, his failure to build a bridge across the Sure, which had caused a slow build-up beyond the river, had caused his superior, General Brandenberger, to call upon Field Marshall Model at Army Group B to send a replacement for Mohring. The Germans continued to fail to bring their engineers up front and replace knocked out bridges. It was standard procedure in the American Army to have their combat engineers up front to build the bridges under fire in close support of the infantry. As it turned out General

Mohring was riding in his command car that evening near the front lines at Beaufort where fire from an American machine gun killed him.

The next morning the steps Mohring had taken to assemble a force at Savelborn served the 276th VG Division well. Before daylight, as the Germans were beginning to attack Savelborn, the 60th Armored Infantry's I & R platoon entered the woods outside the village. German fire killed the platoon leader at the outset and virtually wiped out the platoon.

After daylight the main body of CCA's attacking force followed along the same road through the woods, and to the men in the half-tracks and tanks there appeared to be a panzerfaust behind every tree. In what seemed to be only minutes, the panzerfausts wiped out a light tank and six Shermans. The commander of the leading tank company Captain Arthur Banford, his own tank shot from under him, ordered withdrawal. Pleading insufficient foot troops to protect the tanks, the entire column fell back to Savelborn. An inauspicious first offensive action for those troops of CCA, and it left men of the 60th Armored Infantry to fend for themselves.

In the beleaguered position of that battalion, the artillery forward observer finally managed to repair his radio late in the afternoon of December 18th. By order of Colonel Harrold, the men were to make their way out by infiltration. That night and over the next two nights 400 men made their way back to safety; in the three day fight, the 60th Armored Infantry Battalion lost close to 350 men, most of them during the withdrawal.

The new line to be held by the 9th Armored Division's CCA extended far more than seven miles, from Waldbillig along the Ernz Noire through Savelborn and Ermsdorf and beyond. Yet despite the length of that line a gap between the combat command and the 109th Infantry of four miles still existed. The Regiment's 2nd Battalion soon moved into the gap, a stop gap measure at best, and as it turned out all that was needed.

A new commander of the 276th VG Division, Col. Hugo Dempwolff, made it his priority to reorganize his command, for casualties had been heavy. Still lacking a bridge for the Sure River, he arranged during the night of the 18th to pass his artillery and supplies over bridges belonging to the adjacent German units. When his engineers completed a bridge late on the 19th, he was able to move forward three assault guns that the commander of the 7th Army, General Brandenberger, had scrounged from some where. Only with the arrival of those guns was Colonel Dempwolff prepared for the 276th VG Division to return to the offensive.

By that time the higher command had other plans. By daylight on December 17th, the slight superiority in numbers by the 212th Vg Division over the 12th Infantry's Colonel Chance—five infantry battalions against three—had disappeared. The Commander of the 4th Division, General Barton, had ordered his reserve battalion of his southern most regiment to the threatened sector and his organic engineer battalion into the line to fight as combat engineers and infantry. That made it five against five, and Barton had a decided edge in artillery, tanks, and tank destroyers. The German General Sensfuss had only four assault guns, and as yet no way to get them because of the failure of his engineers and his horse-drawn artillery across the Sure River.

Although Sensfuss's engineers had thrown a bridge across the Sure on the first day, American artillery had knocked it out and his engineers had failed to move up front and rebuild it under American fire. That night the engineers brought down search lights close to the river near Echternach. They planned to build a bridge based on stone piers of an earlier bridge that had served the town since the Middle ages, but American shelling again interfered. Falling back, the engineers had to wait for daylight before building another bridge at a site downstream, and not until late afternoon of December 18th did the bridge serve the division.

The first move that General Barton made on December 17 to meet the continuing German threat was to send the 4th Recon Troop and the 4th Engineer Combat Battalion, before daylight, to an obvious point of danger: the high point of the Ernz Noire not far from Mullerthal. Barton decided to reinforce by creating Task Force Luckett, headed by a former commander of the 12th Infantry, Colonel James Luckett. In addition to the Recon Troop and the engineers, Luckett was to have eight Sherman tanks which Company B of the 70th Tank Battalion had managed to put in order, also the Tank Battalion's mortar platoon, and the reserve battalion of the adjacent 8th Infantry. Calling on that battalion was a risk, for the German offensive might expand southward, but knowledge that the 10th Armored Division's CCA was on the way made Barton's decision much easier. The 10th Armored was part of Patton's 3rd Army.

When the eight Shermans began to arrive in mid-afternoon on the 17th, Colonel Luckett sent them to block the gorge at the Ernz Noire a half mile upstream from Mullerthal. When the 8th Infantry's reserve battalion reached the scene, the 2nd under the command of Lt. Colonel George Maybry, he added the infantry to that block. Yet, ironically, General Barton had created a block against a German force that threatened not only his 12th Infantry, but also the 9th Armored Division's CCA—for the Germans in the gorge were the 276th Volksgrenadier Division, whose zone of advance lay on CCA's side of the gorge. Barton and Luckett would be left to wonder why the Germans made no effort to emerge from the gorge into the 12th Infantry.

Elsewhere the 12th Infantry spent the 2nd day of the German offensive trying to rescue surrounded units and reinforce others. The Regimental Commander, Colonel Chance, again sent Company B, reinforced by a platoon of light tanks and four mediums, to clear the town of Berdorf and rescue the men of Lt. Leake's Company F. That was no easy assignment, for Berdorf was an elongated village extending one half mile along a spine formed by the highway leading from the 2nd Battalion's Hdq's. village of Consdorf. Accompanied by light tanks, half of the infantrymen worked house to house up the spine, while the rest of the men and the four medium tanks by-passed the village over the open ground.

That led to Lt. Leake's little force in the Parc Hotel. As the tanks neared the hotel it looked to Lt. Leake as though they were maneuvering to get into position to fire on it. As indeed they were, for since Lt. McConnell had lost Company F's SCR-300 radio during his fracas with the Germans in Berdorf, Leake had no way to report his position. How to reveal to the tanks that Americans held the hotel? Leake had no identification panels, no flares, nothing. One man suddenly remembered when rummaging through the drawers of a dresser in one of the rooms, he had came across an American flag. He rushed to find it, and a volunteer climbed to the shattered roof and waved it frantically.

As the tanks and accompanying infantry arrived at the hotel, the rest of Company B was pushing the Germans back passed the road junction a hundred yards away in Berdorf, but that was as far as the attack carried before nightfall brought a halt. Leake and his men continued to hold the hotel, for that provided good flank protection for the men in Berdorf.

In the center of the 12th Infantry's sector, in Osweiler and Dickweiler, the third line company of Chance's 1st Battalion, Company C, reinforced the defending companies of the 3rd Battalion and, in mid morning, the reserve battalion of the 22nd Infantry. The 2nd under the command of Lt. Colonel Thomas Kenan detrucked behind the two villages. The men of one company climbed immediately upon the decks of a company of tanks of the 9th Armored Division and headed for Osweiler. On the way they flushed out and routed a company of Germans in some woods alongside the road, and in the process freed 16 men of Company C, captured during the company's move to Osweiler.

The Germans had been on their way to Scheidgen, close to Consdorf and headquarters of the 12th Infantry's 2nd Battalion. There the Germans gained their only success of the day when a platoon of self-propelled tank destroyers abandoned the village without a fight.

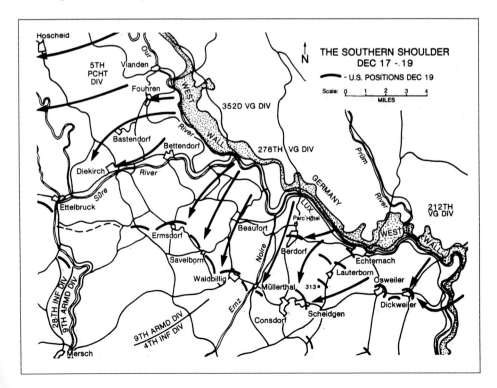

With only a few men from headquarters available to defend Consdorf, the battalion commander, Major John Dorn, spent an anxious night but the Germans made no effort to push beyond Scheidgen.

At the end of the second day of the German offensive, the trace of a new defensive line was beginning to take shape in the 12th Infantry's sector. Osweiler and Dickweiler on the right were firmly held, a fact soon recognized by the German Commander, General Sensfuss, who made no further attempt to take those two villages. On the left, too, Task Force Luckett had firmly anchored the line along the upper reaches of the Ernz Noire. The weakness was in the center where there was a gap between Osweiler and Consdorf along the principal highway through the sector, the road from Luxembourg City to Echternach.

Out in front of the two projections, Company B and Lt. Leake's small band at Berdorf constituted one; Companies A and G in Lauterborn and Company E in Echternach constituted the other. Except for the danger of the men in those positions, the 12th Infantry at nightfall on December 17th was in fairly good shape, and reinforcements were arriving. They consisted of an Engineer Combat Battalion, the 159th, which General Barton placed in reserve near his left flank lest the enemy break through the adjacent sector.

26

The 159th Combat Engineers and the Battle on Hill 313

We were in the 3rd Army of General George Patton and in the battle of the Brest Peninsula, and on September 23rd when the battle of Brest fell we became part of the drive across France through Compiegne and St. Quenten, and on into the Ardennes. We came on into Belgium, and on the 29th of September, we arrived in the vicinity of Bastogne.

We moved down into some woods near Fauvillers, Belgium and were assigned a sector for engineer maintenance. The enemy was about 20 miles away on a line along the eastern borders of Belgium and Luxembourg. In their retreat back into Germany the German Pioneers (Engineers) had demolished bridges, blew craters in roads, and destroyed road net facilities to delay our attacking Infantry and Armor.

The battalion came into Luxembourg on the 7th of October 1944 for what was to be our longest stay in one place in this very mobile war which some called the "Engineer's War". Success depended upon who could keep their Infantry and Armor moving by reinstalling the attackers demolished road net. Thus far the American and British side had been successful. We in the 159th had much to do with restructuring the main routes up to the Siegfried line, but as December arrived the Germans had holed up behind the Siegfried line with its pillboxes, dragons Teeth, and entrenched big guns. We had not figured out how to engineer our way through that supposed vaunted line.

We found the Luxembourg people to be friendly folks, but as November rolled into December, we frequently saw the Germans across the river. We were affected only by some artillery fire or V-1 rockets. We worked around Ettlebruck, Clerf, Diekirch, Wiltz, Arlon, and Martelange. We knew we were in the Army, but the Germans seemed more than 15 miles away, until December 15th when one of our trucks went up to Diekirch for some rock.

They came back and said the rock quarry was under German fire. We got the news later on that day. German General Von Runstedt was on the march. We knew that the VIII American Corps had an enormous front and we knew it was lightly held, but the Germans knew this too, and they came crashing in.

We got the order to move out the next day. Luxembourg City was in danger and what was left was the badly battered 4th Division standing in the path of the attacking Germans. We in the 159th were attached to the 12th Infantry Regiment of the 4th Infantry Division. Our order was quick and fast and on the night of December 17th we were on our way to drive the Germans out of the town of Schiedgen.

The battered and undermanned 12th Infantry had some of its units surrounded already, and the Germans were pouring into Luxembourg. Small task forces and combat commands of tanks had pulled out to the northeast to attempt to remedy the situation, but the Germans could bypass tanks by going through the woods. They were already in Schiedgen, a small but important town a short distance away.

Schiedgen was the battalion's first objective. We were to clear it of Germans and take the high ground around it. Hill 313 was part of the high ground. We thought of our days back in Brittany, France when we had met and beaten the Germans. We had been assigned to task force A and our mission was to hold the Dacoulas Peninsula, and prevent any Germans in or out of Brest. We were part of what consisted of the 1st Tank Destroyer Brigade, the 15th and 17th squadrons of the 15th Cavalry Group, the 705 Tank Destroyer Battalion, one battery of the 23rd Field Artillery, and the 509th light ponton Company.

We remembered the tough German road block that had to be cleared near St. Milo. The road at the site was under heavy enemy fire and under complete enemy observation. Lt Gibb picked out seven men to go up to the block with demolitions. P.F.C. Meyer and Cicola were instantly killed. The rest couldn't move; they were pinned down. Lt. Gibb heard a man cry out for water and as he attempted to reach the man he was shot through the head.

Death surrounded the road block, but it had to be cleared. Lt. Surkamp called for tanks and with his men riding and Sgt. McNally leading his men with explosives they finally blew the road block and evened up the score when A and B Companies, led by Lt. Chapek cleaned the Germans out of the woods. A total of 40 Germans were killed, and 16 captured. Only one of our men was wounded.

We drew our ammunition and grenades and moved out. We were confident and ready. The morning of the 18th the battalion CP moved to Consdorf, about 2 kilometers away from Schiedgen. A and C companies moved into position in the woods south of Schiedgen and B Company was in reserve at Altrier. The weather was currently against us, the air was wet and cold and the sky hung heavy with dark clouds. We needed an air force to get back and break up the big German columns. We needed it to locate them and give us a picture of just what was going on. Sorely needed information was hid by the darkness.

When any man wanted to find our commanding officer, he had best look first where the going was tough. That is where the courier found Lt. Col. Dick Staeffler when he delivered the order for him to take off for the objective. He was up with the lead squad of C Company, and when the order finally came the companies advanced. We had some light tanks and Tank Destroyers with us, but they were road bound and we went up through the woods. A Company on the left received the first enemy fire, but it was small and soon melted away. We continued forward and as we approached Schiedgen from the south the tanks were coming in from the west. We drove into the town, captured a few prisoners and moved onto high ground. The Germans were not ready to fight yet!

Our point from C Company hit heavy small arms fire approaching hill 313. They had run into what appeared to be a rear guard of a larger body of Germans. We were able to disengage the enemy and that night of December 18th both companies assembled in Schiedgen.

The Germans were wicked with those 88s and mortars; it came crashing in all of the time. Consdorf and Schiedgen were getting plastered at regular intervals. The Germans must have felt that we were in there in great force. He could not have realized how thinly the sector was held. He was trying to break up any concentration of our troops by heavy shelling. The roads were getting it too, and any man having to go down them in a vehicle just prayed, crouched low and threw her in high. We really hinged down those roads with the stuff hitting on each side and kicking up dirt and smoke.

In the CPs we were doing most of our work on the floor. The building would shake and the glass would fly and you felt that one was about to drop right on you. They were hitting all around. B Company had been called down to Michelshof to protect a T.D. outfit and later down to Bech where they were attached to Task force Smith. They met no enemy but again there was heavy shelling.

On December 19th A and C Companies, each minus one platoon, went out to secure hill 313. We moved into position on the hill, but the only Germans we found were dead ones from the encounter we had the previous day. We dug in on the hill and it was cold with heavy clouds. We opened our cold K rations up there, checked our ammunition and waited.

By this time we were starting to get some idea of the set-up; it didn't look good. The Germans were really on the move in earnest, as evidenced by the magnitude of their attack in the north. We heard the unbelievable: they were at St. Vith and Wiltz and driving on Bastogne. We had considered these places as rear areas only a few days before.

Luxembourg City was a plum and we now realized that the enemy would be after it in force. We had never retreated before and it was hard for us to think in terms of retreat, yet the stunning fact was that the Germans had actually advanced in force against our armies. We realized that our lines were thin, but it was hard to believe that the entire German Army could even push back one American squad.

The battalion was out on a salient in the line that jutted into the enemy sector. There was a small force of infantry about eight kilometers to our right, and some tanks from a task force about five kilometers to our left. But in between the Germans could parade back and forth at will.

The infantry in Echternach was cut off and surrounded, and the Germans were moving down on Schiedgen. There were too few of us to cover the entire front, so we could only hope to deny the enemy the most critical spots. Hill 313 and Schiedgen were definitely critical.

We could see the enemy moving around on the road in front of the hill, and in the night they could slip right into the towns of Consdorf and Schiedgen. The cold seemed to go right through the men in the foxholes on hill 313.

The night of December 19th is one that we will never forget; that is, those of us who were up there that night. There was one ray of hope. Relief was supposed to be coming up.

Fresh Infantry were on the way that very minute, and by the next day we should be back as engineers again. Well, it was a comforting thought anyway.

By the morning of December 20th, things started warming up again. It wasn't that the weather changed. Those clouds and that cold air seemed to be permanently with us, but it was the Germans coming back up for hill 313! They warmed things up with a barrage of mortars, 88s, and the rockets we called "Screaming Meemies".

They would crash and whine and sing into the hill and the dirt would fly and branches on the trees went helter-skelter. They were coming into the towns too, but it wasn't as bad as it was up on that hill. The foxhole seemed small and inadequate, but right then there wasn't much we could do except lie there and take it. But it sure made you grit your teeth in anger when one of our boys was hit.

Later that day two squads of Germans started up the hill. Those that were able soon did an about face; it was like shooting ducks, but we knew that soon they would be back in force. Those of us not on the hill were doing well out on other missions. A platoon of B Company had to go back in where the enemy was, in order to cover the withdrawal of some tanks. Each group of us was busy at something.

On December 20th B Company, minus one platoon, went into position on high ground about 800 yards from hill 313. A Company remained on the hill and C Company came into Schiedgen for hot food, and what rest they could get.

On the morning of December 21st, C Company went back to the hill and A Company returned to patrol and protect the rear. Our position was such that the enemy could attack from the front and flanks, making it possible for them to infiltrate to our rear.

The enemy made several small attacks on the hill that morning, but we repulsed them easily. They continued to harass the position with mortar and rocket fire and our patrols reported great enemy activity in all sectors of our front and flanks.

A platoon from A Company fought and drove back an enemy patrol trying to get in back of us and in general the entire front was more active than usual. We still expected relief from the infantry.

A radio report from B Company indicated that an enemy column of from four hundred to six hundred was on the road just North of our positions. C Company saw a couple hundred more on the road below the hill headed towards Michaelshof; they were on bicycles.

Tough-looking Germans came at us in waves. They were very close; we just pumped lead into them. The radio man from C Company was walking up and down the line, broadcasting the action like it was a football game.

If you had been on hill 313 that day you would have seen them stack up and fall back, but over towards your left where B Company was in position you would have heard the fire increase in volume and tempo.

The main force of the Germans had hit B Company, less one platoon, with over a battalion of ardent Nazis. They too had came in firing and screaming and when you shot down the first wave another took its place, and so until your gun barrel got hot and wouldn't fire anymore.

The Germans managed to drive between the two platoons that made up B Company. Captain Chapek was with one out on the flank and they were in trouble. Their guns were going out of action and they were running out of ammunition. Lt. Flowers tried to fight his way through to them, but he was far outnumbered.

Captain Chapek was the last man to go down according to those who saw him. They say he just stood there and fired away, and wouldn't budge one damned inch. He always was a determined guy.

We lost a lot of good men in that engagement. A few of them turned up later as prisoners of the Germans, but for the most part the company was badly battered. They certainly battered the Germans; the odds were way up, but again one felt there could be no ratio that could even up the toll.

When the Germans occupied the positions that B Company had been in, they had more or less nullified the tactical value of hill 313. C Company was ordered to withdraw to Schiedgen, and thence along with A Company to positions slightly southeast toward Michaelshof. A heavily mauled infantry company was dug in there to make a final stand before Luxembourg City.

As the companies moved toward the southeast the battalion CP, along with the remnants of B Company, went to Altrier. It was a lucky move; twenty minutes later a direct hit blew up the building in which it had formerly been.

Consdorf and Schiedgen had taken a terrific pounding from enemy shells and they were in shambles. Our artillery was giving it back to them; they had given us wonderful direct support all along, but then the Germans had an enormous concentration of fire power on that sector. They wanted it badly.

By December 22nd the companies were in position and waiting at Michaelshof. The Germans knew that we were there too, and shifted their rockets and artillery over there. Our own artillery was kicking up the woods to our front and in general was discouraging the Germans from concentrating too much stuff at that point.

At about 5:00 p.m. a large force of enemy was seen moving out of a draw in the woods to our northeast. They came out into the field in an enormous "V" formation, and they advanced across our front with confidence. It looked like another mass attack in force. This time they would try to break us once and for all.

Captain Surkamp was in command. We had two companies minus one platoon in the line. To our north was the depleted infantry company, and in the line were two tanks and T.D. Surkamp gave the order to hold the fire until the big "V" came on. They came out of the woods into the open country on our front. Not a shot was fired.

Our artillery had been alerted and we were going to drop them in close, and we all sat nervously sighting down our guns until the enemy was about one hundred and fifty yards away. "Fire!" The order was given and everything on the line opened up: B Company and the guys from C and A Companies, and those from Headquarters Company, too. The big "V" stopped short and fell in its tracks and the bodies flew up in the air as the 10th Armored artillery dropped them in. The tanks fired everything, even their pistols, and very few of the Germans in that "V" formation ever got away.

The observers could count over one hundred and fifty of the enemy stretched out. That night we could hear the others that were wounded, screaming with pain. It was a blow from which the enemy never recovered in that area.

One of the things we remembered about December 23rd was waking up that morning and looking towards the sky and suddenly realizing that it was clear. And then we heard the drone of motors. Our own planes, thousands of them.

They were headed straight for Germany and they left long thin trails of vapor in their wake. This was the thing we sweated out for days and there they were. We then knew that Hitler's jig was up.

By the 24th of December we were in position again up above Schiedgen and it was still freezing weather. The Germans did not show themselves, but this rocket barrage was murderous. It was tough going, but we were tired. We again heard that we were to be relieved, but then they said that many days ago, too.

Well, at last it came; Patton had swung his army up from the south and was pounding on the enemy's southern flank. We could see some of his boys now, part of the 5th Division coming up the road. There were plenty of tanks and artillery and it made us feel that we had not been forgotten after all.

On Christmas Eve of 1944, the infantry came in. We were relieved. Ironically though, just as the last platoon of A Company was ready to leave the Germans threw over a final rocket that killed Lt. Leckman.

Christmas Day the Battalion was back in Billets in Luxembourg City. At this time the German drive in the north had been stopped, but the Germans were in an all out attack on Bastogne.

The men of the 159th had faced forces 15 times greater than they had on hill 313. They had surrounded their hill with mines and concertina wires to prevent the attacking infantry from coming in close. There is a monument on this hill dedicated to their effort to save mankind!

27

The Race for Bastogne

Bastogne was a small village of 3200 people and somewhat of a highway and railway center. The countryside around the area was farmland with rolling short elevation. One could say it was better tank country than the rugged Ardennes to the north. This prevailed to the east and the German border. The only important military installation at or near Bastogne was the headquarters of General Troy Middleton, the VIII Corps Commander.

Hitler's secret war plans did not include Bastogne as part of his main thrust, but a village to be bypassed by the blitzing armor and later mopped up by infantry troops. In fact the main thrust was considerably north of this small village. There were no military supply

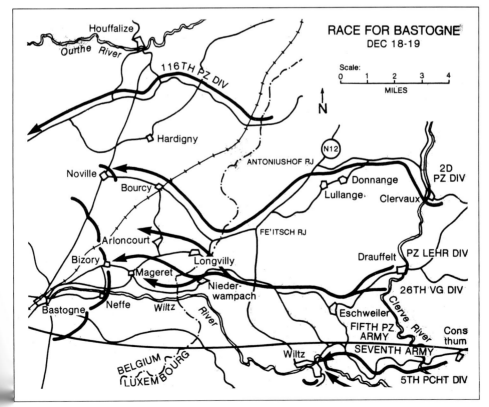

dumps or tank and material shops in the area such as was located south of Liege, the center of the main thrust led by the Panzer Divisions of the 1st SS Panzer Corps of General Hermann Priess.

When Peiper was approaching within a short distance of General Hodges First Army at Spa, the decision to move the airborne divisions to Werbomont caused some delay in the movement of the 101st Airborne to the defense of Bastogne.

With the news that an airborne division was coming to Bastogne, the commander of VIII Corps could relax a little. As he was disturbingly aware early on the evening of December 17th, the center of his front was falling to pieces, leaving him to wonder whether he or the Germans would be in Bastogne to welcome the airborne troops when they got there. Later in the evening Middleton learned that the commander of the 10th Armored Division Major General William Morris was coming to his headquarters. He soon learned from Morris that his division was on its way north from Third Army and would be assigned to VIII Corps. Middleton requested that one of the 10th Armored Division Combat Commands be assigned to Bastogne and the bulk of the division be moved north of Luxembourg City to counter-attack the German penetration there.

Morris then ordered his leading combat command to move to Bastogne from the bivouac near Luxembourg City. Middleton then realized that the race for Bastogne was under way. The German General's 47th Panzer Corps was only 15 miles away preparing to cross the Clerve River against the troops of the 28th Division.

The 110th Regiment was struggling to hold the Germans along the Skyline Drive. The 109th was in the south and the 112th to the north, all battling against the 560th Volkstorm Division, the 2nd Panzer Division, the 26th VG Division, and the 116th Panzer Division. How the Germans were able to mass this heavy force against one American division was unbelievable. The bulk of this German force was directed against the 110th Regiment.

At this point in time the Germans had crossed the Our River in the south and central attack areas, but were still attempting to cross the Our River in the 112th Infantry defensive area. The main effort for Hitler's minions was to assault the Clerve River area and then go on to the Meuse River.

To the south, the 26th VG Division was still waging a war of position against the 110th west of the Our River. When they forced their way into Hosingen against the "B" Company of the 103rd Engineers, they had taken a pounding from the rifles, machine guns, and rifle grenades of the engineers. Also, they had to attack through the mine fields with their infantry and tanks, suffering casualties and knocked out tanks.

Using 2500 pounds of explosives, Corporal George Stevenson, one of the demolition men of the company, had blown a bridge in front of the Germans as their infantry was attempting to cross. He and his men were able to work their way back to the company with no one wounded. In the face of a mortar attack from the enemy the men took cover in the basements of some buildings at the end of a street in Hosingen.

Sgt. "Chuck" Schroeder of B Company indicated that in the four days of battle in Hosingen they had fought as infantry 50% of the time and as combat engineer 50%. Before they surrendered and were overrun they had killed or captured over 700 Germans. At the time of capture they had only 3 killed and 7 wounded Engineers. He did say that they had more killed and wounded in the Huertgen.

The Germans did manage to force their way into Hosingen, but the delays caused by the 110th and the engineers had a great affect on the 5th Panzer Army's failure to reach the Meuse River. The engineers had blown the bridge at Gemund on the Our River which took the German engineers two days to rebuild. Amid a terrible traffic bottleneck when they completed the bridge, the Panzer Lehr Division wormed across the river with its recon battalion, and engaged the 110th at both Holtzthum and Consthum. The overwhelming strength of the German infantry and armor against the Americans who were short of ammunition and artillery support soon prevailed. The Germans finally assaulted the Clerve River area at Kaltenbach where the Wiltz River flows into the Clerve. This German force was the 5th Fallshirmjager (parachute) Division. In each of these battles for the villages the attacking force suffered many more casualties than the defensive force which were dug-in behind roadblocks set up by the 103rd Engineers, along with extensive mine fields.

The only sad thing about the defensive forces were the result of many days of battle and running out of ammunition and other military needs. Many medics remained behind to care for the wounded in the hands of the enemy. The delays caused by the "Bloody Bucket", 28th Division, permitted the commander of the VIII Corps, Lt. General Troy Middleton and the First Army Engineer, Colonel William Carter, time to assemble engineer barrier lines on the road to Bastogne and in the area east of the Meuse River from Bastogne to Marche, Manhay and Werbomont. This line of road blocks created by engineer units would also begin at Monschau and progress in front of Eupen, Verviers, and tie into the barrier line from Butgenbach, Malmedy, and Werbomont. More and more combat engineers were moving from the north to stabilize and reinforce the barrier lines.

Between Clervaux and Bastogne, Middleton placed his meager reserves, a reserve combat command of the 9th Armored Division, and some Engineer Combat Battalions. After two days of fighting the outnumbered forces of the 28th Division completely collapsed after much bloody fighting at Clervaux and the Skyline Drive.

The 47th Panzer Corps claimed 1155 prisoners of war and 22 tanks destroyed. General von Luttwitz's Corps of Divisions were now behind schedule by 48 hours and was still not across the Clerve River. The cost to the Americans had been heavy, and the 110th Regiment with its infantry, engineers, artillery, and tank destroyers had suffered about 75% casualties in three days of fighting. Just as in the Huertgen forests, they had sacrificed themselves for the good of the cause. They had held despite the vast odds against them. For many of these men as prisoners of war, they would go on to suffer many days of hunger, foot marches of hundreds of miles, rides in crowded box cars, and at times witnessing cruelty from their German guards, and all types of diseases and skin infections.

To the north, the 116th Panzer Division was having great difficulty crossing the Our River near the German border. The 112th infantry Regiment of the 28th Division with its "C" Company of the 103rd Engineers fought tenaciously—blowing bridges, laying mines, and fighting as infantry, with great artillery support and some support from American air. The German numbers of tanks, infantry, and fighting equipment seemed endless as the Germans kept coming on despite their losses. They recaptured the span at Ouren, but soon found out it was so badly damaged that it wouldn't support their heavy tanks. Disappointed, von Manteuffel ordered the Division to cross over the 2nd Panzer Division's bridge to the south of Dasburg. Again the defenders with their engineers had caused him valuable time as he watched his troops and equipment get battered by small groups of American soldiers of all branches of the service that overcame his great favorable odds.

The Panzer Division's Recon Battalion with light armored vehicles moved across the Our at the light bridge near Heinerscheid. Almost as soon as they crossed they were engaged by the light tanks of the U.S. 707th Tank Battalion which they defeated in a one sided battle. Three engineer combat battalions that Middleton had at his disposal in his Corps area were the 35th, the 158th, and the 44th. He assigned the 44th to move quickly to Wiltz to help General Cota, commander of the evaporating 28th Division. He assigned the 35th and the 158th to form an Engineer Barrier line in the villages just beyond the eastern periphery of Bastogne. Earlier assigned to general support of the 28th Division, the 58th Armored Field Artillery Battalion also was to support all units in front of Bastogne. Now the combat engineers and the artillery would be working together for the same cause. Generally when the engineers were forced to fight as infantry, they had no artillery support.

Having ordered CCR of the 9th Armored Division to an assembly area closer to Bastogne before the arrival of the 101st Airborne Division, Middleton now had some form of defense to attempt to stop the onrushing Germans who had crossed the Clerve River and had four divisions running clear, heading for the Meuse River. On the south the 5th Parachute Division of the Nazis war machine was moving at Wiltz, the 26th VG Division was aiming at Eschweiler after having been delayed with the crossing of the Clerve River.

The second Panzer Division had destroyed the remaining forces of the 110th Infantry Regiment of the "Bloody Bucket" at Clervaux, and the 116th Panzer Division was heading for Houffalize. Hitler was now raving because of the failure of his Divisions to come anywhere near the original time table but his goal was still to cross the Meuse on each side of Liege and head directly for Antwerp. Little did he realize how badly mauled his key divisions had become. Defensive positions such as Bastogne were to be bypassed by armor and wired out by infantry. He also didn't know how badly battered were his divisions in the 5th Panzer Army of von Manteuffel.

The 28th and the 106th Divisions had lost the bulk of two regiments, each with some of their men escaping to the west on foot. The 7th Armored Division led by General Bruce Clarke had fought a delaying action back towards Vielsalm and were able to keep the division intact by closing with the 82nd Airborne in the Vielsalm-Manhay area. The 7th Armored had been aided by the combat command of General William Hoge of the 9th Armored Division.

28

Bastogne: The 35th Engineer Combat Battalion

When the VIIIth Corps Commander, General Troy Middleton, saw that the German breakthrough would effect Bastogne before the arrival of the 101st Airborne Division, he assigned the 158th and the 35th Engineer Combat Battalions to defend the road net surrounding the village. The battalion had arrived in France on August 7th 1944 and quickly became involved in mine clearance, bridge building, and supporting the 50th Armored Infantry Battalion and the 15th Cavalry squadron and, like most combat engineer battalions, started to receive casualties.

While clearing mines and opening up the road net for the 15th Cavalry Squadron, the second platoon of Company A destroyed two 37 mm. guns and two German bazookas as they were forced to battle a German counterattack. The battalion continued to act as combat engineers across France and into Belgium and had participated in the Brittany Campaign where the cavalry and the engineers had the mission to proceed in force, to capture and neutralize enemy positions west of the main line of resistance.

The battalion entered Belgium on September 28, 1944. On October 4th they moved into Luxembourg where they continued to remove dangerous mine fields and roadblocks

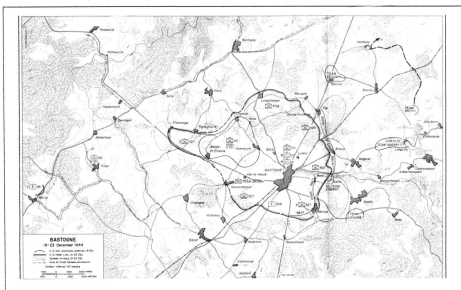

for the advancing American Infantry. Then came the job of rebuilding the vast number of bridges blown by the rapidly retreating enemy.

The 35th became involved in operating saw mills and building timber trestle bridges to support tanks. They learned the road net all over Belgium and Luxembourg as they took care of the main supply routes to the front. They operated saw mills in Clerf and Wiltz and in the November rains learned about the river crossings that were necessary to guard and reinforce due to high water.

Little did they know at that time that this experience would come in handy later in December. During this relatively quiet time the men of the battalion and the people of Luxembourg became acquainted and the homeland persons knew that they had great allies in these Americans who had driven the Germans from their land.

Suddenly on December 17th Lt. Col. Paul Symbol received orders to move to Bastogne and revert to VIII Corps control with the mission of defending Bastogne. The orders indicated that they were to fight as infantry. The area became a battlefield almost before they received the order. Company B encountered a German patrol of ten men while moving out of their bivouac area in the vicinity of Goeblesmuhl. Six men of this patrol were wiped out by machine gun fire laid down by Company B. Companies moved from their respective positions into the vicinity of Bastogne, Belgium. Defensive positions were set up which included all routes into the city.

On December 18th the battalion was relieved of attachment to VIII Corps and attached to Combat Command "B" of the 10th Armored Division. The 158th Engineer Combat Battalion, commanded by Lt. Colonel Sam Tabet, moved into position around Bastogne and relieved the 35th of the northeast sector of the city. This all had been developed as a plan prior to the delayed arrival of the 101st Airborne. Companies A and C were committed while Company B was held in reserve. The battalion commanders of the engineer battalions all planned to use their well trained engineer tactics of setting up road blocks, laying mines, use TNT blocks to drop trees across roads, and use their bazookas and other weapons to fight as infantry.

Battalion headquarters rear echelon plus heavy equipment moved to Neidercolpach. During the evening of the 18th there was some German firing into Bastogne as well as some minor action of German air forces. All vehicles were pulled out of the parking area in the vicinity of Bastogne to a place of safety. Company B supported the 420th Field Artillery Battalion, and H&S Company took up arms and was committed as infantry after the line companies had committed their reserves. Company C held out in the town of Marvie, Belgium, while Company A held out in the town of Mont.

Company A encountered the enemy throughout the night. H&S Company lost two water points in the vicinity of Clerf and Wiltz in Luxembourg. Company C was finally relieved at 11:30 p.m. by the 101st Airborne Infantry against C Company then moved from Marvie into Bastogne itself. The following enlisted men were missing in action: Gerald E. Ice, Orlan Stanphill, John Armstrong, William Turner, Loius Womock, Delbert Clifton, James Gordan, and Robert Lemos. This was only the beginning of the heavy battles in the

Bastogne vicinity for the men of the 35th Engineer Combat Battalion. It was also the beginning of blowing snow storms and temperatures below the freezing point.

On the 20th of December Company A was holding 500 yards of front in the vicinity of Mont until relieved by the 101st Airborne Infantry. H&S Company had 12 men protecting Tank Destroyers with bazookas. Company B and C were held in reserve. At 9:00 a.m. the battalion was relieved of attachment to the 10th Armored Division and reverted back to VIII Corps control. The battalion moved to the following locations: H&S to Libramont, Company A to Recogne, Company B to St. Hubert, Company C to Jenneville.

Lt. Rush from battalion hdqs. along with Lt. Skinner and 20 enlisted men from Company A left for Bastogne. Their mission after reporting to the commanding general of the 101st Airborne Division was to do demolition work for the defense of Bastogne. The battalions mission was to deny the enemy the crossroads in St. Hubert, Jenneville, and Recogne. During this hazardous mission close to the enemy, Ramon Solis was missing in action.

On the 21st of December, as the snows came down and the skies were overcast, Company A blew bridges, built road blocks, and did general demolition work in the vicinity of St. Hubert to cover the withdrawal of other entrapped American units. Then under the cover of darkness they moved to Bouillion. H&S Company had 18 men on guard at an important crossroads and they too were moved to Bouillion. Lt. Joyce and a detachment of men were left behind to execute demolition work on the order of the commanding officer of the 7th Tank Destroyer Group. Pfc. James M. Morris, Company A was killed in Bastogne.

Up to this time in the battle for Bastogne the 35th Combat Engineers of Col. Paul Symbol had not been forced to fight directly in the front lines with rifles, grenades, and bayonets. They had accomplished much in using their combat engineering skills to prepare a defense of road blocks and mines with demolition of bridges in front of American infantry which later would serve the overall defense of the village of Bastogne.

To the east of Bastogne the 5th Parachute Division had crossed the Clerve River and had successfully moved in the direction of Wiltz. The 26th VG and the Panzer Lehr Division had crossed the Clerve River and were driving towards the Meuse in the direction of Longvilly and Niederwampach which moved them directly towards Bastogne or north thereof. The 2nd SS Panzer Division had overran Clervaux, captured Donnange and was headed north of Bastogne. The 116th SS Panzer Division was racing towards the Meuse south of Houffalize.

On the German side at this time the overall plan had always been to send its main thrust directly towards the Meuse and isolate the city of Liege and cross the Meuse River north and south of Liege. This plan had failed with the halting of Peiper and now on the night of the 21st of December Colonel Otto Skorzeny had failed in his attempt to relieve the entrapped Peiper. This meant that Hitler and his generals would have to revise their plan in the south end of the bulge. Hitler did not want to make a major assault into Bastogne, but pass it to the north and south with armor and later wipe it out with infantry.

The 22nd of December found one platoon of Company B under the command of Lt. Nettle being sent to Recogne; the platoon was ready to set booby traps, do demolition work, and remove road blocks if necessary, on the order of the commanding officer of the 7th Tank Destroyer Group. The coordination between the various units in the defense of Bastogne was outstanding.

The battalion mission was changed as Col. Symbol was assigned to use his battalion to secure all bridge crossings along the Semois River in the battalion sector, with A Company at St. Cecile, B Company at Morteham, Company C and H&S Company at Izel.

On December 23, all main bridges were prepared for demolition and guarded. Less important bridges were blown. One bridge in the C Company area was bombed by the enemy using about 20 bombs of the personnel type. One man was hit and evacuated to the hospital. On the 25th of December, Captain Day, commanding officer of A Company was killed by rifle fire.

On the 26th of December, Company B moved from Mortcheam to St. Vincent. The battalion was guarding nine river crossings, all of which were prepared for demolition. Lt. Nettle returned from Libramont with his platoon. Two of his men were missing in action due to enemy bombing.

On December 27th all companies made reconnaissance for secondary defensive positions along the La Chiers River and now the battalion became part of the extensive engineer barrier line created by First Army.

For its action in the Bastogne area the battalion received high commendations from both General George Patton and General Troy Middleton. This was for their devotion to duty and valor for their tremendous stand against overwhelming odds. There were many Silver Stars, Bronze Stars, and Purple Hearts. One citation for the Silver Star reads as follows:

> SERGEANT CHARLES R. CANNON, 32134076. Corps of Engineers, 35th Engineer Combat Battalion, United States Army. For gallantry in action, in connection with military operations against the enemy on the 21st of December, 1944 in Belgium. While setting up road blocks and digging in his position, Sergeant Cannon heard approaching enemy tanks. Upon arriving at a point where he could see the advancing armor, his first bazooka team fired a shot which stopped the lead tank. The two tanks following opened up with machine gun fire, pinning down the bazooka team. With complete disregard for cover or small arms protection, Sergeant Cannon advanced within range and immediately took up a position and fired, scoring a direct hit on the second tank rendering it useless throughout the rest of the engagement. The tenacity of purpose, courage, and attention to duty demonstrated by Sergeant Cannon symbolize the highest traditions of the armed forces and reflect great credit upon himself. Entered military service from New York.

The 35th went on to play major roles in the victory in the battle of the bulge and the attack into Germany.

There were times when they fought directly as infantry during the big battle, but their skillful use of combat engineering went far to bring victory for the American soldiers.

29

The 511th Light Pontoon Company and the Engineer Barrier Line

The first men of the 511th to realize that anything was amiss east of the village of Bastogne was PFCs Leslie and Noble on the 16th of December when shells came at their training site with the 103rd Engineers. The shells came crashing in from the direction of the Siegfried line into A Company of the 103rd's bivouac area.

As the 103rd Engineers moved up to the fighting area the men of the 511th were ordered to move their ponton equipment back to their company sector near Redange, Belgium. They loaded their bridge equipment and moved back to Redange by way of the road through Diekirch and Ettelbruck.

Captain Guenter, their company commander, received word from the Group command post that there was heavy fighting up front in the 28th Division area. The situation in the North and East had changed dramatically and CCB of the 9th Armored Division had been sent towards St. Vith to support an overrun 106th Division.

On December 17th PFCs Noble and Leslie reported in to Guenter on the situation at the front and he responded by quickly notifying his platoons to return to the command post.

On the evening of the 17th Guenter had succeeded in locating all of his troops back in Redange. All had knowledge that the 109th Infantry of the 28th Division at Grosbous only five miles due north of the 511th was waiting the German attack and ordered to hold the line along the Alzette River which runs along the line from Ettlebruck to Luxembourg City.

While the world was collapsing around him on the morning of the 18th, Guenter continued to organize his unit for the necessary action to learn of his mission. Guenter sent an armed patrol to Niederfuelen on the outskirts of Ettlebruck. An outpost was established by Corporal Haggan with Schweitzer, Werry, Barone and Kershaw in a farm on high ground overlooking the town of Ettlebruck. He laid a land telephone link to Redange backed up by the 511th short range radio. By the time Haggan arrived, resistance to the north by the 110th and 112th Regiments of the 28th Division was weakening after being hit by an entire Corps of the German Army. There was no actual established front except piecemeal resistance by almost surrounded and broken units establishing quick battle lines and then retreating.

The 109th Infantry Regiment remained the best organized with the support of some tanks of the 9th Armored Division and A Company of the 103rd Engineers. It had faced east on the morning of the 16th but late in the day on the 18th it faced north, having been passed by the Germans 5th Parachute Division which headed for the southern flanks of Bastogne.

As the 5th moved west the 109th moved west and south until it was strung out for 25 miles and largely non-existent in most spots.

Haggan called in that civilians were evacuating Ettelbruck and elements of the 109th Infantry were passing in full retreat. Haggans outpost was not aware there was no longer any organized resistance between themselves and the paratroopers and the Panzers heading west. The 109th Infantry and A Company of the 103rd Engineers were somewhat south and east. The Germans were rolling farther northwest with little or no opposition as other parts of the 28th and 106th Divisions started surrendering by Regiments. During this period Haggan was the only patched in unit on the VIII Corps front. All units were either out of touch or had scattered, interrupted transmissions. Almost all other land lines were disrupted.

Later on, during the day, the 1102nd Engineer Combat Group as the only major command in the rear of the southern shoulder affiliated directly with VIII Corps, would become a sort of task force. Its primary function was to take combat support and service units and use them to act as infantry. The 35th Engineer Combat Battalion was retreating to Bastogne after serving as infantry. This unit had already been taken from the 1102nd and transferred to a division. The only units available to group were the 511th and 628th Engineer Light Equipment Company.

By the evening of the 18th of December at 1825 hours Company B of the 299th Engineers moved west two miles west of Martelange to Witry, Belgium. Their mission was to set up a barrier line of bridges set for demolitions, running northwest out of Bastogne on route 15. At midnight Company A moved out of La Vacherie which lays about seven miles northwest of Bastogne just off the main road to Marche. To the east lay the critical bridge at Orthueville. At 2029 hours on the 19th they reported that their mission had been accomplished. At 1500 hours the same day Company C moved out to Vaux, leaving the Battalion command post at Hachy. All three companies of the 299th started preparing all the bridges across the Ourthe for demolition.

By early evening a part of First Army's 158th Engineers was helping to defend Magaret against the Panzer Lehr Division of General Bayerlein, later commander of the West German armed forces. The outpost held with help from American tanks and the 158th came directly under VIII Corps control that day. They ended up as part of the surrounded forces in Bastogne. This now left the First Army's 1128th Engineer Combat Group with only the 1278th and the 299th Combat Engineer Battalions to maintain lengthy engineer barrier lines.

Once again Sgt. Haggan of the 511th was sent out on patrol at Eschdorf to act as a lookout station, and with his radio act as a relay for any messages from a missing Corps 707th Tank Battalion.

This battalion had been supporting the 110th Regiment of the 28th Division and they had lost most of their tanks and were now along with the troops of the 110th filtering back through the German lines. Haggan was not able to contact any American units and found himself in a bad position. His position lay directly in the path of the 5th Paratroop and the

352nd Volks Grenadier march to Bastogne. He was called into 511th CP and arrived at 1930 hours on the 19th.

Farther to the east and south the 9th Armored and 4th Infantry Divisions were holding fast on a German attack towards Luxembourg City. The main danger to the 511th was perceived to come from the north and remained the area of greatest concern to Captain Guenter, the Company Commander.

The VIII Corps Engineer had become concerned that the Germans might attempt to capture our bridge equipment and use us to build a bridge in the combat areas. Part of Hitler's plans relied on the captured American supplies to fill his shortages which included bridging and especially fuel. At this stage of the big battle almost all of the German engineer troops had been wasted fighting as infantry in the first days of the campaign and re-placements were not experienced and failed under fire, delaying the advance critically.

Colonel Winslow of VIII Corps advised Guenter to destroy all of the maps in the war room and prevent any knowledge of them from falling into German hands. Guenter did so, keeping only the overlay of the proposed Rhine crossings which they were to preserve at all cost. At this time Guenter realized how important his bridge trains were to the Germans.

He immediately ordered the entire bridge trains of the first and second platoons to move to Habay La Nueve that night. Under complete blackout conditions the bridge trains started to move out at 1800 hours.

Bridge destroyed and rebuilt by Captain Jerry Guenter and the men of the 511th Light Pontoon Company Northeast from Bastogne at route N-15.

Haggan, with Lang, Kershaw, Barone, and Piles went out on a third outpost duty of the day to Rambrouch. The town forms the apex of the inverted triangle with the road from Ettelbruck to Martelange running one half mile to the north. At this road junction he picked up First Sergeant Robert Jacobs and Staff Sergeant Charles F. Salsbury of the 687th Field Artillery who told the patrol that tanks were headed for their position in Rambrouch which lay in the path of the Panzer Lehrs and 5th Parachute Divisions drive on the southern portion of the VIII Corps Bastogne defense line at Martelange. The 687th's firing positions had been overrun after desperate hand to hand fighting. After their companions were killed, wounded, or captured, the two Sergeants slipped into the woods and walked twenty kilometers. They hadn't seen an American until meeting Sergeant Haggan's patrol.

Sometime during the day Haggan was reinforced with others including T5 Doherty from the 511th H&S Company. At 0300 hours on the morning of the 20th of December he reported that he had made contact with armored vehicles and he was ordered back to base. There are stories from the men at the outpost that the enemy tanks or vehicles at one point parked momentarily in front of the house occupied by the 511th. It is probable that this was the column that reached Martelange later in the day and had the 299th Engineers blow the bridges right in front of them.

As is now known, these vehicles were free to move anywhere they wished and were on recon to determine American positions and locations. Haggan retreated and the rest of his patrol jumped into two vehicles and were placed under fire as they rushed out of Rambrouch and towards Redange. Everyone was placed into a truck and Doherty's jeep, including the two artillery men of the 687th Field Artillery Battalion. These survivors of what has to be one of the most heroic units of the VIII Corps were fed, given a place to sleep, and then sent on to Corps at Neufchateau with their information.

On the evening of the 20th the commander of the 299th Engineer Combat Battalion reported to the commander of the First Army's 1128th Engineer Combat Group and suggested a new barrier line. They checked with the First Army Engineer, Colonel William Carter, and the plan was put into action. He proposed that he set up a new line with the help of the 341st Engineer General Service Regiment to the south, incorporating Arlon on its defenses. This would extend the new barrier line west of Bastogne to the south.

The 299th's executive officer was sent out to check the barrier line and he reported at 1500 on the 19th that a pitched battle was taking place north of Martelange. Company B confirmed the reports and they reported that they had blown the Martelange bridges at 1720 hours on December 19th. Tracked vehicles moved into Martelange under the protection of heavy gun fire from the German assault gun brigade. On the receipt of the report, B Company was ordered to retreat to Witry. The Germans occupied not only Martelange but Fauvillers, thus blocking the roads north from Habay La Nueve.

By the afternoon hours of the 20th while part of Company A 299th Engineers was blowing the bridges on the Ourthe one of its patrols ran into several problems. Company A hadn't left a guard at the mined bridge on the N-4 and as the patrol returned with two trucks to blow the bridge it ran into fourteen German tanks. They possibly hit one tank with a

bazooka and the patrol abandoned its vehicles and broke for the woods. Only the patrol leader returned to the Company CP at 0145 hours. By daylight the company was relieved by the 158th Engineer Combat Battalion and managed to return to Hachy before the encirclement of Bastogne.

The situation on the 20th was hardly ideal for VIII Corps. Bastogne was surrounded and held the 101st Airborne, three task forces of the 10th Armored Division, four field artillery battalions, and the 326 Airborne Combat Engineer Battalion. Defending the outer road net with mines, abatis, bazookas, and bridges prepared for demolition were the 299th, the 35th, the 158th, and the 1278th Engineer Combat Battalions, all of whom had held Bastogne's outer road net until the 101st had taken up positions in Bastogne.

Those with specialist combat skills were sent to whatever combat arms were needed the most within the perimeter. VIII Corps headquarters had moved to Neufchateau on the 18th of December and had appropriated the 527th light ponton company as headquarters guard troops. Colonel Winslow, Chief Engineer of VIII Corps had only one Bailey Bridge company left after this arrangement. It too had been assigned to fight as infantry to defend Habay La Nueve.

During the period between the 20th and the 25th of December, Captain Guenter's Bridge Company had became part of a lengthy engineer barrier line on the southern shoulder south of Bastogne where the Germans 5th Parachute Division had captured Martelange and were apparently prepared to move south through the defenses of the 511th, the 299th, and the 1278th engineer units.

These engineer units were at one time ordered by their group command post to defend as infantry the town of Martelange. When Captain Guenter went on patrol to that town on the evening of the 20th he learned that it was heavily defended by the 5th Parachute Division of the Germans, and Guenter wisely refrained from attacking the enemy with his very limited forces. Apparently the very presence of the engineers and their active patrolling made the enemy believe that the area was heavily defended and as a result the German higher command decided to attack north towards the Meuse in the direction of Spa and Liege. If the commander of the 5th Parachute Division had investigated to the south with patrols and found a scarcity of defenses, he would have attacked almost unopposed.

Captain Richard D. Guenter kept his head when he could have lost it and most of his men. He disobeyed, or countermanded an order to move into a town when he knew the odds were impossible based on wrong information of which he had positive proof from his own eyes. In the confusion, he could have easily abandoned the field. By defending the outpost with a show of strength he caused the German Paratroopers to go no further and eventually withdraw from the field altogether.

The VIII Corps gathered more engineer troops to defend the road to Arlon as the Germans remained in the town of Martelange and made no attempt to repair the bridges.

To add to the confusion, the long awaited arrival of Patton's 3rd Army was delayed at Martelange, where the 4th Armored Divisions 25th Cavalry Regiment had to defeat the 5th Paratroopers and take the town away from the Germans. There was a long await in getting a Bailey bridge company to build back the type of bridge needed for heavy tanks. Patton's philosophy was like Peiper's: capture the bridges before the enemy can blow them. This thinking did not work in the Ardennes battle.

30

Bastogne: And the 299th Engineer Combat Battalion

The 299th Engineer Combat Battalion had came in on the beaches of Normandy on D-Day with the mission to clear under water obstacles and dangerous mine fields in close support of the infantry. They suffered many casualties and yet survived as a unit to move on through France and Belgium as Corps Engineers in close support of armor and infantry. They received a Presidential Citation for their courageous actions in Normandy.

Like hundreds of engineer combat battalions they built Bailey bridges, ponton bridges, and timber trestle bridges, sometimes under fire, to keep the armor and infantry rolling as the German engineers blew everything in sight while they were driven back into their homeland in 1944.

The 299th was attached to the 1128th Engineer Combat Group, who in turn was in support of VIII Corps, whose headquarters was located in Bastogne, Belgium. The battalion headquarters at Hachy and Habay, Belgium was now running saw mills and preparing the bridge material for the coming assault into Germany. They had been involved in replacing bridges up to the Siegfried line in Belgium and Luxembourg.

Presidential Citation recipients (from left to right) Lt. Col. Harvey Fraser of the 51st; Lt. Col. David Pergrin of the 291st; and Lt. Col. Jewitt of the 299th.

The first enemy action concerning the battalion came on the 16th of December, 1944 with the shelling of Diekerch, Luxembourg, where the battalion was operating a saw mill. The shelling was so heavy it became necessary to evacuate the personnel and equipment. At 1:30 a.m. on Dec. 17th the battalion was alerted, all observation posts were manned according to our standard plan.

A Company was placed on alert for movement. All the personnel and equipment forward of Corps rear boundary were assembled at their respective command posts at Hachy and Habay.

The enemy threat became worse on the 18th and Company B was ordered out at 6:25 p.m. to establish and man an engineer barrier line running northeast from Martelange and generally along route N-46 to its junction with N-15, a frontage of 12 miles. This would mean preparing bridges for demolition and other road blocks to delay and stop the enemy.

Company B opened up their command post at Witry, Belgium at 55 minutes after midnight on the 19th, and started to establish a barrier line which they completed by noon that day. Company A was ordered out at 11:50 a.m. to establish a 15 mile barrier running northwest along route N-46 in conjunction to the one given to Company B to the junction with N-26, and from there, along the Ourthe River to a point north of N-4. This linked up with the barrier line being established by the 1278th Engineer Combat Battalion which extended on north towards La Roche.

Company A moved out, and established a CP at Lavacherie at 2:15 p.m. and went to work on their barrier line. First priority was given to a Bailey bridge on N-4 in the vicinity of Ourtheuville and other bridges in their vicinity. It had been reported to civilians that the German tanks were seen there. At 3:00 p.m. Company C was ordered to move to Vaux and remain in support of companies A and B. They opened their CP at Vaux at 5:25 p.m. Lt. Colonel Jewitt had learned from the Corps Engineer that Colonel William Carter, the First Army Engineer, was now setting up a continuous engineer barrier line from Monschau near the Siegfried line in front of Eupen, Vervier, and south to tie into the barrier line established by the 291st at Malmedy, Stavelot, Trois Ponts, and Werbomont, where Peiper had been stopped by the blowing of the bridge at Habiemont.

Company A completed the preparations for demolition of six bridges at 10:29 p.m. The southern portion of their sector was taken care of by the 1278th Engineer Combat Battalion. A patrol being sent out by Company A to prepare a bridge for demolition met an enemy armored column of 14 tanks advancing on them. They engaged the enemy, knocking out one tank with a bazooka as they scrambled for cover in the woods when capture was eminent. The patrol leader returned to the Company CP alone at 1:45 a.m. Enemy action early on the 20th of December along the northeast end of Company A's barrier caused them to blow all of the bridges except the Bailey bridge on route N-4. Security of the Bailey bridge was reinforced by eight Tank Destroyers.

Many times during the drive across France and Belgium combat engineers were out in front of the enemy, such as existed in this case. Tank Destroyers were a great addition to A Company's barrier line. Company A was to be relieved of all road blocks north of N-26 by elements of the 158th Engineer Combat Battalion and all blocks south of N-26 and N-15 by C Company of the 299th Engineer Combat Battalion who was still in reserve at Vaux. Company C moved to Morhet, opening their CP at 4:00 p.m. The enemy action was so severe that the 2nd platoon of Company C was not relieved by the 158th Engineer Combat Battalion.

The enemy attacked the Bailey bridge at 9:30 a.m. on the 20th of December. In the ensuing fight the Tank Destroyers knocked out an enemy tank on the end of the bridge, thus making it an effective obstacle. A counter attack by the 158th Engineers with elements of Company A of the 299th attached secured the bridge, destroyed an armored vehicle and pushed the enemy back, opening up N-4 to Bastogne. The second platoon Company C 299th Engineers arrived and relieved the 2nd platoon of Company A on the bridge about noon. Company A, less two squads still missing in action, assembled in the battalion CP at Hachy and went in reserve.

On the evening of the 19th the battalion submitted a plan to Group hdqs. for a barrier line from Martelange to Arlon and west of N-4, a frontage of about 15 miles. The task of manning this barrier was given to the 341st Engineer General service Regiment at Arlon, on the 20th. The 341st had come under the control of the 1128th Engineer Combat Group. Now the preparing and manning of barrier lines was spreading in the direction of the Meuse River where the plan was to set up five Engineer General Service Regiments from south of Namur to Liege. The engineer reaction to the surprise counter-attack of Adolf Hitler had been complete and now the development of armor, infantry, and artillery to form on these engineer barrier lines would result in the overall defeat of this massive surprise attack.

The 299th Engineer Combat Battalion was to supervise the barrier in their area and coordinate it with the barrier in their north. The executive officer was sent out at noon to check the barrier, but on his return he showed concern of the possible by-passes of the bridges and fording of some streams. He also reported that a pitched battle was going on just north of Martelange at 5:20 p.m. and that enemy tanks and Infantry had moved into town under the protection of heavy gun fire.

All barriers in the vicinity of Martelange and all personnel not cut off by the enemy, returned to the Company CP at Witry. Company B was given orders by Colonel Jewitt to stand by at Witry as long as possible.

At 5:45 p.m. on the afternoon of December 20th, the 299th Engineer Combat Battalion was given the order down from Corps Hdqs. "Retake the town of Martelange." This was like saying "Go and fight as Infantry."

Company C of the 1278th Engineer Combat Battalion, less one platoon and 140 riflemen of the 341st Engineer General Service Regiment, were attached to the battalion for this mission. Two forces were organized. Captain Manion, 299th Engineer Combat Battalion was to meet Captain Sullivan, C.O. Company C 1278th Engineers, in Habay and take elements of his company to Witry where he was to pick up remnants of the first platoon of Company B 299th Engineers, who had been on the bridge at Martelange, and attack the town from the west.

This force was to be known as Company "B's Force". Lt. Jenkins, 299th Engineers was ordered to proceed to road junction 9 and N-4 where he was to meet Captain Oldenberg with 140 riflemen. (All engineers are qualified to fire the rifle.) This force was to be known as "Buick Force" and was to attack Martelange from the south with N-4 as an axis for the attack.

At 8:00 p.m. Major Kohlar, Battalion Executive Officer, was sent to the CP at Witry to coordinate the two attacks. He arrived there at 8:30 p.m. and found that Company B task force had not as yet assembled.

Captain Manion arrived at Witry at 11:30 with approximately one platoon of Company C 1278 Engineers. The convoy had been separated in moving forward and it was not expected that the rest of the company would follow.

Company B task force was immediately organized, consisting of a provisional platoon of Company B, 299th, with Captain Steem, Company Commander in charge and two officers, Lt. Donahoe and Lt. Seibert, accompanying him. There was a provisional platoon of Company C 1278th with Lt. Christie in charge, accompanied by Lieutenant Zelenzy. Captain Manion moved out at 1:12 a.m. with a mission of establishing a defensive position on the outskirts of town and then sending patrols into town to determine the strength and disposition of the enemy. He was not to attack the town before dawn. No contact had been made with "Buick".

"Buick Force" had moved up N-4 to the southern outskirts of town and were preparing to send patrols into town at night. This they accomplished very successfully, obtaining information of strength and disposition of the enemy. They did not attack. The remainder of Company C 1278th arrived just as the task force B was moving out. They were joined by Captain Sullivan, Company Commander, Company C 1278th at 2:10 a.m. and moved forward under his command at 2:47 with the strength of one platoon less one squad. The squad led by Sgt. Bersten was sent out by Major Kohlar to patrol the road blocks to the northwest along N-46 and to establish contact with Lt. Russell, second platoon Company B, who was in charge.

The patrol returned about 8:30 the next morning indicating that everything was quiet. Contact was made with elements of the 552nd Engineer Heavy Ponton Company who were along N-45 in the vicinity of Trainment. The 552nd Ponton Company had a Barrier line from Trainment northwest to N-15, and agreed to stand in their Barriers as long as elements of the task force were forward of them. Close communications were maintained between task force headquarters at Witry and the 552nd.

Lt. Zelanzy arrived at the CP at Witry with Lt. Christie, who had been injured in a jeep accident. Lt. Christie was evacuated to the CP at Hachy; Lt. Zelanzy indicated everything was quiet. Patrols had been sent into town and only one patrol had been fired upon. One man was slightly wounded with a bullet in his cheek. Captain Manion planned to attack the town at dawn.

A patrol had been sent out to contact the "Buick Force". Chow, medical supplies, and Scr 284 radio and operators from the 278th Engineers were sent forth with Lt. Zelanzy at

7:30 a.m. Although contact was made with the radio on two occasions for short intervals, no messages were able to be transmitted or received, and all personnel sent forward at this time are still missing in action. It was later confirmed that these men were never able to contact the forward CP and could have been wiped out or captured.

Company C was ordered out of their Barrier line on the afternoon of the 20th by the officers of the 28th Division who had occupied the area. The Division didn't want to have any barriers constructed in front of them that would hinder their advance. Company C, less the second platoon, assembled at the CP at Morhet and turned in to rest. At about 2:00 a.m. on the 21st, Company B was ordered to reinforce the task force at Witry with all available men.

Captain Bunting arrived at the CP at Witry at 9:30 a.m. with about one platoon of Company C 299th Engineers to reinforce the task force. The Company convoy less one platoon had been cut by enemy action while moving from the CP at Morhet the night before. Lt. Koenig and one squad had been dispatched when the convoy reached Vaux, to pick up stragglers. The second squad under Lt. Husch was attached to the 158th Combat Engineer Battalion of Lt. Colonel Sam Tabet, and was guarding the Bailey bridge on N-4 at Ourtheuville. They remained there until orders to evacuate. The second platoon of Company C supported. At 3:00 p.m., December 25th, all men were detached from the 28th Division and proceeded back to Malonne, arriving there about 7:30 p.m.

The First Sergeant Company "C" 1278th Engineers reported in at 9:30 a.m. December 21 that there were paratroopers at Vauvillers, cutting the task force off at Martelange.

Captain Bunting and elements of Company C 299th Engineers then present were sent forward to break through the task force in Martelange and keep the road open. Company C engaged the enemy in Fauvillers at 10:05 a.m. and cleaned out the town, killing at least two and capturing four. They continued their advance towards Martelange. About one-half mile outside of Fauviers the enemy pinned them down with machine gun and mortar fire. The advance point had been cut off. When the enemy began closing in on the flank, the company withdrew to the road junction of N-45-46 where they reinforced the road block with a half squad, the rest returned to the CP at Witry.

Orders had already been received at Witry to evacuate and return to the CP at Hachy. A message was sent to battalion CP informing them that the task force had been cut off in Martelange and armored vehicles were needed to break through and get them out.

In the meantime an officer from the 552 Heavy Ponton Company had come forward to the CP to check on the situation and stated that all was secure behind us and that he had gotten two tank destroyers to support his road blocks. Captain Bunting was sent back to see if he could get the two tank destroyers to support his company which now amounted to two platoons. The Captain desired to use them to attack the Germans in Martelange in order to get through and free the engineer task force.

Major Kohlar ordered everyone to withdraw and return to their respective CPs. The convoy was assembled and a patrol was sent back to pick up the rear guard. In addition to picking up the rear guard they picked up the Sergeant of Company C 299th and two men who had been cut off just east of Fauvillers. Also two men from the forward truck area reported that they had been surrounded that morning about daylight and all of the vehicles had been captured before they could destroy them.

The remnants of the task force left Witry around 2:20 p.m. At 1100 hours on December 21 the battalion received orders to assemble all personnel and proceed to St. Cecil. The battalion had been battling for many days against superior forces without any artillery support, but they had delayed the enemy from reaching the Meuse River.

They had fought as Infantry, and used their combat engineering skills much to the detriment of the attacking Germans. Company A had moved out and relieved "Buick" forces at 6:00 a.m. on the 21st. They took up defensive positions at a road block just south of Martelange on N-4 and remained there until word was received to disengage and return to battalion CP. Company A reblew the crater on N-4 to renew its effectiveness. They returned to the CP with remnants of Company B and C at 3:00 p.m. Three squads of Company "B" had returned from obstacles in the vicinity of RJ N-15 and N-46. Lt. Russell and 19 enlisted men were still fighting on N-15 in vicinity of their road blocks. At 4:30 p.m. the battalion convoy moved out from Hachy, arriving at St. Cecil at 8:30 p.m. where the battalion was billeted in two hotels. Major Perry, the S-3 remained at Hachy to pick up stragglers and later went to Neufchateau to pick up Lt. Russell and his men. The battalion departed from St. Cecil on the morning of the 22nd and arrived at their destination at Malonne, Belgium at 4:40 p.m.

Lt. French arrived at Melonne at 6:30 p.m. after having been picked up by elements of the 4th Armored Division entering Fauviers. The 4th Armored were attacking north from the 3rd Army area to relieve the 101st Airborne Division now surrounded by a 16 mile ring of attacking Germans.

Major Perry arrived at battalion CP at Malonne about 7:30 p.m., December 25th, with Lt. Russell and 19 enlisted men. The battalion was now coming back together to reorganize and become re-supplied with everything from trucks to bulldozers. There were still many missing, however this was reduced in numbers when Captain Steem arrived about 8:00 p.m. on December 25th with Lt. Donahoe and Lt. Seibert. Captain Steem's task force with survivors of the battle at Martelange arrived. These 25 men and 1st Sergeant Bowers had been prisoners and were rescued by the 4th Armored Division.

A check of the 26th of December reveals that there were 41 men missing in action and two wounded. This is from an after battle report signed by Lt. Colonel Jewitt.

The 299th would go on towards victory on the Roer, the Rhine, and other river assaults to the end of the war.

31

Bastogne: And the 158th Combat Battalion

Lt. Colonel Sam Tabet was trained under the R.O.T.C. program and in 1941 found himself at Fort Belvoir, Virginia in a training battalion using his combat engineering skills to train men from all walks of life to become combat engineers. There was mine laying, use of explosives, building all types of assault bridges, and firing the weapons of war such as rifles, bazookas, machine guns, pistols, and carbines. There were 20 mile marches, obstacle courses, and night problems under the cover of darkness. Map reading was a special course and use of radio was also stressed.

After many courses as a leader and instructor, Sam went to a field unit being trained for combat. Basic and intensive training was followed by maneuvers with infantry and armor and real-life river crossings.

Later Sam found himself in England as a battalion commander of a 650 man engineer combat battalion getting ready to invade Europe. The battalion was the 158th and in June of 1944 they were in Normandy clearing mines and aiding the infantry and armor move through

Bridge built and blown by the 158th Engineers of Col. Tabet in the defense of Bastogne.

The newly constructed bridge after the original bridge was blown.

France and into Belgium. They had casualties and they were bombed from the air. They built bridge after bridge up to December 1944. They had covered a wide area in Belgium and Luxembourg, mainly keeping the road net open for the rapidly advancing First Army. They were battle hardened and had witnessed and been part of assault crossing of rivers. The 158th was located near Bastogne, Belgium when on December 17, 1944 at 5:30 p.m. the group commander of the 1128th Engineer Combat Group gave Sam orders to occupy a defensive position in front of the City of Bastogne, from Foy to Neffe—a distance of 3900 yards.

Later on Sam was asked to make a full report of his actions in the battle of the bulge. This is his report on December 26th 1944.

We were advised that we would be attached to the VIII Corps and additional orders would be received. This battalion immediately contacted Colonel Winslow, the VIII Corps Engineer and was advised to not move into position until daybreak of the 18th of December, as the 35th Engineer Combat Battalion was some where in the area, and confusion would result if we would try to move in under cover of darkness.

The commanding officer of the 35th Combat Engineers was contacted and arrangements completed to occupy our defense line at day break. Incomplete information was available about the enemy at this time. Plans were then made for the battalion to move at 0500 hours into our assigned defensive line with A Company on the left flank, Company B on the right flank, and Company C in reserve. The battalion CP was to be located in the village of Luxery. The battalion was there at 0630 hours and in position.

Four M18 Tank Destroyers were received from the 507th Ordinance Battalion and turned over to Captain Gabbs, the S-2 Intelligence officer whose purpose was to reconnoiter a natural barrier line, and to find the information about the enemy in our vicinity. In addition to these tanks from the 507th Ordinance Battalion, we received eight light tanks and two M-4s from 532nd Ordinance Battalion. All the above being manned not by regular tank crews but by repairmen and mechanics. This help proved invaluable.

Four tanks were held in reserve and the others were dispatched on call for help from the Company Commander of Company B, this battalion, along with one platoon of the reserve company.

At 1030 hours 18 December information was received from Colonel Winslow that this battalion would be attached to the 10th Armored Division, Combat Command B, who were to arrive sometime that night. At 2300 hours, a call was received from Colonel Roberts, Combat Command B, was in Bastogne, and I immediately reported to him, giving to him the situation as we knew it. At this time our right flank was under intense small arms and mortar fire, and our CP was somewhat under artillery fire. At 0730 hours, I was ordered to pull out Company A who was on our left flank and send them in support of one of the combat teams known as Desobry, who was located at Noville on Route N-15 and were under heavy small arms fire. Arrangements were made to have the elements of Company C protect the left flank of Company B, and I went to Combat Command Bs CP and informed Colonel Roberts of the situation at that time and strongly suggested that Company A not be pulled out of line; as it would let Company Bs left flank, who were receiving considerable fire, wide open.

Colonel Roberts gave his approval not to let Company A out of line and to stay in their position to protect the left flank on N-15s entrance to Bastogne. At 0930 hours, Colonel Winslow called and informed us that reinforcements were on the way and upon their arrival they would occupy our position which was precarious at best. The 158th Engineers would be relieved and sent back to its CP in St. Ode.

At 1200 hours we were advised by Colonel Winslow that we would be relieved by the 507th Parachute Battalion and two battalions of the 101st Airborne Infantry and an engineer company of the 10th Armored Division. Upon receiving this information, we dispatched personnel to locate the CP of the above organizations and to lead them into line. At 1330 hours, orders were given to the company commanders that we were being replaced in line by the infantry and that they would contact the commanding officers giving them all the information about the road blocks and position of the enemy.

Company A was ordered back to its old CP in Chene. Companies H&S, B, and C were ordered to return to the battalion CP in St. Ode. Group was kept informed at all times. The entire move was completed by 1900 hours on December 19th, 1944. We had acted as a full blocking force in our area south and east of Bastogne against strong enemy forces and we had held until the arrival of armor and infantry. Upon returning to the CP a number of orders were found which had given our adjutant a certain amount of concern. The messages were from the Group Commander.

This photo shows a position in need of a bridge.

Every effort was being made to carry out all orders and some platoons had already been dispatched to fill these orders when we were informed to disregard the above orders as it was the Group Commander's desire to keep the battalion intact to repel the enemy who was then advancing on Ortheville. Every effort was made to recall troops who had been dispatched, but in some cases this was not entirely possible.

The 1128th Group headquarters had now advised us that the German 2nd SS Panzer Division had bypassed Bastogne on the north and were attacking towards Ortheville, while their Panzer Lehr Division had bypassed Bastogne on the south.

This all indicated that we were going to be involved in a major battle in our area. We also had learned from the Group operations officer that Colonel William Carter, the First Army Chief Engineer was establishing an engineer barrier line to prevent the Germans from reaching the Meuse River. The 158th, 35th, 299th, 51st, and the 1278th was to become part of this development of road blocks, craters, mine fields, and bridges prepared for demolition.

At 1730 hours, a platoon of Company A 299th Engineers, who were guarding the Ortheville bridge was relieved by a platoon of Company C of the 299th. The platoon was attached to Company B of the 158th Engineers. At this time the executive officer of the 299th Engineers, arrived at my CP and all available information with regard to his men was transmitted to him. It was suggested that he contact his Battalion Commanding Officer to clarify why his men were at the bridge site. He informed me this would be done. It seemed to me that we engineers may be forced to fight in this area without much help from our own armor or infantry. During all of this activity, all engineer companies were busily laying road blocks, and mining roads in the immediate vicinity.

Two platoons of the 705th Tank Destroyer Battalion, eight in number were found in the vicinity of the Ortheuville bridge; this was good news at 1220 hours. Recon patrols were continually reporting that convoys were trapped from the Ortheuville bridge to the road junction N-4 and N-26, and also south of this road junction and north of the Ortheuville bridge. It was then decided to attack and clear the road from the Ortheuville bridge site to the road junction N-4 and N-26 which would open up the Army main supply route from Bastgne to Marche. This was done, and from the start of the attack until our objective was reached, convoys of gasoline and ammunition went into Bastogne, and convoys of rear echelon non-combatant units used N-4 to Marche.

During this attack one company of Canadians were used to our right flank, but due to their physical condition and inexperience, they had to be withdrawn and our reserve committed to the right flank.

The four tank destroyers received orders to report for the defense of Bastogne. Our objective was reached at 1705 hours on December 20th, at which time we withdrew to our CP leaving strong road guards behind for the establishment of road blocks. There was a lull in the fighting which indicated that the enemy had sent for reinforcements. At 2315 hours, the enemy began to attack in strength. Three attacks were repulsed. On the fourth attack the enemy began to infiltrate our flanks.

The Bailey bridge that had been wired failed to blow, as it is believed that all leads were cut by 88mm fire. The four tank destroyers that were with us were used to fire upon the bridge which resulted in an explosion in which it is believed destroyed the bridge in such an extent that it could not be used by the Germans heavy traffic. Leaving a rear guard, the battalion withdrew in good order to St. Hubert where it reorganized. Orders were then received from the Group to withdraw southwest along N-28 through Recogne. Further orders were received to withdraw to Givet where the Group convoy was to meet and we were taken to our present position in Floreffe.

At the battle at Ortheuville a line of defense was set up with machine guns, rifles, hand grenades, and tank destroyers. The bridges had been prepared with six charges of 96 pounds each of TNT. Mines were put in strings on the bridges. There was much exchange of fire with the enemy, however, the range was too long and our casualties was minimal. The enemy pounded us with artillery fire, however we were well dug-in. With the destruction of the bridge, we had caused the enemy to slow down his advance to the Meuse River.

The following comments are made; The enemy are using troops dressed in American uniforms who can speak English to penetrate outposts and to gain information.

Many of my men earned Bronze and Silver Stars for their courageous action in the battles, however, Private Bernard Michin was awarded the Distinguished Service Cross for his performance on the night of December 18th at a road block near Martelange. Michin was setting on top of a road block with a bazooka when while peering into the darkness he saw the approach of a German tank, he waited until the tank was almost on top of him when

Men just before the battles (from left to right) are: Lt. Col. Jack Jeffrey (deceased), 296th Eng. C. Bat.; Lt. Col. Sam Tabet (deceased), 158th Eng. C. Bat.; Lt. Col. Dave Pergrin, 291st Eng. C. Bat.; Lt. Col. Bud Cameron, 164th Eng. C. Bat.; Major Al Kahn, 164th Eng. C. Bat.; and an unknown Lieutenant.

he fired. At first he wanted to make sure that it was an American tank, he fired and the tremendous explosion finished the tank, but also seared his eyes. He rolled into the ditch and was partially blinded. Soon thereafter the Germans moved up a machine gun and Michin rolled over and threw a hand grenade at the gun wiping it and the crew out of commission.

The men of A, B, and C companies along with many in the H&S were engaged with the enemy constantly for eight days and we had fought at times as Combat Engineers, and at times as Infantry.

Lt. Colonel Sam Tabet's Battalion went on to rebuild the bridges blown by the Germans in their final retreat. Many of these bridges were built under fire and in bitter weather. This again reveals the great and courageous actions of the American soldier and especially those up front with the Combat Engineers.

32

The 51st Engineer Combat Battalion and the Engineer Barrier Line

Commanding Officer: Lt. Colonel Harvey R. Fraser

During World War II, the American Army called together millions of civilians and molded them into units that could work together to go about the business of winning the war. One such unit was the 51st Engineer Combat Battalion. At the beginning of WWII, the United States Army sent its newly inducted recruits to units for training. The engineer military training called for 13 weeks of basic, individual and team training, consisting of eight months of training as a unit. It was followed by training with other units, and culminated in maneuvers with divisions, corps and armies.

One of the 131 units formed in 1942 was the 51st Engineer Combat Regiment, activated at Camp Bowie, Texas. In August of that year Colonel H. Wallis Anderson took over

The bridge at Hotton where the 51st Combat Engineers stopped the Panzers of the 5th Panzer Army at their farthest point of attack.

281

Knocked out Panzer IV at Hotton.

command of the unit and laid the foundation for the development of teamwork and esprit de corps that bound the 51st together.

The unit moved to Plattsburg, New York, located about 20 miles south of the Canadian border. Enlisted men began arriving on Christmas Day, 1942 from all corners of the United States. In March 1943, the regiment was re-designed and the headquarters company became the 1111th Engineer Combat Group and Colonel Anderson then had two Engineer Combat Battalions under his command: the 51st and the 238th. The two battalions scored highly in their training tests as they learned all of the skills of combat engineering. The 51st Engineers moved to Ft. Belvoir, Virginia for two weeks of intensive training. They then went to Fort Dix to prepare for overseas movement. They landed in England on January 20th, 1944 and became part of Colonel Anderson's 1111th Engineer Combat Group. From mid-June 1944, the 1111th Engineer Combat Group supported the First Army through France and Belgium.

The three battalions were operating saw mills to provide critical lumber for the assault into Germany when, on December 17, the Ardennes offensive began. Colonel Anderson's experience in two other wars helped to make his group capable of stalling the German thrusts into Malmedy, Stavelot, Trois Ponts, and Habiemont.

Now, with the First Army engineer barrier line being established and Anderson's Group located at Modave, the Group was assigned a large segment of the barrier line using the 300th Engineer Combat Battalion, A Company of the 291st, and the 51st Engineers of Lt. Colonel Harvey Fraser. The 51st Engineers performed courageously, and their history supports such an assertion:

Lt. Col. Harvey Fraser receiving Bronze Star.

Captain Preston Hodges receiving the Silver Star for his bravery at Hotton, Belgium.

The 1111th Engineer Group assigned the 51st ECB to prepare for demolitions all of the crossings of the Ourthe River from Durbuy to La Roche. The battalion then assigned this task to companies A and B, ordering them to establish obstacles such as minefields, and abatis on the roads toward the river, and plant demolitions on bridges and culverts. The key point for the battalion in the defensive line was the Ourthe River bridge at Hotton. By 0700 hours on December 19th, the battalion had prepared all crossings for demolition. Two anti-tank minefields were laid just 200 yards downstream from the Hotton bridge, and one in the ford under the railroad bridge in Melreux. Below LaRoche, at the extreme south of the barrier line, the Canadian 9th Forestry Company prepared the crossings on the Ourthe River for demolition.

Although the situation was unclear, there was no doubt as to the need to keep the roads clear. Rumors of paratroopers behind our lines kept everyone in a turmoil. As a result, Colonel Fraser instituted a civilian check system. At the 51st checkpoint, 21 civilians were found to have American clothing, cigarettes and other military items in their baggage. All except one spoke German, and one had a German officer's passbook. They were turned over to an interrogation point in Namur.

On December 20th, Company B continued to set up barriers along the Ourthe River. A bridge southwest of Durbuy was prepared for demolition. Further southwest, a detachment with a bazooka and a .30-caliber machine gun defended a weak bridge at Grand Man. At Noisseux, the piers of a destroyed bridge were wired for demolition, and a trench with a .50-caliber machine gun and a bazooka guarded the crossing. The railroad bridge near Melreux was also prepared for demolition.

Second Lieutenant Spearmin of the 440th AAA Battalion arrived at the 51st ECB command post and said he wanted to fight with the engineers. His 90 men made up eight sections, each consisting of a .40-MM gun, a .50-caliber machine gun, and a bazooka. Six of these sections were spread out along the line, and two were assigned to the Hotton bridges. Fraser later regretted that he did not recommend Spearmin for the Silver Star.

Monument to the 51st Engineers on the the bridge at Trois Ponts.

Company A prepared a bridge in Hampteau for demolition and guarded it with one .30-caliber and two .50-caliber machine guns. A short distance down the road in that direction, two footbridges were prepared for demolition and a guard placed. A weak class-10 bridge at Marcourt was prepared for destruction. It was defended by a half-track and a man with a bazooka, two .50-caliber machine guns, and one .30-caliber machine gun. One squad with a .50-caliber machine gun and a bazooka defended the road junction at N-34 and 488.

Company A also prepared other roadblocks. Abatis were placed on N-4 near Tenneville, and 30 mines installed after the trees were blown. Further north, at an intersection called Champlain Crossroads on N-4 and N-28, a platoon of Canadian Foresters and 13 men from the 158th ECB, 13 men from the 51st ECB, and 12 men from the 440th AAA Battalion defended the intersection. Armaments included one .40mm gun, one .50-caliber machine gun, and one bazooka.

Further north on N-4 at Bande, south of Marche and where the N-4 crossed the Hadree, meticulous defenses were prepared. In the event of an enemy attack, all men and equipment were to fall back east of the roadblock and make a stand. Other roadblocks and bridges prepared for demolition were completed at Rochefort. The roadnet from Marche-Aye-Humain-Rochefort and N-35 from Marche to Rochefort was denied to the enemy.

During the day, a continuous recon was made on N-4 toward Bastogne. Enemy armor and infantry coming up N-4 temporarily stopped at Ourtheuville, 2000 meters south of Tenneville. The battalion called for all possible roadblocks that could be established on N-4 northwest of Ourtheuville. Shortly after receiving word of the enemy at Ourtheuville, the 158th ECB said that N-4 was clear all the way to Bastogne. The enemy ground troops had been routed and some armor destroyed. Even so, the battalion had two squads of the 3rd platoon, Company A ready to put in roadblocks if necessary.

On December 21, 1944, at 0700 hours, 25 German infantry men crossed the Ourthe River at Hampteau and drove off two squads of Company A, 51st ECB. These were the first probing elements of the 116th Panzer Division, which had already lost 24 hours in a counter-march maneuver on the 19th. Now, without rest since the 16th and dead tired, they were attempting to break the 51st's line. But on this day, the Fifth Panzer Army's advance would be carried by forward patrols of the 2nd Panzer Division and the 116th Panzer Division only. These patrols were separated by the Ourthe River, so they fought two separate battles.

The Hampteau defense had been organized by the leader of the first platoon, Lt. Floyd D. Wright. On the road to Soy, about 30 yards northeast of the footbridge across the river, his men laid a hasty minefield. Private Stanley A. Driggs guarded it with his M-1 rifle. On the southwest side of the river, about 30 to 40 yards from the footbridge, a bazooka team of three men had a detonator to blow the bridge. Along the Hotton-LaRoche road, two bazooka teams, about 700 yards apart, were protected by daisy chain of mines. A half a squad of riflemen, two .50-caliber machine guns, and two tanks waited west of the Hotton-LaRoche road.

Just prior to the battle of Hotton, jeep patrols from the 820th Tank Destroyer (TD) Battalion received fire near LaRoche. They relayed the message to the 2nd platoon, Company A at Marcourt. The 2nd platoon subsequently blew their bridge. Wright tried to talk the 820th TD into reinforcing the 2nd platoon's roadblock at Marcourt, but failed. He sent

Lt. Col. Fraser (51st Engineer) and Lt. Col. David Pergrin (291st Engineer) Receive Presidential citations on the banks of the Rhine for their units.

his platoon sergeant, Donald A. Bonifay, along with Benjamin Ham's squad to Marcourt; they arrived in an M-8 armored car, at the 2nd platoon's CP at 0130 hours and reported to Lt. Paul W. Curtis Jr., the platoon leader. Curtis put them on line to defend the town. There had been a brief firefight between the two German half-tracks approaching the bridge and his own .50-caliber machine guns, but no casualties. But when the 51st ECB guards tried to halt an American patrol at Marcourt, Cpl. Jerry Stevens was killed and T/5 Clifton M. Pratt was wounded, all because of mistaken identity.

Bonifay left Sergeant Ham's squad at Marcourt and returned to Hampteau for the fighting there. At 0510, Driggs ran across the bridge to report the approach of a German armored car from the northeast. The Armored car shelled the town while the rest of the men

The bridge at Hotton where the 51st Engineers halted the drive of the Germans to the Meuse.

from the car shelled the bazooka teams. An attempt was made to blow the bridge, but the wires had been cut. By this time Hampteau was on fire and the battle of Hotton had started. Lt. Colonel Fraser ordered Lt. Wright to reinforce Company B at Hotton. At 0900, Bonifay took one last look at the burning but deserted town of Hampteau and made his way back to Hotton on foot. At Hampteau, T/5 Floyd Johnson exposed himself to observed enemy small arms fire and .47-mm HE fire to remove his vehicle after enemy infantry had entered town.

At 0730, firing broke out at Hotton, near the critical class-70 bridge; a half hour later a small-scale battle was in full swing. Fraser put Captain Preston Hodges in charge of the defense of the bridge. Hodges had one squad from Bruce Jamison's 1st platoon, Company B; the 1st platoon, Company A, commanded by Wright; a squad of the 23rd Armored Engineers, 3rd Armored Division (AD), with a 37mm anti-tank gun; two 40mm Bofors AAA guns; several bazooka teams; and some .50-caliber machine guns. Captain Barnes later reinforced Hodges with a ten-man patrol from battalion headquarters. Hodges put most of these personnel and equipment in defensive positions on the southwest side of the Hotton bridge.

On the northeast side of the bridge were the 3rd Armored Division trains and some heavy equipment. Additional 3rd Armored Division personnel southwest of Hotton fought off German infantry and tanks from the heights east of the Ourthe River.

Early in the battle, Fraser was in constant telephone contact with Lts. Jamison and Wright getting eye witness description of the fighting. The army telephones between Hotton and Marche did not work, but the Belgian telephone system was still usable.

The return of the commander of the 51st to Hotton, along with Captain Preston Hodges, who won a Siver Star here. Lt. Col. Fraser is in the red cap, with Cap. Hodges to his right, while the remaining members of the photo are Belgian Historians.

The situation in Hotton soon deteriorated and Fraser requested help from the 84th Infantry Division. Part of the division arrived in Marche but had no mission yet. When his appeal was dismissed, Fraser put the Hotton phone next to the Marche phone so the sounds of battle could be heard. The commanding general, Major General Alexander R. Bolling, personally refused aid until the facts of the matter could be brought to his attention. Eyewitness reports from officers were called rumors without a factual basis.

At 0833, the telephone connection went out, so Fraser left his command post in Marche and drove to the scene of battle in Hotton. While there, Private Lee Ishmael, his driver, seeing the crew manning the 37mm gun was hesitant about putting the piece into action, decided to man the gun himself. With the assistance of the crew, Ishmael disabled one of the German tanks, causing its crew to abandon it. While the battle progressed, Lts. Jamison and Wright found an M-4 tank armed with a 36mm cannon in an ordnance detachment on the outside of Hotton. They tried to talk the tank commander into supporting Company B at the bridge in Hotton. But the tanker was reluctant to move his tank to a defensive position without a crew and support. He insisted that he needed three men inside the tank to man the cannon and 15 riflemen deployed around the tank for protection. Once assured that these men would be provided, he moved the tank to a firing position southwest of the bridge. Three men from the 51st went inside the tank and twelve men deployed outside to protect the tank.

One man deployed outside of the M-4 was Wright's driver, T/5 Floyd Johnson. This tank became part of an unorthodox, but effective, combined arms team, along with the 37mm anti-tank gun, the 40mm Bofor, and the bazooka teams. Between them they put four German heavy tanks out of action. By 0900, two tanks from the 3rd Armored Division trains, one medium and one light, occupying Hotton northeast of the bridge also engaged the enemy. A German Mark VI tank approaching the bridge from the Soy road quickly knocked out the light tank. The M-4 knocked out one German tank. Shortly thereafter, a German round missed the M-4. Johnson ran over to the sergeant in charge of the tank and told him that he and another man saw a flash from the shrubbery between two buildings across the river. The Sergeant fired one shot that was too high. Johnson ran back and told him to lower his sights into the bushes. The second shot was a direct hit, sending a cloud of smoke into the sky. Another German tank was knocked out by the 37mm cannon.

Captain Barnes, having sent his squad of volunteers from H.& S. Company to Hotton, went down N 4 to the outskirts of Marche where an M-10 three-inch gun motor carriage backed up a 51st roadblock. Barnes brought the M-10 back through Marche to Hotton for reinforcement, but was stopped by General Bolling of the 84th Division. Barnes explained the situation in Hotton to General Bolling, but Bolling would not take his word for it. Finally one hour later, at 1000, an officer of the 84th accompanied the S-2 to Hotton. When they arrived at 1030, the town was being heavily shelled. While there, the officer of the 84th received additional reports as to the gravity of the situation, but remained unconvinced. Still, he did promise help.

The battle continued into the afternoon. The Germans soon shot out the wiring on the bridge. Jamison and Wright jumped into the freezing water and, while under small arms fire, repaired the wiring. With the appearance of the relief force from the 84th, most of the 51st withdrew towards Marche, having succeeded in defending the bridge at Hotton. Half a squad remained to blow the bridge if necessary. This was combat engineering to the highest degree. This type of action was common throughout the soldiers of the American forces during the "Battle of The Bulge" in all service branches, in particular the Corps of Engineers.

The first platoon of the 84th task force arrived at 1500, some six hours after the first request for assistance. Additional reports of enemy action led the 84th to send two additional companies to reinforce the platoon. By the time they arrived, the fighting was about over. Hodges, with the aid of a full-strength platoon and a tank destroyer, and assisted by some of the 3rd Armored Division's trains fighting north of the river, had already saved the bridge from the Germans. The tank destroyer knocked out two more German tanks, for a total of four. Hodges looked into one of the burning tanks and noticed that the personnel were wearing American uniforms.

By the time the 84th arrived to take over the town, the 3rd Armored Division had assumed responsibility for the east bank of the river and had chased five German half-tracks and 50 men, four large personnel carriers loaded with about 100 men each, and a German tank. These enemy units had evacuated the Hotton area and were headed for Erezee.

The stiff opposition put up by the engineers in Hotton convinced the LVIII Panzer Corps Commander that a continued effort in that area would lead nowhere. General Krueger then ordered the 116th Panzer Division to disengage on the Soy-Hotton road, pull back, and cross the Ourthe at LaRoche. The 560th Volks Grenadier Division continued its attack to the northwest. There was evidence that Hitler's goal was to cross the Meuse River on each side of Liege.

Aided by a few men from the 3rd Armored Division and the 1st Platoon of Company A, the embattled engineers of Company B, in a seven-hour battle, defeated an enemy attempt to take the bridge at Hotton. Their actions had preserved a key link in the Allied supply lines and had denied the German 116th Panzer Division an opening to the Meuse River. This feat of arms was subsequently acknowledged by the German corps and Army commanders. Later, the bridge would play a key role in the American offensive that followed. Captain Hodges was awarded the Silver Star for his heroic achievements at Hotton.

A separate action that afternoon took the life of Lt. Curtis. He led a patrol of 10 men and a half-track to the Ourthe River near Rendeux to destroy a footbridge. The men who guarded the bridge had been sent on another mission. At the bridge site, Curtis, Saunders, Wimberley, Ochson and Kelley discovered that the wires leading to the demolition charges had been cut. The severed wires indicated that the Germans had been there. In fact, they were still there! Small arms fire broke out and Curtis was mortally wounded.

Although heavy fighting occurred at Hotton on December 21, only two members of the 51st sustained wounds. Captain Hodges was hit by a shell fragment in the leg, and Private Ishmael was wounded in the hand.

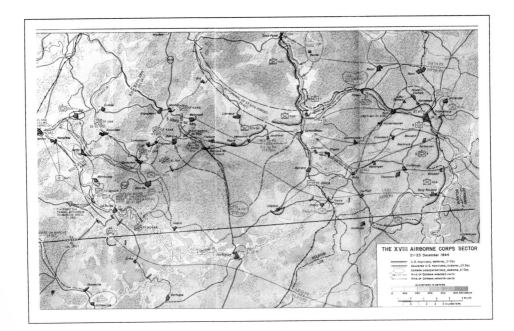

33

The Complete Engineer Barrier Line in the Ardennes: The Actions of Colonels H. Wallis Anderson and William Carter

Colonel H. Wallis Anderson, the veteran now of three wars and the commander of the 1111th Engineer Combat Group, had worked closely with Colonel Mason Young, the VII Corps Engineer, and Colonel William Carter, the First Army Engineer, in setting up the Engineer Barrier line from east of Malmedy through Stavelot, Trois Ponts, and Werbomont. By the evening of the 18th of December, when "A" Company of Captain James Gamble had blown the bridge that stopped Peiper at Habiemont, this Engineer Barrier line had been extended from east of Malmedy through Waimes, Butgenbach, Krinkhelt, and north along the Siegfried line to Monschau.

The engineer combat battalions then involved in the barrier line were from left to right, the entire 291st Engineers (with the addition of one company of the 51st Engineers), the 1st Division Engineers, the 254th Engineers, the 2nd Division Engineers, the 146th Engineers, and the 324th Engineer Battalion organic to the 99th Division. The mission of these eight battalions was to lay mines, prepare bridges for demolition, and other defensive obstacles to thwart the attacking German Divisions of the 6th Panzer Army of General Sepp Dietrich. The plan for this overall defensive strategy was laid out by Colonel Carter and his staff at First Army working closely with the Corps Engineers and the Groups. By the evening of December 19th various Engineer Combat Battalions were given missions to expand these Engineer Barrier lines from Werbomont to Manhay, Marche, Ortheuville, Hotton, and Martelange. This would also include a defense around Bastogne according to how the battles developed in that area. During the battles in the Trois Ponts-Stoumont area with the 1st SS Panzer Division, the 105th Engineer Combat Battalion, organic to the 30th Division, became part of the barrier line along with the 82nd Airborne Division and the 3rd Armored Division. All of these units became part of the hidden strength of the American forces in the Battle of the Ardennes.

All of these units were well trained to act on defense, and then rapidly convert to offense to aid the attacking armor and infantry in this very mobile part of the war. Since the early Normandy stagnant movement of the American forces, the combat engineers had rapidly replaced bridges of all types good for movements of tanks and cleared away the mines and many obstacles that the Germans had left behind in their massive retreat across two countries. Now it was their job to maintain a defense against the overwhelming German forces.

Thus far in a short period of time the German Engineers had failed to assist the Nazi Armor and Infantry. To solidify the American Defense General J.C.H. Lee, the quartermaster general, was assigned by Eisenhower to set up along the Meuse River five Engineer General Service Regiments to protect the bridges from Namur to Liege. Colonel Carter began to insert more Corps Engineer Battalions into the barrier line by moving the VII Corps from its strong defensive sector along the Roer River to the Dueren area of Germany. Colonel Mason Young, the Corps Engineer, had been advised by Colonel H. Wallis Anderson almost on an hourly basis of the situation on the Malmedy front. Colonel Young moved his headquarters from Kornelminster, Germany back into Bassinnes, Belgium along with the Corps headquarters of General Collins.

They rapidly moved the Engineer Battalions and formed a barrier line southwest of Liege-Marche-Hotton-Modave-Mohiville to counter-attack or seal off the westward penetration. The new Corps sector was over 65 kilometers wide on the First U.S. Army's right flank, with the XVIII Airborne Corps on its left and elements of the British XXX Corps on its right. Also, the 29th Armored Brigade (British) protected bridges across the Meuse River with a reinforced tank battalion at each of the towns of Namur, Dinant, and Givet.

As reconstituted, the VII Corps had the 75th and the 84th Infantry Divisions, and the 2nd Armored Division with some of the same Corps troops including engineers, artillery, anti-aircraft, and service troops. This rapid movement was efficient and effective and proved to be most successful in the defeat of Hitler's secret war. All divisions were closed in the new area on the 22nd of December, although some Corps troops were still in route from Germany. The area of the new zone of operations had been liberated by the VII Corps during the first two weeks of September. The German attack was in the Eifel Region in its seventh day; many aspects of the German order of battle and the enemy intentions as gathered from prisoners of war and captured documents began to crystallize. The 58th Panzer Corps (16th Panzer Division and the Grossdeuchesland Division), and the 1st SS Panzer Corps had been identified. With the capture of St. Vith by elements of the 2nd SS Division, the 9th SS Panzer Division had been committed as stated by prisoners of its engineer battalion. These units had failed to crack the 99th and 2nd American Division's lines to the north.

Now they moved south of St. Vith and again were attacking north in the direction of Spa and Liege, in order to outflank the First Army troops on the northern shoulder. On the 23rd of December, the VII Corps began forming a defensive line against the enemy counter-offensive by establishing road blocks and outposts to the south and southwest of the Corps assembly area and stabilized the right flank. Numerous small enemy thrusts from the southeast and southwest were either repulsed or destroyed.

Despite the extremely cold weather a ground haze prevented fighter bomber support of the Corps. At 1600 hours the 3rd Armored Division, less combat command Boudinot, was attached to the Corps, taking up positions on the left flank. The 84th Division occupied the center of the Corps Sector and the 2nd Armored Division occupied the long right flank with the 75th Division in Corps reserve.

The boundary between the VII Corps and the XVIII Airborne Corps was along the Ourthe River, Bomal to Manhay, and along the bend to Werbomont. The Corps operated in the general area south of the Meuse River and east of Namur, Dinant, and Givet. The Corps was operating on a front of 75 kilometers from the junction of the Lessee and the Meuse Rivers to the vicinity of Ansmerme.

Corps Engineers began their march from the Dueren-Aachen area during the early morning hours of the 23rd of December, and all of the units had closed on their new assembly area by 1200 hours on the 24th. The motor marches were somewhat restricted and delayed by enemy action from the air and also long range V-1s and artillery. There was deep snow drifts. The mission of the combat engineers was that of constructing roadblocks, preparing bridges for demolition, laying mine fields, and developing an impregnable defense. A final barrier line was established along the line which extended from the Corps east flank from Hotton, north along the Ourth River, to Liege, and on the south from Hotton along the highway to Marche. Then on to Rochefort, Hans Sur Lessee, and along the Lessee River to Dinant. The movement of engineer units into position along this massive engineer barrier line was quick and decisive. There were several defensive phase lines every three miles. This meant that if the Germans broke through the first defensive line their attack was far from over, particularly if the engineers were able to move in artillery battalions and tank destroyers behind their lines in strategic positions.

The ability of engineer units to load up and move added greatly to this type of defense. This could be developed from small unit action such as a squad. The missions of these engineer squads was to move in, prepare the crater or bridge for demolition, blow it upon the arrival of the unsuspecting enemy, and move out avoiding casualties to these well trained soldiers of great skill.

Bridges on the Ourthe River at Melreux, Noiseau, Durbuy, and Hamoir had been destroyed previously by the enemy in 1944. Corps Engineer Units had prepared all existing bridges for demolitions with instructions that the demolitions be executed only upon division order or when capture was imminent. In the preparation of the barrier line, engineer units were ordered to blow all of the bridges prepared for demolition from Eprave south and to withdraw personnel north of the barrier line along the Lessee and Ourthe Rivers. During the final campaign it was necessary to destroy one bridge in the final barrier line to prevent its capture by the enemy; the bridge at Chanly was destroyed by the bridge guards when the German tanks threatened to seize the bridge. Road blocks consisting of daisy chain mines, road cratering charges, and abatis were prepared on all roads leading from the final barrier line. In addition to the final barrier line, three defensive phase lines were established under the direction of the First Army Engineer, Colonel William Carter, and his staff.

When Colonel William Carter learned at First Army Headquarters that Peiper had been stopped at Habiemont by Company "A" of the 291st Engineers, and he had seen earlier the need for an engineer barrier line for VII Corps, he was anxious for Colonel Anderson to move his group headquarters out of Trois Ponts to Modave, Belgium. Anticipating this, Anderson had advised Major Lampp of the 291st to blow the bridge at Habiemont and move the rear command post of the 291st to Modave and prepare to become involved in the barrier line in that area. Anderson advised Major "Bull" Yates to take over the defenses in Trois Ponts from Major Lampp as established by the 291st and "C" Company of the 51st. Yates had arrived on the scene after the blowing of the bridges by Captain Scheuber and Lt. Walters.

Major Lampp turned over to Major Yates about 95 men of the 291st, including men from "A", "C", and H&S companies. These men were on the defensive line along the Salm River from the lower Salm bridge to the middle of the village of Trois Ponts. Most of the men were from the motor pool located in Trois Ponts.

After assigning the bridge blowing to Captain Gamble, Lampp then moved the rear CP across the Habiemont bridge west to Modave. Soon there was a new barrier line in effect with the 291st and the 51st engineers in front of the Meuse River, which was an extension of the barrier line from Malmedy through Stavelot, Trois Ponts and Werbomont.

The defensive phase lines ran roughly parallel to the final barrier line and at a distance of 10 to 15 kilometers apart. The phase lines were prepared by Corps and Division Engineer units. The bridges along these lines were prepared for demolitions.

Approximately 80,000 British and American anti-tank mines were installed in the final barrier line and in the defensive phase lines. There were 169 individually recorded minefields laid during this operation. There were three American Corps involved: the XVIII, the VIII, and the VII. In the VII Corps there were the following Engineer Combat Battalions that stopped attacking Germans: the 51st, the 291st, the 300th, the 296th, the 297, the 294th, the 298th, the 82nd, the 298th, the 275th, the 237th, and the 49th. On many occasions these engineers were accomplishing these missions right in front of the enemy and under fire from their guns.

Extensive mines had been laid by the Germans as they retreated back into Germany in September of 1944, and their handy work of blowing bridges prevailed throughout Holland, France, and Belgium as well as Luxembourg. It required over 100 Engineer Battalions and bridge companies to clear those mines and build those bridges for tanks of the American Armored and Infantry Divisions to press on to the German border.

No new mines were encountered by our troops. The enemy made use of Teller mines, 35 and 42, Riegle mines, and a great quantity of Holtz wooden box mines. S-mines were widely used. Difficulty was encountered in the breaching of the enemy mine fields due to the snow covered fields. The D-7 bulldozer was used to clear a path by taking a six-inch cut in the frozen-icy earth; by this method the snow, as well as the mines in a snow covered field, was pushed aside. The engineers followed the dozers and dragged the mines aside as they were unearthed.

This hazardous work was made more difficult because it was done out in front of the infantry and the armor. Many Bailey bridges were built when the German artillery pounded the bridge sites. Without the quick action of the engineers building these bridges, the infantry had to fight without tank support.

The enemy became clever in their deceptive use of mines. One armored combat command was held up 24 hours in trying to breach a heavily snow covered minefield. The minefield pattern was clearly visible under the blanket of snow. After friendly artillery forced the enemy to withdraw, it was found that the shape of the mines in the snow-covered field was caused by stale loaves of bread carefully laid in a standard German minefield pattern.

One of the Engineer Combat Battalions that became involved in the Engineer Barrier line development in the bulge was the 164th of Lt. Colonel H.F. "Bud" Cameron Jr. His Battalion would later become heavily involved in the successful crossing of the Rhine at Remagen, Germany. Here is his battalion's story:

After the breakthrough of the final Siegfried line east of Aachen, the battalion moved to the village of Brand just east of Aachen. Work was normal for an engineer unit but our main objective was heavily embroiled in the Arc Project, building and storing supplies for the Rhine River crossings.

On December 17th, Group Headquarters sent the battalion an order to discontinue all operations, except the water points and to be alert for a German Airborne attack which was expected during the night. This unit immediately took defensive action. Patrols were sent out to sort out prospective landing sites and road blocks were established. Sgt. Mario Piciaccio and his squad on a hill where they could observe the surrounding area were hit by a dive bomber so low that they returned the fire with their M-1s. The battalion packed and loaded its equipment on the trucks in readiness to move and remained on the alert all night. On the 18th the unusual German bombing and strafing attacks continued all during the day. Reinforced road blocks were constructed, covering all main intersections, and daisy chain mines covered with concertina and machine guns were dug in covering the road blocks.

Group Headquarters again informed the battalion to expect an airborne attack between 0500 hours and daylight on the 19th. Road blocks were further strengthened and patrols were out all night. Another report was received from Group that civilians had been picked up placing red identification panels on their roofs pointing towards Aachen and the battalion was to search all flat top roofs in the area.

The battalion was assigned to work with the 148th Engineers since they were in charge of the Group defensive plan. This went on until the 22nd of December when at 1530 hours we were alerted for a possible night move. So many times during the war we experienced orders to rapidly load and move out. It now had become a quick and decisive operation.

The 51st Engineers were doing a superb job of delaying the Germans on a broad front. The battalion's order from Group specified that one company be specially loaded and be prepared to go to the support of the 51st Engineers. The movement of one company to the 51st Engineers at Hotton was canceled and at 1950 hours all companies were ordered to pull in their road blocks and be ready to move. Orders finally came through at 2330 hours December 22nd for the battalion to move by way of a series of back roads to the town of Huy, Belgium which was located on the Meuse River between Namur and Liege.

The column was moving along smoothly under blackout conditions when suddenly the Lieutenant leading in a jeep came over the air, "Stop. I've almost gone over the abutments of a blown out bridge." Recon showed a bypass for the demolished bridge.

Getting that half mile of convoy turned around in the dark and back into march formation took several hours and delayed the battalion in getting to its assigned location. The battalion arrived at the town of Huy at 1045 hours on December 22nd.

The weather was miserable with snow, sleet, and temperatures below zero. The roads were slippery and many near accidents occurred. Operations this close to the front were being carried out rapidly. The other two battalions in the Group were ordered forward across the Meuse. One battalion was to lay minefields across the front in the vicinity of Ciney to stop any further German advance. The other battalion was given the job of loading, for demolitions, all bridges and culverts to the immediate front. The 164th was ordered to construct road blocks in the vicinity of Huy and to construct a 410 foot class 40 floating Bailey bridge (good for 40 ton tanks) across the Meuse River near the town of Andenne, about 3 miles from Huy.

To make the situation a little more enlivened, at 2300 hours on the 23rd of December, a message was received from First Army that their security unit had discovered a plan for all German Prisoners of War to plan to escape, with the aid of German Paratroopers. All P.W. enclosures were on the alert, and the battalion was ordered to assist them if the plan was put in operation.

The Meuse River forms a big bend between Dinant and Huy; the only bridge between them was blown by the Germans previously. Should U.S. forces be unable to stop the German advance, several American Divisions would be in a pocket without means of re-supply or evacuation of the wounded.

The floating bridge would be installed just upstream from a bridge the Germans had destroyed at this site. Company "C" was sent back to a depot to load the material and get it up to Company "B" which was to build the bridge. Construction was started on Christmas Eve as building material arrived from the depot. In the meantime, the British Xth Corps had moved in and deployed behind the battalion position on the north side of the Meuse. On December 24th the Germans were still advancing and only four miles from Dinant on the Meuse.

It was so cold the ground was frozen solid and the men were issued T.N.T. blocks to blow their foxholes, as digging in was impossible. It was late at night before the component parts were brought up for the Bailey bridge, but the men never slacked off since they knew that the lives of our infantry was at stake. Lt. Richardson reported that some of his men, who didn't have gloves, had their skin frozen to the Bailey Panels. The only hazard we didn't have building this bridge was German artillery fire. During the night a lone motorcyclist going east on the south side of the river turned left on the destroyed bridge and plunged into the icy stream. There was no way to rescue him.

Christmas Eve was not very festive. Work went on despite the freezing weather. The British did enlighten it somewhat with their sporadic firing of tracers over our heads.

Christmas day dawned bright and clear; it was the first sunshine we had seen in several weeks. There was an unusual sound in the air around mid morning that we could not identify. The answer was soon apparent. In the clear blue sky, as far as one could see, was an endless line of vapor trails marking the flight of the bombers and among them zigzagging vapor trails of the fighter planes that were protecting them. This was one of the most beautiful sites we had ever seen.

The saturation bombing marked the end of the German advance. The forward movement was started again. The forward movement of the American forces was extremely slow. The whole front was a major engineering problem. The roads were heavily cratered, both from artillery fire and mines. All road signs were missing, snow covered most of the area, and everything was frozen solid and roads glazed with ice. For a long period the daily report was monotonous. "Posting the edges of mine cleared roads, erection of road signs on the multitude of small roads, clearing mines, filling craters and assisting forward movement of vehicles."

The Meuse River was full of ice cakes. These cakes, some quite large, endangered the pontoons of the bridge. The bridge was finally assembled and opened for traffic on December 26th. To avoid possible sabotage to the bridge it was decided to install anti-floating mine log booms above the bridge.

The men of Lt. Colonel "Bud" Cameron had almost performed a miracle; to build a 410 foot floating bridge in 50 hours across a river caked with ice seems impossible. However, the American soldier always seemed to rise to new heights in this brutal war.

34

The 101st Division
and the Defense of Bastogne

The small village of Bastogne sets on a plateau with much farmland and slightly rolling hills. There are no outstanding defensive features in fairly open tank country. There are no important American military facilities in the entire area as there exists in the Liege-Spa sector where Hitler had planned his main thrust. If one looks at Hitler's secret war plan one can see that Bastogne is out of the entire thrust of the two major Army attack plans of the 6th and 5th Panzer Armies.

Fortunately when the 101st Airborne Division was delayed, arriving in the Bastogne area from France, there were defenses set up by combat engineer units such as the 158th, the 299th, the 35th and the 1278th who defended with their combat engineer skills to permit the 101st to come into Bastogne and set up their defense before the town was overrun.

The German Generals considered Bastogne a village that could be encircled and later wiped out by infantry troops. This would permit the armored divisions time to get to the Meuse and not be delayed on their way to Antwerp.

The strengths of the attacking German forces were not up to par and even thought they were fighting against weaker American divisions. Their drive to the west was slow and plodding with many tactical mistakes with regard to river crossings and defensive strong points set up by Engineer units at Hosingen, Wiltz, and Schiegden.

The 47th Panzer Corps consisted of the 2nd SS Panzer Division, the Panzer Lehr Division, and the 26th Volksgrenadier Division, all reinforced by one volks mortar brigade and the 600th Army Engineer Battalion for bridging purposes. The 2nd Panzer Division had only 80% of its forces and equipment and the other two divisions only 60%. Despite the weakness on both sides due to previous battle losses, the 101st Airborne won the race to Bastogne by a hair. The German forces were known to have been battered during their many years at war, and their units had been replaced many times.

Two teams of the 10th Armored Division's CCB had gone a long way to consolidate their hairbreadth victory in the race for Bastogne. When it received the assignment to defend Bastogne, the 101st Airborne Division had 805 officers and 11,035 men. Included in its organization were four infantry Regiments and all supporting arms including four artillery battalions and the 136th Engineer Combat Battalion.

The Division under the command of General Anthony C. McAuliffe first headed for Werbomont and learned that they were assigned to Bastogne. They made the move of 25 miles into Bastogne where they began arriving in the assembly area near Bastogne about midnight on December 18th. The men were cold and wet, having ridden in big cattle trucks through rain without any overhead cover. Many of them had no weapons or ammunition and hardly anybody had overcoats and overshoes. They would have little sleep and little time to prepare for the battle ahead, but what mattered was that they were there.

As McAuliffe's columns moved through heavy traffic toward Bastogne, forty tanks from Combat Command B (CCB) 10th Armored Division, the 705th Tank Destroyer Battalion (with 76 mm self-propelled guns), and two battalions of 155 mm artillery were ordered to Bastogne to be attached to the 101st. These organizations and a makeshift replacement pool of stragglers from the 28th, and the 106th Divisions who had escaped capture from the Germans, would bolster the defense of the 101st Airborne Division throughout the critical period in the battle for Bastogne.

Even as the 101st and its attachments were moving into Bastogne, the German advance had moved rapidly down the Wiltz-Bastogne road to a point just three kilometers from the town. There they collided with the first elements of the 101st. With VIII Corps evacuating the area, the defense of Bastogne became the Division's task. The paratroopers had barely won the race for the town; now the problem was to hold it. Fortunately, the combat engineers had held and were still holding a barrier line around Bastogne, and there was strong engineer support between Bastogne and the Meuse River.

In the early stages of the German advance, supply difficulties had not been a critical issue. The Germans had counted on capturing American supplies; however, there were no major supply dumps in the Bastogne area and as the German thrust moved forward they moved farther away from supplies. Fuel supplies were running short and due to the high consumption rate it had become a major problem for the Germans.

Unanticipated high water across the Our River, the blowing of the bridges in their faces, craters in the roads, and minefields had caused great delays for the Germans. The German Generals were quickly becoming skeptical as to the success of the mission.

The stiffening American resistance prevented the Panzer Lehr division from arriving in Bastogne at the appointed time, 1800 hours on December 18th. Had the Germans arrived on schedule, the 101st would have been five kilometers west of the town.

As the 101st and its attachments formed a perimeter defense in the villages around Bastogne, formerly held by the engineers, the tide of events had begun to turn. German troops, pressed by their commanders for a faster rate of advance, were near exhaustion. Previous losses of men and equipment and the prospects for more of the same sapped their will to fight. They had learned in the past that the attacking force generally suffers more casualties than the dug-in defending forces. The American forces they now faced were fresh, motivated, and in control of Bastogne. But Bastogne would be hotly contested in the week ahead.

By any comparison, the Americans, with a light infantry airborne division, some additional artillery, forty tanks, and a tank destroyer battalion, should have not been a match for the superior German forces, which consisted of two Panzer Divisions and a volksgrenadier division. Their ability to resist the Germans was their timely occupation of the town. Low German morale also strengthened U.S. resolve. The Germans of Army Group West and the Fifth Panzer Army had no choice but to sustain the momentum of the offensive at all costs to keep with Hitler's demands. Ultimately, German commanders who were too far removed from the action would make fateful decisions that would allow the lightly equipped defenders of Bastogne to survive.

The first steps to save Bastogne were taken on December 18 when the VIII Corps Commander, General Troy Middleton, dispatched the recently arrived Combat Command B of the 10th Armored Division to the northeast, east, and southeast of town with orders to hold at all cost. Such action indicated to the Germans that Bastogne would not be surrendered. In the week that followed the Germans squeezed the perimeter tighter and tighter, but it did not break.

Throughout the defensive sector, McAuliffe organized the 101st and its attachments into regimental task forces. Each had a proportional share of artillery, tanks, antitank, and anti-air forces. Thus, light infantry received supplemental firepower in their defense. With the exception of their artillery, the Germans were similarly organized. Their artillery was kept primarily in general support.

On December 19, small unit German infantry-armor forces, both with and without artillery support, infiltrated at night with tanks but the Americans resisted strongly and the Germans had been contained along the line Noville-Bizory-Neffe. The inadequate road network and the American artillery around Bastogne was slowing down and crushing the German advances.

The 10th Armored task forces set up strong points in an arc to the east. Team O'Hara (Lt. Colonel James O'Hara), pushed southeast to Wardin on the Luxembourg road. Team Cherry (Lt. Colonel Henry T. Cherry), and team Desobry (Major William R. Desobry) moved toward Longvilly in the east, and northeast to Noville, on the road to Houffalize. The 501st Parachute Infantry Regiment was sent due east toward Team Cherry on the road to Longvilly, late on December 18. Unknown to these teams, spearheads of Panzer Lehr had already cut that road at Margaret where they had tangled with the 158th Engineers. This point formed a solid block between the two American formations. The Paratroops were therefore stopped on the 19th at Neffe and Team Cherry was forced to attempt a withdrawal to link up.

Results were mixed. Team Cherry was caught in the open east of Neffe and destroyed, but the 501st, in a classic three-battalion attack, managed to push Panzer Lehr units out of Bizory to the north of Margaret, consolidating a defensive line that would hold firm until the following day. Elsewhere, the situation was much the same. In the northeast Team Desobry, supported by the 506th Parachute Regiment, beat off an attack by the 2nd SS Panzer Division at Noville, while team O'Hara was forced to give up ground including Wardin itself, in the southeast. The Germans were clearly probing for weak spots, but a clear defensive line was beginning to emerge by the 19th of December. The period of American confusion, during which major German advances should have been made, was already coming to an end. The artillery battalions were coordinating their fire power against the

Germans and the 136th Engineer had assigned one company to each task force to lay mines and set up roadblocks. This action had good effect elsewhere on the same day, for while the defenders of Bastogne were sorting out their defensive plans, top level Allied commanders at Verdun were making some major decisions. Eisenhower was now convinced that one way to destroy the German assault was to contain it between the already solidifying shoulders around Elsenborn and Echternach, preparatory to attacking from the north and south. Bastogne was part of the south flank just as the Malmedy shoulder was part of the north flank.

The Supreme Commander canceled Patton's projected attack in the Saar and extended the front northward. The Third Army, released from both offensive and defensive commitments, could then turn north toward Bastogne. Patton was anxious to comply and when Eisenhower directed him to re-deploy on December 19th, he ordered the 4th Armored Division to move toward Arlon and the 80th Infantry Division to move towards Luxembourg, while the 26th Division was directed to concentrate as a reserve, facing north. All three formations with its artillery, tank destroyers, and combat engineers were to head north and close on the German Corps units attacking northwest towards the Meuse.

Patton's forces could not be expected to begin their advance until December 22, but if it could duplicate the reaction of First Army to the German Offensive on the northern shoulder by establishing a solid defensive line from Monshau to Werbomontin in 48 hours, there was a great possibility that the "Battle of the Bulge" could be turned around and in favor of the Allies.

On the 20th of December Team Desobry (now under Major Robert F. Harwick of the 101st Airborne since Desobry had been wounded the previous evening) came under supreme pressure from panzer grenadiers of the 2nd SS Panzer Division, and although the initial attacks were repulsed, the American position became untenable. Harwick was ordered to withdraw to link up with the 502nd Parachute Infantry Regiment to his south, a movement completed by darkness. Unopposed, 2nd Panzer swept through Noville to Ortheuville and crossed the Ourthe River, outflanking Bastogne to the north. At the same time Panzer Lehr units managed to dislodge the paratroops of the 501st from their positions at Bizory in the east, forcing them back to within two miles of Bastogne.

Fortunately for the Americans, the following day, December 21st, saw an easing of German pressure. This was due to a temporary break in the weather which allowed Allied aircraft to fly in supplies and hit ground targets. According to Sgt. Tom Jones a military policeman inside of Bastogne, the German artillery was now pounding the village with long range artillery and Screaming-meemie fire. Many civilians and American soldiers were being wounded or killed and some buildings were on fire. The German command felt that Bastogne should have fell on the 18th, but despite Panzer Division breakthroughs to the north and south the town's defenses were still holding out, principally in an arc from Noville to Wardin. This was in the area where the 158th, the 299th, and the 1278th engineers had originally set up roadblocks.

German Corps Commander, General von Luttwitz, made the decision to reorganize his forces because he was frustrated at not being able to overrun the small village of Bastogne. He decided that his main mission at this time was to get on with the attack to the Meuse River with his armored divisions and let his infantry with the support of some tank destroyers wipe out the American forces in Bastogne.

He sent the Panzer Lehr Division south of Bastogne, and kept back the 901st Panzer Grenadier Regiment as a reinforcement to the 26th Volksgrenadiers now charged with taking the town. In addition, he shifted the attack from the east right around to the southwest and west, a policy which completed the encirclement of the American defense. The siege of Bastogne began late on 21 December with the odds theoretically in the Germans' favor.

The 2nd SS Panzer Division was cutting off communications to the north and Panzer Lehr and 5th Parachute Division, newly positioned astride the Arlon road, were in the south. Therefore, the 26th Volksgrenadiers, comprising a reconnaissance battalion, an engineer battalion, the 39th, 77th, and 78th volksgrenadier Regiments as well as the 901st Panzer Grenadiers, could devote all its energies to a quick victory.

Early on the 22nd, the commander of the 26th Volksgrenadiers, General Heinz Kokott, offered to negotiate a surrender for the town. McAuliffe refused by saying "Nuts!" to one of his supporters, who then passed on a "No!" to the German surrender contingent. At this time news had come through to the Americans in Bastogne that Patton was to send troops to reinforce the 101st. This gave them more confidence, despite the cold and snow, along with the battering by German heavy artillery and the constant reduction of the perimeter defense.

Kokott's troops attacked strongly around Assenois in the south and in the northwest around Champs, but the defensive positions held with only slight withdrawal and the killing and wounding of many of the attacking forces by American artillery. Once these attacks had been repulsed and some tanks knocked out in the engineer mine fields, Kokott seemed to go over to the defensive.

Mounds of Panzer Lehr infantrymen were now piled up on a hillside in front of the paratroopers. Trapped between barbed wire fences laid by the engineers, they had been slaughtered by even spaced lines. McAuliffe's biggest ally was the commander of CCB of the 10th Armored Division, Colonel Roberts. He combined the remnants of Team Cherry and Team Desobry, eight tanks, into one team and organized a second force of fifteen light tanks and four tank destroyers which could be sent at the moment's notice to any threatened sector. Roberts had a third force, sixteen half-tracks each mounted with four .50-caliber machine guns, also ready for quick counterattack.

Against the defenders of Bastogne, Baron Hasso von Manteuffel, the 5th Army Commander, was maneuvering an almost equal force: the 26th volksgrenadiers and one regiment of Panzer Lehr. Although he knew that Bastogne in enemy hands could influence all of his movements, he couldn't hold up his attack to the Meuse.

The remaining two regiments of Panzer Lehr were already finding little opposition in their sweep below Bastogne. That morning they had captured a convoy bound for the encircled Americans, fifty-three trucks and fifteen jeeps, all undamaged. But after this easy victory the Panzer Lehr commander, General Bayerlein's lead tanks slowed down and finally stopped at a log barrier hastily set up by the American engineers who were starting to plague the higher commanders of the German Armies.

Manteuffel heard this and hurried to the front. He was furious. All that was needed was a little dash and determination. He jumped into the first of five stalled tanks. His men warned him to look for mines and before the column could move forward they had to clear the mines surrounding the road block. After a long delay, Manteuffel yelled at the driver, "Head for St. Hubert." The driver headed on, followed by the three other tanks and for an hour Manteuffel led the patrol into what was supposed to be heavily defended enemy territory. Not a shot was fired or an American seen. At last they stood on heights overlooking St. Hubert, an important town twenty five miles from Bastogne.

That morning a thick white mantle covered the somber buildings of Bastogne, giving the town an atmosphere of peace and security. The firing of artillery into the town by the Germans had suddenly stopped. In the northwestern outskirts, at McAuliffe's command post, there was an atmosphere of confidence. Two important messages had just arrived. One read, "Hugh is coming." This meant that General Hugh Gaffey's 4th Armored Division was driving up toward the beleaguered town on the left flank of Patton's III Corps attack. The other message was from VIII Corps: "Resupply by air will start at 2000 hours."

The men in the foxholes and in lonely company command posts on the edges of the defensive circle felt a growing confidence too, but for a different reason. When word spread that they were surrounded, rivalry amongst the various units was suddenly forgotten. The Paratroopers now grudgingly admitted that the 10th Armored Divisions teams had put up one hell of a fight and had saved the bacon on the first two days. The sharp rivalry among the various regiments of the 101st had vanished also. At midnight on December 22nd in Bastogne, McAuliffe and his staff again were down in the dumps; the air drop promised for 10:00 p.m. had been canceled because of bad weather. They reviewed their situation and found three things that had prevented the Germans from overwhelming Bastogne: lack of artillery, uncoordinated attacks, and the stubbornness of the defenders. As yet the Germans had only hit one sector at a time, giving the defenders time to rush reserves to the threatened spot.

The situation report showed there was bitter fighting at Marvie; reports of rumbling traffic at other points presaged other attacks. When these came McAuliffe thought he would have little to stop them. Infantry commanders all around the perimeter were calling for artillery and getting about none due to lack of ammunition. Ammunition was limited to ten rounds of shells per gun.

Colonel Robert's big 105s, the heavy punch of the town's defense were so low on ammunition that two of his tanks and half-tracks were now making a break for the south. This desperate force led by Captain McCloskey hoped to fight its way back to Bastogne with an ammunition train. But before McCloskey had gone a mile all the vehicles had been wiped out. As news of this reached Bastogne, the unfamiliar hum of German bombers could be heard. Their roar grew louder, then deafening. There were shrill whistles, followed by explosions. Manteuffel was carrying out von Luttwitz's threat to devastate the town. The men in the foxholes behind Bastogne were bitter. If the Germans could fly over, why not the Allies? The confidence of that morning was waning. This bombing was an indication that the end was near.

On the morning of December 23rd in the foxholes surrounding Bastogne the bright sun was bringing welcome warmth to the town's cramped defenders. They had never before been so glad to see dawn. It had been a night of misery. Their foxholes had been like refrigerators. Awake all night, they had danced up and down to keep from freezing. Rifle mechanisms were frozen.

Distant hums in the west became shrieks. Sleek American fighter planes knifed overhead, bound northeast for missions in the Fortified Goose Egg. The men in Bastogne stood up and cheered. At 0935 hours there was a deeper roar as several lumbering transports appeared and circled the town. Parachutists drifted to a snow covered field. They explained they were pathfinders who were to guide in re-supply planes which should start arriving in an hour and a half.

While the pathfinders were assembling their radar sets, Captain James Parker, an air force officer who had made his way into Bastogne the day before the encirclement, was getting more good news by radio. Supporting planes were on the way. At 1000 hours Parker, whose radio jeep was parked outside of McAuliffe's command post, was talking to the approaching planes, telling them where to strike. Without warning they dove at German Columns converging on Bastogne, knocking out scores of tanks and armored cars.

At 1150 hours sixteen C47s approached the encircled town. German anti-aircraft threw up a wall of flak. Several planes plunged to the earth in flames, but the oncoming flight never wavered. Over Bastogne hundreds of gaily colored parachutes blossomed and drifted to the open fields.

In spite of regulations, civilians poured out of their cellars and stared up in awe at the carnival sight. The Americans were like people from another world. GIs seized each other. They shouted and danced in the streets.

The battle in and around Bastogne was now turning back to the American side with supplies of medicines for the wounded, ammunition for the guns, and known support from the air. The defenses in Bastogne were now on the mend.

35

The 23rd of December
and the Turning Point of the Battle

When the men of the 101st in Bastogne came out of their foxholes cheering the arrival of American air forces they knew that the Germans had finally been halted in their effort to take Bastogne. They knew that they had accomplished the task of preventing the Nazis Panzers from breaking down their engineer designed defenses of minefields, blown bridges, and craters.

Now they knew that ammunition and shells for the artillery battalions was going to be on hand, as well as for Colonel Roberts' tanks and tank destroyers. There was joy that food and medical supplies would help their wounded as well as the brave civilians who had suffered through this period of disaster.

By late morning the strategic withdrawal of General Bruce Clarke and the 7th Armored Division and the survivors of the far-flung battle of St. Vith were now passing in a steady orderly stream through Vielsalm. They went across the Salm River and joined the forces of

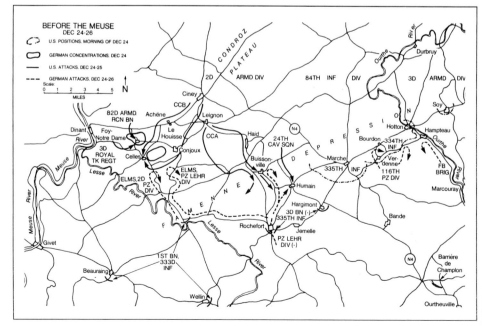

General Jim Gavin's successful Paratroopers who had taken over the defenses at Trois Ponts and along the Salm River to Vielsalm and thence towards Manhay.

Threatening these men from the south was the 2nd SS Panzer Division. Originally scheduled to follow General Sepp Dietrich's main thrust of the 1st SS Panzer Corps, it had been routed below the salient to exploit Manteuffel's breakthrough. It had suffered losses from the 28th Division as well as at Bastogne. Though this unit could have burst through the 82nd Airborne Division protecting the American withdrawal from St. Vith, the German high command had a much greater objective since they passed up taking Bastogne. Their plan was to drive the 2nd Panzer SS up N-15, the fine road from Bastogne to Liege. This highway was about 10 miles west of Vielsalm and into the First Army area where Peiper had been attacking.

The first step was to head for Baraque de Fraiture, a tiny isolated settlement where the N-15 intersected the road from Vielsalm. This intersection was guarded by Major Arthur Parker III who had set up three 105 mm. guns and a small force to protect this important spot. He had an anti-aircraft battalion with three guns, three multiple .50 caliber machine guns, self-propelled 37-mm. gun, a recon company, and several dozen assorted stragglers from the east. After Parker was seriously wounded in the first German attempt to take the crossroads on the morning of the 23rd, a much more serious attack was made. When General Gavin learned of the battle at the crossroads, he sent Captain Woodruff of Company "K", 325th Glider Infantry to rush to Baraque de Fraiture. That morning a great German victory hung on the actions of a few men and a few guns at a dreary road junction. For two days nothing happened, then German General Kruger's 58th Panzer Corps swept south of Baraque de Fraiture and to the extreme right flank and moved towards the Meuse River without eliminating Parker's valiant force. Again, this was the American soldier taking over where Generals made no plans or gave orders. Parker's force held off a dozen raids and Major Elliot Goldstein, Parkers Executive officer took over for the wounded Parker.

When ammunition became scarce at the crossroads and the wounded were prevalent, Major Goldstein took the two German prisoners north to look for help. But finally the Fraiture roadblock had served its purpose and quietly faded away.

On the 23rd the battles along the Northern shoulder had become quiet. The men of the 99th and 2nd Division had repelled every attack by the badly mauled 6th Panzer Army in their repeated attacks to drive through their defenses and cross the hills north of Malmedy to the Meuse River north of Liege.

The 12th SS Panzer Division and the 3rd Paratroopers of the 6th Panzer Army had tried to crash through the U.S. Army 1st Infantry Division, but after an all out battle at Butgenbach and east of Waimes, the two German divisions were badly mauled and had failed to penetrate the engineer designed barrier line. The coordination of twelve Field Artillery Battalions had pounded the attacking Nazis into failure.

The situation in Malmedy had become solidified since the defeat of Skorzeny's brigade. We in the 291st were still developing road blocks and still in line as infantry. Considering what we had been through our casualties were minimal, with only 3 killed and 9 wounded. Our roadblocks were still receiving attacks of recon nature from the Germans; at Sgt. Walter Smith's road block three of Baron von der Heydte's paratroopers surrendered.

The Norwegian soldiers of Colonel Hansen had fought bravely throughout and had suffered many casualties as had the men of the 526th Armored Infantry and the soldiers of the 825th Tank Battalion.

Food arrived and there was no shortage of ammunition, but then at 1520 hours six B-26's of the 326th Bombardier Group approached a town nestled in a hilly forested area. The flight leader glanced down and hadn't been able to locate his primary target, Zulpich, Germany, a railhead for General Brandenberger's Seventh Army. He concluded he was over Lammersum, only six miles northeast of the target. As the plane swept over the town, thirteen 250-pound general purpose bombs dropped from the bomb bay. The other five planes of the flight dumped their loads. The streets of the town erupted from the bombs. All pilots noticed with pleasure, that the results were excellent. Dazed American soldiers and I, along with hysterical civilians, were crawling from the wreckage of Malmedy, Belgium—39 miles away was Lammersum. Many were no longer able to crawl. Our boys had bombed Malmedy!

Moments later, General Hobbs, commander of the 30th Division, was angrily talking by a phone to an air force General. Hobbs was bitter. It wasn't the first time he had been bombed by the 9th Air Force. His men had already dubbed it "the American Luftwaffe." The air force general was dismayed, "It can't happen again."

To those of us in the 291st we had seen it happen before near St. Lo at the time of the saturation bombing in July, and now we had seen it again in Malmedy where we had set up an all around defense and had held it through some very trying days. For now our mission had expanded in Malmedy. There were hundreds of Americans, civilians and even some Germans buried in the debris and it was up to our engineer soldiers to rescue the wounded and remove the bodies of the dead out of the debris.

The situation remaining on the shoulder, which General Omar Bradley had called the "Malmedy Shoulder" in his book "A Soldier's Story", showed that on December 23rd Peiper had been badly defeated by the 30th Division, the 82nd Airborne and two Combat Commands of the 3rd Armored Division. Peiper went out on foot with only 800 men and no tanks. Essentially on the evening of the 23rd the Sixth Panzer Army had been defeated badly by the First American Army of General Courtney Hodges, even though he had to move his headquarters twice to avoid having it overrun.

When Eisenhower decided to place General Montgomery in charge of the American northern shoulder, already the units had been so organized to prepare to counter-attack and drive the Germans back into Germany. In reviewing the overall situation, Montgomery decided that the Americans should start to tidy up their lines before ever considering reversing the form of the battles from defense to the attack. Many of the Divisions on the Malmedy shoulder were in the attack from the very beginning, such as the 82nd Airborne of General James Gavin and the 30th Division of General Leland Hobbs. The 3rd Armored Division had been on the attack since they came into the area to attack Peiper.

Montgomery proposed that the 82nd Airborne had too much front and should pull back its forces to shorten the front line. General Gavin's troops had never given up ground that they had captured with blood and they didn't want to comply at this time.

The situation on this 23rd of December showed the Germans surrounding Bastogne. They were moving towards the Meuse just south of Bastogne near St. Hubert and north of Bastogne with the arrow pointing directly at Hotton, Belgium—after taking Houffalize. As yet, Patton had not been in the picture.

36

The 238th Engineer Battalion
and the 2nd SS Panzer Division

Commanding Officer Lt. Colonel Jay P. Dawley

Prior to December 16th, 1944 the 238th Engineer Combat Battalion was engaged in close engineering support of the 104th Infantry Division west of the Roer River in Germany. The battalion had been active in building bridges, clearing mines, and keeping the road net open for the advancing American armor and Infantry units.

On the 15th of December 1944 the Battalion Commander, Lt. Col. Jay P. Dawley held a briefing at which the Non-Coms and officers were told to plan for a possible movement to

Officers of the 238th (Front row, left to right): Capt. Leo Smith, Company A; Capt. Edward Blumenstoin, Co. B; Lt. Col. Jay P. Dawley, Commander 238th; Capt. Brown H&S Co.; and Capt. John B. Wong, Company C.

Bridge built under fire at Targnon on the L'Ambleve River Dec. 29-31

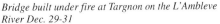

Front view of the Targnon Bridge.

the Ardennes in case of an attack in that lightly held area. For the next several days the battalion was busily engaged in laying an extensive, hasty mine barrier across the Division's entire front in the Inden-Lucherberg area. In the area south of the 104th's front, Hitler's forces had started a major counter-attack.

On 21 December, the 1106th Engineer Combat group, including the 238th was relieved from attachment to the VII Corps and attached to the XVIII Airborne Corps. The battalion was then placed in direct support of the 82nd Airborne Division who at that moment was heavily embattled with the leading spearhead of the 1st SS Panzer Division. The unit convoyed through Verviers, Spa, and My to Xhoris. There it received orders to proceed to Werbomont. The commander, Lt. Col. Dawley, who had gone ahead, met it there with instructions from the Engineer, XVIII Airborne Corps to construct a major engineer barrier line across the Corps front which at that time was changing hour to hour. Colonel Dawley had learned when he arrived at Corps headquarters that the 82nd Airborne was battling to help wipe out the 1st SS Panzer Division's Kampfgruppe (Combat Group) Peiper only a few miles east of Werbomont. Also the 7th Armored Division had been driven out of St. Vith by three divisions of the 5th Panzer Army.

He assigned Company A to the road from Manhay to Bra; Company B the road Manhay to La Fourche; and Company C the road Manhay to Grandmenil to La Forge. The Battalion forward CP was established at Chene-al-Pierre. After a reconnaissance of their respective areas, all companies started early on 23rd December to prepare defenses, including minefields, abatis, daisy chains and other barriers. Mine laying started promptly, using organic loads, while Captain William S. Sweitzer, supply officer, was securing much larger quantities from Army depots. Almost 10,000 mines were laid in the three company areas. Sweitzer's concern at this time was that First Army had already moved their Headquarters twice due to the breakout of Kampfgruppe Peiper.

At noon on the 24th, barrier work was nearing completion. Lt. Col. Dawley inspected the entire line. While in Manhay his jeep came under observed German Artillery fire. He and his driver hit the dirt, but were not hit. Since the bulk of the 7th Armored Division was

Trois Ponts, Jan. 6-7 under fire.   *Bridge at Trois Ponts built under fire Jan. 6-7 1945.*

still south of that location, he reasoned that the German forces must have infiltrated to a spot nearby. Thus, he had direct evidence that the enemy was near, and might attack within hours.

At 4:00 p.m. that day, the companies reported completion, and most units were relieved of guarding the barriers they had constructed. They were prepared to return to base at Xhoris. Yet there appeared to be little organized defense in the sector. Lt. Col. Dawley held a meeting at Battalion Forward and stated that he and the line company commanders would remain in the threatened area. He instructed each Company to take defensive positions in its assigned area using machine guns and bazookas, employing at least one platoon. Companies were free to keep more than a platoon in the assigned area if they felt more force was needed. By this action on his own authority, and since the 1106th Engineer Group had put its two battalions directly under XVIII Airborne Corps control and there was no time to consult the Corps (by messenger), the battalion commander committed the 238th Engineers as infantry in the defense.

Hence, the 238th Engineers filled in the defenses in the sector of the weary, disorganized 7th Armored Division. The 7th had made a gallant stand for four days at St. Vith and after being battered by three Divisions of the 5th Panzer Army, made a strategic withdrawal with support from a Combat Command of the 9th Armored Division. The sector was rather narrow for a division since the Division was strung out over a long distance and had been heavily engaged all the way from St. Vith.

At about 1900 hours, the situation on the Manhay to Werbomont road, RN-15, took on the appearance of a rout, with units of the 7th Armored Division rushing rearward with little semblance of order. The 238th Engineers were the only organized defense on the three routes out of Manhay. Lt. Col. Dawley drew up a message to the commanding general of the XVIII Corps and the 1106th Group advising them that there was much confusion near Manhay but the 238th Engineers were in position and would hold the line until driven out or relieved. He reasoned that Company B and battalion forward, being astride the main road to Liege and Antwerp, would take the brunt of the imminent German armored attack. He then set up a straggler line at Chen-al-Pierre, placing disorganized elements, halted from rushing north, into a defensive line just north of Manhay.

At 2300 hours, German tanks of the 2nd SS Panzer Division and infantry of the 560th Volkegrenadier Division attacked Manhay in force. Company "B", under Captain Edward J. Blumenstein took the brunt of the German armored attack. T/4 Jesse P. Winkles, manning a 50 caliber machine gun of Company "B" south of town, reported that he got in a fire fight. His actions resulted in casualties among the attacking ground troops. He withdrew to the north of town leaving his gun as ordered by an officer of another unit. Company "B" could not execute daisy chain road blocks as they were ordered to leave forward barriers and friendly tanks were still using roads. The Germans captured Manhay, then turned left (west) onto the secondary road to Grandmenil. One of their tanks hit a daisy chain of mines west of Manhay and was abandoned on the road. Meanwhile Company A platoon under Lt. Ernest James, east of Manhay, heard firing to its right rear and believed itself bypassed. They nevertheless stuck to their position under light artillery fire and were not otherwise attacked.

Westward out of Manhay were the fixed defenses manned by "C" Company under Captain John B. Wong. Small elements of the 3rd Armored and 75th Division were moving in the area. Captain Wong, a former instructor of mine warfare in England, had supervised erection of a tough belt of thousands of mines in his assigned area. He and his troops manned a tenacious defense even under heavy mortar and artillery fire. Lt. Bob Latchaw's platoon, positioned in Grandmenil and the cemetery between Manhay and Grandmenil, were fired upon by infantry, artillery and tanks. Though advised to withdraw by an officer of the 75th Infantry Division which had troops in the vicinity, it stayed in place, defending, until forced by enemy tanks to withdraw.

Having passed through the daisy chains at Manhay, and having passed the cemetery, the German tanks surged towards Grandmenil, but unexpectedly encountered mines again, concealed under a heavy snowfall at the approaches to the town. Five tanks stopped at the approaches to the town. Five tanks were then stopped in rapid succession before Grandmenil

Bailey Bridge being built at Namur on the Meuse Sept. 7, 1944.   *German tank knocked out in a minefield.*

German armor knocked out by mines.

The 238th built this floating Pontoon Bridge 564 ft. long on Sept. 6, 1944, at Namur on the Meuse River.

with treads blown by mines guarded by Company "C" on a winter night in trackless snow was all but impossible. This defeat stopped the spearhead. It was the high water mark of the final German thrust to Liege.

Halting the attacks of the 2nd SS Panzer Division and 560th Volksgrenadier Division was largely the result of the 238th Engineer defense and the barriers the unit had constructed almost in the face of the enemy. This gave sufficient time for the 82nd Airborne and 3rd Armored Divisions to counterattack and later retake Manhay. The mines had been laid prior to the heavy fall of snow in the area and when the 2nd Panzer Division attacked there was over a foot of snow covering the mines. The crews of the German tanks were well into the minefield before they realized and the result was the loss of tanks.

The arrival of the 238th was very timely for they were able to close the engineer barrier line to conform with the engineer barrier line created by the First Army Engineer, Colonel William Carter.

Late on Christmas day the situation was stabilized in the area and the Germans had failed to penetrate through the Manhay-Werbomont area to the Meuse River. The objective

of the 2nd Panzer Division and the 560th Volksgrenadier Division was to swing south of St. Vith and head northwest to penetrate the First Army lines in the vicinity of Grandmenil.

General Matthew Ridgeway, the Commander of the XVIII Airborne Corps was most appreciative of the 238th Engineer's effective defense and called Lt. Col. Dawley to Werbomont on Christmas day to hear his

German armor knocked out by mines.

report and commend him and his unit. General Ridgeway commended the unit in writing through the 1106th Engineer Combat Group:

1. The Corps Commander desires to commend you and the units under your command for the manner of performance of their duties under his command. Your Group came under the control of the Corps at a critical time. The work of the 238th Engineer Combat Battalion in the construction of the initial Barrier in the vicinity of Manhay was outstanding and materially assisted the Corps in holding off the attack of the enemy in that area.

2. It was a pleasure to have this unit with the Corps. I wish you continued success.

M.B. RIDGEWAY
MAJOR GENERAL U.S. ARMY
COMMANDING

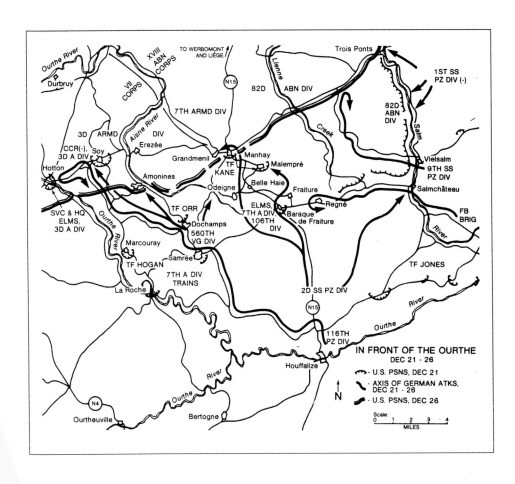

37

Patton and the Battle of the Bulge

In Chaudfontaine, General Courtney Hodges awaited the arrival of General Bernard Montgomery, recently appointed by Eisenhower to take charge of the northern half of the bulge. Bradley would command the southern half. Hodges was considered colorless compared to Patton, but his army moved faster than Patton's 3rd Army; in fact, Hodges led the way across France and Belgium. Hodges was a man of natural dignity and not colorful copy for the news media, especially when compared to the ebullient and controversial George Patton, with his fancy uniform and bold approach.

As a result, the First Army achievements received far less publicity than Patton's Third Army. Hodges was directly responsible for this lack of publicity. He shied away from the media and sought only to run a smooth First Army.

On December 17th, Hodges realized more than any of the high brass that the German attack in the Ardennes was serious. Without wasting time making excuses, he immediately switched over from the offense to the defense. Within hours, thousands of men and machines turned toward the danger zone. This movement was so decisive that a strong defense quickly formed from Monschau to Werbomont. Hodges, now ready to attack, had Ridgeway's corps strike southeast to Vielsalm and into the German salient. Moments later, Montgomery stepped into Hodges' headquarters. Montgomery appeared confident, cheerful, and willing to take control of the battle. After Hodges briefed him, Montgomery claimed he had the Germans in position for an attack by the First Army that would close the goose egg at its eastern end, through Vielsalm. At this time Hodges was forming a corps to attack east to Marche. The corps would consist of the 84th Infantry Division, the 75th Infantry Division and the 2nd "Hell on Wheel's" Armored Division.

Montgomery said the Germans would wheel north across the Meuse near Liege. Therefore, an American counterattack was out of the question.

Farther south, in the 3rd Army's area, Patton busily prepared to assault the Saar by "bouncing" the Moselle and then the Rhine. The Saar offensive began on November 8, 1944 and progressed to Saarlautern, where the XX Corps crossed the river and prepared to exploit the imminent breach of the Siegfried line. Various crossings of the Saar took place in the XII Corps' zone, which attacked in a northwesterly direction, parallel to the river Blies. Plans began for an attack on the Siegfried line on December 19.

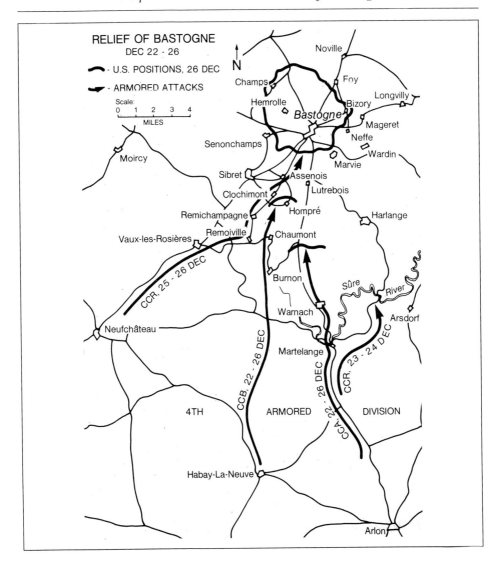

A saturation bombing of the German defenses would precede the attack. On December 15, the 87th Division replaced the 26th Division which had been badly battered in the battle for the fortress city of Metz, France.

George Linthicum, a recon officer in the 26th Division, reported that the division lost over 4000 men who were either killed, wounded or captured. They withdrew from the line to reform ranks using replacements from the Third Army. The 5th and 80th Divisions were complete, but the whole army lacked nearly 12,000 men.

On December 16, the 12th Army Group ordered the temporary attachment of the 10th Armored Division to First Army's VIII Corps to help prevent a serious enemy breakthrough.

Patton's words, on the 18th of December: By the request of the Army Group Commander, I go to the general staff HQ in Luxembourg accompanied by the generals of the 3rd Army's 2nd, 3rd and 4th Groups. The object of my journey is to give a detailed explanation of the breakthrough according to the information that we have. General Bradley asks me when I could intervene. I declare that I would be able to do it very soon by means of three divisions.

I then phone to the Chief of the General Staff, 3rd Army, and give the following orders: the 4th Armored Division and the 80th Infantry Division are to stop their attack and to prepare adequate means for moving the 80th Division at any given moment after sunrise on December 19th.

The 4th Armored Division should be ready to set off during the night from the 18th to the 19th of December. At the same time I inform the 19th Tactical Air Command that the planned raid is to be canceled at the Siegfried line.

General Bradley phones me at 2200 hours to tell me that the situation has become much worse since lunch time and that we will have to evacuate our troops as quickly as possible. General Milliken draws up and mans the new front line of his headquarters. I suggest Arlon as a good possible starting point and this suggestion is generally accepted. General Bradley charges General Milliken to personally prepare an account of the situation of the morning of the 19th to be submitted to the General Staff of the 12th Army Group. As for myself, I have to set off, accompanied by a staff officer, to a rendezvous with General Bradley as we were to attend a conference with the Supreme Allied Commander, General Eisenhower, at Verdun at 1100 hours that same morning. One unit of the 4th Armored Division moves toward Longwy at midnight and is followed by the remainder of the Division at daybreak. The 80th Infantry Division consolidates its position in Luxembourg at dawn on the 19th. This operation has been facilitated by the G-4 of the Army Group due to a very [large] concentration of Com. Z. lorries.

The 19th of December a meeting between the general commanding the tactical air command, the Corps leaders, and the staff of the 3rd Army has taken place at 0800 hours. The new position is under discussion. I am saying that the 3rd Army's and the 19th Air command's reputation for speed and efficiency is largely due to its officers, here present, and that I am counting on them to do still better.

On the supposition that the VIIIth Corps shall be joined to the Third Army, we develop a plan for making the best use of it as well as the III Corps. We envision three possible lines of attack: Neufchateau-St. Hubert, Arlon-Bastogne, and Luxembourg-Diekirch-St. Vith.

The Chief of the General Staff and myself agree on a small secret telephone code for the Third Army. Departure for Verdun at 0930 hours, arrival at 1045 hours.

Following the conference, the Supreme Allied Commander orders that the 6th Army Group shall establish itself on the southern front as far north as it can go in that sector. The 6th Armored Division should remain in the vicinity of Saarbruecken and should there wait to be relieved by elements of the VIIIth Corps. General Eisenhower questions me on the possibilities of a 3rd Army attack towards the north, and I declare that this Army could attack with three corps on December 23rd.

After the Verdun interview, I telephone the 3rd Army's Chief of Staff to give him the following instructions: the 26th Division should be moved to Arlon on the 20th of December; advance units should set off immediately. The XII Corps should disengage itself and the Corps Staff HQ and the artillery should move toward Luxembourg on the 21st, leaving a skeleton staff at the old HQ until it could be relieved by the XV Corps of the 7th Army. The 35th Infantry Division should be withdrawn from the lines and be reassembled at Metz. The tactical echelon of the 3rd Army's staff HQ is leaving for Luxembourg on the 20th whereas the advanced echelon of the II Corps should leave immediately for the vicinity of Arlon.

I am paying a visit to the XII Corps in Luxembourg and then to the generals commanding the IIIrd and VIIIth Corps and the 4th Armored Division at Arlon. Thereafter I visit the staff HQ of the 4th and 26th Infantry Divisions. I inspect the advance echelon of the 80th Division, which has just arrived at Luxembourg.

As it is quite clear that at the present moment the VIII Corps is not in a position to engage in offensive action, it is decided that they shall play a defensive role in Bastogne, assisted by the 101st Airborne Division and the following detachments: the Combat Command of the 9th Armored Division, the Combat Command of the 10th Armored Division, the 705th Tank Destroyer Battalion minus one company and some units of the artillery Corps, the engineer combat skills of the 158th, the 299th, the 35th, the 136th and the 1278th Engineer Combat Battalions, and the 511th Engineer Bridge Company. The Engineers to set up mine fields, use demolitions and at times fire their combat weapons.

The master plan as outlined by Eisenhower at the Verdun meeting of the 19th turned into a major effort to plug holes in the north and to launch a coordinated attack from the south.

It was clear that Patton would be responsible for knifing into the German southern flank, which would employ at least two of the Third Army's corps. On December 20, Patton learned that his VIII Corps was in bad shape from the battle for Metz, so he chose not to use it.

Patton instructed his Chief of Staff to move the 26th Division north and, along with the 4th Armored and 80th Divisions, they would become part of General Milliken's III Corps in the Arlon sector south of Bastogne.

When the American XII Corps, in Luxembourg and southeastern Belgium, took control in this sector on the 21st, the German thrust into Luxembourg had been checked. The three German divisions thrown into the initial attack had suffered drastic losses. The Germans were concerned about an American counterattack there. The American units involved were the 4th Infantry Division, the 109th Regiment, 28th Division, and task forces from the 10th Armored Division. CCA, 9th Armored was also involved in this successful endeavor.

Before Bradley ordered Patton to attack to relieve Bastogne, Eisenhower formulated an overall plan for a major counterattack to drive the Germans back into their homeland once and for all. This attack required detailed coordination between the United States, Canadian and British Armies. For this plan to work, Patton's III Corps had to relieve Bastogne.

Eisenhower had already set the direction for the attack: north from an assembly area in Arlon. The immediate mission, assigned after the Verdun meeting, was to relieve Bastogne and use the roadnet as a sally port for a Third Army drive to St. Vith. The closing of the First and Third Armies would occur near Houffalize. The Third Army would attack on D-Day, December 22. The Third Army order issued the day before was rather ambitious and typical of Patton. The plan contained a Patton flourish that prescribed an eventual wheel to the northeast and seizure of the Rhine crossings 'in zone'. The forces employed knew their tasks as early as the night of December 18, when Bradley and Patton agreed to move the new and untried III Corps to Arlon from Metz. The divisions given to Major General John Milliken all occupied a quiet sector when the Third Army was ordered north. These out-of-line units were Patton's first choice.

The area chosen for the III Corps counterattack extended from the Alzette River to Neufchateau in the west, a thirty-mile front. This zone, with the eastern part in Luxembourg and the western part in Belgium, contained some of the most rugged terrain in the Ardennes. East of the Arlon-Bastogne axis, two deeply eroded corridors cut by the Sure and Wiltz Rivers formed effective barriers to mechanized and motorized vehicles. Rivers and streams sliced into this terrain everywhere. Here, as in other parts of the Ardennes, dense woods alternated with rolling fields and clearings, making road junctions the key military features. Bastogne, despite its size, had some important roads that led in and out.

Charles MacDonald, the noted U.S. Army historian wrote of Patton in his book "A Time for Trumpets". His summation is worth repeating; most of us who were there concur with his analysis:

By late 1944, George Smith Patton Jr., at 59 years of age, was already something of a legend in the United States Army and a darling of the American press. It had not always been so. After word had leaked out that in Sicily Patton slapped two American soldiers whom he suspected of malingering, newsmen had gone for his jugular. An impolite remark before a ladies' club in England before the invasion had set the jackals to howling again, but Eisenhower stuck with him, confident of his ability on the battlefield.

His dash across France from the Normandy beachhead in late summer appeared to justify Eisenhower's loyalty; and a fickle press, suddenly adoring his posturing, his profanity, his singularly flashy uniforms, glistening helmet, pistols on each hip, nicknamed him "old Blood and Guts." His men, whom he frequently visited up front, stated, "Yeah, our blood and his guts." The press turned him into an idol of the American public. Soldiers who hated him in Sicily came to love him. All they had to say was that they were in Patton's Army; everybody knew which army that was. A man of independent means, married to a woman of even greater wealth, George Patton had no economic need to devote his life to the United States Army.

He was a man given to extreme ups and downs. Thus he could kick and scream like a child deprived of a toy when, on December 16th, General Bradley ordered him to relinquish an armored division to the First Army in the Ardennes, then three days later enthusiastically embrace the sending of a major portion of his Army into the Ardennes. The difference was that in the second case, he, George Patton, was to be the star.

Relieving Bastogne to Patton was as irritating as a burr under the saddle to a horse, for Patton was not after Bastogne but the bigger piece of pie: St. Vith, thereby cutting off the German forces that had penetrated far to the west and destroy them.

George Patton made good on his promise to attack on December 22, not only in the direction of Bastogne but farther east to relieve the threat to Luxembourg City. Yet the American attack only involved one regiment, for not until late on December 23rd did the commander of the Third Army's XII Corps, Major General Manton Eddy, get his supporting artillery in place and all of the veteran 5th Infantry Division forward. Thus, it was not until the morning of the 24th that an attack began in earnest to drive the Germans across the Sure River.

The 5th Division advanced northward on both sides of the Ernz Noire, while the 10th Armored Division's CCA and a task force of the 9th Armored Division's CCA extended the attack towards the west. The advance moved across ground and through villages recently relinquished by the 4th Division's 12th Infantry and the 9th Armored's 60th Armored Infantry Battalion.

By nightfall of the first day, the armor reached that part of the Sure River that flows west to east and forms an angle with the junction of the Our, where men of the 109th Regiment defended at the start of the German offensive. By Christmas Day they reached high ground overlooking the part of the Sure that forms the boundary between Luxembourg and Germany. They pounded the 212th and 276th Infantry divisions of the Germans with artillery until they had been reduced down to only 25 men to a company as German bodies lay throughout the battlefields. In Echternach, the first patrols arrived on the 26th and soon were in control of the town.

In addition to the 4th Armored Division, charged specifically with breaking through to Bastogne, Patton's main attack was supported by the 26th and 80th Infantry Divisions, both fairly well rested after being out of line for a short period. However, both had suffered great losses in the battles for Metz and had about 3500 men on board.

The task assigned to the infantry forces was to clear territory between the Alzette River and the Arlon-Bastogne highway, thereby protecting the right flank of the 4th Armored Division and advancing the line so that when relief came to Bastogne, there would be no narrow corridor leading into the town but a broad expanse of American controlled territory extending eastward. That also conformed with Patton's ambition to proceed beyond the relief of Bastogne with a general movement of the entire southern flank in a drive on St. Vith.

The 26th Division, commanded by Major General Willard Paul, sported mostly inexperienced riflemen replacements. The 80th Division, commanded by General Mcbride, was in good shape; it was one of the units primed for the assault of the Siegfried line. The two divisions were to attack on the morning of December 22. On December 10, the 4th Armored Division withdrew from the line after five months of incessant fighting; the 4th had earned an enviable reputation during the autumn battles in Lorraine. The last phase of combat, the attack in the Saar mud, had been particularly trying and costly. Replacements in men and material were not to be had, and trained tank crews could not be found in the replacement centers. In fact, these specialists no longer received their training in the United States. When the division started for Bastogne, it was short 713 men and 19 officers, all from the tank and infantry battalions and the cavalry squadron.

The state of the material was much poorer, for there was a shortage of medium tanks throughout the European theater. The division could replace only a few of their losses and were short twenty-one Shermans when they were moved north.

Fortunately for the Americans, the Germans were not only ill-prepared but totally incapable of meeting an attack. Except for troops in front of the American armor, where the 5th Parachute Division had attached, nobody manned the ramparts. The commander of the Seventh German Army's 85th Corps, General Kniess, managed to get his other division, the 352nd Volksgrenadier, forward from Ettelbruck over a road that turned off the Ettelbruck-Bastogne highway and meandered west and eventually connected with the Arlon-Bastogne highway. As the American infantrymen plodded through the snow before daylight on December 22, the 352nd VGD's infantrymen were not defending but on the march.

American artillery observers and tanks and tank destroyer crews could not believe their eyes. Germans in vehicles and on foot were passing before them in columns, unaware that their foe was nearby. The 26th Division fired at the front of the column, and the 80th Division hit the middle and tail. Although the German regiment bringing up the rear quickly deployed near Ettelbruck, a regiment of the 80th Division broke through farther west and, under a bright moon, took the village of Heinerscheid and cut the Ettelbruck-Bastogne highway. Before nightfall on December 23, a company seized a bridge over the Sure river.

The leading German regiment hit by the 26th Division fought for Grosbous and, in the process, drove out a company of the 28th Division's 109th Regiment. Yet it was farther west that the more significant development occurred, for there fresh units of the Germans appeared.

These units were advance elements of the Fuehrer Grenadier Brigade, created around a nucleus of 6000 men, many of whom fought on the Eastern front. The brigade had two battalions of infantry mounted on half-tracks and trucks, an assault gun battalion, and a battalion of forty Mark IV and Panther tanks.

The going was tough through the rugged country between the Alzette River and the Aron-Bastogne highway. To add to the Seventh Army's newly acquired strength, the commander, General Brandenberger, received the 79th VGD. With those forces, Brandenberger attacked south of the Sure River to drive the Americans back and to regain control of the Ettelbruck-Bastogne highway. As the attack began, the commander of the 80th Division had to send two battalions of infantry to the 4th Armored Division.

The brigade turned out to be less of a threat, for the venom of American fighter bombers, finally flying in clear weather, strafed and bombed the German brigade, creating a bottleneck out of the Our River.

It was a grim fight, as bitter in the brutal cold as any that occurred anywhere during the battle of the Ardennes. Scores died on both sides, but by the day after Christmas the two American infantry divisions had carried the field. Except for a few points, they controlled all of the rugged countryside south of the Sure River, held two small bridgeheads over the river, and regained Ettelbruck. There the attack halted to await General Patton's drive northward. The engineer combat battalions of both divisions cleared mines out in front of the infantry as they moved in freezing and snowy conditions. The fine close support of the engineers, the artillery, and the tank destroyers in the drive to erase the bulge proved admirable.

The 4th Armored Division not only lost many tanks, but they lost their division commander for health reasons. General Gaffey was the replacement and this battle was his first fight as a division commander. There were also many replacements for key division positions.

The armor began its advance in two columns, one combat command up the Arlon-Bastogne highway, another up secondary roads adjacent to the highway. Demolitions executed earlier by the 4th Armored's combat engineers, placed as a precaution against German attack, delayed both columns. By mid-afternoon, December 22, CCA approached Martelange and the deep gorge of the Sure River, not quite half way from Arlon to Bastogne. There, a company of the 5th Parachute Division tenaciously held the two demolished bridge sites. Not until well after midnight did a company of armored infantry succeed in getting to the far bank. The 4th Armored's combat engineers discovered that the banks were too steep for either ponton or treadway bridges. They would have to build a Bailey bridge, which would not be ready until early afternoon on the 23rd. Patton charged the 4th Armored to "drive like hell," but it was not working out that way. Patton told the exhausted troops in Bastogne they would be relieved before Christmas.

Progress was better with CCB on the secondary roads west of the highway. Only when coming abreast of Martelange did that column encounter enemy fire, and then only small arms fire from outposts that quickly fell back. By nightfall of the 22nd, CCB reached the village of Burnon, just seven miles from Bastogne, but that column too had to replace a demolished bridge. Before daylight, CCB resumed its advance across a bridge successfully erected by the combat engineers. CCB found the next village, Chaumont, defended by a company from the German 5th Paratroopers. In a combined tank-infantry assault that afternoon, CCB's tanks bogged down in ground turned soft by the sun, but the armored infantrymen rooted the paratroops. Hardly had the infantrymen reported success when ten German assault guns, which fired on the engineers building the bridges and what the GIs believed were five Tiger tanks with paratroopers clinging to them, opened up with deadly fire.

At the headquarters of the 26th Volsgrenadier Division near Bastogne, five Ferdinand tank destroyers, mounting long-barreled 88mm guns on a Tiger tank chassis, had arrived.

They belonged to the 653rd Heavy Panzerjaeger Battalion, recently arrived from Italy and committed to Alsace. Somehow those Ferdinands had been diverted to the Ardennes. The division commander, Colonel Kokott, cared not from where they came, for they seemed heaven sent. These Ferdinands could prevent the American drive from cutting into the rear of his division at Bastogne.

Kokott sent the tank destroyers south along with ten assault guns. They arrived at Chaumont in time to support the paratroopers in retaking the town. The German guns exacted a heavy toll of the American tanks mired just outside the village.

That night, General McAuliffe sent a concerned message from Bastogne to the 4th Armored Division: "Sorry I didn't get to shake hands today. I was disappointed." A short while later, somebody on his staff sent another: "There is only one more shopping day before Christmas!"

On December 22, during the afternoon briefing at the Ninth Air Force's HQ in Luxembourg City, Major General Hoyt Vandenberg listened gloomily to the prediction of his chief meteorologist, Major Stuart Fuller. A low pressure front had settled in the general vicinity of the Rhine River, and he could see no break in the clouds for four more days. They were anxious to give air support to the 101st in Bastogne.

At breakfast the next morning, Fuller happily acknowledged that he was wrong. The cold winds of a Russian high had blown the clouds away. All morning officers and airmen gaped at the sky and, by noon, one parade after another of Medium B-26 Marauders, seemingly everywhere, darkened the sky. P-47 Thunderbolts and P-38 Lightnings flew 1,300 sorties by nightfall.

Before it was over, 241 planes had dropped 144 tons of supplies. That day, and for the next four days, McAuliffe's support needs were more than met, including field surgeons who landed in gliders. During that five day period, the Germans shot down nineteen planes and damaged fifty more.

The snow helped the pilots tremendously, for the Germans left tell-tale tracks of their vehicles leading to assembly areas in the forests. Before day's end, fires circled the American positions so that the smoke made it seem like the fog was closing in again. With either bombs or napalm, the fighter bombers hit every village within a mile of the perimeter, some of them several times. They flew over 250 sorties each day.

The clear weather enabled the commanding officer of the Ninth Air Force to plan an aerial action he devised soon after the German offensive began. The first priority was to blunt the enemy's armored spearheads and supporting motor transport by every available means while simultaneously knocking out his railheads and communication centers in the Eifel-Prum, Nideggen, and Bitburg. Other high priority targets were the bridges used to bring supplies and reinforcements across the Rhine.

Early on the 24th, General Manteuffel asked Hitler about Bastogne. At that point Hitler had lost interest in the village. He said, "Use all available forces to get to the Meuse." Hitler nevertheless remained concerned about Bastogne, for he found it galling that what he believed was a small American force could hold the town. Hitler then decided to attack Bastogne on Christmas Day with fighter bombers followed by a massive infantry and tank destroyer blitz.

The Fifth Panzer Army commander, General Manteuffel, also decided to attack Bastogne on Christmas day. Hitler had reinforced the 5th with the 9th Panzer and 15th Panzergrenadier Divisions from the German strategic reserve.

Inside Bastogne, the foxhole-bound GIs were concerned, especially military police-man Tom Jones and 101st Airborne trooper Van der Slice, both of whom had experienced the terrible pounding of American soldiers and Belgian civilians. Many of these brave civilians helped the troops in many kind ways, including caring for the wounded.

On Christmas Eve, everyone believed that Patton and his troops would be there; however, quickly disillusioned, they couldn't understand why he failed. They knew he was only a few short miles away and that liberation would come before Christmas—but that wasn't the case!

In command posts and in cellars, everyone read a Christmas message from General McAuliffe. Van der Slice and Jones clearly remember this message, even as they now live and enjoy the holidays in Philadelphia on the 50th Anniversary of the Battle of the Bulge.

What's merry about all this you ask? We're fighting, it's cold, we aren't home. Yet, wrote McAuliffe, every man in the Bastogne perimeter could take comfort from the fact that the defenders of Bastogne had stopped cold everything thrown at them from every direction. They were writing a page in world history and, in the process, giving our country and our loved ones at home a worthy Christmas present. The 101st's G-2 periodic report that night depicted a set of enemy positions and activity around Bastogne in red ink and, in the center (the hole in the doughnut), in green ink, were the words "Merry Christmas."

Earlier in the day, McAuliffe received a message from General Patton: Xmas Eve present coming up. Hold on! Yet there was to be no Christmas Eve present. McAuliffe returned to his command post and spoke with General Middleton at Neufchateau. The finest Christmas present the 101st could get would be relief tomorrow, said McAuliffe.

As Middleton was aware, there was little chance of that. Indeed, of all the problems the 4th Armored Division was encountering, General Patton was ill-advised to send his message, for it raised false hopes. It had taken CCA until midday on the 24th to clear the first village beyond the Sure River on the Arlon-Bastogne Highway—the village of Warnach, still nine miles from Bastogne. Although CCB was less than five miles from Bastogne, they still battled the assault guns and Ferdinands that appeared the day before at Chaumont. The threat posed by the arriving Fuehrer Grenadier Brigade prompted General Gaffey to commit CCR to protect the division's flank. Hopes of a quick, bold thrust to Bastogne faded.

The basic problem was the stubbornness of the German paratroopers. When the tanks gained ground or a village, the paratroopers counterattacked. It took the GIs time to clear them out. This problem prompted General Millikin to ask for two battalions from the 80th Infantry Division to join the fight on Christmas Day. At midnight, he shifted the boundary of the 26th Division to the west to give that battalion responsibility for the Fuehrer Grenadier Brigade; he ordered CCR back to Neufchateau to make a supporting attack along the Neufchateau-Bastogne highway.

Inside Bastogne, at 2030 on Christmas Eve, men heard the drone of planes. They soon learned they were not American. Railroad stations with both civilians and soldiers within bore the brunt of the German bombs. What remained of the buildings was soon in flames.

The medical officer, Major Prior, and others worked as the German planes strafed and bombed. Medics went through the debris with the help of men from the 35th and 326th Engineers locating the wounded and taking them to aid stations. The engineers used their dozers to open up the clogged roadways and build firebreaks. Twenty of the wounded at the aid station died in the bombing. Days later, GIs dug their bodies from the debris.

All during Christmas Day, German armor and infantry hammered the perimeter at Neffe, Wardin, Champs, Hemrolle, and Foy. Panzerjaegers and volksgrenadiers waded into the American line. American tank destroyers and artillery hammered them back, though. Minefields and roadblocks, defended by combat engineers with bazookas and machine guns, further thwarted the attack.

Two companies of the 502nd Parachute infantry were advancing on the beleaguered Champs when German tanks met them. Two tank destroyers of the 705th fired. The panzers burst into flames; once again, the Germans failed to get through. Colonel Kokott, under pressure from his Army and Corps commanders, had failed again. He was also concerned that the American forces driving up from the south would add to his problems. For this reason, he had dispatched assault guns and heaven-sent Ferdinands to the 5th Parachute forces battling the 4th Armored Division.

Kolkott also sent the grenadiers of the Panzer Lehr Division and some of his own men to defend south along the highway to Arlon. That road and the highway from Neufchateau were his principal concerns. But late on Christmas Day, when he learned that an American armored column had entered Hompre, less than four miles from Bastogne, he became greatly concerned. That night, he sent a battered volksgrenadier battalion to Assenois.

The 4th Armored Division's Combat Command Reserve (CCR), with Lt. Colonel Creighton Abram's 37th Tank Battalion and Lt. Colonel George Jaques' 53rd Armored Infantry Battalion, was on its way. Both units were greatly under strength. Jaques was 230 men short and Abrams had only 20 medium tanks. Like the rest of Patton's forces, this division fought brilliantly in Lorraine and at Metz.

Also available to CCR were a platoon of self-propelled tank destroyers, the self-propelled 94th Armored Field Artillery Battalion, and attached battery of 155 mm howitzers from the 177th Field Artillery Battalion.

Abrams and Jaques pushed toward Neufchateau on Christmas Eve along the highway to Bastogne, where they arrived on Christmas Day. CCR's commander, Colonel Wendell Blanchard, badly wanted their first objective: the village of Vaux-les-Rosieres. General Cota's 28th Division HQ occupied this town until the Germans attacked.

A German pioneer battalion occupied the village; they heavily mined the surrounding area. The pioneers also staffed an outpost near Sibret further north. CCR crashed into the town with tanks and guns blazing. Although they lost several tanks, they forced the German engineers to surrender after a brief fight.

A platoon of the 4th Armored Engineers came west to Remoiville with a bulldozer to fill in the bridge blown by the German engineers. The American engineers took fire as they worked the bridge site, but the delay proved minor.

CCR's artillery fired on the village with four battalions before the column moved ahead. As the rapidly moving CCR burst into town, they overwhelmed an entire battalion of the 5th Parachute Division, although they did have some knocked-out tanks and casualties.

Darkness soon fell. Clouds rolled in and, with several feet of snow on the ground, the German engineers blew a road crater that the 4th Armored Engineers leading the attack quickly found and repaired. The difficulty in locating mines surrounding the crater forced the column to halt and provide counter-battery fire for the working engineers. The Germans always fired on their roadblocks with artillery as they retreated.

Early that morning, the day after Christmas, Colonel Blanchard intended to continue until he came abreast of CCB at Hompre, then he would attack Sibret. This appeared to have the makings of a major battle.

Soon, sixteen P-47's of the 362nd Fighter Group pounded the Germans at Remichampagne. The air strike made the job much easier for the GIs. They rapidly took the village and cleared the nearby woods.

Colonel Abrams didn't want to expose his flanks, so he sent a recon team north on both roads to determine the best approach to Sibret. One tank recon went snooping towards Assenois and the other towards Clochimont.

As Abrams and Jaques stood at a road junction discussing their next move, they saw C-47 Aircraft dropping supplies at Bastogne. That sight so vividly underscored the plight of the men at Bastogne that Abrams took an ever-present cigar out of his mouth and proposed that they say to hell with Sibret and barrel-ass through to Bastogne by the shortest route. The road through Clochimont and Assenois was it. Strangely enough, they failed to inform Colonel Blanchard of their decision.

Abrams radioed his operations officer, Capt. William Dwight, to come forward with his C team, which consisted of Company C, 37th Tank Battalion; Company C, 53rd Armored Infantry Battalion; and one platoon of Company C, 4th Armored Engineer Battalion. He also radioed for three battalions of CCB's artillery to assist. When Captain Dwight arrived, Abrams showed him his objective and put him in charge. Abrams barked, "This is it!"

In front of the column were combat engineers with mine detectors. At 1620, with darkness approaching, 1st Lt. Charles Boggess moved out in the lead with six Sherman tanks followed by the armored infantrymen in their half-tracks. At 1645, Lt. Boggess radioed for artillery support and Abrams himself relayed the request. Four artillery battalions and a separate battery of 155's opened fire. The 155s and three light battalions fired ten volleys each on the village center, while one battery of the 94th Field Artillery Battalion hit the forward edge, hoping to knock out any anti-tank guns. The other two fired on woods flanking the village. It was an intense bombardment; the guns fired a total of 420 rounds.

Lt. Boggess called for the artillery to cease. They approached the village. Abrams also entered the center of the village as the lead tanks passed through. Many buildings were burning. Unfortunately, many civilians were killed or wounded. Germans emerged from the cellars and fought hand-to-hand with the arriving American infantry. The fight for control of Assenois raged on amongst the foot troops of both sides.

As Lt. Boggess, in the lead tank, neared the woods on the other side of town, his machine gunners maintained a steady rate of fire to keep the Germans pinned to their holes. So fast were the tanks moving that the half-tracks and tanks following were left far behind. That afforded time for those Germans in the woods to toss a few anti-tank mines onto the roads. The half-track hit one and exploded.

Captain Dwight immediately directed the tanks onto the shoulder and, while they suppressed with fire the Germans in the woods, the engineers removed the mines.

Meanwhile, as Lt. Boggess emerged from the woods, just over one hundred yards ahead of him at a point where a farm track crossed the road, he saw a small pillbox and American troops preparing to assault it. With a quick round from the tank's 75, Boggess's gunner knocked out the pillbox and sent the American troops diving for cover. Standing in his open turret, Boggess shouted, "Come here! This is the 4th Armored!"

As the men emerged, their commander, 2nd Lt. Wayne Webster of the 326th Airborne Engineer Battalion, came forward. Boggess leaned down and shook his hand. At 1650 on December 26, Lt. Boggess and his men ended the siege of Bastogne.

Oddly enough, Lt. Webster and his men were part of a solid engineer barrier line that formed the Bastogne perimeter.

Someone in the 326th Engineer Battalion quickly reported to General McAuliffe the approach of three light tanks that appeared friendly. McAuliffe hurried to the spot and Captain Dwight found him and saluted. "How are you General?" asked Dwight. "Gee," said McAuliffe, "I'm mighty glad to see you."

Meanwhile, as Lt. Colonel Abrams moved forward, he received an ironic radio message from the commander of CCR, Colonel Blanchard. What did Abrams think of the possibility of breaking through to Bastogne that night?

Not until an hour after midnight did the 53rd Armored Infantry clear out the Germans from Assenois and the surrounding woods. In the process, the armored infantry took 428 prisoners.

Yet even before the route was minimally secure, 260 of the most seriously wounded men in Bastogne departed in 22 ambulances and 10 trucks. The others soon followed, and the next day the first supply train entered town with 4th Armored Division tanks providing escort. Having arrived in Paris from the United States on the 26th, the commander of the 101st Airborne Division, General Taylor, declined an offer from General Gaffey to send him into Bastogne in a tank. With his driver, he made the trip in a jeep.

The siege of Bastogne was over. It had cost the 101st Airborne Division 1,641 casualties; the 10th Armored Division's CCB 503 casualties; the 9th Armored Division's CCR considerably more; and among the 4th Armored Division's artillery and engineers 1400 casualties.

As the men in Bastogne soon learned, the end of the siege did not spell an end to the fighting. Hitler's world and his counteroffensive collapsed all around him. His main thrust had failed, and his generals wanted to pull the rest of their weary, depleted divisions out of Belgium and Luxembourg. American and British aircraft were again starting to pound the German armored and infantry columns. Ironically, heavy snows on December 21st helped the Allied Air Forces to locate the lengthy German columns.

The 1st SS Panzer Division and Corps had been reduced to an ineffective force of a few tanks and men. The Allies now added more armored and infantry divisions in preparation for a major counter-attack. But most of all, the deep engineer barrier lines around the German "Bulge" in the American lines was complete. This meticulous and effective defensive line proved to the German generals that they had no chance to get to the Meuse River.

Hitler almost agreed with his generals; however, he decided to make a last great effort to take Bastogne!

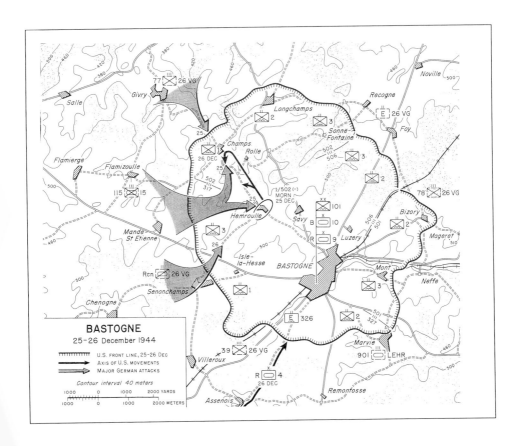

BASTOGNE

25-26 December 1944

U.S. FRONT LINE, 25-26 DEC
AXIS OF U.S. MOVEMENTS
MAJOR GERMAN ATTACKS

Contour interval 40 meters

38

General Gavin and the Critical Period
of December 21-26

The officers and men of the 291st worked closely with the 82nd Airborne Division in the Normandy beachhead area, clearing mines and locating their men who were killed in the minefields. We also learned that General Gavin was an up front leader who always went

where his troops were heavily engaged. Now, here in the Ardennes, we were to experience his crack division again.

Gavin's headquarters were at Werbomont, and his division, after three days of battle with Peiper, was in good shape. The regiments were in line, beginning with the 504th on the left. The 504th faced Peiper's Kampfgruppe, which was across the Ambleve River heavily engaged with the American 30th Division. The 505th defended from Trois Ponts to Grand Halleux. That regiment faced off with the remainder of the 1st SS Panzer Division, which desperately tried to link up with Peiper. The 508th extended the front from Grand Halleux to Salmchateau and then Thier Dumont. Part of the 325th was on the 508th's right and part stayed in reserve. By the evening of December 21, only the 504th and the 505th had exchanged shots with the Germans. The division recon platoon sent patrols south and established contact with some German Panzers moving west. Gavin tells the rest of the tale:

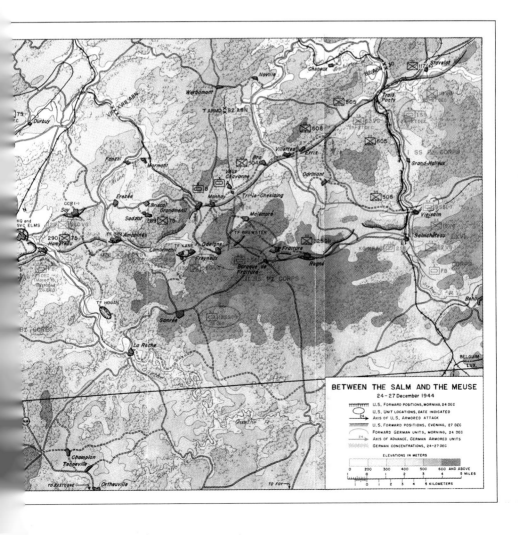

BETWEEN THE SALM AND THE MEUSE
24-27 December 1944

"On December 21, I discussed the situation with General Ridgeway. He expressed the view that the St. Vith forces would probably be withdrawn through the 82nd. He then instructed me to make a recon of the divisional area with the view of withdrawing to a good defensive position after the extrication of those forces who had fought a delaying action from St. Vith to Vielsalm. When I completed my tour of the area, I recommended to Ridgeway that the line of defense should be from Trois Ponts-Basse Bodeux-Bra to Manhay. I went to General Maurice Rose, commander of the 3rd Armored Division, at his command post at Manhay and asked for protection of my right flank, which he agreed to do. I returned to my division and ordered the 325th to extend its right flank and seize and hold the small town of Regne.

"On the afternoon of December 22nd, we had our first contact with the Germans coming from the south. A force of some one hundred vehicles, preceded by twenty-five tanks, advanced north through Ottre. The tanks entered the town of Joubieval, and the column closed up. All the artillery we could bring together was brought down on the column. It inflicted tremendous damage, scattering the Germans through the woods both sides of the road. It was later identified as the Fuehrer Begleit Brigade. Despite the effectiveness of the artillery, an outpost of the 325th was forced to withdraw. An examination of the map revealed that there was a small road with a bridge over the river near the small town of Petite-Langlir in the middle of the sector of the 325th Glider troops. If they were going to use armor against the 325th, it was the only suitable passage between Salmchateau and the Fraiture crossroads. It was obvious that this bridge had to be blown.

"During the night of the 22nd-23rd, the division's combat engineers, led by Major J.C.H. Lee Jr., made it behind enemy lines carrying large quantities of explosives. It detonated the bridge while enemy vehicles were using it. The patrol returned safely. The battle at the crossroads waged hot and heavy, and I had to add a battalion of the 325th out of the reserve.

"The reinforcement arrived just in time, for the enemy overran the town of Regne with infantry and armor. The 325th was ordered to counter-attack and retake the town, which it did. In the midst of the fighting, a German regimental adjutant of the SS Division's Panzer Regiment came into town on a motorcycle. He assumed that the Germans still held Regne. He was captured, and on his person were the march orders for the 2nd SS for the following day. It was to pass through Werbomont on its way to Liege. The orders were sent back to Corps and Army headquarters right away.

"I ordered Colonel Billingslea of the 325th to put a battalion of the 504th and a company of the 325th into the action to quell the zealous Germans. It seemed to me that the integrity of our own position, now extending 25 miles, was most important. Major Edward Wellem's 2nd Battalion of the 504th Parachute Infantry was ordered to move several miles to the woods northeast of the Fraiture crossroads.

"In the meantime the 508th at Salmchateau-Vielsalm-Their Dumont came under heavy attack from the 9th SS Panzer Division. December 23rd found the 7th Armored Division's Combat Command B of General Clarke, the 28th Division's 112th Regiment, the one remaining regiment of the 106th Division, and Combat Command B of the 9th Armored Division of General Hoge, all who had performed gallantly for five days against the German assault of St. Vith, all of these units coming with honor moved through the Vielsalm-Salmchateau gateway.

"As the afternoon of December 23rd waned, I became increasingly concerned about the Fraiture crossroads. At that time Billingslea's regiment was deployed with riflemen 100 to 200 yards apart, very little anti-tank defense, and a serious threat was developing. I went down to the crossroads and encountered such a volume of fire that it was suicide to go any farther. Small arms fire was ricocheting in all directions interspersed with artillery, mortar, and tank fire. F Company was in the command of Captain Junior Woodruff. When he first moved into position on December 22nd, he was confronted with the 560th Volksgrenadier Division. That division was just holding a covering position for the 2nd SS Panzer Division, which was having difficulty closing up the jump-off line.

"The 2nd SS launched an attack just before dawn on the 23rd of December, employing the 4th Panzer Grenadier Regiment, reinforced by a battalion of artillery and some tanks. The attack was driven back after a bitter fight with the troopers. Surprised by the setback, the Germans settled down on pounding the small garrison into submission with mortar, artillery and tank fire. The company stood its ground until Colonel Billingslea gave it orders to come out. Ultimately, 44 of the 116 who had gone to the crossroads returned to their own lines.

"By darkness Major Wellem's 2nd Battalion of the 504th had moved across the rear area of the division and was getting into position to protect its right flank. He had already gotten in touch with Captain Woodruff, and the survivors made a stand at the crossroads. He told me he never saw men who were withdrawing with such high morale. They claimed that they had inflicted tremendous casualties on the Germans. I put Wellems in position to cover the flank and went directly to Manhay, where I learned the 238th Engineer Combat Battalion had taken over the defense of the town and were setting up an engineer barrier line.

"I went to the Corps Headquarters at Werbomont and advised them of the need for forces from Fraiture to Manhay to prevent the Germans from moving up the highway to Liege. I stated that the German attack was certain to come up the main highway through Manhay. The Corps command post had no troops to offer at this time. I then headed to my Division Command Post at 2200 hours.

"I told Colonel Tucker to be prepared to move the 504th command post and one battalion to the right flank of the division and be prepared to engage the Germans there at night. In the meantime I located two tank destroyers, which were moved southwest of the command post to give it some protection from the direction of Manhay. About this time I received information from Corps that the Germans had taken Manhay.

"This information was given to all our troop units, and orders were transmitted to them to be prepared for an all out defensive battle at daylight the following morning. We were now engaged with three Panzer Divisions and part of a fourth; the decisive battle would be fought on the right, provided the 2nd SS could get up enough troops to make a fight of it. It may have been prudent to have executed a withdrawal during darkness the night of the 23rd-24th. The Germans had decided to resupply the beleaguered Colonel Peiper by parachute. Most of the containers landed in the 504th and the 505th areas. This caused rumors of paratroop landings in the area.

"At 1300 hours General Hoge reported to me that he was holding Malempre and that the 238th Engineers had stopped the movement of the 2nd SS Panzer Division. This had been accomplished by the use of mines. We were also given orders by XVIII Corps to shorten our lines by withdrawing. It shortened the sector allocated to the 82nd by 50%, thus enabling us to do much better on the defensive.

"The withdrawal was planned for Christmas Eve. Covering forces were left in position until 0400 hours, when they would be withdrawn. The 307th Engineer Combat Battalion supported the withdrawal by blowing the bridges over the Salm River, laying minefields, establishing roadblocks, and guarding them with bazookas and machine guns. The 504th and 325th withdrew without incident. The 508th, however, was attacked in great force by the 9th SS Panzer Division in the vicinity of the bridges over the Salm River. It also had a platoon on Thier Dumont as a covering force that was cut off during the withdrawal. It managed to return, however, without the loss of a single trooper.

"I was with the 508th as its columns began to move north, and I stayed with them until about 2200 hours, when I decided to go to the 505th. The movement of the 505th was not difficult; it simply had to hinge its movement on Trois Ponts and withdraw its right flank back to the new line. The 508th, incidentally, had a withdrawal march of seven miles.

"Close to 2300 hours, I started to drive back, in an open jeep, to the 505th area. I met a platoon of paratroopers deployed along the road. They told me that they had reports of a large German force in the area and that they were looking for them. I went to the Regimental Command Post and there discussed the situation with Colonel Ekman.

"An unusual situation was developing. Earlier in the night a jeep driver reported that he was driving in the vicinity of Basse Bodeux [the location of my 291st command post before the battle] when he encountered troops in full field equipment walking towards the east in the woods. They hit the ground, took cover, and acted very evasive as his jeep neared them. Another trooper, a telephone lineman who was out checking his lines, reported that his jeep was shot up by what he thought were Germans in our rear area. The Regimental commander asked me what I thought we should do. He estimated that there was a force of around 500 Germans in our rear area. He should stop his withdrawal and search out and destroy the Germans.

"We then decided to complete our withdrawal and be ready to defend our position by early morning against a possible attack of four German Divisions. We had identified at least four who we could expect to be used against us. I therefore ordered him to move on with the withdrawal without delay. Several hours before daylight one of the platoons along the Salm river, just north of Grand Halleux, was attacked from the rear by a German force of great strength—approximately 800 men. A heavy fight ensued. A number of Germans were killed and wounded, as well as a number of the troopers of the division. Among those rescued at this time was an American major of the U.S. 30th Division [The 30th Division was the first one to bottle up Peiper at La Gleize after the 291st Engineers blew the bridge at Habiemont]. He had been captured in earlier fighting at Stoumont by Peiper's force. They took him with them as they withdrew on foot. They had been shot up a bit by random encounters with the 505th as they made their way during the night. Most of them, however, escaped across the river to rejoin their division, including Colonel Peiper.

"So, on December 25th, we realized that we had just succeeded in withdrawing through a hostile force which was itself withdrawing. It had been a novel tactical experience. At daylight of that Christmas Day, all of the regiments were in their new positions, well-organized and ready for whatever might eventuate.

"It didn't take long for the Germans to regain contact!

"Two days later an attack was made by the 62nd Voldsgrenadier Division in the 505th. It was a poor division, not well trained, and its patrols wandered into the 505th area only to be destroyed. The 9th SS came up on our center against the 508th and 504th, and it was of much better quality.

"The 9th SS Panzer Division was charged, by its Corps headquarters, with breaking across the Salm River at Salmchateau and Vielsalm, and there rolling up the southern wing of the division along the river. The night of the withdrawal, its 19th Panzer Grenadier Regiment attacked with great spirit, whooping and hollering. There were only two platoons of the 508th near the Vielsalm footbridge; one managed to stop the grenadiers before they could reach them and the other was engulfed. Under the capable leadership of First Lieutenant George D. Lamm, they fought their way out and back to the regiment. The German 19th Panzer Grenadier Regiment had earned a reputation as the best in the 9th SS Panzer Division. It was an aggressive regiment and followed rapidly the 508th in its withdrawal. The remainder of the 9th SS was strung out for miles, caught up in the chaos of the German rear area.

"On the night of December 25th, the 19th hit the 508th again, this time on its left flank with two battalions in the attack. After a three hour fire-fight, they were beaten back. Again they regrouped, were reinforced, and joined by the remainder of the 9th SS in an all-out divisional attack on the night of December 27th. The division used as the main axis of its thrust the road from Lierneux to Habiemont and hit the 504th at Bra and the 508th at Erria. The Panzers came in screaming and yelling in a mass attack. There were more Germans in the attack than we had ever seen before. The 504th stopped them in their tracks. The 3rd Battalion of the 508th was overrun. The battalion commander, Lieutenant Colonel Louis G. Mendez, borrowed a reserve company from an adjoining battalion and the following morning, during darkness, counterattacked through the town of Erria, capturing a number of the panzers asleep in their bedrolls. The American position was restored.

"I did not hear of the attack for several hours. I then at once went to the town of Erria. The small town was ideal for defense. The troopers told me they had never been in a situation like it. The Germans came across open fields, screaming, and the paratroopers kept cutting them down. The Germans finally engulfed the paratroopers, who stayed in their places and continued to fight them at close quarters. After Mendez restored the situation, they counted 62 dead Germans in one field in front of their machine guns. The troopers informed me that the panzers they captured told them that some Americans turned and ran after their screaming attacks but not our paratroopers. According to the German account of the 1st Battalion of the 119th Panzer Grenadier Regiment, the unit was "cut to pieces" by the American defenders. As far as the 82nd Airborne Division was concerned, that brought the German offensive phase of the Battle of the Bulge to an end.

"It seemed to me that the von Rundstedt offensive was waning in its intensity. Already we had engaged four of their best divisions and defeated them decisively. The latest, the 9th SS, came on with great élan, well supported by artillery, and they had hardly made a dent in our positions by the time the battle was through. Other divisions continued to flow toward the west, but the numbers available for the western thrust towards the Meuse diminished seriously as the Germans turned north towards Liege and the final objective of Antwerp. Blocking them following the efforts of the combat engineers, after December 19th, had been the 82nd, then the 3rd Armored Division, then the 84th Infantry Division, and Major General Ernest Harmon's 2nd Armored Division (Hell On Wheels). Nevertheless, the reconnaissance of the westernmost German division, the 2nd Panzer, reached a point within a few miles of the Meuse. With their tanks going dry, and the long tenuous supply route behind them under constant air attack during the day, they lay vulnerable to Harmon's final counter-offensive, which was launched on Christmas Day.

"During Christmas week, when our front was quite stable, I was invited to First Army Headquarters to dinner with General Hodges and his staff. It was a very pleasant affair. Everyone was relaxed. The first phase of the Battle of the Bulge was over, and now it was only a short time until we would go on the offensive.

"The dinner conversation seemed to return again and again to Montgomery, Patton, and the daily newspaper Stars and Stripes. The staff spoke of Montgomery with amusement and respect. One officer described him to me as 'optimistic, meticulous, precise, and cautious.' They were a bit unhappy about Patton because he seemed to be getting all of the publicity—Patton and Bastogne. One would think that that was where the Battle of the Bulge had been decided and that Patton had been the victor. It had begun to irk First Army staff. They were aware, and the record now shows, that it was the First Army who took the brunt of Sepp Dietrich's Sixth Panzer Army attack and then Manteruuel's Fifth Panzer Army as they sought to break through in the direction of Liege. The fighting had been bitter from the outset and very costly, not only to all of the combat divisions but to all of the higher headquarters, who were constantly, day and night, confronted with the most difficult tactical decisions as they sought to cope with the German onslaught."

Many of the writers who wrote of the Battle of the Bulge indicated in their writings that Patton had done his part for the overall American success. However, writers who were there throughout the battle, such as Robert Merriam, indicated that the Patton story was a myth and that his drive to the little village of Bastogne could not compare to the quick and smooth reaction of the First Army Divisions against the well-equipped crack SS troops on the northern shoulder. Hitler had beefed up the Panzer Divisions of the Sixth Army for his main thrust through the very center of First Army: Malmedy, Spa, and Liege on the way to Antwerp. Hitler's plan shows that Bastogne was on the very southern outskirts of his poorly equipped Seventh Army.

General Gavin continues. "Actually, Patton had been doing extremely well. On thinking over his situation in early December, he decided that there was a possibility of a German attack somewhere in the vicinity of the boundaries between his army and the First Army. So Patton directed his staff to give some thought to the prompt organization of a counterattacking force if such an eventuality occurred.

"He followed the early initial successes of the von Rundstedt offensive with intense interest and began to anticipate a role for Third Army. He decided early that there were two battles: the main one being fought against First Army on the north, and a holding action against Third Army in the south. His thinking was correct, for here in the north the First Army was prepared to go over to the offensive against a badly defeated 6th and 5th Panzer Armies."

We in the 291st would soon make the assault into Germany with General James Gavin's 82nd Airborne Division in close support of his troops.

39

Captain Harold "Bud" Leinbaugh
and the Men of Company K

Captain Bud Leinbaugh commanded Company K, 333rd Infantry Regiment of the 84th Division. On December 21, 1944, he and his company found themselves located near Serinchamps, Belgium. Bud's company had already been reduced to 150 riflemen because of the fighting in Germany near Aachen. Bud and his men knew that the 84th Division had moved to this area because of the German counterattack. The 84th now defended against this German onslaught. At best they knew the Germans were ten miles east. This is Bud's story:

"New messages verifying the murder of GIs by the SS at Malmedy had come in. According to wounded survivors, SS troops had lined up at least 70 American prisoners at the Baugnez road junction outside of Malmedy and proceeded to mow them down. The killers were tankers from SS Kampfgruppe Peiper, last reported in the vicinity of Stoumont, thirty miles northeast of us.

"If K Company's reaction to the atrocity was typical, the Germans had committed their worst mistake of the war on the western front. We had fought by rules of a sort. In the heat of battle, prisoners were sometimes killed. We knew that, but this was murder, and the SS was going to have to pay for it heavily.

"Clayton Shepard wanted revenge, 'When Leinbaugh told us about the massacre, everybody got pissed off. I just wanted to get down to Belgium and start killing Germans'.

"On the 22nd, the division front was fluid. The 84th had received orders to hold a defensive line between Marche and Hotton, six miles towards the northeast, at all costs. The first regiment in the division's convoy, the 334th, had outposted Marche and established road blocks at intersections, bridges, and neighboring villages. The 335th occupied the ground south and west of Marche and sent one battalion ten miles beyond Marche, to Rochefort and nearby villages. Our own regiment's First Battalion probed 14 miles west of Marche looking for Germans. Small jeep patrols were sent out along our entire front to try to find the enemy's line of advance. The lucky ones returned to our lines, some with dead and wounded. Other patrols simply disappeared.

"Rumor had it that the division's flanks were wide open, but the 2nd U.S. Armored Division was coming down within the next 24 hours to fill in on our right. In our book, they were the best: real professionals. It was the only good rumor of the day.

"No sooner were our foxholes dug in the cold and snow when we received orders to move again to defend the country crossroads on the highway running north from Marche. We wiped our shovels, knocked the mud and snow from our boots, lined up and marched off again. We were told we could expect German armor from any direction, so we laid our defensive positions in a closed circle with the command post in the center.

"The cloud cover that had blanketed the Ardennes since the first day of the massive German attack finally broke on the morning of the 23rd. Hundreds of planes, both German and American, mostly American, as far as we could tell, crisscrossed the sky. They left large contrails from horizon to horizon. The dogfights were fascinating. Near noontime five smoking planes went down simultaneously. Flight after flight of Thunderbolts, Mustangs, and Lightnings roared overhead, heading for German lines to our east. The planes gave a big boost to our morale.

"On the 24th the Company made another move to the village of Waillet. So far we had escaped any heavy combat and had seen our engineers lay out minefields and prepare road blocks for our defensive lines. We were now thinking about a peaceful Christmas dinner, but at 2100 hours a jeep from battalion headquarters roared in, and we learned that we were to lead off in a night attack to take a town overrun by the Germans. We had experienced this in Germany and the platoons formed up along the village's main road, and we were loaded in trucks to be transported to the village of Bourdon, a couple of miles east of Marche. There was a meeting in the schoolhouse among the officers and the noncommissioned officers with the messenger from Battalion. It lasted only a few minutes, and the platoons were formed up along the villages main road as there was artillery bursts in the near vicinity. The sergeants were briefing their squads when the Colonel came out and told us to get moving, the attack was already behind schedule. We noticed a squad of engineers among our forces.

"We learned this much in the briefing. The 334th's Third Battalion had been defending a series of villages and strongpoints east of Marche, and some hours earlier German tanks had overrun the village of Verdenne. Heavily outnumbered, the GIs pulled back in good order, setting up new defensive positions along a wood-line between Verdenne and Bourdon.

"A sergeant from the 334th came down to lead K Company up the hill and to the objective. According to the last radio message, four or five tanks were with the riflemen in the woods. They were to follow us in the attack. Our staff thought that the Germans also had tanks and a company of infantry defending Verdenne. The tanks were our big concern. The Colonel told me our regiment's attached artillery battalion would lay down a barrage on Verdenne just before the final assault, which was to begin at midnight. L Company was to follow K Company and help consolidate in reserve."

As the Company moved out, Brewer was setting up a CP in the village. He called a quiet greeting to Phelps: "Merry Christmas, Don. Take care of yourself."

"Don't worry," Phelps replied, but he had a feeling that he was going to be hit that night. It was his turn.

The Company columns went up a hill and crossed over railroad tracks and when Leinbaugh read his map they took a road to the left. Heading left and uphill, the company moved on, traversed a horseshoe curve, the direction seemed right and after a hundred yards entered a dense forest.

Just ahead a tank loomed out of the darkness, its huge bulk nearly filling the narrow road. The men at the front of the column stopped several feet away and passed back word to hold up. The ground mist had thickened after entering the woods, so it was impossible to see more than a few yards. The time was exactly midnight. As the column halted Leinbaugh turned to Phelps, "Tell the tankers to follow the tail end of the company through the woods. We'll work out details for the attack on the far side."

"Phelps felt his way slowly along the side of the tank and soon he heard a voice say when the hatch opened up, 'Was is los?' In a second the men of Company K hit the ditches. Phelps fired a shot at the dark figure opening up the hatch. The man screamed as he collapsed from view. Phelps yelled, 'Get down, they're Germans!' And almost as an echo German voices from the woods screamed warnings. 'Amis, Amis!'"

Leinbaugh realized immediately that the Company was in trouble. Men at the head of the company column fired blindly into the woods and hit the ditches. Machine guns on the German tanks opened up and then everything began to happen at once.

"Streams of tracers lit up the road, giving enough light for Bratten, the radio man, to see the large black cross at the front of the tank. J.B. Cole, standing next to the tank, ran several steps and hit the ditch. 'I ended up amongst a bunch of German infantrymen dug in to protect the tanks.' Pope's platoon had been in the middle of the company column, 'We heard this German yell and they started firing down the middle of the road. We parted just like that.' The tanks remained in place, making no attempt to move forward.

"Phelps yelled for a bazooka man, grabbed his rocket launcher—the man gladly gave it up—and ran forward along the edge of the road. He fired one round, which hit the second vehicle, an armored personnel carrier. It exploded! Phelps reloaded and fired again, but his round bounced off of the side of the vehicle. As he stepped back into the woods to check the bazooka, there was a sudden blast, and fragments from a German shell hit him in the hands and arms and ricocheted off the bazooka tube.

"More German machine guns opened up, and the lead tank fired its big gun, firing round after round of 75mm high explosive shells down the road. Tanks further back in the German column angled fire into the woods and bounced machine gun rounds off the thick steel of the first tank to prevent us from closing in with bazookas or grenades."

As the firing increased, Leinbaugh grabbed the handset of the SCR 300 from Bratten in time to hear the battalion commander ask what in the hell was going on. Pressing the talk switch he yelled above the noise, "Colonel, we've run into the German tanks and have one hell of a fire fight on our hands!"

The Colonel was unimpressed. "Clear those Krauts off the road and get moving." The muzzle blast on the Panther tank's long 75mm spewed flame fifteen feet behind the men at the front of the company column. Holding the switch open, Leinbaugh raised the handset to Bratten. He yelled to the men around him, "Get the hell out of here."

Less than a minute had passed since Phelps had set off the little battle, but a half a dozen men of K Company were wounded in that first exchange. Men began inching their way back along the ditches. Every man along the forest road between Bourdon and Vendenne on Christmas Eve brought back his own story. It was a night of vivid memories and the night that K Company came of age.

"After our medic, Sabia, and an aidman bandaged Phelps' arm, he crawled towards the rear until it was safe to stand. Cradling his wounded hands to his chest, he took off on a slow run toward the aid station and the bottom of the hill, calling out, 'Merry Christmas!' as he headed back.

"Bill Parsons and his squad were no more than thirty feet from the German tank when the firing commenced. 'They would have blown our brains out except they could not depress the gun enough. Thank God there was a depression angle on those babies.'

"Parsons had several new replacements in his squad. 'I rolled over and yelled to those new kids: Get down! Get down! As I turned around, wammo! It was one of those blue concussion grenades, about the size of a lemon.' Parsons was hit in the face. 'It was a small fragment and came across and zapped out my eye.' As Parsons told it later, 'If it would have been a fragmentation grenade I would have had my head blown off.'

"Parsons called on his platoon leader, Lieutenant Zadnick, telling him he couldn't see and had to leave. 'Curly Hoffman, a real good man, came up to take over. Then I crawled down the ditch talking to the fellows as I felt my way along, wishing everybody a Merry Christmas.'

"On the way down the hill Parsons ran into Ybarra. 'He was hit in the elbow, and another guy got hit in the heel. I said, I can't see. So there are the three of us—the crippled leading the blind.' On Christmas morning Parsons was in a field hospital, where surgeons removed his eye.

Back in the woods the rest of the company was inching towards the rear. Campbell's second platoon across the road was to lead in the attack on Verdenne and he and Leinbaugh made the plans for the attack by radio. Harvey Augustin and the company machine gunners were near the rear of the column when the Germans opened up. "We all hit the ground and everyone was prone, but the guy behind me got a bullet in the head. Two German tanks were firing machine guns at us. The Platoon Sergeant asked Clayton Shepard to get bazooka ammunition. The machine gun bullets were coming so close you could feel the heat coming from the tracers. Shells came in and knocked holes in the bazooka. Shepard was not hit but was concerned about all the fire the men were receiving."

"Lt. Zadnick stood up and fired away with his pistol. When the tanks opened fire, Mel Cline's squad broke from the road and into the woods. They found themselves in the middle of a German position. The fellow next to me had his helmet knocked off during the time he bumped into a German gun, and my helmet was hit by a grenade. The Germans started to scatter, and we fired, hitting the two who decided to run. Before joining the exodus down the hill, Cline and the other fellows decided to make sure that all of the German foxholes were empty.

"An officer sent Amici's squad into the woods to protect the company's rear. We saw a German patrol trying to get to our rear. They were trying to be quiet and come around our flanks. We could see five or six before we opened fire; the squad held its fire before the Germans came around the curve and then all hell broke loose. Well, it was like shooting ducks. We were sitting about forty or fifty feet away when the firing broke out.

"We banged them pretty good. The fight lasted only about ten minutes and they had had enough. K Company's only lasted 15 minutes. K Company's engagement with the German tanks lasted less than 30 minutes. Pulling back slowly along the ditches and the shoulder, the company captured a dozen Germans and killed or wounded a dozen more.

"Moving down below the bend in the road, the company prepared defensive positions centered in a rock quarry on the side of an escarpment—less than two hundred yards from the German tanks. So George and I found a bazooka and worked our way up the hill and fired one round. We got an explosion; we thought we got a tank. Both of us felt pretty good about that. The nearest houses in Bourdon were only forty yards below the company's position and the main east-west highway between Marche and Hotton, only another hundred yards away. That was the road that was to be held open at all costs. As K Company withdrew, battalion and regiment reacted with uncharacteristic swiftness. While K Company moved in to block the road into Bourdon, L Company, which was behind K, moved up the secondary road on the right, the one K Company should have taken, and was given the mission to take Verdenne. Locating the American tanks, L Company joined forces with K Company of the 334th Regiment, which was down to 40 men. Following close behind a heavy barrage, the GIs rushed the village. A grim house-to-house fight ensued with heavy losses on both sides.

"With daylight, heavy fighting around the village intensified. Tankers from the 84th's 74th Tand Battalion knocked out nine counterattacking Panthers, and the rifle companies in Verdenne, although heavily outnumbered, hauled in between three hundred and four hundred German prisoners. It was one of the outstanding performances in the Railsplitter's combat history. As it turned out there were 40 German tanks in Verdenne, and Kampfgruppe Bayer was an infantry regiment with an artillery battalion and supporting engineers. K Company's role in the battle prevented the 116th Panzergrenadiers and tanks from breaking out on the Marche-Hotton road and running free and clear to the Meuse.

"Battles raged throughout Christmas day and December 26th in the vicinity of Verdenne, Marenne, Menil and Hampteau, four small villages strung along a secondary road east of K Company's positions. Snow fell much of the day, and cold intensified. Here as elsewhere in the Ardennes, the villages controlled the roads and dominated tactical considerations. On the 26th all four villages were in American hands, but each was under pressure from probing attacks by company-size German units, infantry, artillery, tanks and engineers. The war was turning into an engineer's war with both sides laying mines and setting up roadblocks with bridges to blow on the defense. On the offense it was just the reverse: the clearing of mines in deep snow and clearing the snow in front of the infantry and tanks was a must in order to advance. Many bridges would be built under fire for attacking units.

"Defended by our battalion's Item and Mike companies, Menil was the site of the next crucial engagement. During the evening of the 26th, a strong enemy armored force coming up the road from Marenne entered the outskirts of Menil. The lead tank swiveled in a wide arc and ran over a pile of anti-tank mines that had been roped together as a daisy chain by our engineers of the 84th Division. The giant explosion knocked the tank on its side and tore a hole in its underbelly. Blocked by the knocked out Panther, the rest of the German column left the road, swung into a pasture, and found themselves in the middle of a minefield.

"The GIs defending Menil called for heavy concentrations of artillery and swept the German force with machine gun and rifle fire. Due to the deep snowfall, the engineers had to develop safe roadways and hardstandings for the artillery emplacements at key positions. German tanks and armored personnel carriers were soon burning in the fields, and scores of German infantrymen were killed or captured and hauled off to prisoner of war facilities by the engineers.

"While the battle was still in progress, K Company was rushed in trucks to support the defenders, but our luck was changing; by the time we arrived the fighting was over. German tanks and APCs were still burning, and medics were ministering the German wounded. The Germans lost twenty-six vehicles, including six tanks to mines, engineer bazooka fire, and artillery.

"The mission of Kampfgruppe Bayer was to pierce the Marche-Hotton highway and then proceed northwest and attack Ciney. Following the encounter with K Company, the German tank force in the woods received new orders: 'Hold position; defend against all sides and at all costs block the Hotton-Marche road.'

"At midnight on New Year's Eve, American artillery let loose a mighty salvo on German positions all along the front. Thirty seconds later the Germans replied in kind. The only damage to Menil was broken windows.

"On New Year's Day, we were relieved by British troops of the 53rd Division, who had sat out the fighting behind the Meuse River. The company headed for Hotton in trucks for our next mission. The first week of fighting in the Ardennes had cost us forty casualties, but only a dozen replacements and hospital returnees bolstered our ranks. Like other rifle companies in our 84th Division, we were considerably under strength.

"Rumors floated down from division that we were going over to the attack. We didn't know it, but the Battle of the Bulge was half over."

40

The Crisis Before the Meuse
and the 2nd Armored Division

One of the principal waterways of Western Europe, the Meuse River rises in Northeastern France, meanders through Sedan, and enters Belgium near the French town of Givet. Hitler's secret war plan indicated that Peipers forces should arrive at the Meuse River by the evening of the 18th of December. Leading the spearheading armor of Peiper was to be the regiment of Col. Otto Skorzeny whose mission was to capture the bridges across the big river.

Within Belgium the river is over 500 feet wide with a very swift current, and as it flowed north to Liege it became wider still. The Belgians limited the number of bridges over the Meuse, having used it as a great trench in case of attack. Hitler's plan was devel-

General Eisenhower.

oped to capture the bridges prior to American engineers demolishing the spans and causing great delays to his blitzkrieging forces.

On the second day of the offensive, General Eisenhower became concerned about the possibility of the Germans crossing the Meuse. This was almost a certainty when the 1st SS Panzer Division led by Peiper had reached Werbomont on the second day. When Peiper was stopped by the 291st Engineers at the Lienne river, the 30th Division and 82nd Airborne had not quite arrived nor were in position to attack.

General Eisenhower gave the job to protect the Meuse to the commander of the communication zone, Lt. General John C. H. Lee. To do the job, General Lee called on general service regiments for the bridges considered to be the most critical; the engineers prepared them for demolition. The 29th regiment of infantry was assigned as armed guards.

Thus General Lee ordered the 29th Infantry not only to cover the bridges in Belgium but those in France as far south as Verdun. Starting on December 18th, the regiment sent small contingents to all the bridges and a platoon to a radio repeater station at Jemelle, near Marche, with orders to defend the station against paratroopers and patrols. If threatened by a large attack, the equipment was to be sabotaged before falling back.

Even before General Montgomery assumed command in the north, he sent a scratch force of three hundred men to the bridges from Huy to Givet with an assignment to delay the Germans as much as possible.

By the 20th when Eisenhower gave Montgomery command in the north, the staunch American stand at various points, particularly on the Elsenborn Ridge where the 99th and 2nd Infantry Divisions had formed a solid defense, was as British General Horrocks concluded, "The enemies hopes of bouncing the Meuse crossing have almost vanished." The line to the Meuse was to be held.

Montgomery ordered the 29th Armored Brigade, consisting of three regiments, to defend the three crossing sites from Huy to Givet, the 3rd Royal Tank Regiment at Dinant, and the 2nd Fife and Forfar Yoemanry at Namur. Patrols from yet another British unit, the 2nd Household Cavalry, crossed the river and probed as far east as the road center of Marche. Those deployments freed the bulk of the 29th Infantry to move to Liege, there to guard the bridges and supply installations.

With those dispositions, the chance of the Germans getting a bridge across the Meuse by a coup de main was remote. There remained a real possibility that German armor might reach the river and force a crossing.

Senior German field commanders had begun to voice despair for the prospects of the offensive as early as December 18th, due to the entrapment of Kampfguppe Peiper in the Ambleve River valley by the engineers. On December 22nd Field Marshall Von Rundstedt's staff prepared an optimistic estimate of the situation. Not until January 1 would the American reserves be able to mount major attacks from either the north or south.

Not until the end of December would the Americans be able to defend the Meuse in strength. There was time for General Manteuffel's Fifth Panzer Army to get across the

Meuse. This was in Hitler's mind the next day, the 23rd, when he released the 9th Panzer and 15th Panzer Grenadier to the 5th Panzer Army.

Hitler was continuing to demonstrate that his goal was to continue to outflank the First American Army to the north by slipping his divisions south and then north against the right flank of the most westerly First Army Division. Thus he would be able to have his main thrust of the 6th Panzer Army attack across the Meuse north and south of Liege and on to the port of Antwerp.

The reasons for the failure of his original plan were: The strong defense of the combined efforts of First Army's 99th and 2nd Infantry Divisions from Monschau to the Losheim Gap; the delay of the penetrating Kampfgruppe Peiper by the engineers along his assigned route of advance; the failure of the 12th SS Panzer Division to penetrate on their routes of advance through Butgenbach, Malmedy, Spa, and Liege; the complete failure of the 1st SS Panzer Corps to break out across the mountains north of Malmedy.

The original plan considered the parachute drop of Col. von der Heydte's paratroops, whereby he was to protect the flanks of the blitzing Peiper and the 1st SS Panzer Division. This operation was totally ineffective.

The plan of Skorzeny's regiment of men and equipment camouflaged to look like an American force, also failed in its original mission to capture the bridges across the Meuse River and create havoc behind American lines. This was rather disruptive in the beginning, but the Americans quickly wised up and forced the German planners to use Skorzeny to make an all out attack into Malmedy to free the entrapped Peiper in the Ambleve River Valley.

With only three hours advance notice, the entire 2nd Armored Division packed up, turned its Roer River line over to the 29th Division, and staged an amazing forced march by night on 21-22 December from Germany to Huy, Belgium. All combat elements covered the 75 miles over strange roads within 22 hours, in spite of a shortage of maps and a prior recon.

Von Rundstedt's spearheads were threatening Liege, Dinant, and Nemur at that time. Upon arrival at Belgium, patrols immediately moved out to the south and east, making contact with the enemy on 23 December at Haid Belgium, uncomfortably close to Namur. Their enemy units had penetrated within three miles of the Meuse River at Dinant, and were only six miles from the French-Belgium border at Givet.

In the five-day battle 24 December to 28 December, in which "Hell on Wheels" gained the upper hand by unrelenting shock attack, the Division effectively destroyed the German 2nd SS Panzer Division which had paced the enemies 60 mile advance. The American VII Corps summarized the Division's smashing victory as one that "may well be remembered as having one of the most reaching effects of any action of World War II."

Lt. General Hodges, commanding First U.S. Army, said the defeat of the 2nd SS Panzer Division is regarded as "an outstanding and distinguished feat of arms."

An official count of enemy equipment in the Celles pocket (where CCB trapped and then wiped out a large part of the 2nd Panzer) included 81 tanks, 7 assault guns, 405 miscellaneous vehicles and 74 artillery pieces. Thirty Belgian towns in the Dinant-Ciney- Marche-Rochefort quadrangle were liberated and 100 square miles of Belgian soil were freed of Germans. CCB concentrated its efforts around Celles and the area west of Ciney during this battle, while CCA, first to be committed by General Harmon late on December 23, struck the enemies' flanks at Leignon, Buissonville, Havrenne, Humaine, and Rochefort.

At 1330 December 23, the 1st Battalion 41st Armored Infantry Regiment arrived in their forward assembly area near Ciney, and the battalion passed to the control of CCB. The attack jumped off at 8:00 am. with the 1st Battalion attacking south as part of task force B; A and B companies of the 1st Battalion were in the assault behind a company of medium tanks. C Company was following in support with two platoons of light tanks of A Company, 67th Armored Regiment.

The attack progressed swiftly with devastating effect on the enemy, as our forces caught them completely by surprise. B Company, the right flank Company, encountered a strong enemy armored column driving up the highway headed for Ciney. The company at once dispersed and engaged the enemy armor in a terrific fire fight, which halted the enemy column. At the same time, they were pinned down by the heavy fire power of the enemy.

At this time when enemy and friendly forces were unable to advance, the motor platoon leader at headquarters company, 1st battalion, realized immediately the dire need of artillery support. He crawled out to the outer extremities of the woods bordering the road on which the enemy armored column was halted, within 50 yards of the enemy. From this position he called for the fire of his 81 mm mortar column. In so doing, the platoon leader called for fire close to his own position, and he had to hug the ground to escape the flying fragments. This devastating mortar fire scattered the enemy personnel from many of their vehicles and so decreased the enemy fire. Then, B Company was able to attack and destroy the enemy vehicles, and continue on their mission.

At 1030 hours on December 27th, a company of the 41st Armored Infantry made an attack upon the woods between Conjoux and Celles, supported by a section of Medium tanks. The attack was well-coordinated and swift, and moved completely through the woods, reaching Celles about 1500 hours. During this attack the esprit de corps and fighting spirit of the 1st battalion was exemplified by the personal bravery and initiative of a number of individual soldiers. One of these men was a platoon sergeant from B Company. In the initial stages of the attack enemy anti-tank fire was encountered, and we were unable to advance. This platoon sergeant crept forward to a position near the AT gun and within range of his bazooka.

He fired two rockets at the AT position, destroying the gun and forcing the crew to withdraw. The heroic action enabled the tanks to move forward and neutralize the enemy machine gun positions.

From 29 December to 1 January came another brief pause, then the Division rolled on again, shifting this time to the east over icy roads. On January 3, 1945, working with the 84th Division, they launched another powerful assault against the German's Ardennes salient.

Through snow waist-deep in places, over ice-coated highways and steep trails, the two Divisions struck south from the Hotton-Grandmenil road, operating on a nine mile front. The fiercest winter weather encountered in Europe failed to halt the combined efforts of infantry and armor, which reduced the road centers of Douchamps and Samree. The advance accelerated and on 16 January the Division reached the Ourthe River and captured the important town of Houffalize.

By linking up with the Third U.S. Army troops near Houffalize, the division sealed off the entire western half of the German Salient. Here too, the division took a heavy toll of the enemy, knocking out 43 more tanks, and taking 1800 prisoners, making a total of 3000 in the Bulge. Division losses for the month exceeded 2300. Colonel C. J. Mansfield, commanding the 66th Armored Regiment, was killed in action during the battle for Samree.

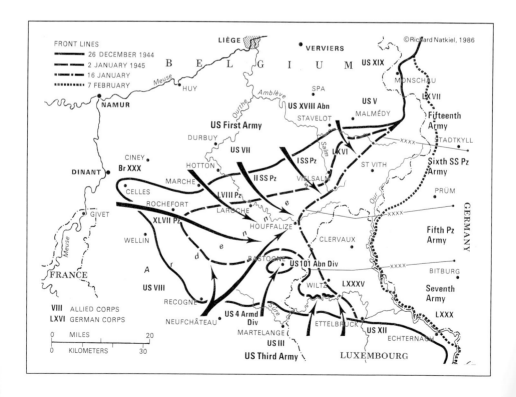

41

The American Forces and Their Engineers
Go Over on Offense

As my new driver, Technician 5th Grade Mike Popp, drove me back through the Ardennes he filled me in on the state and deployment of the portion of the battalion which had become heavily involved in the Engineer Barrier line in front of the Meuse. The headquarters was at Modave near the command post of the Group Commander, Colonel H. Wallis Anderson. Elements of Company A and Company C were manning 15 road blocks along the roads leading out of Marche to Huy, Namur, and Liege.

These tied into the roadblocks in the barrier line laid by the 300th Engineers and the 308th Engineers. Mike said that some of the A Company men who blew the bridge at Habiemont that stopped Peiper had not shown up yet. Company "B" and one platoon of Company "C" were still on the road blocks in Malmedy, but soon would be relieved by the 105th Engineers of Lt. Colonel Dunn.

The road blocks close-in to the city of Marche were close to the front line, but thus far we had received no casualties there. Mike did make me aware of the casualties we had received since the bulge battle started.

291st Engineers Silver Star recipients Sgt. John Noland, 1st Sgt. William Smith, Sgt. Ralph McCarty, Sgt. Floyd Writght, and Sgt. Frank Dolcha.

Battalion photographer Calvin Chapman bravely took all the photographs of the action.

We rolled into the battalion command post in Modave, and I felt relieved that we had contributed much in this battle and still were able to get by with so few casualties. Warrant Officer John Brenna was at the door said, "Colonel, you've lost weight. The K-rations didn't do much for you!"

I could tell by the looks in the eyes of Lampp, McKinsey, and big Max Schmidt that they were glad I finally returned home. There was a look about them that something big was up, but I needed sleep badly; without food or even coffee, I was shuffled off to bed. It is amazing what the human body can put up with when it is under fire for nine continuous days!

Ten hours later, I was staring at the burr haircut of Colonel H. Wallis Anderson. He had his usual slight friendly grin and asked me if I had slept out my stay in Malmedy. He told me that Colonel Bill Carter wanted us to know that General Leland Hobbs had submitted papers to have the 291st receive the Presidential Citation and the appropriate French and Belgian awards. Anderson said that we had been assigned directly to the 30th Division at Malmedy at the request of General Hobbs on the 20th of December, and as far as he knew now this assignment hadn't been changed.

Next, Colonel Anderson provided me with my first overview of the 1111th Group's unparalleled contribution to the containment of the German breakthroughs in the Northern Bulge. He told the story of the defenses at Stavelot on the hill by Sergeant Hensel, and in Trois Ponts by Majors Lampp and Yates, Captains Gamble and Scheuber. He also mentioned the stopping of Peiper by Lt. Edelstein's platoon of the 291st's A Company. He also told me that the main body of the 51st, under Lt. Colonel Harvey Fraser, had held the barrier line from Barvaux to Hotton, and from south of Marche to Rochefort.

Lt. Colonel Harvey Fraser was a West Pointer, and took command of the 51st on December 14th. Since December 17th, he had overseen the destruction of three foot bridges, two highway bridges, and a railroad bridge while holding a 25 mile front against German and Infantry attacks. According to Anderson the barrier lines shaped by the 291st and 51st Engineer Combat Battalions were now in the hands of five Infantry and three Armored Divisions, from Malmedy all of the way back to the Meuse River.

The Battalion staff was anxious to meet in McKinsey's staff room where all of the maps existed showing the overall situation at this time in the Ardennes "goose egg" created by Hitler's forces. Don Garrity, our adjutant started it off by indicating that we had four known fatalities, and that a dozen officers and men had been wounded and evacuated. Unbelievably with such close contact with the enemy there were no known 291sters captured. Some recommendations for medals were sent to XVIII Airborne Corps and others through 1111th Group. One of Edelstein's men, Pfc. John Rondenell received a bronze star for his heroics in the action of blowing the bridge at Habiemont from the XVIII Airborne Corps.

Captain Bill McKinsey briefed us on the battle situation from maps and daily after-action reports furnished by Group and the Infantry units in our area. Present at the meeting was Don Garrity, Adjutant, Major Ed Lampp, Operations officer, Captain Max Schmidt, H.&S. Company Commander, and Captain Jim Walton, the Battalion Supply officer.

(left to right) Captain Gamble, Captain Rhea, Lt. Col. Pergrin, Captain Rombaugh, and Captain Walton.

Battalion staff of the 291st.

The map showing the situation from Malmedy to Dinant on a line through Stavelot, Trois Ponts, Manhay, Hotton, Marche, and Dinant, reveals that we are about ready to go over on the offensive. The 2nd Armored Division has smashed up and almost obliterated the 2nd SS Panzer Division at Celles. The 9th SS Panzer Division has been hit by American air power and is being faced by the 84th Infantry Division near Marche. Bastogne is still surrounded, but air attacks have reduced the forces of the Germans in that area. The 116th Panzer Division is also crippled by air attacks and the U.S. 3rd Armored Division is in line to move against them.

The American 75th Infantry Division has moved into the Manhay area. Naturally since the demise of Peiper's Kampfgruppe, the 82nd Airborne and the 30th Division are now preparing to go on the offensive in the Vielsalm to Malmedy line. Along the rest of the "Malmedy shoulder", as General Omar Bradley calls it, the 1st, 2nd, 99th, 9th, and 78th Infantry Divisions are preparing to go over on the offensive. Along the southern shoulder Patton is ready to go on the offensive from the Bastogne salient with eight divisions, 4th and 6th Armored, 26th, 35th, 87th, and 90th Infantry, and the 17th and 101st Airborne. At first the emphasis was on the German pocket concentrated against the eastern shoulder of the corridor west of Bras. For this there is a combined assault, delivered by 6th Armored and 35th Infantry from within the Bastogne perimeter and by the 90th Infantry.

McKinsey brought out a map showing the tremendous Engineer Barrier lines that had prevented the Germans from being able to get to the Meuse River. There were 32 engineer combat battalions in this type defensive action at this time which included the organic engineer battalions to the Infantry, armored, and Airborne Divisions. Many thousands of mines had been laid, bridges blown in the face of the attacking Germans, and tanks knocked out by bazookas and daisy-chain mines. Just as the barrier line around Bastogne, Malmedy, St. Vith, Hill 313, Wiltz, and Honsigen had delayed or stopped the pursuit of the German Columns, such was the defensive positions three deep in front of the Meuse from Dinant to Liege and in front of Spa from Malmedy to Monschau.

Engineer Combat Battalions were the 296, 82nd, 300th, 307th, 309th, 311th, 237th, 178th, 163rd, and 249th to mention a few. There were six Engineer Combat Groups involved: the 1106th, 1110th, 1111th, 1123rd, 1128th, and the 1159th. McKinsey stated that to gather up the stories of the actions taken by the combat engineers in these units would take a long time, but Hitler's biggest error was his failure to realize the importance of the combat engineers from D-Day up to this very moment when the Allied side of the battle lines were preparing to make the final drive to wipe out the bulge and drive the Germans back into their homeland and beyond.

Several hundred bridges had been blown to prevent the Nazi forces from reaching the Meuse and now these bridges would have to be built back quickly for the attacking Infantry Divisions tank and artillery support, many of them Bailey bridges under fire. The Germans would blow many more bridges and lay thousands of mines as they retreat back into the fatherland.

The going for the combat engineers will be doubly toughened by the heavy snows and the below zero temperatures. They will in many cases have to use bulldozers out in front of the infantry and armor to clear mines and uncover the iced and snow-filled roads. Engineers with blocks of TNT will have to explode foxholes in the frozen ground and cut through snow and ice for artillery gun emplacements. More than at any time during the war in Europe the combat engineer soldier will be out in front of the infantry to construct a wide path on the way to victory.

When I and my staff had looked at Bill McKinsey's maps and Major Ed Lampp was ready to put his attack plan overlay on top we all realized that our work ahead of us and for many other Engineer Combat Battalions would be most difficult and severe. The Germans would have the opportunity to retreat and create obstacles that only engineers could have the opportunity to eliminate in front of the Infantry.

Michael J. Popp of Elizabeth, PA, was the driver for the battalion commanding officer.

Major Lampp then described the overall situation and stated that shortly armor and infantry units were going to take over the engineers position in the Meuse engineer barrier lines and we in the 291st and 51st would have a brief period of rest and rehabilitation. Lampp pointed out the mine laying patterns which would have to be turned over. It was a very impressive picture.

Lampp said that the bulk of the First Army was maneuvering so it could push the 5th Panzer Army back from the nose of the Bulge, to drive the Germans back from the Meuse as far as possible. The Third and Ninth Armies, to the south and north respectively, were to try to cut through the Germans on the two shoulders and bag as many German divisions in the resulting pocket as possible. Closer to our immediate interest, the 84th Division was on the move towards Marche, which was in our zone of responsibility and the relief of our units on the barrier line was imminent. Soon Major General J. Lawton Collin's VIIth Corps—the veteran 84th Division, the 2nd and 3rd Armored Divisions, and the newly arrived 75th Infantry Division—were ready to establish headquarters east of the Meuse astride the Huy road. We had nominally and temporarily been attached to the 84th Infantry Division. McKinsey and Lampp had then released the blockbuster news for the end of the briefing: As soon as the elements of the 51st, 300th, and the 308th Engineer Combat Battalions had relieved elements of our Company A and Company C along the Meuse Barrier line, the entire 291st was to move back to Malmedy, Trois Ponts, and Spa to support the attack into the German rear.

The relief of our troops on the Meuse Barrier line was accomplished on schedule and the last of our troops from Malmedy arrived at Modave on December 31, as had all other platoons. All of the men were re-equipped with clothing, and broken and marginal equipment was replaced. On January 1, 1945, following two days of frantic work, the refurbished 291st was ready to undertake its new assignment.

I had to make some changes at this time to fill some vacant slots. Captain Larry Moyer was made Major and became the Executive officer. Lt. Warren Rombaugh was made Captain and became the C Company commander and Lt. Tom Stack took over Rombaugh's platoon. Battlefield commissions were given to John Brenna, Coye Self and Robert Bryant.

We were somewhat rested and thus we moved back to the Malmedy area on January 1, 1945. We had learned that on December 28th General Eisenhower had met with Field Marshall Montgomery to plot the role of the First United States Army in the coming counter-offensive. First Army's task was to link with the Third Army at Houffalize, nine miles northeast of Bastogne, then drive on to Bastogne. The attack would be shortly after the new year.

The First Army's XVIII Airborne Corps, Under Major General Mathew Ridgeway, held a portion of the line from Waimes through Malmedy, to Stavelot, and then along the Ambleve to Trois Ponts. From there the line went across country to Bra. The VII Corps took over where the line crossed the Lienne River near Bra, on the southwestern flank of the XVIII Corps. It would carry the burden of the First Army's attack. Two of its infantry divisions, the 75th and the 84th held a fourteen mile front running from Bra southwestward to the Ourthe near Hotton. These divisions along with the 83rd Infantry Division, and the 2nd and 3rd Armored Divisions, were scheduled to trap the Germans at the point of the Bulge. Major General James Gavin's 82nd Airborne Division would protect the left flank of the VII Corps.

The terrain in the area where the fighting took place was difficult and made worse by the weather. Only one major road led directly to any part of the objective, leaving a network

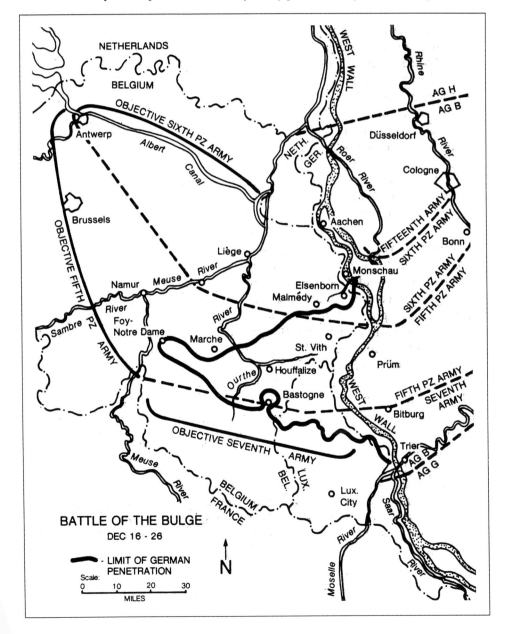

NETHERLANDS

BELGIUM

WEST WALL

Rhine

AG H
AG B

OBJECTIVE SIXTH PZ ARMY

Antwerp

Düsseldorf

Albert Canal

NETH.

GER.

Roer River

River

Cologne

Brussels

Aachen

FIFTEENTH ARMY

SIXTH PZ ARMY

Bonn

OBJECTIVE FIFTH

Liège

Meuse River

Monschau

SIXTH PZ ARMY

FIFTH PZ ARMY

Namur

Elsenborn

Malmédy

Sambre

River

PZ

ARMY

Foy-
Notre Dame

River

Marche

St. Vith

Prüm

FIFTH PZ ARMY

SEVENTH

ARMY

Ourthe

Houffalize

Bastogne

WEST

WALL

Bitburg

OBJECTIVE SEVENTH ARMY

LUX.

BEL.

Trier

AG B

AG G

Meuse

River

BELGIUM

FRANCE

BEL.

Lux.
City

Saar River

BATTLE OF THE BULGE

DEC 16 - 26

Moselle

River

— - LIMIT OF GERMAN
PENETRATION

Scale:

0   10   20   30

MILES

N

of secondary roads connecting the villages to serve as main avenues of advance, though cluttered by numerous bridges, defiles and curves. When the operation began on January 3rd, the fog was so heavy that there was no air support. During the period there were snow-falls and the kind of weather that made it very difficult for tanks to keep from slipping off the roads into minefields along the shoulders, so this made it quite necessary for the engineers to lead the way with their mine detectors and bulldozers. When we moved the battalion away from the 1111th Engineer Group at Modave, we set our Battalion Comand Post up near Spa and traveled through the villages of Werbomont, Stoumont, La Gleize through Stavelot and on to Spa. We were amazed at the destruction rendered to these villages as a result of the battles with Peiper's Kampfgruppe.

I had no sooner set up in a building in Spa when I had a visit from Colonel William Carter, the First Army Engineer. Carter had with him Helena Huntington Smith. She was part of the press and wanted to write the story of the 291st. Carter thought it was a good idea to go into Malmedy and have me tell our story to Helena. We traveled in Carters command car and witnessed a village almost completely totaled from the bombing from our air force. She learned about the massacre and the destruction of the Habiemont bridge and the 7 bridges that stopped or delayed Pieper and aided in the defeat of Skorzeny. Carter said that she would proceed from here and then interview Sam Tabet of the 158th Engineers, as well as others who were heavily involved in the engineer barrier lines as established by Colonel Carter for First Army's defense. Carter then told me that both General Leland Hobbs of the 30th Division and General James Gavin had requested that the 291st be assigned directly to their divisions in the offensive against the Germans. They knew of our great knowledge of the area with its bridges and road net and felt that we had worked closely with their engineers against Peiper and Skorzeny. Carter left me off at my command post and stated what an excellent job the First Army Engineers had done in the face of unbelievable odds. He also pointed out that what was ahead of us would be even tougher.

42

The Disastrous Bombing of Malmedy by Our Own Air Force

Following the defeat of Skorzeny's brigade in Malmedy on the 21st of December we in the 291st expanded our minefields and took care of our wounded and I checked with Lt. Colonel Greer to make certain that he had knowledge of our improved roadblocks. At this time he had also brought up some of his reserve riflemen to take care of the losses in the lines during the battle. He also advised me that one of his men, PFC Fran Currey, had been recommended for the Congressional Medal of Honor for the battle at the west end with members of the 291st.

As I was talking to Colonel Greer, I received a message from Colonel Banner Purdue, the 120th Infantry's commander, to meet him at the 3rd Battalion's Headquarters. The Colonel was so complimentary about the successful battle we had at the defense of the vital bridges at the west end.

The men of the 291st digging out their Commander and Captain Moyer.

Christmas toast in Malmedy.

He then told me, "Colonel Pergrin, we have to blow the bridges at the west end! Our intelligence section expects an all-out attack in the morning to take Malmedy. It is to be a stronger effort than the assault by Skorzeny's forces." I told Colonel Purdue, "Its no easy task and will take away opportunities to move over to the attack once the bridges are blown." But Colonel Purdue insisted and Lt. Frank Rhea was given the job of blowing the three bridges which included the railroad viaduct over the highway.

We blew the Warche River bridge and the Rue de Falize bridge with ease and then tackled the massive stone railroad span. It was an enormous job and had to be completed by sunset. In all, 1800 pounds of TNT were put on one of the stone piers and 500 pounds were put on the crown. I arrived at the site with Lt. Rhea just before Sgt. Charles Sweitzer was given the order to blow the bridge. Just before the detonator was pulled artillery fire struck the site, but no person was struck by shell fragmentation.

At 1400 hours on the 22nd of December the order was given by Rhea and up she went in a cloud of dust. It was a perfect blow. All of the stone structure fell on the road and blocked it almost to the top of the embankment. It was also the biggest boom that the men had ever heard. But one thing was dead sure: Nobody could approach Malmedy up the Stavelot road again. Now the road blocks at the west end did not have to be maintained.

Lt. Frank Rheas platoon extended the minefields far out into the area towards Stavelot along the Rue de Falize and Sergeant Ralph McCarty and Squad Sergeant Sheldon Smith wired the bridge on the S-bend over the railroad and set up a guard to blow it in case of an attack. Sheldon Smith and one of his men, Pfc. Zaleski dug foxholes and set up the guard.

A little after 1430 hours on December 23rd on the first clear cold day on which the air force could fly extensively, the first U.S. planes had appeared over Malmedy. This was a great sight for all of us in the village and everyone went out to follow the contrails through the sky.

Suddenly a heavy and intense fire opened up on the planes from the German guns south of Malmedy, and all the planes flew away. Around 1600 hours a small flight of six medium bombers with fighter escort flew over Malmedy. Unbelievably, before the astonished eyes of everybody watching, they dropped their bombs in the heart of Malmedy! It couldn't be! Their own planes? Bombing their own men in Malmedy!

But it was. A carpet of bombs was rained down on the town and several homes were totally destroyed. The streets were blocked with debris.

The wounded and the killed were everywhere. People were buried under the rubble and muffled cries came from beneath the masses of debris. The spectacle was horrible. The men of the 120th pitched in to help dig people out, and a cry went up for us to clear the streets, and soon the men who had manned the road blocks were clearing the streets with bulldozers and rescuing civilians and soldiers alike out of the debris. The buildings started to burn. The men of the 291st such as Raymond Nice, Don Cresswell, Bernie Koenig, and Sgt. Walter Smith set up groups of men to remove the dead and take the wounded to our medics for Captain Kamen and his men to dress their wounds and then have them transported out of Malmedy to field hospitals.

Among the first to help was our engineer fire brigade run by our 291sters who operated the water purification plant: Technician 5th Grade John Chapman, Private First Class Camilio Bosco, and Private First Class John Iles. The makeshift fire brigade came with first class fire trucks and hoses.

As our line engineers converged on the ravaged area, Larry Moyer and John Conlin organized rescue teams to sift through the rubble in search of survivors. They even found

Remains of a V-2 Rocket.

1,000 pound V-1 rocket damage in Malmedy.

some German soldiers in the debris. This was especially ticklish work near the center of the bombed-out area, for rubble blocking the streets was likely as not to contain survivors.

At the far edges of the blasted area, Sgt. Charles Sweitzer's demolition team blew fire lanes to contain the further spread of the uncontrollable fires. Within minutes of the detonation of the last bomb, Captain Paul Kamen's battalion aid station was receiving the first of many military and civilian casualties.

My troop leaders and troops were magnificent. As I walked through the rubble, there rose in me a sense of pride. Their reaction to the unbelievably frightening disaster had been so quick, so thorough, so giving. Almost without let-up, those combat-hardened young men worked straight into the night, gingerly sifting the rubble of countless buildings for some sign of even the most tenuously maintained spirit of life.

Locating the living and the dead in the rubble was more difficult than it sounds. The detonations of the five-hundred-pound bombs had ground many parts of many buildings to a fine, powdery dust which covered everything in sight. A living unconscious body looked much the same as dead stone, and more than a few survivors were located after they gave way under the foot of the rescuers. There was no red blood visible, only dusty splotches of a dark liquid. The men had to put on masks as they worked long hours in the gray dust.

Master Sergeant Ralph McCarty and Sergeant John Noland lifted some heavy rubble from the ruin of one house and found several live children arrayed around the cold, stiff bodies of their mother and father. Children and adults whose clothing had been reduced to gray, dusty rags wandered aimlessly through the area of the worst destruction, all no doubt driven temporarily over the edge by the shock and grief that had burst upon their orderly lives (It is one thing to see a war going on, and quite another to have the war explode in your family's sitting room).

We eventually learned that beneath cloudy skies, 28 medium B-26 bombers of the U.S. Air Force's IXth Bombardment Division got confused on the way to Zulpich, Germany, which was thirty three miles from Malmedy. Twenty two of the twenty eight pilots eventually realized that they were off course and aborted their bombing runs. However six of the pilots thought that Malmedy was Zulpich and six of the medium bombers dropped a total of eighty-six five hundred-pound general-purpose bombs on Malmedy. To this day when I have returned to Malmedy, I cannot imagine what would have befallen us if had all or most of the B-26s dropped their loads. This was the second time in the war when the 120th Infantry had been bombed from the air by friendly aircraft. Hundreds of casualties had been sustained by the regiment in July during the carpet bombing that marked the beginning of operation Cobra, the Normandy breakout. We were fortunate then and now for we were in close support of the 30th Division then and now. God was with us both times for we had no casualties either time.

Major General Leland Hobbs, the Commanding General of the 30th Division, raised holy hell with First Army Headquarters, and the 1st Army raised hell with the 9th Air force. The air force said: we will not do it again!

Adding considerably to our woes that December 23rd was a particularly fierce German rocket and artillery bombardment against the lines of Lt. Colonel Hansen's 99th Norwegian Battalion. Even before the bombing quite ended, German infantry tried to storm the

Hole caused by a German 240 mm shell.

291st Engineers fighting fires in Malmedy Dec. 24, 1944.

Norwegian's lines but they were beaten off rather easily as Lt. Davis' men rendered fire support from their weapons.

Well after sunset, I took measures to organize shifts so we could pull relays of my hard working engineers off the job for hot food and soup. However the work never ceased. Late in the morning of December 24th, I finally stumbled from the work site, intent on catching a few winks at my command post. At this time we had been assigned directly to General Hobbs as an integral part of his division.

I had no sooner nodded off than Sergeant Bill Crickenberger shook me awake to tell me that a rescue team directed by Captain Larry Moyer had located a 30th Division kitchen buried close to the town square. I grabbed my driver, Corporal Curtis Ladet, and headed to the scene in my command car. By the time we arrived, Captain John Conlin had brought in an air compressor and Corporal Jesse McGhehee was busting his jackhammer through a concrete wall so we could gain access to the basement in which the cooks were entombed. Progress was maddeningly slow.

As soon as McGhehee had made some progress into the concrete wall, Private first class Jim Coupe, Conlin's driver, organized a small group of Company C engineers to begin lifting the debris from the excavation. As the men worked, news arrived from the 120th Infantry's CP that up to 10 cooks might be trapped in the basement.

At 1430 hours the hole got big enough to crawl in, so Larry Moyer and I did. Before we could make a move to free the entrapped cooks, eighteen IX B-24 heavy bombers unloaded on Malmedy.

Little of what the B-26's had left standing remained in the wake of the thoroughly efficient B-24 strike of Christmas Eve. Many of the 120th Infantry's companies and platoons were struck by the cascading bombs. Casualties went through the roof, or would have had there been a roof left standing anywhere in the central part of town.

The bombs knocked me for a loop. The first thing I knew, Larry was saying "Lets get out of here," as he climbed out from the debris of a collapsed wall. He moved a beam that had me pinned down, and we crawled a few feet and saw no opening. I was only semi-conscious but could hear a jack-hammer at work.

As though by magic another hole appeared in the wall and McGhehee pulled Larry and I to safety. I was still collecting myself when we found John Conlin in a heap in the street. A long tear in one of his legs was bleeding freely onto the cobblestones. We saw John Coupe and others lift the unconscious Conlin into the command car and head to the medics. Larry Moyer was not seriously injured and took over the rescue job which had become far beyond reason.

I knew that we had lost Conlin and I hoped that we had not lost many others. What we had been through with the Skorzeny battle and now a battering from our own air force was beyond belief.

Soon the medics had me in tow and found that I had a severe concussion and a punctured ear drum and should be evacuated. I refused and appointed Lt. Frank Rhea as "B" Company commander. Master Sergeant Ralph McCarty was the recipient of a battlefield commission and I appointed him to take over Frank Rhea's platoon. I hobbled over to the

Fire fighting in Malmedy after the bombing.

Fire fighting and rescue work for soldiers and civilians at Malmedy, Belgium, Dec. 24,1944.

A command car in Malmedy after the bombing.

Malmedy after three days of bombing from the air.

command post of Lt. Colonel Howard Greer of the 120th Infantry and was happy to find his CP was undamaged. I then radioed General Hobbs and gave him a description of the devastation. When I headed to my command car, I found it in a totaled condition, never to run again and learned that my driver had been evacuated. I then moved slowly through the debris to my own CP and found it intact. No one there had been wounded but I learned that Private Edward Barker of "B" Company had been killed by a bomb, and Private John McVay had been seriously injured.

I also learned that Private Edward Gutowski had been seriously wounded by German artillery fire on December 23rd. In all, thus far, our battalion's casualties in Malmedy had been three killed and nine wounded. It was not good, but I knew how much worse it could have been.

It was not a merry Christmas for we were again pounded by our own air force, when for a third time at 1430 hours four B-26 Medium bombers dropped a total of sixty-four, 250-pound, all-purpose bombs on Malmedy instead of German-held St. Vith.

We continued to rescue soldiers and civilians and kept piling bodies in the school yards until the 26th when one of our men, Technician 4th Grade Bernard Hebert of B Company, lost his leg to Artillery fire. We were also notified to move back to Modave and become rested and rehabilitated to prepare for the counterattack to drive the Germans out of Belgium.

Civilian victims of the U.S. Air Force's Christmas Eve air raid against Malmedy.

I was asked to report to General Leland Hobbs before I left, at his CP near Franchorchamps. There I received the Silver Star and a letter of commendation which later awarded us with the Presidential Citation, The French Croix de Guerre with Silver Star, and the Belgian Fourragere. And later still, the Magneu de Makeye from the people of Belgium. Before I left Malmedy I received a new command car and a new command car driver to replace the wounded Corporal Curtis Ledet.

43

The High Point in Hitler's Secret War in the Ardennes

The day after Christmas when the 4th Armored Division arrived at Bastogne the over-all situation on the American side of the goose egg created by Hitler's attacking divisions was beginning to change around the perimeter of this huge semi-globe. All along the northern shoulder of the big battlefield there was a solid defense which had stopped the main thrust of the Sixth Panzer Army. The 1st SS Panzer Corps had failed miserably in its mission, with the 1st SS Panzer Division wiped out almost completely by the 30th Division. The 82nd Airborne, and the outstanding attacks of the 3rd Armored Division that completed the demise of the Kampfgruppe Peiper.

Despite many attempts by the Sixth Panzer Army to penetrate the northern shoulder, the armored and infantry forces were unable to breakthrough the likes of the 99th, the 2nd, the 1st, the 30th and the 82nd Airborne Divisions from Monschau at the Siegfried line. The Germans particularly tried to crash into these defenses or outflank them repeatedly from the 21st of December until Christmas, but only took a pounding from the artillery and tank destroyers. They sent Panzer divisions south of St. Vith and thence attack northwest to crack this well established engineer barrier line defense.

The 2nd SS Panzer Division, which had been in the reserve awaiting the Sixth Panzer Army's breakthrough north of Malmedy, through Spa and cross the Meuse on each side of Liege along with the 12th SS Panzer Division, had broken through south of St. Vith and was embattled with the 109th Regiment of the 28th Division. They broke out and blitzed towards Bastogne where they lost men and equipment when ordered to attack into Bastogne.

Their next orders from General Manteuffel was to strike up the Bastogne Liege Highway which was known as N-15. No other German Division had gained as much ground as the 2nd SS Panzers. Its success was the result of avoiding attacking heavily defended positions and moving around these difficult positions and heading on to the Meuse. The 2nd Panzer had shot the gap between St. Vith and Bastogne, brushing the Bastogne perimeter at Noville where they overcame the Americans at that point in a day of fierce fighting.

They split their column into two combat groups with one group heading for Celles and the other heading directly towards Manhay and the route to Liege. The division had served on the right flank of Manteuffel's Fifth Panzer Army, but were now heading Northwest aiming for the crossroads of Baraque de Fraiture.

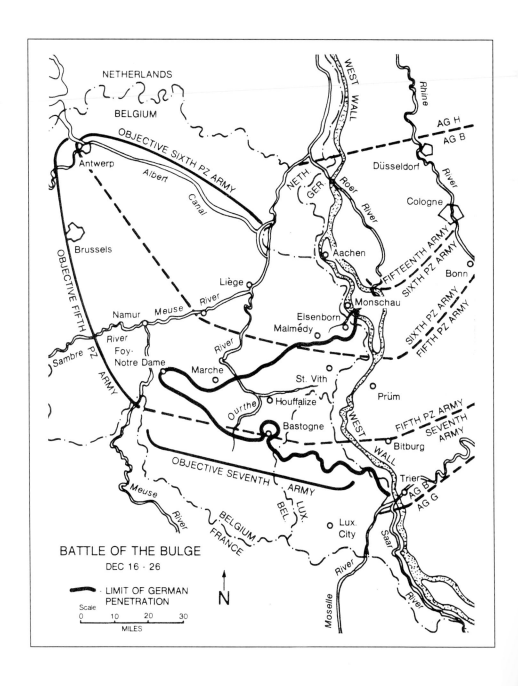

BATTLE OF THE BULGE

DEC 16 - 26

LIMIT OF GERMAN
PENETRATION

Scale

0   10   20   30

MILES

N

This force was hoping to be on the way to Liege by moving up N-15 through Werbomont and Targnon, but they became entangled in the minefields of the 238th Engineers and eventually had to give up the attack on N-15.

The Allied Commanders were convinced that the German plan was to swing northward to Liege so General Hodges on the 20th of December decided to withdraw General Collins VIIth Corps from the Dueren area in the north and swing it over onto the Marche plain west of the Ourthe River. This Corps would have three Divisions to attack against the three attacking German divisions in the area between the Ourthe and the Meuse. Already the 3rd Armored Division of General Maurice Rose was split into three Combat Teams in that area. To add to Collins force would be the 2nd Armored Division (Hell on Wheels), the 84th (Rail splitters), and the 75th Infantry Division.

When the 2nd SS Panzer Division overran Manhay and were later driven out, this armored combat team headed west towards the Meuse. The development of Panzer attacks toward Dinant and Namur at right angles to the imagined German axis was a surprise.

The second armored and the 84th Infantry were situated in the front line around Dueren, and had to be moved south through some narrow winding roads loaded with snow. When the 75th Division came into the area on the 25th of December they were assigned directly to the defense of Manhay east of the Ourthe. The vital area between the Ourthe and the Meuse was handed over to the 2nd Armored Division and the 84th Infantry Divisions only, occupying a series of strong points rather than a continuous line. The first units of the 84th Division, the 334th and 335th Regiments arrived on the 21st of December, despite the prevailing snow conditions. They were deployed in battalion groups on the road between Hotton and Marche, with one battalion moving down to Rochefort, eight miles southwest of Marche, the following day. They were only just in time. Responsibility for capturing Marche and opening up the road to Namur lay with the 2nd SS Panzer Division, aided on their left by Panzer Lehr and on their right by the 116th Panzer from the 48th Corps. By the 22nd of December all three divisions were closing on the Ourthe-Meuse gap, having successfully by-passed the defensive blocks of St. Vith and Bastogne. The 2nd Panzer was in the lead, pushing hard towards its objective despite a number of Allied air strikes against its lead formations.

They skirted Marche to the south, leaving the capture of the town to a detached panzer grenadier group, and headed straight towards the Meuse. This was ill-advised because of the strong engineer barrier line supported by Artillery, Armor, minefields, bridges prepared for demolition, and craters prepared for demolition. Between Marche to the north and Rochefort to the south there were strong American defenses. When the lead units encountered probing Allied patrols late on the 22nd of December they halted in a wide part of the road from Bastogne to Marche in an area with woods and trees along the road. Their objective was to go on to the Meuse through Celles, but the very success of the 2nd SS Panzer Division in closing on the Meuse only 15 miles away was causing it to approach the massive engineer barrier line established by Colonels Carter, Anderson, and Young.

It was traveling without protected flanks since they had out-distanced the Panzer Lehr Division on their left flank and the 116th Panzer Division on their right flank. They were running short of fuel and, coming up in the rear of their column which was greatly exposed, the American Air Forces had destroyed much of the supplies of ammunition and equipment.

General Manteuffel, commander of the Fifth Panzer Army realized the 2nd SS Panzer's situation and ordered the Panzer Lehr Division to break off its attack on Bastogne and make its way forward to aid the 2nd Panzer on its way to the Meuse. Manteuffel was with them when they broke off and headed from St. Hubert to the Rocheforte area about 15 miles from the big river on December 23rd.

Manteuffel then visited the 116th Panzers who were in trouble trying to break out through the engineer barrier line north of Marche. Also the patrols of the Panzer Lehr, the 2nd Panzer, and the 116th Panzer were learning that every patrol was finding that there was a strong engineer barrier line blocking the approach roads to the Meuse. This included minefields, craters, and bridges prepared for demolitions. Also sighted by German airforces was the arrival of two infantry and one armored division east of the Meuse.

When he heard the reports of his division commanders, Manteuffel felt that the German counter-offensive was about to reach its high point. Bastogne was still holding and the Americans had fresh Divisions coming into the defenses. Soon he knew that the Allied side would be making an all out attack to again drive the now failing Germans back where they came from.

44

The Second Half of the Battle of the Bulge

Charles B. MacDonald was a company commander in the 23rd Infantry Regiment of the 2nd (Indianhead) Infantry Division. His company was I Company which he took over at the age of 21 years. The 2nd Division came ashore under the command of General Walter Robertson on Omaha beach on D-Day plus 1. The Division was outstanding and from the beaches through France and Belgium had an impeccable combat performance right up to the Siegfried line where they found themselves in December 1944. The unit had been on defense on the line from Losheim south for about 10 miles. Then they were given an assignment to take over positions to the north and prepare to attack towards the dams on the Roer River in Germany.

Charles MacDonald and his Company I had been in position just along the dragons teeth and pillboxes of this Hitler planned defensive wall. Company I had suffered many casualties up to the vaunted wall and in their position in the woods had suffered shellings from the Germans and watched V-1 rockets go clattering overhead and experienced the shock of rocket explosions.

Monsier Gerard Gregoire and daughter, Marie, in France. Gerard is an author and museum founder who wrote a story of the Battle of the Bulge.

I Company was subjected to German attacks early in December as they were marched north to take over new positions not far from the town of Bullingen. Just before Hitler kicked off his secret war, I company under Charles command had been heavily attacked and suffered casualties from the greatly outnumbered forces and tanks of the Germans. MacDonald who had never been under fire before this was now dirty, tired, and frightened, but he knew that he was responsible for other men's lives and any mistake by him could mean their death.

At this point in these writings, I think of Charles and what he went through to survive the war and have knowledge of the many soldiers he commanded in the thick of many battles, especially the battles at the Elsenborn Ridge area where the 99th and 2nd Infantry Divisions held off the bulk of the Sixth Panzer Army for many days until just after Christmas when we came to the point of counterattack by the Allied forces. Having gone through the same situation with my men of the 291st is one reason that Charles and I got together as charter members of the Veterans of The Battle of the Bulge. VBOB as we are called.

Charles had been heavily involved with the Office of the Chief of Military History, Department of the Army, researching and writing material about the European War of WWII. Charles was dedicated to this type of work, because he felt that the more the American people knew about war, possibly the following generations may find ways and means to prevent war. At the time I met Charles, I had been active with the men of my battalion and

Charles MacDonald and Marie and Gerard Gregoire at La Gleize, Belgium. The Gregoires have developed a fine museum in tribute to the Americans in the village of La Gleize.

Janice and Henry Giles, writers who had done the 291st story in the two books "The Damned Engineers" and "The G.I. Journal of Sergeant Giles." Charles had learned about the story of the 291st through these two books and apologized that in his writings with the Chief of Military history he had failed to tell the story of the Combat Engineers in the Battle of the Bulge.

At this time he was writing a new book entitled "A Time for Trumpets." He assured me that he would cover the engineers in this book, and after long hours of interview he taped the 291st story, studied the tapes and covered the contents with after-action reports and sent it to me for edit. His book really told much more of the story of the 291st and combat engineers who had performed similar war-time actions.

After several years of working with MacDonald and other writers on the battle of the bulge, I now am in the same position as Charles, trying to bring out the history of war so that anyone can examine the contents of war written material and someday be in position to deny the need for one country to attack another.

Charles died of cancer and is buried at Arlington Cemetery, and his actions from the time of writing a book entitled "Company Commander" with many others about the war in Europe up to and including "A Time For Trumpets", certainly brought to the attention of many people throughout the world the direct horrors of war. We in the Veterans of the Battle of the Bulge are continuing to tell the story of all departments of the army in the bulge battle and have found several methods of bringing it out to the public: reenactments, writings with maps and pictures, and videos developed from signal corps film found in the national archives.

We are hoping to develop a museum of research at Valley Forge Military Academy where we have placed a permanent monument in memory of the soldiers who died or served in the battle of the bulge. We have also placed a large-size scholarship fund at the Academy.

To be placed in the museum will be all of our writings, after-action reports, and other allied material which can be used for scholarly study about wars.

If Charles were living, he would have wanted to start this chapter of the big battle, for at this point the Germans have been stopped and the men and equipment have been battered by air, artillery, rifle fire, machine gun, bazooka, mines, craters, and blown bridges. Each branch of our service has played a large part in the overall 15 days of brutal, cold, snow-drifted roads and fields of war.

The cloud cover and deep snow beginning on December 21st have made it a large-size engineer war. As a result of conditions, it has been the engineer war and the German side at this point has failed as a result of complete failure of their Pioneers (Engineers). The main thrust of the Sixth Panzer Army failed because of the Panzer thrust of the 1st SS Panzer Corps with Kampfgruppe Peiper in the lead; they were stopped at first by the 254th Engineer Combat Battalion at Bullingen at a strong road block with mines. The Pioneers never arrived there. They were delayed by a blown bridge near Lanzerath where the Pioneers failed to replace the bridge and Peiper made a perilous crossing down the hill, crossed the tracks and went up the hill into a minefield where he lost tanks.

After the massacre at Baugnez, they were halted on the hill south of Stavelot by the squad of Sgt. Charles Hensel with Goldstein out on point. They lost 12 hours. There is a monument at this location, placed by the people of Belgium, in memory of Goldstein and Liparulo who were killed there. Peiper's Pioneers were never there.

The next location where the German Engineers never showed up was in Trois Ponts where three bridges were blown just before the arrival of the Kampfgruppe. These bridges were blown by C Company of the 51st and A Company of the 291st. This prevented Peiper from obtaining his assigned route to the Meuse. There is a monument to C Company of the 51st Engineer Combat Battalion where the bridge over the Ambleve was blown. The Pioneers of Peiper again failed to move up and build a quick assault bridge at one of the three locations. There is a monument at the Ambleve River Bridge where the 51st Engineers forced Peiper into the Ambleve River valley.

There is a monument located at the bridge over the Lienne at Habiemont where Lt. Edelstein and his platoon blew the bridge in Peiper's face on December 18th that stopped completely his progress to the west. This monument was placed there by Emile Lacroix and the Belgian people to honor Edelstein and the 291st Engineers. Should Peiper have brought up his engineers, they would have had plenty of time to build an assault bridge to keeping moving before the arrival of the 30th Division.

There are monuments in Stavelot, Wanne, and Waimes along Peiper's route of advance. However, the one in Malmedy where the 291st had placed 15 road blocks and blew three bridges marks the spot where Peiper and his column could never break through from December 17th to the end, nor could Skorzeny crash through these road blocks on December 21st.

The race across the center of the bulge goosehead where the 103rd, the 44th, the 159th, the 81st, the 158th, the 299th, the 511th, the 35th, and the engineer battalions organic to the armored and infantry divisions, laid mines blew bridges and delayed the entire 5th Panzer Army for days as a result of the failure of quick and decisive engineer action on the German side. The actions and engineer defences of the 51st, the 164th, the 138th, and the many other engineer units who defended in the overall engineer barrier line, as set up by the First Army Engineer planned by Colonel's William Carter and H. Wallis Anderson, had been highly successful at the river crossing on the Sure, the Ourthe, the Our, the Clerve, and the Wiltz rivers.

Unfortunately at this point of the battle, the shoe is going on the other foot. The American side goes on the offense and the German battered Divisions will be subjected to the defense.

It will be much more difficult for the American engineers to lead the Armor and Infantry Divisions through 2 feet of drifted snow and ice, rebuild blown bridges, and clear mines covered with snow. Generally in the German assault to the west there was little or no snow until the 21st of December. The big advantage was that the skies would be clear for American air force activity.

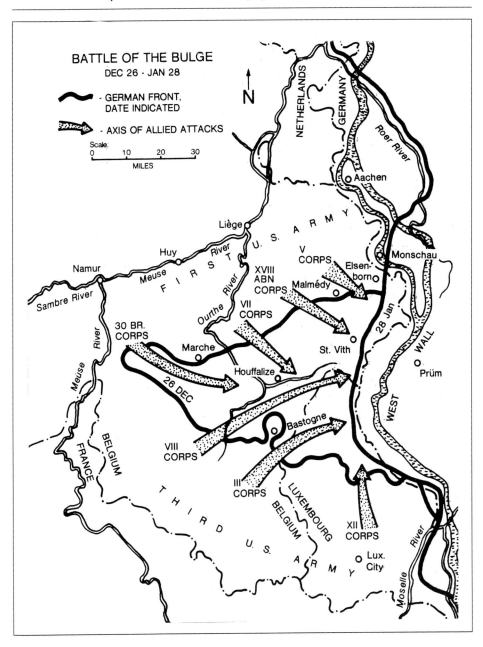

BATTLE OF THE BULGE
DEC 26 - JAN 28

- GERMAN FRONT, DATE INDICATED

- AXIS OF ALLIED ATTACKS

Scale:
0   10   20   30
MILES

N

NETHERLANDS

GERMANY

Roer River

Aachen

Liège

Huy

Meuse River

Namur

Sambre River

Meuse River

FIRST U.S. ARMY

V CORPS

XVIII ABN CORPS

Malmédy

Ourthe River

VII CORPS

Elsen-born

Monschau

28 Jan

WEST WALL

St. Vith

Prüm

30 BR. CORPS

Marche

Houffalize

26 DEC

Bastogne

VIII CORPS

III CORPS

FRANCE

BELGIUM

THIRD U.S. ARMY

LUXEMBOURG

BELGIUM

XII CORPS

Lux. City

Moselle River

45

The Attack to St. Vith
and the Malmedy Massacre

We had until January 10th to get ready to give close up engineer support of the 120th Regiment of the 30th Division. We had met with their 105th Engineers and had worked out an agreement that we would take care of all blown bridges, use our bulldozers to clear roads of ice and snow and also clear mines. We both knew that most of our work would be up with and in front of the infantry.

The first order of business was the plotting of the huge restoration job that faced us across our former and immediate area of operations. Following Captain Bill McKinsey's survey of the 30th and 82nd Airborne Divisions zones of action we now had a plan for the location and types of bridges that we knew had been blown, and we would have to build an assault bridge. We also placed advanced orders for Bailey bridge material and the use of bridge companies we would need in the XVIII Airborne zone of attack. Bill McKinsey's reconnaissance teams prepared to move out with the infantry and contacted the artillery's Piper Cub planes to spot blown bridges when they flew over the front lines.

Captain Max Schmidt went into perpetual motion lining up every bridge company that was available. The Company commanders knew that the Germans would blow bridges and line up their artillery to fire on the sites as they retreated back. The offensive in our sector began on the evening of January 10th, 1945. Since our arrival from Modave much had happened in the XVIII Airborne Corps area as far as a build up before going over on the offensive. The remains of the 28th Division had moved their command post into Trois Ponts and the 106th Division had moved into Stavelot. Each division had only one remaining regiment which had survived the assault of the Fifth Panzer Army.

These remaining men had gone far beyond the average units of soldiers at war, and they along with their comrades who were wounded, captured or killed, had delayed and halted the Fifth Panzer Army whose race to Bastogne and the Meuse failed.

Setting off mines with Bangalor torpedo.

374

The 424th Infantry Regiment of the 106th Division and the 112th Regiment of the 28th Division were now in line to make the attack against the failing German forces as part of the XVIII Airborne Corps. Each of these two regiments had a company of combat engineers to clear mines and open up the snow and ice covered roads and replace blown bridges when the opportunity occurred. These were the organic engineers who had survived the break-through.

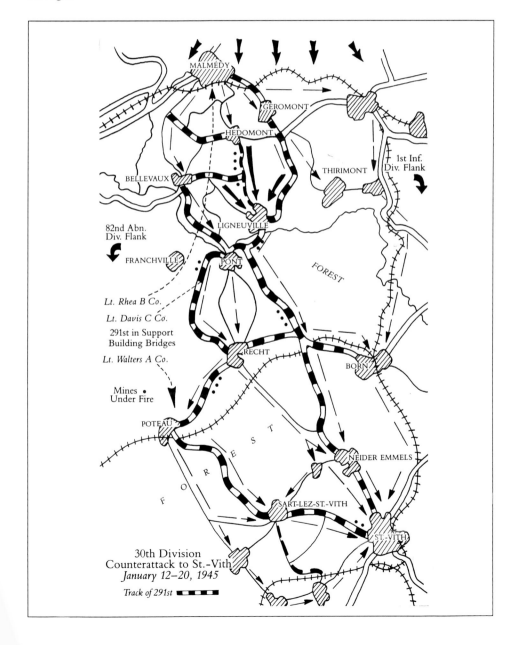

30th Division
Counterattack to St.-Vith
January 12–20, 1945

Track of 291st

The Petite Spa bridge was overloaded.

When the 291st was assigned to act in close support of the 30th Infantry and the 82nd Airborne Divisions, the 51st Engineers of Lt. Colonel Harvey Fraser had been heavily involved with the barrier line breaking through the Marche-Pessoux-Maffe-Hotton area by maintaining road blocks and bridges prepared for demolitions. Shortly thereafter on January 4th, 1945, the battalion moved to Modave to begin a long promised rest. The respite lasted just six hours. Colonel Anderson commander of the 1111th Engineer Combat Group, assigned the 51st a new mission: close engineer support of the 82nd Airborne Division.

From January 5th to the 10th the battalion operated in close association with the 307th Engineer Combat Battalion, organic to the 82nd Airborne. They also provided close support to the 275th ECB of the 75th Infantry Division when the 75th relieved the 82nd on line from January 11th to the 19th.

The battalions new assignment began the night of January 2nd, while the first platoon of Company A was guarding a double-double Bailey Bridge at Noiseux. The bridge had been prepared for demolition. Fraser had knowledge that the 2nd Armored Division was to cross the bridge in the morning, so he had it tested by a medium tank and it proved capable. At daybreak on January 3rd the 2nd Armored Division safely crossed the bridge without a hitch. This was a case whereby the 2nd Division was able to continue its attack with this type engineer support.

During the first part of the Allied offensive, the 51st ECB kept the division main supply routes open despite the heavy snow. It also maintained a barrier line along the Lienne, a river which flowed north into the Ambleve near Stoumont where Peiper's Kampfgruppe fought its last battles. The weather made the battalions mission all the more difficult, for the

Remains of Coolonel Anderson's headquarters in Trois Ponts.

Houffalize, Belgium, 2nd Panzer Division tank knocked out in the final battle with the U.S. Armored.

Sgt. Dolcha and his men clear mines on the way to Baugnez.

winter of 1944-1945 proved to be very severe. The extreme cold accompanied by heavy snow added greatly to the difficulty and hazards of constructing bridges sometimes under enemy fire, removing mines, and clearing snow from the roads with metal shields protecting the operators. Without the engineers performing these missions the infantry could not advance.

The 51st, and the 238th Engineer Combat Battalions, the 501st Light Ponton Company, the 629th Light Equipment Company, and the 994th Engineer Treadway Bridge Company all joined or re-joined the 1111th Engineer Combat Group by January 4th. It marked the first time that the 51st and the 238th were back under Colonel H. Wallis Anderson since the training days in Plattsburg, New York. The 51st and the 238th were the original battalions of the 51st Engineer Combat Regiment before reorganization and the activation of the 1111th Engineer Combat Group.

The 300th ECB was already part of the 1111th Group at the time these units were attached. That brought together Lieutenant Colonels Jay P. Dawley, 238th ECB, and Riel S. Crandall,300th ECB, along with Harvey Fraser, all classmates at the United States Military Academy. Upon graduation from the academy, all three had been assigned to the 3rd Engineer Regiment in Hawaii. Bachelors at the time, they were known as the "Three Musketeers."

Probably the most hazardous duty of the 51st during the period was the removal of numerous minefields and barriers placed by various units, both enemy and friendly. Many of the enemy mines were booby-trapped. Records of minefields were vague and sometimes didn't exist. Even so it fell to the engineers to find or even mark or remove the minefields or demolitions. The 51st was one of those engineer units expected to accomplish the job despite snow and extreme cold.

On January 8th the battalion established a new command post at Stoumont, co-located with Company A. Company B moved to Chevron, and Company C to Lorce, west of Battalion headquarters and north of Company B. In addition to maintaining roads in the new area, Company A had to clear a minefield in the Trois Ponts area, construct a culvert in Basse Bodeux, and maintain and guard a Class 10 bridge near Fosse. It completed the culvert the following day at noontime, and finished removal of the minefield without casualties at 1900 hours on January 9th.

On January 11th the general mission of the 51st was changed from close support of the 307th ECB to close support of the 275th ECB of the 75th Infantry Division who were attacking. The 51st was to be prepared to build bridges in support of division operations against the enemy. From January 15th to the 18th the 51st built back five bridges that had been blown against the attacking Kampfgruppe Peiper.

One of the five bridges was a class 40 double-single Bailey bridge put across the Salm River at Grand Halleux. The Germans had blown this bridge in their retreat in September, and the 291st ECB had built a timber trestle bridge there in early October. When General Bruce Clarke moved through the 82nd Airborne's lines on December 19th, Major J.C. Lee

Lt. Edelstein built this Beiley Bridge with his men of Company A in the assault and under fire for the 82nd Airborne.

The 30th Division moving out of Malmedy to attack to St. Vith.

Jr. of the 307th ECB blew the bridge in the face of the 116th Panzer Division's attacking forces. Now the 51st was to rebuild the bridge for the attack of the 75th Infantry Division.

Located in the west half of town was an infantry battalion of the 75th Division. One of the rifle companies had crossed the easily fordable river and occupied a line along the eastern edge of the village. From there the infantry could observe across the open farmland to the forested ridge line.

The Germans controlled the ridge line, which gave them direct observation for mortar and artillery fire on the bridge site as well as on the road leading to the village from the west. If more than one truck or jeep used the road at a time, the Germans shelled it. For this reason the platoon moved into Grand Halleux by infiltrating one truck at a time. The infantry battalion command post was in a building located on the north side of the main road about 200 feet from the bridge site. The 1st platoon moved into a building on the south side of the road about 100 feet from the bridge site.

They brought bridge material in at night, one truck load at a time. After it was unloaded, each truck went to the rear. During the effort to move material into town the 3rd squad truck driven by Private First Class Earnest F. Minyard was hit by an 88 shell. Eight pieces of shrapnel tore into the back of the cab and destroyed a tire. Nobody was wounded, but Minyard's ears were damaged by the concussion. The area was covered by several inches of snow and the soldiers used bed sheets from the empty buildings to cover the bridge material, hiding it from the Germans. By January 12th all bridge material was at the site, camouflaged and ready for construction.

Staff Sergeant Bonifay, with the first squad led by Sergeant Benjamin C. Ham, laid out the bridge site and identified the centerline of the bridge with tracing tape. Shortly after the layout crew left the site, a German mortar shell exploded on the centerline tape. The Germans had zeroed in on the bridge site.

The Germans bombarded the village several times a day as we waited for orders to build the bridge. The timing of the shelling was unpredictable. When the shelling came in everyone dove for the cellars of the buildings. On January 13th, the third day of the wait, Pfc. Emile B. Doucet was struck on the left elbow by shrapnel. Doucet was evacuated, eventually receiving a medical discharge from the army. His left arm remained stiff for the rest of his life. On the fourth day came the phone call ordering the construction of the bridge from the division G-3 at 2200 hours. Fraser was notified immediately. The night was pitch dark and cold with the temperature 15 to 20 degrees below zero. The panel crew, consisting of Ham's 1st squad and Sergeant Charles Kroen's 3rd squad, began work immediately. The transom was given to Sergeant John Stiftenger's 2nd squad. Three days of rain, snow and freezing weather had left ice on all the bridge material. The men used hacksaw blades to scrape off the ice, which slowed down the work. The bitter cold prevented the men from working long periods. Fraser came along and told the men to use torches to remove the ice, for as soon as the infantry were across the river they would need tank support and in turn a quickly built bridge.

Baugnez, site of the Massacre.

30th Division, 120th Regiment cover tanks and uniforms with white sheets on way to St. Vith.

30th Division fighting snow on the way to St. Vith.

Baugnez-The remains of the café at the massacre site.

The first torch that was lit caused the Germans to open up fire on the bridge. As the shells exploded the men hit the ground and took cover. Miraculously there was no one wounded or killed from the heavy shelling. Fraser himself picked up a rack stick and helped place panels in the bridge. At 0800 hours on the morning of January 15th, the division launched the attack with a hail of small arms fire, mortar fire, and artillery. The bridge was ready. The first tank across started down the approach ramp on the far shore and took a direct hit from a 88 shell. The disabled tank blocked the bridge from further use. The follow on tanks veered to the left, forded the river, and continued the attack. After the assault wave had passed the tank was removed, permitting normal use of the bridge.

Company B built a class 60 double-single bridge at Salmchateau on route N-28. The Germans harassed the engineers with mortar, small arms fire, and artillery. Although two vehicles were badly destroyed there were no casualties. The construction crew finished the most hazardous and difficult job the next morning.

The same day Company C built a Bailey bridge at La Tour, Company A built a bridge south of Trois Ponts on N-28, and Company B another tank assault bridge at Vielsalm where a large amount of mines with booby traps had to be cleared.

On January 27th Colonel Anderson assigned the battalion to provide close engineer support to the 504th and 508th Regiments of the 82nd Airborne Division in their attack towards the Losheim Gap where Peiper's Kampfgruppe broke out. In performing this mission the 51st worked side by side along with the 307th Engineers.

The snow was deep and the infantry could only advance behind bulldozers. The men had difficulty finding mines, so the dozer operators plowed ahead, often running over mines and disabling their vehicles. Almost every day the battalion had to replace a bulldozer. The dozers had been outfitted with armored cabs for the protection of the operators, but the men soon learned that when an operator hit a mine he would be blown into the top and either killed or hurt. So they kept the top open. The operator would be blown out of the dozer and land in the snow with only minor injury.

From January 29th to February 4th, the 82nd Airborne advanced much faster than the unit on its right flank, the 87th Infantry Division. This latter Division formed the left flank of Patton's Third Army. The result was an unprotected gap of 20 miles on First Army's southern flank. The 32nd Cavalry Recon Squadron had to cover that gap. The 1st platoon of Company A provided engineering support. That support consisted of removing mines and obstacles so that the 32nd could move forward, make contact with the Germans, and keep the contact until the 87th Division could move up and close the gap.

While moving on a trail in a very dense part of the forest a troop of the 32nd ran into a roadblock defended by several German infantrymen and an anti-tank gun. The roadblock consisted of log posts and cribs filled with rock and dirt. The obstacle with about 10 inches of snow on the ground and dense woods on either side of the trail, blocked any forward movement. Early in the afternoon the squadron commander decided to eliminate the road-

Engineers of the 105th Combat Battalion approach the massacre field at Baugnez.

The Warsh River Bridge rebuilt for the attack of the 30th Division in Malmedy.

block with the forces at his disposal and not wait for the 87th to move up. He brought up two more troops and the attached platoon of the 51st.

His plan of attack was simple. One of the troops would move by foot through the forest and come in on the right flank of the roadblock. Another troop would do the same on the left flank. The 3rd troop would be in the reserve. The engineer platoon was given the mission of leading the frontal attack, sweeping for mines as it advanced down the trail. In support of the engineer platoon, and ten feet to its rear, was an assault tank which was to fire on the Germans as the attacked progressed. The plan called for the two troops on the flanks to move into position close to the roadblock as the attack progressed and to report in by radio when in position. If radio contact failed, they were to set off a green flare to show they were in position. The engineers put two mine detector crews in front to sweep the trail, and one squad in reserve behind the assault tank.

With one hour of daylight left and a heavy snow falling, the squadron commander, having received neither word nor signal, decided to launch the attack without them. The engineers opposed the order: they would be leading an exposed frontal assault and no apparent assistance or support from the flanks. This was a no-win situation for the engineers. But, on command from the squadron commander, they launched the attack.

As they moved down the trail, each man fired his M-1 rifle into the roadblock while the assault tank behind them fired its howitzer and machine guns as rapidly as possible.

The assault had advanced 200 feet when, through the falling snow, several men could be seen standing in front of the roadblock waving their arms over their heads. The platoon

Corporal Charles Bissell locating victims of the massacre.

leader gave the order to cease fire and the assault force moved to the roadblock. They found the Germans had withdrawn and the Cavalry flank troops had moved into position and no casualties were reported. Once the exposed flank was closed by the 87th, the 1st platoon rejoined Company A on the 4th of February.

During the first week of February the battalion continued to work with the 82nd Airborne in the Ardennes. In that wooded sector north of St. Vith and north of the Luxembourg border there were no paved roads, and the task of opening up forest trails, firebreaks, and an unimproved road to take the pounding of the division traffic fell to the 51st. In many instances dozer operators took their dozers out in front of the infantry to complete required tasks, leaving themselves open for enemy attacks.

By the end of 1944, the enemy in the Ardennes had passed to the defensive. During the last few days of the old year, he had attempted to drive north through Manhay towards Liege, but had been stopped. A large portion of his power was engaged in counterattacks to contain the Third Army near Bastogne. No longer attacking, Field Marshall Von Rundstedt had a new battle cry: "We have succeeded in disrupting the enemy's planned winter offensive." He was quite right, the thankless job of compressing the Germans back into the Siegfried line had to be completed before the Allies could strike into the Reich. The burning question was: Can the Ardennes debacle be converted into an asset?

The German bulge in the Ardennes was about the same size and shape as the Falaise pocket in France. The comparison was a tempting one. However, the plan that emerged called for a general attack all along the north flank of the bulge, beginning in the west where the British XXX Corps and the American VII Corps were in line then rippling eastward to eventually involve all the troops facing south along the flank of the bulge. The first objective was the road center of Houffalize, in the center of the German salient where the Third Army troops advancing from the south and First Army troops advancing from the north

Grave registration numbers marking the bodies from the massacre-81 in all.

The six witnesses and survivors of the massacre return to the site.

were to meet. St. Vith controlling the main road network in and out of the bulge would come later.

On January 3rd the drive for Houffalize from the north began, with the 2nd and 3rd Armored Divisions leading and the 83rd and 84th Infantry Divisions following up. Progress was slow through snow and minefields and soon the order was reversed: the infantry division led the way and the armored followed. On January 6th the 117th Infantry Regiment of the 30th Division and their 105th Combat Engineer Battalion sneaked bridges along the Ambleve River east of Trois Ponts and the 291st Engineers and 238th of Lt. Colonel Dawley placed bridges across the Ambleve and Salm Rivers in Trois Ponts.

These bridges were in close support of the 82nd Airborne Division. General James Gavin and General Mathew Ridgeway were at the site when Captain Jim Gamble's Company A built a Bailey Bridge that was fired upon by the Germans. At this bridge site, Sergeant Joe Geary of the 291st saw the bodies of 12 civilians that had been massacred by the troops of Kampfgruppe Peiper.

The troops of the 112th Infantry Regiment crossed the bridge east of Trois Ponts and joined up with the attacking troops of the 82nd Airborne who had crossed the bridge that the 291st had built in Trois Ponts. The 112th was a regiment that had been resurrected from the ruins of the 28th Infantry Division along with a company of engineers of the 103rd Engineer Combat Battalion. When the 112th and the 82nd Airborne troops matched up and drove the Germans from the high ground south of Stavelot toward Grand Halleux, the engineers had been out in front of the infantry, clearing mines and opening up the snow and ice-covered roads.

Lieutenent Don Davis's platoon of Captain Warren Rombaugh's C Company went to work on a 140 foot Bailey Bridge to replace the timber trestle bridge across the Salm below Trois Ponts that Lt. "Bucky" Walters's troops had blown to stop Peiper's attacking troops. The bridge was built in three and one half hours despite the presence on the heights of elements of the 9th SS Panzer Division. A number of cold, miserable Waffen SS men were rounded up by our infantry as soon as they crossed the new bridge, and they told their interrogators of their mission to plant mines to cover the retreat of a much larger force. At Malmedy, Captain Frank Rhea's "B" Company worked on the west end of town, rebuilding the blown Warche River bridge and clearing the underpasses around which Skorzeny's attack met its end on December 21. This was Company B's third bridge installation at this site. First at our arrival in the area earlier in the Autumn, the company had built a Bailey bridge. In November, the Bailey had been replaced by a timber trestle, which Rhea's former platoon of Company B had blown, per orders on December 23rd.

On January 13th, at Malmedy, the 30th Division was preparing to jump off and drive the Germans back into their homeland. The attack was to be to the south in the direction of St. Vith. The "Old Hickory" Division would have on its right flank the 82nd Airborne Division, and on its left flank the "Big Red One" 1st Infantry Division. General Bruce Clarke's CCB of the 7th Armored Division was to give tank support. This would be the drive to St.

C Company built this bridge at Ponts, Belgium, under fire for the attack to St. Vith.

Lt. Walters and his platoon built this bridge at Poteau under fire.

Vith and General Clarke's Armor would be the unit to make the final assault into the village where Lt. Colonel Tom Riggs had made a great stand with his 81st Engineer Combat Battalion.

To us in the 291st we were anxious to locate the bodies of the 285th Field Artillery Observation Battalion's Battery B in the field of snow at the crossroads where Peiper's men had performed the massacre. I was certain that we could locate the bodies based on information I had collected from the battered survivors we had aided in the wake of the barbaric massacre. Lt. Virgil Lary and Corporal Al Valenzi were concise and accurate about the story as was William Merriken in recent years. In fact since the war I have met with many of the survivors each year and am just as convinced now as I was when I interviewed 17 victims of the disaster on December 17th 1944.

As the 120th Infantry was about to get underway toward Geromont, Mike Popp drove me down that way so that I could follow the assault close behind the infantry. As we neared the little village we ran into Colonel Banner Purdue, the 120th's commanding officer, who was also aiming to move closely behind the infantry's advance elements. As I climbed out of my command car to greet the Colonel, he jokingly asked me if I would like to liberate the village with my troops. I responded in a dead serious tone that we had no time to fight as infantry, that we would have enough to do opening up the roadnet, clearing mines, and building bridges under fire so his tank support could get to the front.

As feared, the Germans had time to lay tons of mines along the roadways and in the fields around Malmedy, particularly in B Company's sector, west of town.

The 30th Division's assault went off through two feet of snow in zero degree weather where the wind-chill factor measured out at minus-twenty degrees. As Colonel Purdue's 120th Infantry moved to seize Geromont and Five Points, Lt.'s Tom Stack and John Perkins

The Poteau Bailey Bridge.

moved their platoons towards the field of the massacre. A platoon of the 526th Armored Infantry also moved out through a pasture south and east of Malmedy.

This situation for the attacking American divisions was much worse than the Germans in their defensive positions where they were holed up in the buildings of villages and farms. They were able to lay their mines and blow the bridges and set up their tank destroyers and artillery to fire on the blown bridge sites, roadblocks and mine fields. The only solution for the Americans in the attack was to make full use of the organic and Corps Engineer combat battalions.

The heavy armored vehicles had great difficulty on the slippery and severely damaged roads of the Ardennes. The infantry had many problems with the severe weather conditions: Their fingers at times froze to the trigger of their M-1 rifle and digging a foxhole at times required the assistance of the combat Engineer with his blocks of TNT. Needless to say the long marches with full field pack through 2 feet of snow was exhausting. The infantryman was always concerned about mines and booby trapped mines, particularly when he was attacking towards a bridge or the entrance to a village. Many of them were killed or wounded by the German mines.

The "Battle of the Bulge" had been an "Engineers War" when the American side was being attacked, but now it was even more so when the infantry and tanks could not attack without the engineers out in front. The 30th Division's objective was the city of St. Vith. Before it lay the rugged terrain of the Ardennes, a seemingly endless series of narrow valleys cut by swift meandering streams. It was country very similar to that faced by Kampfgruppe Peiper, and it was defended by wily Germans every bit as determined to stop our push as we had to stop theirs. Nevertheless, the weather and topography plagued the

The bridge at Poteau, overloaded with a tank and a tank retreavor.

30th Division's attack more than the dogged Germans, including all the mines and blown bridges. Mines aside, the road conditions all but stopped our modern wheeled and tracked army. Lateral roads that might have been used to skirt or bypass tough defensive blockages were often rendered impassable by snow too deep for our vehicles to breast.

Captains Gamble, Rhea, and Rombaugh's engineer line companies employed all of their bulldozers to cut fresh attack routes through the heavy snow. Bulldozers with their makeshift armored cabs had to precede the infantry, assaulting snow-bound German blocking positions.

The German forces in front of us were the 293rd Volksgrenadier Regiment, who held the best ground overlooking all the avenues of approach. The terrain and the snow tended to canalize our assaults across ground that had been mined to excess by the 1st SS Panzer Division. The mines we faced were invisible to our magnetic mine detecting equipment because by the time we attacked they were sheathed in ice.

The attack to the killing ground was roundabout through the village of Hedomont which was atop a ridge overlooking the field where the bodies of the victims of the "Malmedy Massacre" lay. On the right flank of the 120th Infantry were the men of the 526th Armored Infantry and they had run into a German minefield not too far from Hedomont and had several casualties from the German fire.

When Tom Stack and John Perkins platoons arrived at the scene of the massacre, they cautiously approached the field with mine-detectors. They went about locating the bodies and uncovering them. There was a graves registration team to help uncover the bodies and tag them for identification. The mine detectors helped locate the bodies through the heavy layer of snow due to the belt buckles that were metal. The bodies had frozen stiff and we found many of them that had bullets through the skull from the front of the forehead to the rear. We later learned that of the 81 bodies we dug out, there were 41 who had been shot through the head. We found only a few bodies were along the roadway ditch and not in the field. These were the men who had been killed in the initial attack by the Germans. None of these were shot through the head, which indicated that 90 percent of the men were killed in the massacre field and then were finally shot through the head if the Germans thought they were still alive.

There was no question in the minds of my men who uncovered the bodies or those that I interviewed of Battery B who survived, that this was an out and out violation of the Geneva Convention. Sergeant Melton, Lieutenants Tom Stack, and John Perkins said as they uncovered the bodies they were frozen stiff in the position they were in when they were machine-gunned and shot through the head at close range. No bodies were removed yet from the positions where they were found. A placard bearing a number was placed on each body in the order of which it was found, and signal Corps photographers took pictures as evidence for lawyers and future generations that a ghastly crime had been committed there. Sergeant Calvin Chapman, our battalion photographer also took pictures and they were placed in our battalion photograph history.

As American men went about their grim duties, a squad of 30th Division military policemen marched a group of 50 German prisoners through the adjacent Five Points crossroads. All work in the killing field ceased and a great wave of hatred went through our ranks

The bridge at Petite Spa was only good for a five ton load!

The men of Company F, 2nd Battalion, 117th Infantry, 30th Division lie prone in the snow waiting for their supporting armor to move up to Pont, Belgium

and reached out to the passing Germans. It is a wonder that none of our troops opened fire. When the last German had passed the grisly work resumed. At length after the last body had been located, and after the last photograph had been taken, the graves registration technicians began lifting the bodies into trucks. Eventually, except for an eerie stillness, a passing stranger would never have known that this was a place of death.

On the 30th Division side of the attack towards St. Vith, the 105th Engineer Combat Battalion Commanded by Lt. Colonel Carrol H. Dunn was organized with a company of engineers in each Regiment. Company A was assigned to assist the 117th Regiment which was on the left flank of the attack; Company B on the right flank; and Company C in the center with the 119th Infantry Regiment, and 'B" Company with the 120th. Each regiment had a company of the 823rd Tank Destroyer Battalion, and the 118th, the 197th, and 230th Field Artillery Battalions. The 531st Anti-Aircraft had a Battalion with each regiment. Last but not least each Regiment had a company from the 105th Medical Battalion.

The 291st was assigned directly to the 30th Infantry Division for this entire attack to St. Vith, just as we had been assigned to General Leland Hobbs upon his request in Malmedy.

Testifying at the War Trials are (left to right): Virgil Lary, Carl Daub, Kenneth Kingston, Sam Dobbyns, Homer Ford, and Kenneth Ahrens.

Captain Lloyd Sheetz, my liaison officer made contact with division headquarters and the regimental and battalion command posts of the 120th Regiment. The operation in the attack to St. Vith was such that we were so involved with the division that we had no contact with an engineer combat group.

One of the points worth noting at this time since we had been in close support of the 30th Division from Carenton to the bulge during several periods of time, was the high rate of turnover to the basic arm—the Infantry. Each of the three infantry regiments of the 30th had combat losses in eleven months of fighting equivalent to twice the table of organization strength. Losses, of course, were more severe in the infantry companies, which had an even higher turnover rate. For us in the 291st we learned that the changes in all of the key leadership positions such as Company and Battalion commanders were constantly happening; for instance, Lieutenant

Joachim Peiper at the War Trials.

Emile LaCroix placed a monument to the 291st at Habiemont, shown here with Lt. Tom Stack (left) and Pergrin (center).

Colonel Howard Greer, commander of the 2nd Battalion of the 120th Regiment had moved up from platoon Sergeant to Company Commander and later Battalion Commander in six months. Of course Colonel Greer had been a great combat soldier, having been awarded the Distinguished Service Cross.

Despite the rigorous defense and the disadvantages of the weather, the 30th Division ground slowly forward with battalions attacking in columns of companies because of the canalizing nature of the terrain. There were some good roads to be found, but they were few in number and did not necessarily run in the right direction, and invariably ran afoul of Germans holding ridges as much as six or seven hundred feet above the valley floors. It stood to reason that the roads paralleled the low-lying stream beds.

Often our thrust up one valley was outflanked by Germans the next valley over. Mike Popp and I were negotiating the ridgeline above Ligneuville in our command car when we spotted a lengthy German column, complete with horse-drawn artillery, on the river road between Bellevaux and Pont. American forward artillery observers spotted them and called on a fire mission that obliterated the enemy soldiers, horses and all. Long after the scene ended before my eyes, I was stunned by the ferocity of the death struggle and sickened by the carnage, even though it was meted out against the Germans who had massacred the men of the 285th's Battery B in the field near Baughnez.

The 30th jumped off at 0600 hours on the 13th of January with the initial task of reducing the enemy's main line of resistance along a six kilometer front north of the Ambleve River. The operation soon developed into a two phased problem: that of maneuvering troops and weapons through the snow to positions from which they could reduce the well sited defenses of the 293rd Volksgrenadier Regiment to the south; and that of securing the left flank uncovered as the Division moved. The first phase of the problem was solved in two days trudging and fighting. None of it was easy, mainly because of the terrain and the snow. There were even more consistently dangerous enemies than the cold, discouraged, Volksgrenadiers manning the enemy machine guns and observation posts. During the first morning, a tank and then a wrecker was knocked out blocking the main route of the right column. Several hours were consumed rerouting the tanks over an alternate route to support the renewal of the infantry assault. Mines were everywhere. These half iced-in explosives were proof against mine detectors and often were detonated only after many vehicles had passed over them and worn down the protective coating of ice. During the first three days of the attack, despite the engineers diligent efforts with mine detectors and tank bulldozers, 15 American tanks were disabled by mines.

Hedomont had been vigorously defended by the enemy on the 13th, despite two out-flanking attempts by the 3rd Battalion, 119th Regiment. A company of infantry and a platoon of tanks from the regimental reserve advanced along a forested trail to the east to intervene but didn't arrive until after dark.

Hedomont, an initial objective, did not fall until 2330 hours, when the renewal of the attack preceded by a heavy artillery preparation forced them to withdraw.

By nightfall of the first day the infantry, tanks, and tank destroyers of the 2nd Battalion, 119th Infantry, were overlooking the Ambleve River from the high ground back of Bellevaux, on the right flank of the attack. The next morning the battalion advanced in strength to the river bank and routed the enemy from Bellevaux. They then crossed the river at Planche

The annual remembrance ceremony by the people of Belgium.

Annual salute to those who lost their lives.

where the engineers had replaced an eight foot gap in a blown bridge. Opposition was mainly from artillery, mortar, and Nebelwerfers. The infantry battalion command posts of the enemy were being overrun and his will to fight had diminished considerably.

The Germans failed to blow the bridge at Ligneuville and our 117th Infantry rushed across it and seized a three hundred yard corridor on the south bank of the Ambleve. Other elements of the 117th Infantry captured the town at 1830 hours on January 14th. This victory all but ended the German 293rd VG Regiment and weakened the adjacent sector of the German 3rd Parachute Division. Late on January 14th, Sergeant Ed Keoghan's platoon of "C" Company of the 291st was hit from the air by the Luftwaffe. The platoon was removing mines and roadblocks at the entrance to Born, Belgium. Pfc. John Stackhouse and Pvt. Stanley Reed were wounded. While its sister battalions were plowing over the hills to the Ambleve River, the 120th Combat Team was locked in a three day struggle for Thiramont, a ridge town which controlled the eastern entrance into the flank of the attack. Thirimont was held by the Germans 1st Battalion, 9th Parachute Regiment, considered the best in the German fighting forces. Most of the 1st Battalion was in the town, with another company dug in atop of Hart-Sarts Hill, which controlled the Thirimont and Malmedy-St. Vith highway. They also had excellent artillery support. The 120th attacked with two battalions abreast at 0800 hours on January 13th. The 3rd Battalion on the west drove through the little towns of Geromont and Baugnez and on up to positions on the hills above. The second battalion attacked on the left for Thirimont.

The enemy action was not long in coming. The Germans attacked with about 100 men, but were driven off. The road from the north of the town was loaded with German artillery and as the German artillery pounded the town G Company of the 120th was being whittled down and by 1800 hours forced to withdraw with losses of over 100 men.

About 0030 hours on January 14th the 1st battalion of the 120th attacked Thirimont, after an artillery barrage into the German lines. The battalion's leading riflemen captured the ten westernmost houses in the village, but were held up by strong arms and artillery fire. The 3rd battalion had attempted to cross from Houyire Hill to Hauts-Sarts Hill but had been driven back by strong fire. Meanwhile the 1st battalion was being counterattacked vigorously. The first attack by 30 paratroopers was led by a tank. This was easily knocked out by American artillery fire. A fresh battalion of paratroopers plus an assault gun battalion was stopped short of its objective by 500 yards. American howitzers pounded the paratroopers, but they still kept coming on. Four enemy assault guns were knocked out in this action— two by bazookas fired by the 105th Engineers, one by a minefield and one by artillery.

January 15th provided the climax of the battle. Both sides planned early attacks; the Germans jumped off first, at 0600 hours, with a mixed battalion representing all three regiments of the German 3rd Parachute Division and the 348th Assault Gun Battalion.

Only driblets of American tank destroyers and tanks had been available for the close-in work the past two days because of minefields and uncrossable terrain. The 105th engineers came up and cleared hundreds of mines to aid the attack. B Company of the 823rd Tank Destroyer Battalion led the American attack knocking out three German assault guns, and B

The monument to the 81 victims of the massacre at Baugnez.

The railroad vinduct at Malmedy.

Company of the 743rd Tank Battalion destroyed two others. The pounding artillery took care of more. Then the tanks and tank destroyers went to work with the infantry on the sinking Germans. By 0130 the town was cleared. The battle in Thirimont was the fiercest in the 30th Divisions experience.

The first of two bridge sites to fall into our hands was at Pont, just south of Ligneuville. Work began just at the moment the near approaches fell into the hands of our infantry. In fact our Company B Engineers went to work while intermingled with the first wave of attacking infantry. The Bailey bridge began the night of January 15th; we were supporting the 119th Infantry's attack down the Pont-Recht road, early in the morning.

Out ahead of even our forward most line squads and platoons, Captain Bill McKinsey and his intelligence reconnaissance teams often went into the assault with the infantry so that they could instantly assess the condition of recaptured bridges that appeared to be intact. Bill and his troops were feeding a stream of vital information to Major Ed Lampp, who had to marshal our assets and schedule our work. Every minute we gained in getting news from the front was a minute gained in building and repairing bridges over which the infantry and armor could attack and be supported and resupplied. Minutes meant lives.

On January 16th, the 119th Infantry attacked out of Pont towards Recht across Company B's new Bailey Bridge. Our troops helped the infantry Regiment's vanguard clear an abatis roadblock comprised of thirty eight trees that had been felled across the highway, on the 119th Infantry's right flank. The 117th Infantry reached the heights of Wolfsbusch by nightfall again with the help of our engineers. At that point the Germans threw in their fresh 326th Infantry Division. However, despite the infusion of new regiments, the 30th Division

B Battery comrades who survived the Massacre at Malmedy 1944 at the 1987 reunion: (front) Eugene Garrett, Alber Valenzi, Leon Scarbrough, Leroy Scheaf, and Kenneth Ahrens; (back) William Summers, Michael Seiranko, Ralph Logan, Robert Mearig, William Meriiken, and Edward Batsman.

maintained pressure towards Recht. It was rewarded for its persistence on the night of January 18-19 when the cold and weary Germans had left and laid mines throughout the approaches to the village and drove 24 inch logs into the roadway as a roadblock.

The engineers of the 105th Engineer Combat Battalion, under the leadership of Captain Leland E. Cofer, cleared the mines. Captain Cofer was the Lieutenent who blew the bridge at Stavelot, Belgium that prevented the Germans from reinforcing the entrapped Peiper at La Gleize. Once the mines were cleared, Captain Frank Rhea moved in some 291st Engineers and chain sawed the log road block clear of the approach to the town. Generally the Germans pulled back and fired artillery shells at blown bridges and roadblocks of these types, but in this case their hurried departure obviated the shelling at Recht.

The 117th Infantry's soldiers sprang forward into the abandoned Recht, ready to use the houses in the town for warmth and rest and to move through and on to the next village on the route to St. Vith.

On the evening of January 19th, Captain Bill McKinsey radioed the battalion CP to tell us that the bridge at Poteau had been blown. Poteau was the village just southwest of Recht, about two miles on the way to the objective of St. Vith. The 117th Infantry had not captured the bridge site as yet, but he could see from his vantage point with the forward troops that bridge was blown. This was bad news, for this bridge was the key to the successful attack into St. Vith. Its replacement was badly needed by the attacking 117th Infantry and their tank support. Major Ed Lampp gave the job to Captain Jim Gamble and he soon had Lt. "Bucky" Walters' platoon on the way to Poteau.

Early in the evening of January 19th, I witnessed Colonel Banner Purdue's 120th Infantry capture the village of Born which was heavily defended, and then rushed over to Poteau to see how well Walters' Platoon was doing for the movement of the 117th Infantry. Mike Popp drove through battered Recht, but all hell had broken loose at Poteau. A barn north of the bridge was on fire and the Germans were firing in artillery shells in bursts, but had not hit the half finished bridge nor wounded any of the men who were taking cover under the concrete bridge abutment.

Soon the shelling stopped and Sergeant Elio Rosa had his men back to work emplacing the Bailey Bridge panels on the bridge over a very cold looking stream of water, half full of ice. The town of Poteau was dead black and the American Infantry had taken over, but needed their tank support as they would move ahead.

The fire in the barn was put out, but the Germans again fired at the bridge site. Sergeant Rosa and his troops were well experienced in building bridges under fire, but by 0200 hours on January 20th the bridge was completed and shortly thereafter the tanks of C Company of the 823rd Tank Destroyer Battalion crossed the bridge and joined the 120th Infantry on the way to St. Vith.

Along with the engineers of the 105th Engineer Combat Battalion they cleared snow from the roads for the 119th Infantry; cleared mines ahead of them; kept the airfields swept so the liaison planes could land and take off; and built two landing strips at Monteneau, Lieutenant Arch Taylor's home.

On January 23rd, exactly one month to the day the 7th Armored Division had withdrawn from St. Vith, they took it. Brigadier General Bruce Clarke, a former combat engineer, had the honor of marching his Combat Command B into the shattered little town. St. Vith was a snow covered, totally destroyed village and when one looked at the ruins there was a feeling of frustration and sorrow. How many civilians were beneath all of that rubble? How many German and Americans had died in the battles here? Why does man go to war?

I had now seen the two most demolished towns ever during the war thus far, Malmedy and St. Vith.

The fight for Thirimont and for the control of the vital highway was won but the cost had been high. Total battle casualties for the 120th Infantry had been 450 men. At dusk on the 15th the 3rd Battalion had a fighting strength of only 150 men—less than that of a single full-strength company-in its three rifle companies. The 2nd Battalion, which had taken the brunt of the first day's action was only slightly better off; "G" Company had only 53 men left. The 1st Battalion, numerically stronger, had just finished the toughest day of its career and was critically tired. Everyone was cold, wet, and miserable.

The 30th "Old Hickory" Division ended the drive to St. Vith in a blaze of glory as the sun beat down on the hills of snow. The 7th Armored Division had passed through the attacking "Big Red One" 1st Infantry Division, which had made a gap for it down on the line of the Ambleve River on the 30th Division's left flank and was pressing south past Born. On the way south the Combat Engineers of the 1st Division and the 254th were superior in their performance for the infantry.

On the 22nd both Divisions continued to move south, and in the Old Hickory zone the enemy opposition showed signs of chaos. Attacking into Sart-les-St.-Vith with a very brief artillery preparation, the 117th swept into town so fast that one group of enemy soldiers were captured at the breakfast table. The 119th had similar success with Hinderhausen, while the 120th killed or captured most of the 250 German defenders in seizing Ober Emmels and then turning east to seize Neider Emmels.

The same day, the reason for the enemy's persistence in holding onto St. Vith became apparent. The east west roads through the ruined city provided Division's artillery observers with the juiciest targets many of them had ever seen—roads packed with enemy troops of all types struggling eastward, with traffic snarled at several points. The artillery vied with the Ninth Air Force's P-47s in slashing at these columns.

There were still plenty of enemy groups left as the 30th Division moved south of St. Vith; however, they were pinched out by Third Army's VIII Corps advancing from the southwest. The enemy's feverish struggle to pull back into the comparative safety of the Siegfried line lost him 1000 men a day in prisoners alone.

By midnight of January 27th, VIII Corps troops had advanced all the way across the Division front, cutting it out from all contact with the enemy since the battle in the Ardennes began. The "Old Hickory" had earned its just rewards of rest and recuperation with warm baths and to get rid of many frozen feet. Battle casualties had cost the 30th 1,390 men in Infantry alone—the best part of three of its nine rifle battalions. Trench foot and frozen feet caused 463 more casualties. The doughboys had been hardest hit by weather as well as bullets, despite the efforts of regimental commanders to provide warm rooms where the men not fighting could be defrosted. The main reason why many line soldiers kept fighting was to get houses in which they could bed down. All the American soldiers infantry, engineers, armor, or artillery fought the battle to victory.

Monument in Stavelot to the men of the 30th Division.

46

The Assault to the Siegfried Line and the Losheim Gap

When we went beyond St. Vith to the south and the 30th Division closed with the Third Army forces moving northeast, we were ordered to form our battalion on the lines of the 82nd Airborne Division whose mission was to attack across our old battle ground at the beginning of the bulge battle. We turned over to the 105th Engineers of Lt. Colonel Dunn all of our roadblocks and minefields. We had served with them constantly ever since the 18th of December when General Hobbs found us defending Malmedy with only 180 men. We said our good-byes and moved over with the 82nd and their combat engineers with whom we became well acquainted earlier in the battle.

The objective of the 82nd Airborne Division at the end of January was achieving a breakthrough of the Siegfried line at Losheim. In that we were so familiar with this area, General Gavin had requested that we be assigned to his division for this attack.

We would be working with his engineers and Major J.C.H.Lee, their operations officer. The area was more of the hills with heavy snow and difficult roads for tanks and heavy

The Lanzerath Bridge.

Engineers at work to destroy the Siegfried Line.

armor. The men of the 291st did not follow the lead companies of the 82nd Airborne into the Losheim Gap as we had followed the lead companies of the 30th Infantry Division toward St. Vith. Now, we mostly led the paratroopers through the hip-and-thigh-deep ice and snow.

From the outset we faced a howling blizzard and minus degree temperatures through a dense forest that lacked all but rudimentary footpaths. The problems and hardships we faced were surmountable, but only by battle-hardened troops with stout hearts and iron determination. Fortunately, the 291st had those in abundance.

Particularly noteworthy were the heroic efforts of Technician 5th grade Herbert Helgerson, a Company "B" bulldozer operator, near Wereth on January 29 as he was clearing heavy snow from a supply road along the front lines. Often working ahead of the Infantry, he was once pinned down by a German machine gun and almost constantly exposed to mortar and artillery fire called by German forward observers who seemed to have him under observation throughout his mission. Despite the unnerving proximity of fire, Helgerson got the road cleared so the infantry could get the needed support from the rear.

The blowing of the railroad viaduct in Malmedy by the platoon of Lt. Frank Rhea.

Generals Hobbs, Bradley, and Simpson.

The viaduct before the bombing.

Another great performance was by Private Edward Woertz, who got so wrapped up in his work that he worked eighteen hours or more at a time for four consecutive days. Woertz kept working even though German machine-gun fire was hitting the body of his dozer.

Technician 4th grade John Noland, whose exemplary leadership had done so much to save the day against the Skorzeny Brigade at Malmedy, constantly drove his armored dozer directly into the face of enemy emplacements. John was seriously injured by a flurry of German rifle fire as he cut a trail for the troops of the 325th Glider Infantry in front of German defensive positions. Also working far and above his expected performance, Lieutenant Wade Colbeck took miserable, life threatening turns in the cabs of the armored dozers when his platoon's cold-dazed operators needed relief.

We had as many as ten dozers and five road graders in constant operation behind the lines cutting supply and evacuation trails. The Germans had mined every possible route through the forest, but our mine-sweeping teams seemed to find every mine along the routes we opened and used.

The 504th Parachute Infantry advanced seven thousand yards on January 28, capturing Herresback after killing 65 and capturing 201 Germans without sustaining any losses. The 325 Glider Infantry faced stiffer opposition in its zone and suffered losses accordingly, but wound up the day far ahead of its line of departure. On the 29th the two airborne units were restricted to gains of only two thousand yards. The 505th Parachute Infantry eked out only fifteen hundred yards in the direction of Honsfeld.

The Dragon's teeth at the Losheim Gap.

The Lanzerath Bridge over the railroad.

On January 30th, the 325th Glider Infantry jumped off at 0500 hours and by 1500 hours had reached Bucholtz, abreast the Honsfeld-Losheim railroad line. By nightfall they were into Germany. On that day the newly committed 508th Parachute Infantry captured Lanzerath and the damaged highway bridge over the railway line. American troops were thus in possession of Kampfgruppe Peiper's original jumping off position. On January 31, the 505th Parachute Infantry bullied its way forward to Losheimergraben against moderate resistance.

As Technician Mike Popp and I toured the frontier area visiting my operating platoons, we noted how many German vehicles and horse-drawn artillery units had been knocked out by our tactical air. Many of the villages had been extensively damaged at the hands of our fighter-bomber pilots. There was no evidence of German civilians in the area.

Captain Bill McKinsey reported that the Germans had blown the Lanzerath bridge as they retreated. We had to build a 180 foot Bailey bridge over a 80-foot-deep railroad cut. The location of the new bridge would be on the Belgium-German border. The job was a typical rush. General Gavin wanted to bolster the 508th Parachute Infantry's positions with the self-propelled guns of the 629th Tank Destroyer Battalion. The 508th had already repulsed one German counterattack with its light infantry weapons. No one knew what the Germans might throw in next in symbolic defense of their border.

On February 1, the 291st Battalion CP moved forward from Malmedy to Meyerode and Company's "A" and "C" were assigned to build the bridge. Before advancing to the bridge

The Lanzerath Bridge where Peiper crossed the tracks and the 291st rebuilt the bridge in the attack with the 82nd Airborne.

The 82nd Airborne's route to the Losheim Gap is opened up by the 291st Engineers' Dozer.

site, our mine sweeping teams had to probe forward and clear all of the approaches. The Germans had mined all of the shoulder areas with antitank and antipersonnel devices. They had wired in various booby traps whose only purpose was to kill or maim engineers clearing the mines. As usual we suffered no losses.

The bridge was started at 0030 hours on February 2nd under the cover of darkness. Beginning at sunset, the two engineer companies moved into the holding areas within a mile of the bridge site. For the next six hours, all the troops worked feverishly to prepare for the massive, miserable job ahead. At 0030 hours right on schedule, Captain Warren Rombaugh's Company C advanced on the bridge site to begin the first continuous twelve hour shift. Because it was below zero, Warren would work his platoons on four hour shifts. This was about the limit for human beings to endure the tasks of wrestling the frigid five hundred pound steel bridge panels into place.

Sleet fell steadily upon the men whose duties prevented them from seeking even rudimentary cover. The Germans quickly learned that we were there and started to pound the area with artillery fire. One of the greatest dangers was in the potential for slipping or sliding off of the glazed steel bridge panels into the eighty foot deep railroad cut. There were many heart stoppers before the ordeal was over. All of this was done with the knowledge that the lightly armed and relatively unsupported troops of the 508th Parachute Infantry were waiting for their tank destroyers in vulnerable infantry fighting positions about a mile in front of the bridge.

Mike Popp wrestled our command car to the bridge site at 0300 hours, February 2nd, in the immediate wake of one of the artillery barrages. As I watched the miserable, cold, battle-hardened Company "C" troopers wrestle the five by ten steel panels of the double triple Bailey bridge across the 80 foot deep chasm in the midst of a vertical ice storm, I became convinced that these were men who would finish anything that anyone could conceivably dream up to be accomplished by combat engineers.

The bridge, which would be two panels thick and three panels high with a single span treadway floor required the placement of 216 five hundred pound panels. When completed, the span would be able to support a forty ton load moving at six miles per hour.

We opened the bridge for traffic at 1700 hours, February 3rd, forty and one half hours after work began. We did so after a round-the-clock effort by two complete combat engineer companies and without suffering any wounded or injured engineer soldiers. The men of Captain's James Gamble and Warren Rombaugh did the job under incredibly dangerous working conditions and incessant German Artillery fire. Our first customers were all the self propelled Tank Destroyers of the 629th Tank Destroyer Battalion. The payoff soon arrived: a coordinated attack, amply supported by way of the Lanzerath bridge where Peiper chose to go down the railroad embankment, and thence cross the tracks and up the bank on

Engineers building a ramp over the Siegfried Line.

Taking cover at the Dragon's teeth.

the other side. The 325th Glider Infantry and the 504th Parachute Infantry Regiment quickly and decisively cracked the Siegfried line between Neuhof and Undenreth, just north of the Losheim Gap.

As soon as possible, the 291st followed the 82nd Airborne through the dragons teeth and the formidable array of bunkers and pillboxes comprising the Siegfried line. Behind us lay the long sought breach in the enemy frontier and ahead of us lay victory, but not without privation and struggle, hope, and glory as we had never seen them before.

The road back on the southern half of the Hitler created goose egg became a most difficult part of the "Battle of the Bulge."

Most of the American divisions that had fought in the defensive phase joined in the drive back to the Siegfried line. As a part of the First Army were the 1st, 30th, 75th, and 84th Infantry Divisions; the 82nd Airborne Division; the 2nd Division's 23rd Infantry; the sur-

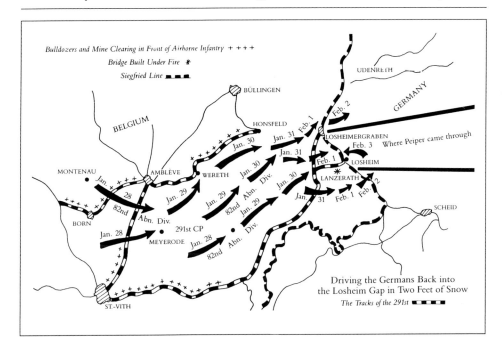

Bulldozers and Mine Clearing in Front of Airborne Infantry + + + +

Bridge Built Under Fire *

Siegfried Line ▪ ▪ ▪

UDENREfH

GERMANY

BÜLLINGEN

BELGIUM

HONSFELD

LOSHEIMERGRABEN

Feb. 3 Where Peiper came through

Jan. 31 Feb. 1

Feb. 2

Jan. 30

Jan. 31

MONTENAU

AMBLÈVE

WERETH

LOSHEIM

Jan.

Jan. 30

Feb. 1

LANZERATH

Jan. 28

82nd

Jan. 29

82nd Abn. Div.

Jan. 30

Jan. 29

Jan.

Jan. 31 Feb. 1 Feb.

Abn. Div.

BORN

82nd Abn. Div.

291st CP

SCHEID

Jan. 28

MEYERODE

Jan. 28

82nd Abn. Div.

Driving the Germans Back into
the Losheim Gap in Two Feet of Snow

ST-VITH

The Tracks of the 291st ▬ ▪ ▪ ▪

viving regiment of the 106th Division; the 4th Cavalry Group; the separate 517th Parachute Infantry; and the 2nd, 3rd, and 7th Armored Divisions.

As part of the Third Army, the 4th, 5th, 26th, 35th, 80th, and the 87th Infantry Divisions; the 101st Airborne Division; and the 6th, and the 11th Armored Divisions. Joining them were four units new to the Ardennes: with First Army, the 83rd Infantry Division; with Third Army, the 6th Cavalry Group, the 17th Airborne and the 90th Infantry Division.

This was a considerable force to throw at the heavily battered forces on the German side which now had the difficulty of supplying the units so far from their supply points back in Germany. For both sides the snow and below zero weather would play a major role.

47

The Road Back to Victory

The snow was deeper than ever in the Ardennes, the temperatures lower, the fog thicker, the chill winds more penetrating when the VIII Corps of General Joe Collins sent the 3rd and 2nd Armored Divisions attacking southeast toward Houffalize along the bottom Manhay highway. They were attacking into the 12th and 560th Volksgrenadier and 2nd SS Panzer Divisions.

Leading the attacking American Divisions were the 23rd and 17th Armored Engineer Battalions, clearing mines and working with the 300th engineers and their bull dozers to open up the snow and ice filled roads. The going was slow as many of the tanks slid off of the roads and into uncleared mine areas. The German engineers were blowing bridges as they retreated towards the east.

Delays were met as the engineers built back the bridges many times under German fire. The goal was to close with the First Army's VII Corps at Houffalize. Another goal was to cut off the retreating Germans by having Patton's III and XII Corps cut them off from the south. Tanks stalled on icy hillsides. Trucks towing anti-tank guns or artillery pieces skidded, jackknifed, collided, and blocked vital roads for hours. Bridges everywhere were out, the sites defended. The Germans at times counter-attacked with a company or battalion of infantry. Advances of two miles per day was a maximum.

For the men of Third Army it was even rougher, for the foe around Bastogne was still trying to wipe out the battered village and its troops. Patton's troops were still battling the Panzer Lehr, the Fuhrer-Begleit and Grenadier Brigades, also the 5th Parachute Division, the 26th Volksgrenadier Division, the 1st, 9th, and 12th SS Panzer Divisions. Thus far these German forces had lost much men and equipment, but they were still formidable opponents. The Germans had failed to penetrate the engineer barrier lines of the 158th, the 35th, and the 299th Engineer Combat Battalions.

Von Manteuffel tried to penetrate to the north and then from the south into Bastogne but failed miserably. On January 4th Von Manteuffel gave up and a threat to Bastogne was ended.

On January 8th, Hitler finally agreed to a withdrawal from the tip of the bulge. He had now realized that the offensive in the Ardennes had failed. Patton now became anxious to cut into the Germans from the south with his III and XII Corps forces.

The American side now had over 600,000 soldiers involved in the battle and had the upper hand. The German forces had inserted over 500,000 troops into the attack, but were now suffering from heavily battered armored and infantry divisions. Their losses trying to take Bastogne and losses to American air didn't prevent them from making a stand when Eisenhower had given the orders to erase the Bulge.

The attacking forces generally lose more men in battle than well dug-in defensive forces. The Germans in all sectors of the Ardennes area had put their engineers to work laying extensive mine fields and never failed to blow key bridges as they fell back to their fatherland.

The heavy snow on the narrow roads and the many rivers and streams to cross required the use of all of the combat engineer units to lead the assaults of the infantry and armored Regiments. Generally the organic engineers were active in the mine clearing task and the attached and assigned engineers were responsible for clearing the snow and ice with bulldozers up front, knocking out road blocks and building the Bailey bridges, often under fire.

When the counterattack began on the northern end of the Ardennes bulge on January 3rd, the odds shifted decisively in favor of the Allied Armies. Responsibility for the assault lay with General Collins' VII Corps, comprising the four Divisions assigned to him in December. They were concentrated to the east of the Ourthe River with the 82nd Airborne protecting their left. British troops had been moved in to relieve the 2nd Armored and 84th Infantry west of the river. These two units joined the 3rd Armored and the 75th Infantry to drive down the Bastogne-Liege road from Manhay to Baraque de Fraiture, preparatory to a link-up with Patton's forces at Houffalize.

The 2nd Armored Division and the 84th Infantry Division had made a gallant and decisive drive led by their organic combat Engineers and the combat Engineers of the 51st, the 300th, and the 308th. Mines were cleared out in front of the Armor and bulldozers followed the Infantry clearing the ice and snow for the armor attack. The drive was slow but methodical as the engineers built Bailey assault bridges many times under fire.

The 84th Infantry of First Army had a thirty three-man patrol cross the Ourthe River near the village of Houffalze. The 306th Engineers quickly built a treadway bridge across the river for tanks. All of the approaches to the village of Houffalize were heavily mined by the retreating Germans. Their engineers had driven wooden piles at the entrances guarded by anti-tank guns used to fire on the approaching American soldiers.

The village had been shelled by artillery from the American guns and bombed from both sides' air forces. The villagers had long ago departed to escape the terror of the war. The shock that these Belgians would receive when they returned.

The soldiers on both sides were suffering casualties from both the weapons of war and the below zero weather. The American soldiers were always glad to capture a village to gain a respite from the cold in warm buildings, but here was a case of little or no relief from the cold.

On January 16th the First and Third American Armies closed at Houffalize when the 84th Infantry and the 11th Armored had a meet along with a task force of the 2nd Armored Division.

The night that the 2nd Armored Division moved into Houffalize, the First Army moved back into the open arms of General Omar Bradley.

On January 12th Hitler had ordered the four SS Panzer Divisions pulled from the line to be in reserve positions at St. Vith. This was the beginning of pulling the entire 6th Panzer Army out of the bulge and turning the fighting over to the 5th Panzer Army.

Once the First and Third Armies had joined at Houffalize, the drive of Third Army with its armored, airborne, and infantry divisions turned to the east from January 12th to the 28th. The fighting was dogged and slow movement on a day to day basis. Higher headquarters never came to realize the sheer brutality of the war in unbelievable weather.

Here is the story of Ed Bredbenner 80th Infantry Division, 318th Regiment, Company B: "We were attached to the 4th Armored Division's Combat Command B. The 4th Armored Division requested 80th troops to support their drive into Bastogne. Our Colonel, Col. McVickar, sent the 1st and 2nd Battalions of the 318th. We all knew the story of the weather in those woods and the lack of support needed. Some men spent 6 and 7 days without camouflage, blankets, overcoats, waste deep in snows, near zero. Medics could not get through because of the snows and the enemy closed in behind us. If wounded you stayed with the company or tried to walk out or froze to death. Many did and in March after the snows melted U.S. and German bodies were found in large numbers, in the thousands. There were no buildings and no fires.

"If you were lucky to attack a village you might get out of the cold for a few moments, and then had to move on, always attacking. On the 28th-29th of December, the 35th Division relieved us and we had to move back to Ettelbruck, Luxembourg. Our part in the battle was like most. Not much has been written about our role in the battle. Our company coming off a sixth day rest period started with 220 men on December 22nd and on December 28th, 20 men were left in the company. The 80th Division had two of their Medal of Honor awards in the Ardennes, one in Belgium, Christmas Day. Many of the over 70 DSC were awarded in the Ardennes.

"When we were relieved by the 35th Division, many men were evacuated because of wounds, but had stayed with the company because of little Medical support or freezing to death if lost in the deep snows and heavy woods. There were no roads in those woods. When we returned to Ettelbruck we had no officers or non-coms. A PFC was our acting company commander. Three days later we were back in action, our ranks filled with new replacements or returning wounded. Despite all of this we worked to defeat the enemy."

The Juncture made at Houffalize gave Patton the opportunity to return to his original concept to reduce the original penetration, to attack the base of the Battle of The Bulge.

Accordingly, he ordered preparations for the attack by XII Corps to attack across the Sure River.

48

The Attack of the 26th Division
into the Siegfried Line

The final thrust of the Third Army of General Patton to drive the Germans back into their fatherland can best be described by using the example of the actions of the 26th Infantry Division. The 26th was part of the III Corps which had deployed its troops with the 4th Armored Division on the left, 26th Division in the center, and the 80th Infantry Division on the right.

The III Corps instructions were to move to the north and northeast, find the enemy, fix his position, and maneuver to destroy him.

On the 22nd of December the 26th Division moved out on foot towards the north with the 328th Regiment on the left and the 104th Infantry on the right. The 26th Reconnaissance Troops with George Linthicum, the trooper who verifies this action of the 26th, moved on vehicles ahead of the foot troops. The recon troops were screening to the front and maintaining contact with the troops on the flanks. They operated smoothly and efficiently, moving rapidly across the area as they advanced.

Contact was made by the troop in the area of Rambrouck, about 16 miles from the line of departure. The two infantry regiments made contact with the enemy, and the 328th knocked out two tiger tanks as they advanced. The 104th Infantry stopped near Grosbous and   captured a very much surprised German Colonel and several marked maps. The infantry units ran into scout parties in armored vehicles, which opened fire on them with automatic weapons and mortars. As the infantry continued to advance the fire increased in intensity, and finally, troops were diverted from the flanks to wipe out the German forces.

The going was rough as the 101st Engineers had to move forward and clear the mines in front of Arsdorf and Eschdorrf on the right, where the 104th was attacking after a heavy shelling of the village by the 101st Field Artillery Battalion. The two villages were captured on December 24th after two days of heavy fighting and losses of men and material on both sides.

There was no let up on Christmas Day as the 101st Infantry was moved in on the left flank and the 328th fell back in reserve. The enemy had persisted so strenuously against the attackers that there was little left standing in the town of Eschdorf.

During the resistance Lt. Colonel Tilsen's 3rd Battalion, 328th had pushed vigorously towards the Sure River and had driven the enemy out of Isenborn. As George Linthicum's vehicle moved ahead of the attack, one of the recon vehicles struck a German mine and was

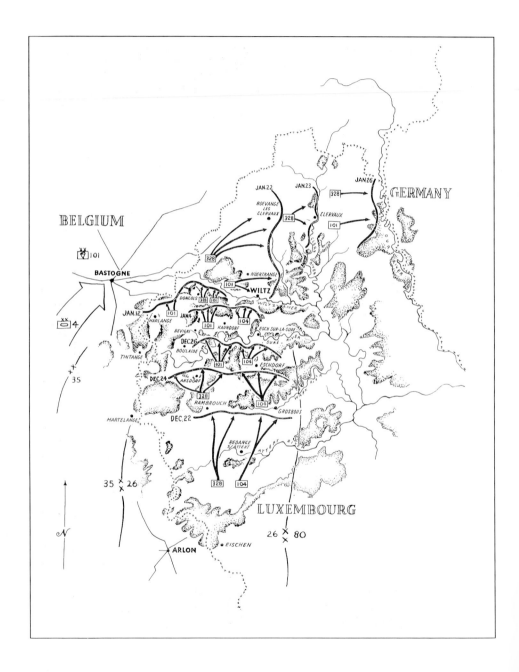

BELGIUM

GERMANY

LUXEMBOURG

BASTOGNE

WILTZ

CLERVAUX

BOEVANGE
LES
CLERVAUX

JAN.22   JAN.23   JAN.26

NOERTRANGE

WILTZ RIVER

DONCOLS

HARLANGE

JAN.12   JAN.4   KAUNDORF

BEVIGNE

BOULAIDE

DEC.26

ESCH-SUR-LA-SURE

SURE RIVER

TINTANGE

DEC.24   ARSDORF   ESCHDORF

RAMBROUCH

GROSBOUS

MARTELANGE   DEC.22

REDANGE
ATTERT

ATTERT RIVER

35   26

ARLON   EISCHEN   26   80

N

35

demolished and the occupants wounded and evacuated. The mines had been covered with snow and ice.

Meanwhile the 101st Infantry had patrols across the Sure River and a footbridge constructed by the combat engineers of Lt. Colonel Richard Free. During the night of December 25-26 Captain Redheffer of the engineers crossed the river in an assault boat on a bridge reconnaissance. In the zone of the 3rd Battalion, 101st Infantry, troops were hesitant about crossing in the face of small arms and mortar fire. The Regimental Commander, Colonel Scott called for an assault boat to be made ready for his use, and taking a body guard they pioneered the first crossing in the zone. The Division now had two crossings and with the 104th and Captain Spencer's Engineers playing a prominent part at Esch Sur La Sure, it was rapidly developing a third.

The crossing of the Sure was quite successful and Colonel Scott received a Silver Star. The 249th Engineer Combat Battalion built a Bailey Bridge across the Sure under fire at night. The 1st Battalion captured Bavigne, and the 3rd Battalion captured La Fringe and Kaundorf, rolling back slightly under two vicious counter-attacks, but then recovering to capture the bridgehead. This was combat engineering at its finest along with dogged infantry attack.

Gladings 1st Battalion, 104th pushed up the line and recaptured Kaunsdorf. The 2nd and 3rd Battalions, 104th crossed at Esch Sur La Sure and clung to the Division's over exposed right flank. Once the Sure River was conquered the Division had advanced well into the determined enemy's flank position.

Every effort to move forward was met with determined resistance and a numerically superior force that counter-attacked to take back lost ground. The 101st Field Artillery Battalion, commanded by Lt. Colonel Burton had its fire direction center about 1500 yards from the front lines. That fire direction center was a busy place that day as they directed fire on any group of the enemy that may have broken through.

The Division had made sizable gain on the enemy's position and was threatening his supply point at Wiltz, where the 44th Engineers had made its great stand.

The 80th Division had advanced abreast of the 26th until the Sure River had been reached. They were unable to cross and remained at the river line. The 35th Division was sent in line on the 26th Division's left flank. The 2nd Battalion of the 104th Infantry suffered many casualties as a result of an exposed right flank.

During the initial period the 35th Division ran into fierce resistance and into difficulty in coming abreast of the 26th.

As the enemy situation became clearer, it was evident that any additional forward movement by the division, without additional assistance, would place them dangerously out of position. Such progress would over-stretch the flanks and present to the enemy an opportunity to wipe out the bridgehead that was a constant annoyance to him. That had forced him to divert three divisions to contain it. The Third Army was aware that the division had gone its limit, and a few days later brought in the 90th Infantry Division to expand the bridgehead and destroy the southern flank of the bulge.

Just ahead of the 26th Division was the awesome task of capturing hill 490 and moving on to the Wiltz River through rough terrain and the heavily defended villages of Monshuman and Nothum. It became necessary to put the B and C companies of the 101st Engineers out in front of the 101st and 328th Infantry, clearing mines and opening up the narrow winding roads with bulldozers. At times they had to fight as infantry to move slowly ahead to their objectives.

The movement forward on each day was at times only hundreds of yards and the capture of well defended villages depended upon the artillery fire to soften up the enemy in advance. Even the movement of the artillery pieces required the assistance of the combat engineers.

In the assault every attack mounted by units of the division was met by an immediate counter-attack. The enemy was willing to pay any price to keep the Americans off of Hill 490 in order to deny them the observation advantage that this hill would provide on enemy supply activities. On the night of January 4-5, the 101st was relieved by the 328th and returned to division reserve. The 101st Engineers were used continually throughout the period. They held ground, resisted counter attacks, and prepared defensive positions in depth. The Battle of the Bulge had become an engineers war with the many obstacles caused by the German engineers and the -06 degree weather. They became an admirable outfit and were greatly appreciated by the men in the infantry.

Task Force Eaves, consisting of companies A and C of the 101st Engineer Battalion, was formed and secured a large section of the division's left flank during the period when the division was shuffling troops in order to provide space for the 90th Division's attack. They were in position later to protect flanks with their mines, bazookas, machine guns and daisy chains of both the 90th Division and 6th Armored Division as they progressed.

The crossing of the Wiltz River was made by the 328th and the 101st Regiments in assault boats manned by the 101st Engineers under the cover of darkness. Then the corps engineer combat battalions built Bailey bridges for their tanks in order to attack into the heavily defended and mined village of Wiltz.

The men of the 26th Infantry entered Wiltz on the 22nd of January after a two day battle. The village was a total mass of demolished houses. The frozen bodies of the 44th Engineers were found there along with some civilians and even German soldiers.

A picture like this makes one wonder why people can't live in peace.

During this drive, Major Spencer Mattingly's Battalion of the 328th Infantry captured Hill 490 overlooking the Wiltz River valley, despite determined enemy resistance. He was killed after reaching his objective.

In almost every instance the methods of reducing these points of resistance was a movement around the flanks to pinch out support. In a few hours the enemy would fall back fighting in utter confusion.

By January 22nd, the situation had become rather fluid with substantial gains being made daily. The offensive spirit of the troops was high and the men passed off the rigors of winter fighting with little or no comment—but they all thought of many long time buddies who had been left in a frozen heap in the snows of Belgium and Luxembourg. On January 25th, the division was notified that it was passing to the control of the XX Corps back in France.

The Battle of the Bulge was over and Hitler's badly battered Armored and Infantry divisions were heavily reduced of men, equipment, and fighting material. First and Third Army were both butt-up against the Siegfried line and now ready to attack towards the Rhine River.

There were many other Third Army Divisions both Armored or Infantry which had fought gallantly as did the 26th. They all depended on their engineers both on the defense and particularly the offense in this rugged weather. They all suffered with great losses of men, but one could say that the American soldier won the battle with courage and determination. The actions of bravery are so numerous that this book would go on forever just citing the writings on the Silver and Bronze Star medals.

I chose the 26th Division to tell their story in detail because the crossing of three rivers in one month of fighting is almost an impossibility. A river assault is the most hazardous of all military actions, with the enemy dug-in on the far banks equipped with all the weapons of war. The engineers and infantry in assault boats are defenseless.

It was bitter winter fighting for all soldiers and all branches of the service. The only solace gained from the bitter cold was that it kept the dead Germans that littered the area from decomposing and consequently the nausea of the Lorraine campaign was not here. However, troops were cold and frozen, and morale was at its lowest ebb. Combat fatigue and shock increased. Soldiers took on the appearance of stupefied hairy animals. Yet out of this "Valley Forge" the stamina of the American soldier roused itself to take another step and shoot another round. This huge battle was not won by Generals, many who had made mistakes before and during the battle. It was not won at the Corps or Division level, but it was won by the dogface up front.

Epilogue

The end of the war in Europe found the American soldiers slipping quietly back into civilian life. Many went to college on the government's "G.I." bill. Some stayed in the military, but all carried with them the horrors of war, especially if they were up near the front.

The civilians in Europe all had a massive rebuilding of their homes and villages, their roads and bridges, and especially their lives where family members were lost during the battles.

In America, as time moved on men became interested in knowing what had happened to their buddies. This all resulted in the formation of unit associations and annual reunions of these divisions, battalions, and company units. Then came the thoughts of the old battle sites and returns to the battlefields.

For history's sake most of the units developed the writings of their history from materials in the National Archives, which included "After Action" reports, photographs, and even 16 mm movies filmed by the signal Corps.

The returns to the battlefields were often many years after the war when the peoples of Europe had built their homes and surroundings back to the point that the markings of war had disappeared. The Marshall plan was put to use by the American government to supply funds, materials, and equipment to aid this purpose. This was done in all countries, including Germany.

For the American unit associations who returned to Europe's old battlefields it was unique to find that the Belgians, the Hollanders, the French, and the people of Luxembourg greeted the returnees with open arms. This was for the sacrifices of the American soldiers during the war. The German people also treated the Americans with open arms, for it was "this time in peace".

There are very few momuments to the American soldier or soldiers of WWI in America. In Europe, however, the memorials dot the land throughout. This is particularly true in the

Ardennes and the area where the Battle of the Bulge was fought. These wonderful people in Belgium and Luxembourg have gone all out to show their great joy and love for what the American soldiers did for them during the long war.

These monuments for the civilians in the Ardennes were placed with great ceremony and kindness, for the battles in the Ardennes were during the most awful period of their lives.

How was this battle possible?

After landing in Normandy, the Allied Armies pushed through Northern France, Luxembourg, and Belgium, and their first troops entered Germany on September 11th, 1944. They were stopped by a strong German resistance on the Siegfried line, and for the first time the Germans were fighting on their own soil.

Moreover, the Allied forces were handicapped by a lack of supplies. The ports in Northern France had not yet been liberated, and all of the American supplies were to come from the beaches of Normandy, some 400 miles away, by heavily damaged roads and railways. The nearest port, the port of Antwerp, had only been reopened on November 26, 1944.

What were Hitler's objectives?

- To retake the newly reopened port of Antwerp, which was now the main supply source for the Allied forces. In order to do so the Germans counted on reaching the Meuse in two days' time.

- To destroy the Allied forces north of the Antwerp-Brussels-Luxembourg line.

Once these objectives were achieved, he hoped that the English and Canadian forces would ask for a separate peace. This way he could turn back the Americans and head towards the eastern front.

The preparation for this counter-attack was a real success for the Germans, and the Allies were completely surprised just when they saw victory over the horizon.

Three mighty German armies of which two were armored—about 22 divisions— launched their attack on December 16 at 5:30 A.M. under the cover of thick fog and darkness. The attack developed on an 80 mile wide front stretching from Montjole to Echternachin, the wooded and hilly Ardennes where the Americans were thinly spread. The Germans threw confusion into the American forces by using Allied vehicles and soldiers dressed in American uniforms.

The front was held by four American divisions; two of the divisions were "green" and had never been in battle before. Two other divisions had been decimated during the weeks of bloody fighting in the Huertgen forest and were at rest, waiting for reinforcements. This thin defending line was quickly overwhelmed, and all the while the northern (Elsenborn region) and southern (Echternach region) held their ground.

The American reaction was quick, and General Eisenhower immediately sent from France two airborne divisions which were in operation on the night of December 18 in the Bastogne and Ambleve sectors. An armored division sent from Holland was able to defend St-Vith on December 17. By another route, an armored battle group was making its way from the south and engaged itself in the Echternach sector and another one in Bastogne.

The following days, Eisenhower threw in the battle several other infantry and armored divisions which were called back from other parts of the European Theater of Operations. It involved the division located in the north, more particularly in the Aachen and Roer sectors. General Patton's Third Army, which was fighting in the Saar River and Lorraine sectors, made a 90 degree turn to go up to Luxembourg City and Bastogne and attack the left flank of the German advance.

The thrust of the German Sixth "Panzer Army" on the north was stopped along the Ambleve and Lienne Rivers by combat engineers, and on the Houffalize-Liege road again by combat Engineers.

The Seventh German "Army's" thrust on the south was stopped southwest of Bastogne again by blown bridges.

But the Fifth German "Panzer Army" went as far as Celles, a few miles from the Meuse River with an Armored Division halted at the bridge at Hotton by, again, combat engineers. The Germans, having completed the encircling of the American units in Bastogne, became heavily involved in the outer defenses of Bastogne established by three engineer combat battalions.

By Christmas 1944, the German advance was completely stopped, and the Allied forces were preparing for a mighty counter-attack which started on January 3, 1945, in the morning.

The First American Army under General Hodges came from the north and the Third American Army of General Patton came from the south, and made their junction in Houffalize on January 16th, 1945, sealing the fate of the Germans.

By the end of January, 1945, the Americans had pushed the Germans back to their departure line of December 16, after fighting mile after bitter mile, town after town, and, in many places, house after house.

The military and civilian losses were very high.

American casualties: about 80,000 men, 10,000 killed and the rest prisoners, wounded or missing in action. 81 American prisoners of war were assasinated in cold blood by SS troops in Baugnez (Malmedy) on December 17, 1944.

German casualties: about 80,000 men, more than 12,000 killed and the rest prisoners, wounded, or missing in action.

About 2,500 civilians were killed and 600 severely damaged, and others utterly destroyed, such as Malmedy, St-Vith, Houffalize, La Roche, Wiltz, Clervaux, Vienden, and Echternach. In other historical towns, little remained.

Economic resources, tourism, farms, and forests were heavily and durably damaged. Thousands of acres of forests, roads, bridges, construction works, electric lines and waterworks were lost.

Livestock were decimated. More than 20,000 houses were destroyed or uninhabitable. The devastation was awesome, and much worse than that from hurricanes or tornadoes. The ability to go from one side of towns and villages was nil until bridges could be rebuilt.

Tens of thousands of victims lived in destitution for months. They were afraid to move around out of fear of walking on a mine or an explosive snare or booby-trap. Plowing a field was extremely dangerous, particularly around the outskirts of towns and villages.

Through their willfullness for which they are known, the citizens, after having dressed their wounds, rapidly began to reconstruct their cities and farms. They had the consolation of seeing an immense burst of solidarity from all of the Belgian and Luxembourg regions that were spared from the offensive and the stand of the American soldiers.

This was just over fifty years ago. Nothing about the landscape today gives any clue as to the destruction the territory experienced except the monuments, the graves, the landmarks, the plaques and machinery, that you will discover by means of the pictures I have placed in this section of "Engineering the Victory".

This part of these writings has been developed by many returns to the Ardennes by me and the men of the 291st. Each return has been highlighted by the kindness of the Belgian and Luxembourg people, and at times a meeting with persons from Holland who visit the Ardennes.

These wonderful people suffered through the occupation of the minions of Hitler after the invasions of 1940. Many of their young men had been taken back to Germany as workmen in factories and mines. Some never came back.

The Battle of the Bulge appeared to again be a repeat of the same series of events until the end of January 1945. We found the people had much faith and at times saw their churches demolished such as the one in La Glieze where Peiper made his last stand.

There are well over 100 monuments over the entire Ardennes area, and if one carefully traveled the roads and read the story told by each monument, he or she would finalize the trip through the colorful and circuitous former combat avenues of attack, as a story of brave soldiers and equally courageous civilians. All of these people suffered from mines, artillery fire, bombing from the air, as well as one of the worst winters ever in the Ardennes. The highlight of the battles came at Christmas time when the battles had not been decided in favor of either side.

From the time when the American units drove the German forces out of the Ardennes in September of 1944 until the beginning of the German offensive, the relationship between the soldiers and the folks in the Ardennes became one of great mutual friendship and admiration.

The monuments began to develop generally after the civilian population had cleared the mine fields, destroyed the enexploded bombs, built back homes, villages, and all communication, water supply, and electrical facilities. Airports had to be made serviceable. We in our country never experienced this sort of thing except at the time of inclement weather, but not on such a large scale even in our battle at Gettysburg.

A quick glance at the map shows large monuments and museums located at La Gleize and Bastogne, Belgium and Diekirch, and Luxembourg. The museums show the full story of the battles in the respective areas along with mannequins dressed in the uniforms of each side. At each museum there are photographs on display that tell the story of the battles, along with sand tables that even locate the position of each tank during and after the battle. The writings of the history of the battles are available at each location. These were all developed by local citizens who have devoted much time and energy to preserving this period of their lives for all time to see. This in hope that such a disaster will never happen again. They have also accomplished these fond remembrances to honor the brave soldiers who died in the area and those who brought their lives back to normal.

There are monuments to all branches of the service and one at Pironpre near Bastogne reads: Where the 35th Engineer Combat Battalion stopped the advanced guard of the "Panzer Lehr" Division on December 24, 1944. During the first eleven days of January 1945, the 87th Infantry Division fought a hard battle with the 5th Panzer Army to liberate the area around St. Hubert.

There is a monument at Grupont near Rochefort which reads: Around here the American, British, and German belligerents left a profusion of mines and shells of all calibers. For long after the Battle of the Bulge these devices took their toll in the civilian population, and the Belgian mine detecting soldiers had the deadly task of clearing the area. The monument in the center of the village remembers their wonderful accomplishment that was often at the cost of their lives.

At Bure near St. Hubert: The commemorative plaque is located on the Church. The 13th Battalion of the 6th British Airborne Division counterattacked with XXX Corps in early January 1945 in atrocious climactic conditions with hand to hand furious fighting against Bayerlain troops. "Red Devils" losses for Bure only reached 110 men killed, wounded, or missing.

* * * * * *

There are several monuments at St-Vith One reads: On December 16, 1944, the 168th Engineer Combat Battalion took position on the Prumerberg Hill, east of St. Vith. The German troops coming from Schoenberg attacked the following noon, but they suffered heavy losses. The Americans held for four days against German attacks coming from Schlierbach road. The memorial stands along this road where the 81st Engineer Combat Battalion also held forth.

There are monuments to the 106th and 2nd Infantry Divisions in St. Vith dedicated to the Infantry and Engineer soldiers of these divisions.

The monument to the civil victims of St-Vith is located at the entrance of the town cemetery. The violence of the fight and the extreme density of the air bombings of December 24th, 25th, and particularly the 26th, 1944 took the city off the map for a while. This third raid was the most terrifying; one where more than a thousand tons of explosive was dropped on the city. In the St. Joseph hospital ruins, more than 100 people died.

All of the village strong points, such as Hosingen, Wiltz, Echternach, Ettlebruck, Diekirch, and Consthum have long lasting monuments of stone and brass. The one at Consthum is dedicated to Lt. Colonel Daniel Strickler of the 110th Regiment of the 28th Division for his leadership against overwhelming odds. The others honor the 80th Infantry and the 17th Airborne Division as well as the 4th, 5th, 76th, and 83rd Divisions. Each monument is intended to not only honor the infantry but to thank the Engineers, the artillery, and the medics.

HENRI -CHAPELLE CEMETERY ★ 38 YD Men Buried Here

The monuments along Peipers attacking roads are many and begin with the most formidable one being located at Baugnez (Malmedy) where there is an annual ceremony conducted by the people and the government of Belgium and the military forces of the United States. This monument at the crossroads between Malmedy and St. Vith is dedicated to the memory of the American soldiers massacred on December 17, 1944. Taken prisoners by the men of the 1st SS Panzer Division commanded by Lieutenent Colonel Joachim Peiper, the disarmed men lined behind the Bodware cafe were then slaughtered by machinegun fire without reason.

The monument has the names of the 81 men who died in the massacre, most of them members of "B" Battery of the 285th Field Artillery Observation Battalion.

In Malmedy there is a huge stone monument on the left hand side of the Cathedral which shows the different U.S.Army units that liberated the city in September 1944 and those that defended it during the Battle of the Bulge. On the face is also engraved the 5th Battalion volunteer Belgian Fusiliers that assisted the U.S. forces. Since December 16th defensive road blocks were built and held at the south and east end of Malmedy. Various American units reinforced the defensive perimeter and participated in the January 1945 counterattack.

Five black marble plaques stand in the park to the right of the Malmedy Cathedral. They were erected after the public subscription to the memories of the 214 Malmedians and other refugees from the Border Zone who lost their lives on December 23, 24, and 25, 1944.

THE LUXEMBOURG CEMETERY

THE LORRAINE CEMETERY

These bombings also killed a number of American soldiers. How many is still unknown. Why was Malmedy, uninterruptedly held by American troops, bombed by the U.S. Air Force on three different times? This question remains unanswered today.

The repeated battles in Stavelot, Belgium and the delays caused by Sgt. Charles Hensel's squad of "C" Company of the 291st Engineer Combat Battalion, resulted in several monuments in and around the village. There is a memorial where Private Goldstein was wounded and P.F.C. Liparulo and soldiers of the 825th Tank Destroyer Battalion were killed on the hill south of Stavelot.

In the city park near the town hall, a memorial plaque by C.R.I.B.A. was inaugurated in 1989 by two veterans of the 117th Infantry Regiment of the 30th Division. On December 18th, 1944 the 1st Battalion of this regiment took position to the north and west of the city to prevent the capture of this part of town by SS troops.

There are other monuments to the "workhorse" 30th Division at Stoumont as well as Malmedy.

The bridge over the Ambleve River in Trois Ponts where the 51st Engineer Combat Battalion blew the bridge on December 18th has a large plaque honoring the 51st of Lt. Colonel Harvey Fraser.

The 82nd Airborne Division of General James Gavin are honored on monuments in Wanne, Trois Ponts, Chenaux and Werbomont.

There is a plaque on the monument near the Ambleve bridge in Trois Ponts which remembers the civilians shot to death on December 18 and 19, 1944 by the German soldiers during the Battle of the Bulge in the hard winter 1944-45, without reason.

There is hardly a cruelty performed by the Germans or an act of bravery by the Allied forces that has not been honored or indicated on these permanent monuments of the war placed by the folks who lived through it.

At Neufmoulin is a large stone monument placed by the group of historians led by Belgian Emile Lacroise. This is the location where Lt. Al Edelstein and his platoon of Company "A" blew the bridge which stopped Kampfgruppe Peiper completely on December 18th, 1944.

The inscription reads: Here, where the "Rollbahn D" assigned to Peiper crosses the Lienne River and the Lierneux-Targnon road, some "Damned Engineers" of Company "A", 291st Engineer Combat Battalion, U.S.Army blew the Neufmoulin bridge, stopping sharply and definitively the advance of the 1st Panzer Division towards the Meuse River. As in Trois Ponts, the leading German Panzers were only a few yards away. The monument stands just beside the bridge.

Located in the center of the village of Cheneux, the monument celebrates the heroic action of the 504th Parachute Infantry Regiment when they dislodged on the 20th and 21st of December, heavily entrenched elements of the 1st SS Panzer Division. The final assault was carried on by Colonel Tucker's 3rd Battalion with heavy losses. B and C companies together lost 225 soldiers, among which 23 were killed in action.

Stavelot, Belgium: A large number of innocent civilians were assassinated during the Battle of the Bulge in 1944, along the way followed by the 1st SS Panzer Division. In the townhall, at the entrance, one can see the memorial to the 130 civilian victims of Stavelot, Parfondruy, Renardmont and vicinity. These dead are distinct from the mere twenty war victims among civilians in this area.

* * * * * *

There are many events which occurred during the battle in the Ardennes which leave some untold stories. Of course the one about Peiper and the massacre of the men in Battery "B" of the 285th FAOB is of prime importance.

Colonel Joachim (Jochen) Peiper was tried at Dachau and sentenced to hang. This was not completed when our Senator Joseph McCarthy took actions which permitted Peiper to be freed from prison and return to a very difficult world for him to exist. Peiper was let out on the 22nd of December 1956. He had spent nearly five years in solitary confinement, and a total of eleven and one half years as a prisoner. But for some people this was not enough;

they thought he had got away with murder. And at the end of the day, many of the people in three countries-America, Belgium, and Germany-were left with a feeling that justice had been served.

Certainly many innocent people had died and suffered as a result of the events of December 1944 in the Ardennes.

Peiper was a bitter and disillusioned man in 1956. He had witnessed the collapse of his whole world and the Third Reich, as well as the Leibstandarte. These were his comrades of six years of fighting.

On June 1st, 1958 he was released from parole and began a few years working for Porsche and Volkeswagen but found he was still considered a Nazi and decided to buy a plot of land in Traves, France, out of Germany in the quiet Alps. Peiper chose to move out of Germany and made a statement to a French writer: "I was a Nazi and I remain one. The Germany of today is no longer a great nation, it has become a province of Europe. That is why, at the first opportunity, I shall settle elsewhere, in France no doubt, I don't particularly care for Frenchmen, but I love France. Of all things, the materialism of my compatriots causes me pain."

Peiper and his wife Sigi moved permanently into their chalet styled house which had been built by the river Saone in Traves.

Their children had been raised and they started a new life which became quite comfortable. Peiper began the translation of writings on history and used the pen-name of Reiner Buschman. He stayed out of touch with former SS comrades and appeared to have covered up his history of being "Blow Torch" Peiper during the war.

His peace never lasted long. On June 21th, 1976 his peaceful life in Traves was shattered when leaflets were passed out in Traves calling for him to be expelled from France as a former Nazi War Criminal. The roads and walls were posted with swastikas and signs with Peiper's name as a Nazi SS killer.

Even though he reported to the French police and to the German Ambassador in Paris that he needed help, his remains were found in the fire-destroyed chalet along with some weapons he had fired. At the time his wife was in Munich and he had bravely decided to remain and overcome this period of travail. He did not believe the people making the threats were particularly courageous. Thus at 0100 hours on 14th of July, Bastille Day, the Peiper home was set ablaze and his identified remains were found there. No one was found guilty of the crime.

What happened to the men of the 285 Field Artillery Battalion? It was their Battery "B" that Peiper's men massacred at Baugnez and of the 160 men that were either killed, escaped, or became prisoners of war, there were 33 men of Battery "B" that escaped. There were men of the 32nd Armored Recon Company, the 197th AAA Battalion, the 86th Engineers, and the 200th FA Battalion that also were part of the troops involved in the massacre.

Of the 33 men who escaped, there were 26 men that were saved and given aid by the medics of the 291st. This included the first three men that I personally rescued. These three men are still living today and have led normal lives.

Since 1970 the men of the 285th Field Artillery Observation Battalion have been enjoying reunions under the leadership of former Sergeant Charles Hammer. Many of the victims of the massacre attend the reunions. I have become an honorary member of their battalion and meet with them each year. Most of them have led normal everyday American lives and have enjoyed assisting the Belgium people to establish the monument at the massacre site. There has never been any doubt in any of our minds that the men of Peiper had them surrender, removed their weapons, and lined them up in a field, where they were mowed down with machine guns and those that moved shot through the head with machine pistols.

Six of these men testified at the war trials in Dachau. Charles Hammer passed away in 1993, but before he died he had arranged with the Congress of the United States and Lancaster County to present five of these brave men with the American service medal.

I also received this medal for the actions of my battalion in the discovery and giving aid to the victims.

One of the most remarkable odysseys of the entire battle was the capture and escape of Lt. Colonel Thomas J. Riggs. He was the biggest hero of the 106th Infantry Division as he held St. Vith for five days with only about half of his 81st Engineer Combat Battalion and some tank destroyers of Major Donald Boyer and the men of the 168th Engineer Combat Battalion.

When Riggs battalion was finally overrun he was wounded and found unconscious by the Germans who marched him and forty others towards a railroad 110 miles away. They were in a Stalag at Limburg where the treatment was fairly brutal. They were fed hardtack and snow.

At the railhead they were put in freight cars and moved to another Stalag at Dresden. He was then sent to a camp in Poland where he escaped and on foot and weary from the cold and no food, he met up with the Russians who treated him kindly and sent him on a train to Odessa on the black sea. He went on board a ship for 500 miles to Istanbul, Turkey. The Captain on the British ship placed him on a British Freighter bound for Port Said in Egypt, some 1000 miles away. From Port Said the Red Cross put him on a ship to Naples, Italy.

There for the first time in nearly three months, Riggs checked in with the American military. When he spoke of his desire to rejoin his 81st Engineers, he was crushed to learn that they wanted to hospitalize him. They relented and he was flown to Marseilles, France, then to Paris for a few days of rest and debriefing.

His final move back to his outfit is described in this manner; "My first night in Paris, something unbelievable happened to me. I went to a bar frequented by Americans. I had just taken a seat when a man from my outfit, the last person I'd seen around St. Vith, came over and stuck his big nose in my face. 'You big Devil,' he said, 'we've been looking for you or your remains ever since December.'

A day or two later, Riggs was driven to a place in Brittany, 350 miles from where he was captured. He was back with his 81st Engineers and the remains of the 106th Infantry Division.

Over the many years after the war and having been involved in the writings of two books about the 291st, "The Damned Engineers" and "The G.I. Journal of Sergeant Giles", I was approaching retirement age when Peggy and I thought seriously about returning to the old battlefields in Europe. This came about in 1977 when our five children were mostly in college and we could make the trip.

We traveled the old battle route from the beaches through France, Belgium, Luxembourg, and Germany. We saw all of the old bridge sites. We visited Bastogne and Malmedy and on to Remagen and viewed the remains of the Ludendorf. Then through Germany to the Danube and saw the bridge site where we built a bridge under fire for the 99th Division. We met wonderful people in all four countries, but of great interest was the treatment we received in Malmedy where they remembered what the 291st had done for them there. We learned that in La Gleize there was a museum which told the full story of Peiper.

This was the beginning of many trips back to the Ardennes and meeting with the fine people of the Ardennes.

* * * * * *

The return to the battlefields in 1977 resulted in an invitation from the Belgian people in the area of the Ardennes where Kampfgruppe Peiper had been halted and finally defeated. This group of people were headed by Francois de Harrenne and Gerard Gregoire. Peggy and I were invited to fly into Brussels and stay in the fine inn and restaurant in the village of La Gleize.

Peggy thought that the trip should be made by me and one of the members of the 291st reunion association. Former 1st Lieutenent Thomas Stack was selected and we were greeted in La Gleize by Francois and Gerard and enjoyed one of the finest weeks and attended ceremonies honoring the 291st for what the battalion had done for the people of Belgium.

We met the Georges de Harrenne family who lived in the castle Froidcouer where Captain Larry Moyer's "C" Company were set up at the time of the Battle of the Bulge. We also met the Edourd de Harrenne family who lived in the castle near Cheneux. These folks would become solid long time friends of the men of the 291st for our actions in the battles in their area.

During this visit we were able to see the fine museum in la Gleize developed by these folks and headed up by Gerard Gregoire. The museum told the story of the defeat of Peiper and Gregoire wrote a book entitled "Les Panzer De Peiper Face a L'us Army".

The book told the full story of the defeat of Peiper and the stopping of his forces at Neufmolin by "A" Company of the 291st. The book also cited the civilian victims in LaGleize during the battles.

The de Harrennes took Tom and I to the villages and we were presented the silver plates of each village by the head of the village.

The final dinner was held with many of the villagers present and there was a group of twelve Belgians dressed in costumes that went back to the early days of 1100 A.D. Francois de Harrenne and the group of twelve conducted us through a ceremony whereby we were to eat the cream cheese and be indoctrinated into the "ORDER OF THE CREAM CHEESE". At the end of the ceremonial, we were decorated with the soldiers medal and presented the plate "des Magneus d' Mackeye". The kindness of these folks of the Ardennes has always been remembered by the men of the 291st since the days of the war and especially when they return for visits.

One of the visits back with the Ardennes people was to attend the ceremonial honoring the 291st with the Belgian Fourragere for its actions in the Ardennes and the unveiling of a monument to the 291st at Neufmolin where the bridge was blown that stopped Peipers forces. This act by the people of Belgium was headed up by Emile Lacroix, a renowned Belgian historian.

There were many highlights of the return of the men and their wives to the La Gleize area in 1980. At this time we met Major General Mike Reynolds, commander of the mobile NATO ground forces. Mike was British and he had written a book entitled "Exercise Pied Peiper". He had been assisted by Major Peter Crocker. This book was used for the maneuver forces. This was the beginning of a long friendship with General Mike Reynolds.

We all visited the museum of Gerard Gregoire and gave him and all concerned copies of our book "The Damned Engineers". The museum showed sand tables with the final position of Peiper's tanks at the end of the battles.

We visited Malmedy and were honored by the Mayor and the people of the village at a ceremony headed up by M. Jaques Goffin. He had been a boy of 10 when the battles occurred and our men had rescued him after the bombing of Malmedy.

There were many more returns to the battlefields and during the years of the eighties the cold war with Russia caused the people in Luxembourg, Belgium, Holland and Germany to worry about an attack by the Russians similar to the Hitler attacks through Europe. The NATO forces were far less in numbers than the great Russian units. The NATO forces were trained for small unit action similar to that used by the combat engineers in the Battle of the Bulge. Major General Mike Reynolds was an exponent of this type action.

On the 50th anniversary of the war in Europe former Sergeant Joe Geary and I returned to the Ardennes to meet with now retired Major General Mike Reynolds. This was in September 1995, fifty years since we drove the Germans out of Belgium. We stayed with Marie Berthe and Edourd de Harrenne at their home "Vaux Renard".

Mike Reynolds was also there and we had the honor of meeting an English unit which was studying the actions on Peiper's route through the Ardennes under the instructions of General Reynolds.

We learned that Mikes book, "The Devil's Adjutant" was ready to go to the publisher.

During the week we were there Joe Geary and I traveled Peiper's route and took pictures of key points of interest. The Siegfried line at Losheim gap was hardly visible, however the dragons teeth were still showing in spots and some evidence of pill boxes.

We went through Famonville and Thirimont and then came upon the massacre site. Malmedy had grown and the three bridges we had blown were now intact. We saw many monuments at all places on the route. We stopped at the one south of Stavelot where Goldstein was wounded and Liparulo killed. We saw the site where Johnny Rondonell pulled the Daisy chain mines in front of Peipers half-tracks and then the monument at Neufmolin.

In his Epilogue in the book "The Devil's Adjutant", Mike Reynolds finalizes his well researched manuscript in this manner: Hitler's last great offensive in the West in general and the attack of the 1st SS Panzer Corps through the Ardennes in December 1944, in particular, beg the same question: did either of them have any real chance for success?

It is not the intention of this author to try to answer the first, strategic question. It would merely entail a repetition of the many theories and those presented in many books written on the "The Battle of the Bulge". The only thing that is worth pointing is that whilst it was, after Von Manteuffel called it after the war, a brilliant concept, it surely lacked the logistic backing to make it a realistic proposition at that stage of World War II.

At the tactical level, the same logistical weakness pertained, but these did not preclude the chance that at least some German forces would reach the Meuse River by D+3. Given the complete surprise achieved and the strength of attacking forces, particularly in armor, all that was needed was a bit of luck. Unfortunately for the Germans that element was missing.

The reasons that none of the 1st SS Panzer Corps Kampfgruppe got anywhere near the Meuse were numerous and cumulative. And only the Leibstandarte KGs will be considered in detail, since the KGs of the 12th SS Panzer Division Hitlerjugend never really got started. In the case of the Hitlerjugend, it has to be said that the stubborn and brave resistance put up by the 99th and 1st US Infantry Divisions and the various defenders of Malmedy, was clearly the reason why the German onslaught failed in this very important northern area.

But why did the KGs of the Leibstandarte also fail? The following reasons can be deduced:

1. The refusal by Hitler to allow the heavy tank forces of the 6th Panzer Army to attack further south where the road network was more favorable. This also applies of course to Hitlerjugend.

2. The refusal of 6th Panzer Army to allow 1st SS Panzer Corps to lead their break-in attack with armor.

3. The initial 12 hour delay in launching both KGs Peiper and Hansen due to infantry attacks and the failure to cope quickly with forgotten mine fields. This could also be called a failure of intelligence.

4. Peiper's decision, albeit understandable, not to attack Stavelot on the evening of the 17th.

5. The decision to halt KG Hansen on 18th December and relieve him with the 9th SS Panzer Division so that he could reinforce KG Peiper.

6. Peiper's decision to use a quarter of his tank force to move on Trois Ponts via Wanne on 18th December.

7. The demolition of the Trois Ponts and Neufmolin bridges by American Engineers on 18th December.

8. The critical delay caused by air attacks on KG Peiper on the afternoon of 18th December.

9. The failure of the 1st SS Panzer Division to resupply Peiper's KG with fuel at the stage during his advance and his own failure to capture sufficient American stocks.

It should be realized, however, that if any one of these factors had not applied, Peiper, or even Hansen, might well have reached the Meuse. For example, if Peiper had attacked Stavelot on the night of the 17th, he would have found no troops to resist him and the Americans would have not had time to prepare the Trois Ponts bridges. Similarly, if his column had not been spotted and attacked from the air on the 18th, he certainly would have crossed the Neufmolin bridge. But these are the 'if's' of history and at the end of the day it can be said that the essential which Peiper lacked, particularly and poignantly on the 17th of December, was luck. That should not detract from the bravery displayed by the American soldiers who stood up to the panzers and panzer-grenadiers of the Leibstandarte and later destroyed Peiper.

And Jochen Peiper? Clearly he was a charismatic leader and a very capable soldier; it is easy to become mesmerized by his dashing exploits. But it should be never be forgotten that he spent three years with one of the most notorious and odious men in the history of mankind: Heinrich Himmler. And it is probably due to the fact that a 'Phiadelphia Bulletin' reporter named Hal Boyle, was in Malmedy on 17th December 1944 and was able to publicize the 'Malmedy Massacre' that Peiper became famous, or infamous, depending on one's nationality and point of view.

Mike Reynolds and I had talked about the actions of Peiper, Skorzeny, and Von der Heydte on many occasions and had summed up the conclusions of why we won and the Germans failed. His account in the Epilogue of his book is superior and if I had to add to it, I would say that Peiper's biggest failure was to bring his Pioneers (Engineers) forward and rebuild the bridge at Neufmolin.

He had six hours available to do the job before the arrival of the troops of the 30th Infantry Division.

Bibliography

The books that I have read about the Battle of The Bulge are too numerous to mention in this part of the overall story of this greatest battle in history. Those books that I have reference to are written by Authors who were there in the battle area. These people who had experienced the war zones could well relate to the real live up-front soldier.

"A Time For Trumpets" by Charles B. MacDonald Is certainly one of highest quality. Charles was a Captain and Company Commander of infantry in the 2nd Division. He was heavily involved in the battle of the Ardennes and spent many years as a historian for the Department of History, U.S. Army. We became charter members of the Veterans of the Battle of the Bulge. (V.B.O.B.) at the same time and then enjoyed our writings over the next several years.

Prior to publisher's day for Trumpets, he audio-taped the story of the 291st in the big battle and then permitted me to review it prior to the publishing of the book. He later introduced me to his publisher's editor, Bruce Lee. This got me started down the road to publishing " First Across The Rhine." The publisher was William Morrow. We also worked together developing video tapes on the Ardennes battle.

Robert E. Merriam wrote " Dark December" in 1947. He was a member of the Ninth Army Historical team in Europe during the war and in the course of his duties he spent much time with the 7th Armored Division. He was always free to wander in the battle areas and interview who he pleased. He sat in conferences among Generals, Sergeants and privates to obtain his materials on the Division's battles. The on sight historians could piece together very adequate accounts of the operations.

Merriam told about several myths of the bulge battle and one of interest was "THE PATTON MYTH"; A great, great many people believe that the battle of the bulge was won by General Patton's Third Army, which did indeed liberate the consecrated town of Bastogne. We knew that the major German forces during the first ten days of the fighting were attacking northwest against steady, but unspectacular, Hodge's First Army. Fewer realized that the heaviest fighting around Bastogne occurred not when the town was surrounded, but ten days later, when the Germans turned south with sudden fury, after Hitler had abandoned his grandiose scheme. His main thrust had been stopped, and the 1st SS Panzer Division was mauled and went out on foot with only 800 men.

Hitler could no longer capture Brussels and Antwerp.

Always the swashbuckling, spectacular General, Patton was sure fire news copy. Old "Blood and Guts" executed one of the neatest turning movements of the war when, on several hours notice, he called off his gigantic attack planned for December 18th which was to carry him through the west wall behind a ripping attack of 3,000 bombers, swung 90 degrees, and within four days had his first divisions attacking the southern penetration of the Germans. Six days later, his two Corps had advanced ten miles over extremely rugged terrain, and the 4th Armored Division had freed the garrison at Bastogne. Perhaps it was only the gains we were making in those days, perhaps it was the defense at Bastogne, or it might have been the colorful Patton attracted so many newspapermen who were always sure of a good story from him, that many a civilian thought he held the key to the Battle of the Bulge.

In the north the 30th Division moved more miles over rugged terrain and were in line from Malmedy through Stavelot and Werbomont attacking against the 1st SS Panzer Division in 36 hours. The troops of General Leland Hobbs had also made a right angle turn out of line near Aachen.

As we know now Patton's initial fighting was conducted against the German 7th Army composed of four mediocre divisions of the Germans sent to the south for the express purpose of blocking Patton. Meanwhile in those nightmarish ten days, both the Sixth and Fifth Panzer Armies, punched slugged and battered through the First Army in the north., getting ever nearer the Meuse River.

While Patton was battling the infantry divisions of the 7th German Army, four Panzer Corps with 1200 tanks and 250,000 men were pounding 60,000 Americans of the First Army. Here was the great crisis of the entire German counter attack. The Germans continually tried to turn the flank of the First Army forces, who were always trying to build up an east-west line from the Elsenborn Ridge through Waimes, Malmedy, Stavelot, Trois Ponts, Werbomont and Hotton.

But new American units, the 3rd Armored, 84th, and then the 2nd Armored, were fed into the brittle Allied line, and they always managed to keep one road ahead of the leading German columns. Only later on December 26th, after the crisis in the north had been met and Hitler had realized his great dream was going up in smoke, did the Germans turn towards the south to attack Bastogne in force. Then the defenders, by this time greatly reinforced, in a magnificent stand beat off eight battered German divisions. The crisis had passed, however, and the Germans were trying to buy time by capturing Bastogne, which would have given them a more adequate defense line behind which they hoped to sit, and tie down more Allied divisions. Patton's Army performed well; his true glory was part of a team , directed by Eisenhower, which was flexible enough to rebound from a completely surprise attack.

Robert Merriam and Janice Holt Giles each formed a foundation for other authors to review and write the history of many units that were prominent in World War II. Janice became known for the excellence of her research and for the integrity of her writing about the American frontier. She has brought both of these qualities to bear in the story of the 291st Engineer Combat Battalion.

The writing of the "Damned Engineers" was accomplished over a period of five years. The research and interviews of the men of the 291st developed a high degree of accuracy. Following the writing of the story, Martin Blumenson penned the introduction to the book for publishers day in 1970. Blumenson was an historian for Patton's Third Army and has written many books on WWII.

Since the late seventies, I have enjoyed the association with Major General Mike Reynolds, former British Commander with the NATO forces and assistant director of Plans and Policy Division, International Military Staff, NATO. Mike's maneuver writings en-titled "Exercise Pied Peiper"and the published writing of "The Devil's Adjutant" have added much research and accuracy to the history of the battles of the Ardennes.

Secondary sources, in the form of books already published about the Battle of the Bulge are John D. Eisenhower, "Bitter Woods", Omar N. Bradley, "A Soldier's Story", John Bauserman, "The Malmedy Massacre", Jean Paul Pallud, "Battle of The Bulge, Then and Now", M. Gerard Gregoire, Belgian author who wrote the full story of Peiper in "Fire, Fire, Fire".

The following is a listing of other books which have been published about the greatest battle in U.S. history:

Blumenson, Martin, *THE DUEL FOR FRANCE*, 1944, Boston; Houghton Mifflin Company, 1963.

Cole, Hugh M., *THE ARDENNES: THE BATTLE OF THE BULGE*. Washington Office of the Chief of Military History.

Parker, Danny S., *THE BATTLE OF THE BULGE*. Combined Books Inc. Conshohocken, Pa. 1991.

Patton, George S. *THE WAR AS I KNEW IT*. Bantom Books, New York, N.Y. 1980.

Gallagher, Richard., *MALMEDY MASSACRE*. Paperback Library Inc. 1964.

Weigley, Russell, *EISENHOWER'S LIEUTENENTS*, Bloomington, 1981.

Toland, John, *BATTLE; THE STORY OF THE BATTLE OF THE BULGE*, New York 1959.

Fowle, Barry W., and Wright, Floyd D., *THE 51ST AGAIN*, White Mane Publishing Company Inc. Shippensburg, Pa. 1992.

Smith, Helena Huntington, *A FEW MEN IN SOLDIER SUITS*. August 1957

Merriken, William, *THE MASSACRE AT MALMEDY AS TOLD BY ONE OF THE VICTIMS*.

Gavin, General James, *ON TO BERLIN*, Viking Press, New York 1978

Clarke, General Bruce, *CLARKE OF ST. VITH*, Diller/Liederbach, Cleveland 1974.

Also from the publisher

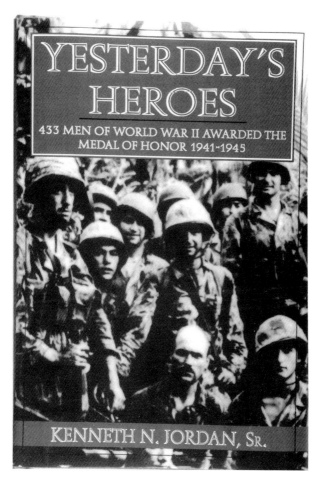

YESTERDAY'S HEROES
433 MEN OF WORLD WAR II AWARDED THE MEDAL OF HONOR 1941-1945

Kenneth N. Jordan, Sr.

YESTERDAY'S HEROES contains all 433 Medal of Honor citations such as this excerpt:
. . . Although machinegun bullets kicked up the dirt at his heels, and 88mm shells exploded within 30 yards of him, Pfc. Dutko nevertheless made his way to a point within 30 yards of the first enemy machinegun and killed both gunners with a handgrenade. Although the second machinegun wounded him, knocking him to the ground, Pfc. Dutko regained his feet and advanced on the 88-mm. gun, firing his Browning automatic from the hip. When he came within 10 yards of this weapon he killed its 5-man crew with 1 long burst of fire. Wheeling on the machinegun which had wounded him, Pfc. Dutko killed the gunner and his assistant. The third German machine gun fired on Pfc. Dutko from a position 20 yards distant wounding him a second time as he proceeded toward the enemy weapon in a half run. Along with the citations are Official Communiqués from the front, and newspaper accounts of various battles. Yesterday's Heroes is a dramatic look at the courage of the American soldier in World War II. Kenneth Jordan is also the author of *Heroes of Our Time: 239 Men of the Vietnam War Awarded the Medal of Honor 12964-1972,* and *Forgotten Heroes: 131 Men of the Korean War Awarded the Medal of Honor 1950-1953* (both titles are available from Schiffer Publishing Ltd.).

Size: 6" x 9"   ISBN: 0-7643-0061-X $35.00
624 pages, hard cover *Available August*

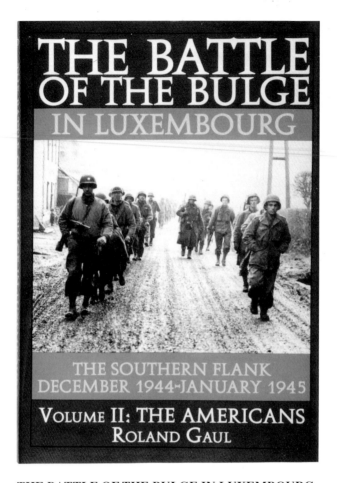

THE BATTLE OF THE BULGE IN LUXEMBOURG:
The Southern Flank - Dec. 1944 - Jan. 1945
Vol.I THE GERMANS

Roland Gaul

These two new volumes offer new insights into the events
of one of the fiercest battles of World War II. Volume I cov-
ers the events from the German point-of-view.
Size: 7" x 10" 48 pages of b/w photographs, maps
320 pages, hard cover
ISBN: 0-88740-746-3 $35.00